HAND BUILT

BUILT

A Potter's Guide

Quarto.com

Paperback edition published in 2024

First Published in 2019 by
Rockport Publishers, an imprint of The Quarto Group,
100 Cummings Center, Suite 265-D, Beverly, MA 01915, USA.
T (978) 282-9590 F (978) 283-2742

EEA Representation, WTS Tax d.o.o.,
Žanova ulica 3, 4000 Kranj, Slovenia.
www.wts-tax.si

ISBN: 978-0-7603-9300-0

Digital edition published in 2019
eISBN: 978-1-63159-599-8

Library of Congress Cataloging-in-Publication Data is available

Design: www.traffic-design.co.uk
Page Layout: www.traffic-design.co.uk
Photography: Elijah Ferguson and Melissa Weiss

HAND BUILT

A Potter's Guide

Master timeless techniques, explore new forms, dig and process your own clay.

Melissa Weiss

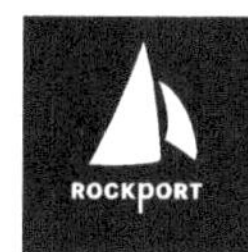

CONTENTS

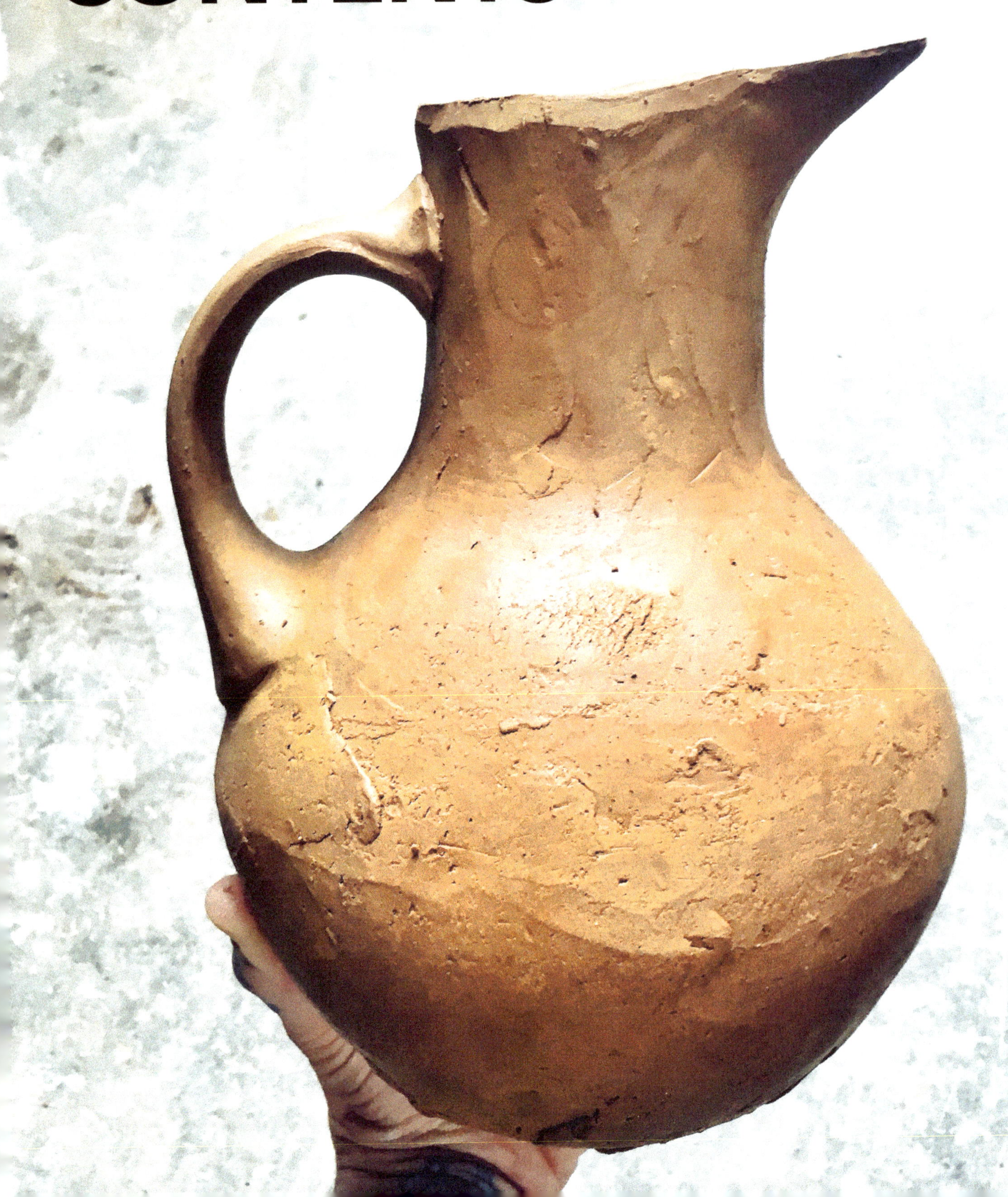

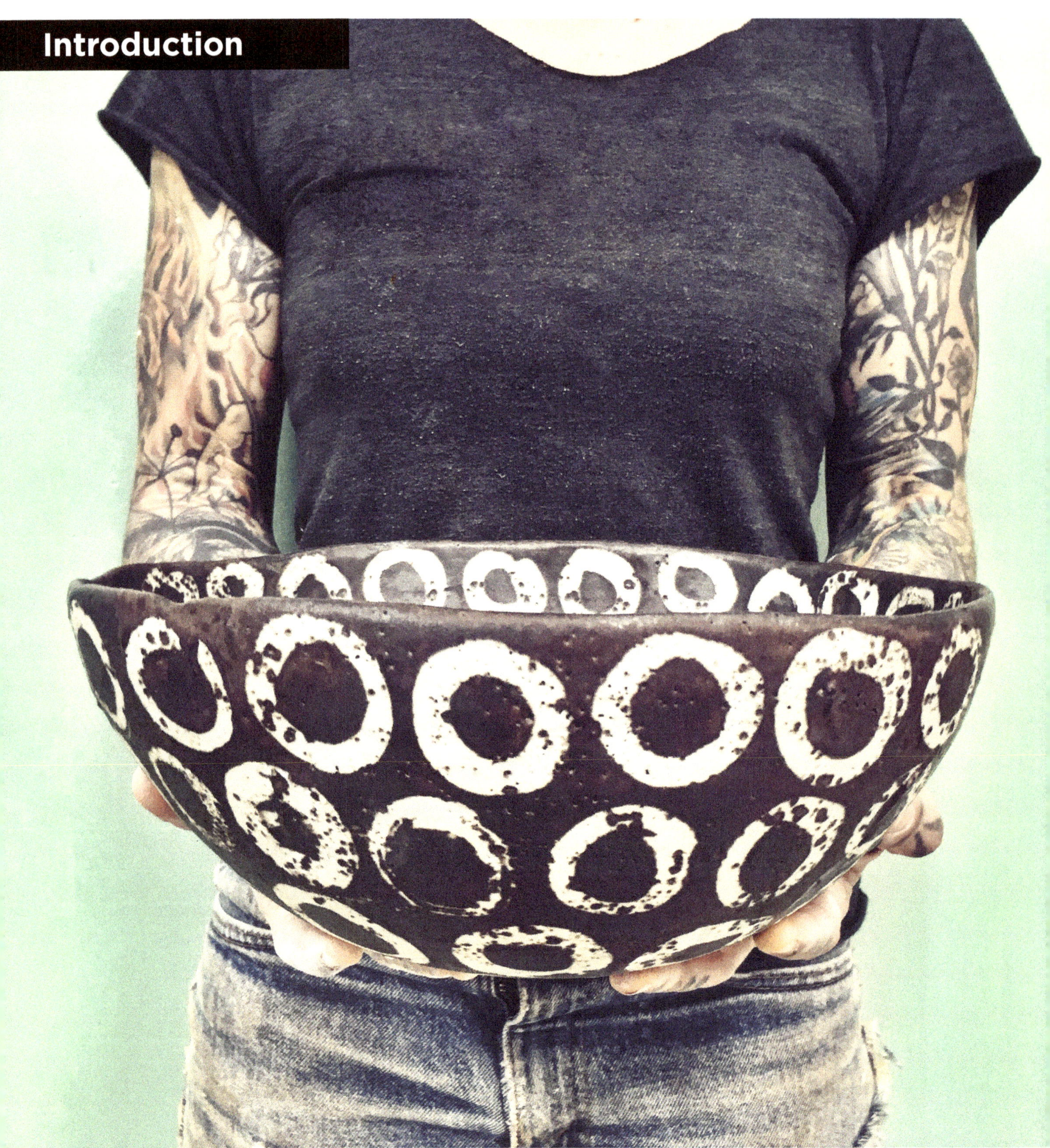

This book is for potters working at many different levels. If you're just getting started with clay, you'll find the basics you need here and, I hope, the answers to many of your questions about clay and firing. If you're an experienced potter looking for new options for your work, and new ways to work contemplatively with handbuilding, then this is the book for you.

Do you have clay in your backyard? Lucky you. I'll give you directions on how to test and use that wild clay. We will make slips and glazes with detailed instructions and recipes. And we'll talk about the different ingredients in glazes and the roles they play in the finished look.

In *Handbuilt: A Potter's Guide*, I've covered some familiar methods of handbuilding, and some not-so-familiar methods as well. We'll carve cups using a Japanese technique called *kurinuki*. This is a subtractive method of carving a pot out of a solid block of clay. We'll make trays and buckets by combining slab and coil methods and build vases and pitchers by putting together two slab-built bowls.

In other chapters, we'll take on the challenge of creating bisque molds and then use them to make platters and dishes. We'll explore different techniques for creating feet and handles and how to attach them to your pots. We'll talk about surfaces and try out a variety of decorating methods, including wax resist, sgraffito, and carving to make each pot one-of-a-kind, reflective of you. And, of course, we'll take a look at the different firing methods—electric, gas, and wood—and discuss what each has to offer.

In each chapter, I'll also introduce you to the work of some very talented contemporary potters from around the country. They'll take you into their studios for a look at their pottery and to share some of their tips, advice, and techniques.

> "This book is for potters working at many different levels."

My Winding Path to Studio Pottery

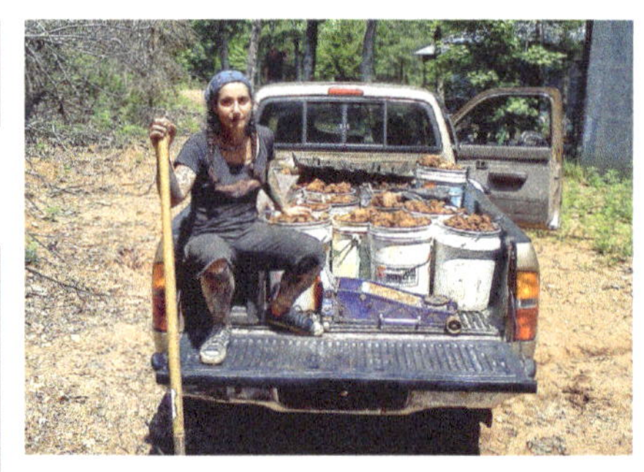

Welcome, I'm Melissa Weiss. I'm a studio potter in Asheville, North Carolina, where I run and work in an 8,000-square-foot warehouse housing twenty artists in various media. It's been a long and interesting path getting here.

I took my first pottery class in the fall of 2004 when my daughter was five months old. I had never before worked with clay and had very little exposure to ceramics. Basically, I knew nothing. It was a beginning wheel-throwing class in Fayetteville, Arkansas, about an hour from Kingston, where I lived and owned a piece of land. The class wasn't much, in terms of instruction or inspiration, and yet it turned out to be extremely significant—it exposed me to a medium I loved instantly. The class only lasted a few weeks, and it would be a year until I would get the chance to take another.

Six months later, I moved to Asheville, North Carolina, and in the fall of that year I took a pottery class at a local technical college, and then another at a nearby ceramics center. This time I got lucky—the class at the ceramics center was taught by the amazing Becca Floyd. Along with being a brilliant teacher, Becca conveyed such a convincing confidence in me and my pottery that it made me believe in it too.

In the spring of 2007, Becca presented me with the gift of a free workshop at the John C. Campbell Folk School. It was taught by Michael Hunt and Naomi Dalglish, and it transformed the way I saw and made ceramics ever after. The workshop introduced me to digging and working with wild clay, to using slips and glazes that are layered and sheer to show the layers of material underneath, and to the challenges and rewards of wood firing. At this point, too, I started learning about the wood-fire traditions of the humble potters of Korea and Japan, and the American potters who were influenced by these traditions. The path I had been following suddenly branched off in many new directions.

I joined a co-op called Clayspace in the River Arts district in Asheville that proved to be invaluable to my ceramics education. I now occupied a studio with a small group of potters who generously shared their knowledge, answered my never-ending questions, and participated in wood firings. There was a gallery in our studio, in which I was able to start selling my work.

In 2008, on a trip to Arkansas to visit my friends and my land, I dug a bucket of the sticky red clay to take home. I spent weeks testing different variations of recipes incorporating this wild clay until I came up with a clay body that was workable, durable, and aesthetically what I wanted. I've used this custom clay body that includes 25 percent of the clay I dig from my land in all my pots ever since.

Beginning in 2013, I had the opportunity to rent the warehouse where I currently work. It has enabled me to grow and be more efficient: I can make clay, make pots, and fire my work all in one place. I spend thirty to sixty hours a week in my studio. My boyfriend, Elijah Ferguson, quit his job in construction to run the pottery with me. We work in cycles: make clay, make glazes and slips, make pots, glaze and decorate pots, fire pots. In between is all the work it takes to run a small business.

"Everyone can take these methods, add what they bring to the craft, and make pots of their own."

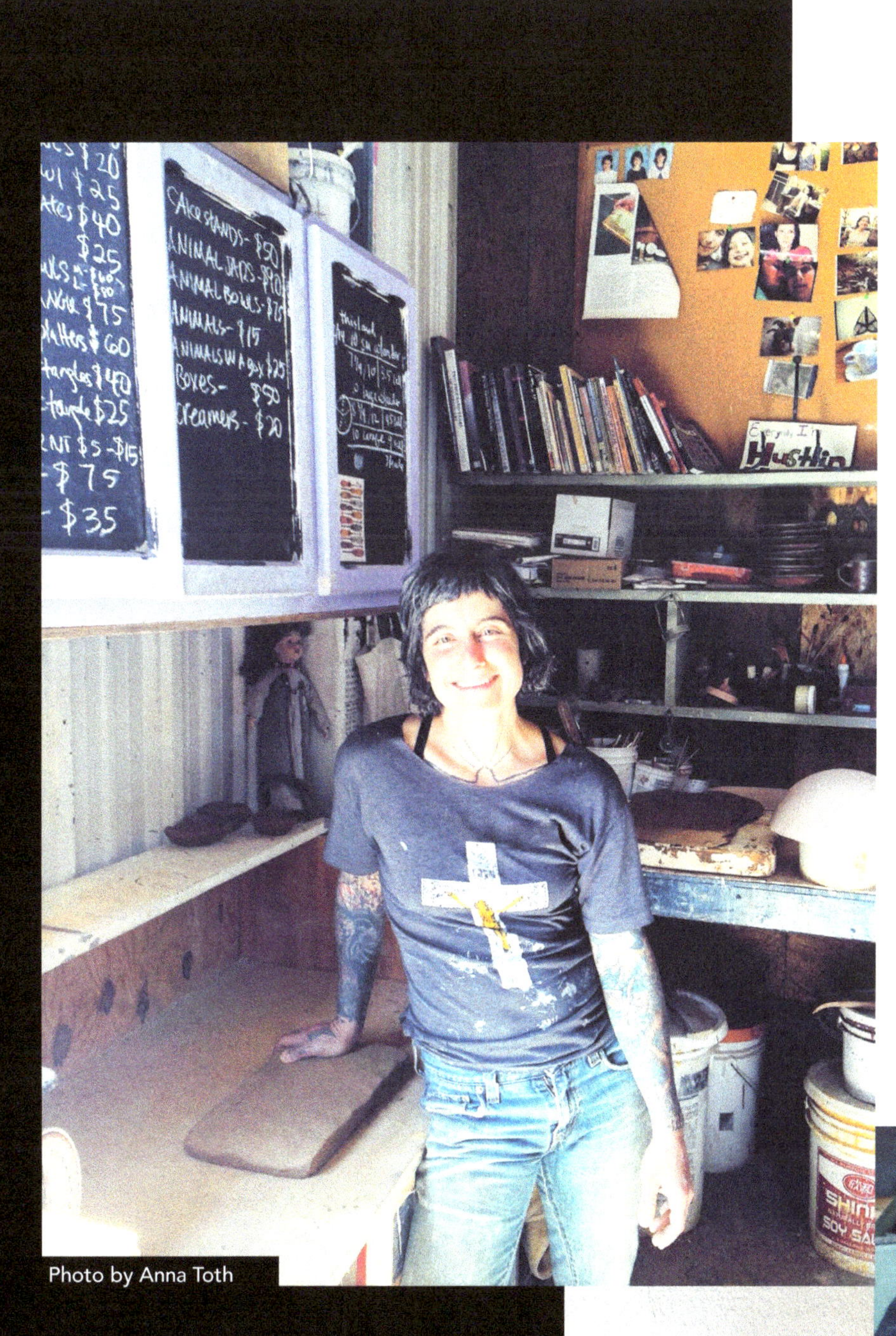

Photo by Anna Toth

Over the past thirteen years I've collected and saved little pieces of knowledge, techniques, and recipes from every branch of my path of learning and built them into my own practice. I use a variety of methods, including carving, coil, slab construction, and combination techniques that I will show you in this book. I try to make pots that feel primitive and look modern by using a minimally processed wild clay body, thin slips, and ash glazes, and by leaving the marks of the maker. I don't "fuss" over my pots. They're not painstakingly perfected and honed. They're meant to be inviting and used in daily life.

When I teach my classes, I find my methods are easily transferred to beginning potters. The pots and methods I use are not intimidating. Everyone can take these methods, add what they bring to the craft, and make pots of their own. Pottery is a humble craft that teaches many lessons. I'm grateful for what it's given me.

Tools and Materials

CLAY You can handbuild pottery with any type of clay, but for me, handbuilding is most successful with a groggy clay with a little bit of texture, called "tooth." This clay shrinks less and has fewer issues with cracking. Typically, if you buy a clay advertised as a handbuilding clay, it will have more grog than a throwing body.

Clays vitrify at different temperatures; make sure you use the clay that corresponds with the temperature you will be firing to.

CARVING TOOLS There is a wonderful selection of tools for carving clay available from many different companies. My favorites are Kemper Pro-Line and Dolan. Most clay carving tools have a wood or metal handle with a steel tool or loop at one end. These might be shaped as a teardrop, oval, triangle, bird beak, or circle, which allows you to carve broad, fine, angled, or curved areas, or get into tight corners. Be sure to get the professional series, as the others will not be sharp enough.

THE BASICS | Kemper Pro-Line: 300 series—PT325, PT 345; 400 series—PT445, PT430, PT480L; S series—PTS10, PTS20, PTS60, PTS80; M series—PTM 80; Dolan: DPT110

KNIVES

FLEXIBLE KNIFE | Knives with a thin, flexible blade make sharper and more precise cuts. These are great for detailing handles, rims, and spouts. I use my flexible knife all the time. I like Dolan DPT 220C and DPT 240.

RIGID KNIFE | I typically use the rigid knife only for cutting clay slabs off molds. Knives come in many styles and widths. If you have only one, I find the Dolan DPT 250 very versatile.

NEEDLE TOOL | As its name suggests, this tool is a steel needle with a wood or metal handle. The needle tool is great for cutting through clay when you don't need a precise cut, marking the clay, and poking the bottom to gauge thickness.

RIBS

PLASTIC RIBS | These are tools for shaping, sculpting, scraping, and adding details. They look a little like the end of a rubber spatula and are available in a variety of shapes. I prefer Sherrill Mudtools for ribs. They color-code their ribs to designate soft to hard, with red being the softest, then up through yellow, green, and blue. The essential ones are R0, Y0, G0, B0, Y3, and G3. Ribs are also available in metal and wood, but I like the flexibility of the plastic ones. I typically use a flexible metal rib only for scraping the surface of pots for texture.

SERRATED RIBS | Serrated ribs are available in the same shapes as plastic ribs, but they have a serrated edge. I use the serrated edge for scoring clay when I add attachments, such as handles.

OTHER IMPORTANT TOOLS

ROLLING PIN | A rolling pin is an option for slab work if you do not have a slab roller. There are rolling pins available from ceramic supply companies, but a kitchen rolling pin will work just as well.

SHEET OF FOAM | You'll use this often. Place a sheet of foam on your work surface when you turn your pot upside down to work on the foot. This will protect the lip of your pieces from getting flattened or damaged.

SLAB STICKS | Slab sticks are a primitive way of making slabs. Notches in the sticks allow you to wrap a wire around the sticks and slice slabs of an even thickness from a block of clay.

STURDY CYLINDER / HALF-GALLON MASON JARS | When I'm using molds to shape slabs of clay, I place cut PVC pipe or mason jars under the molds to raise them off the table. When you lay your slab on top you will need to get under the mold to cut the clay.

SURFORM OR RASP | This is a rasp with a handle. It's a great tool for shaving clay to make an even surface.

WIRE TOOL | This is essentially a length of wire with a handle at either end so that you can get a good grip on it. It's the simplest tool in the world, but it's amazingly useful for cutting a hunk off a large block of clay. This is a tool you can make yourself if you don't want to buy one. All you need is a 2-foot (61 cm) length of fishing line and a washer to tie onto each end.

WARE BOARDS | Make these from pieces of plywood cut into squares, or from pieces of drywall with the edges taped. Place these on your work surface and build your projects on them. When you're done working on a project, you can simply pick up the board to set the project aside for drying, minimizing the risk of damaging the moist clay. Plan on 12" × 12" (30.5 × 30.5 cm) squares for smaller projects and larger for bigger work.

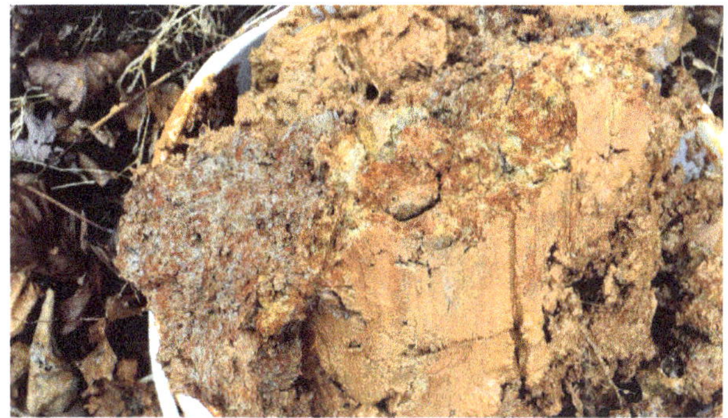

CLAY

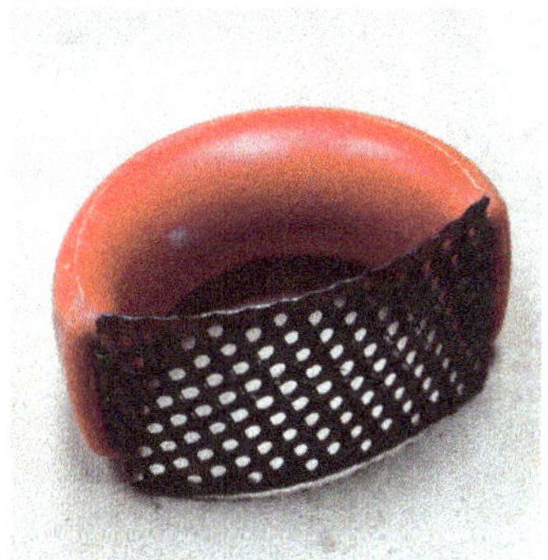

SURFORM

ROLLING PIN

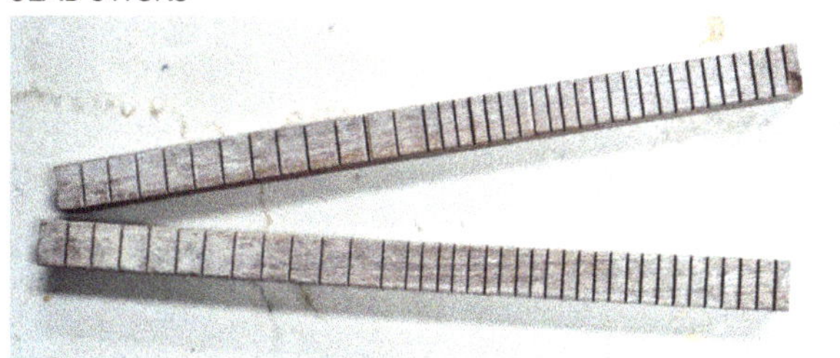

SLAB STICKS

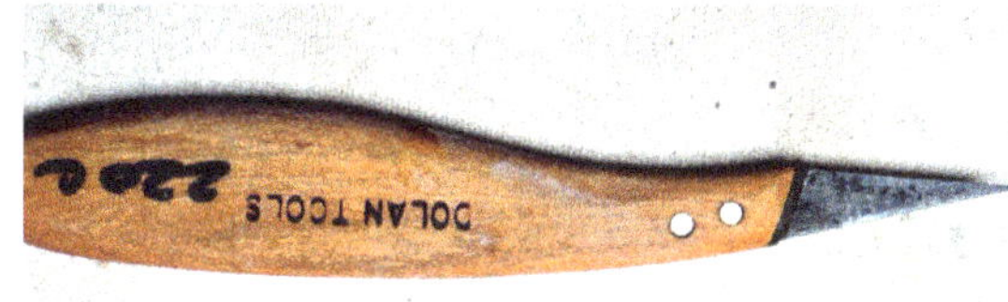

KNIFE

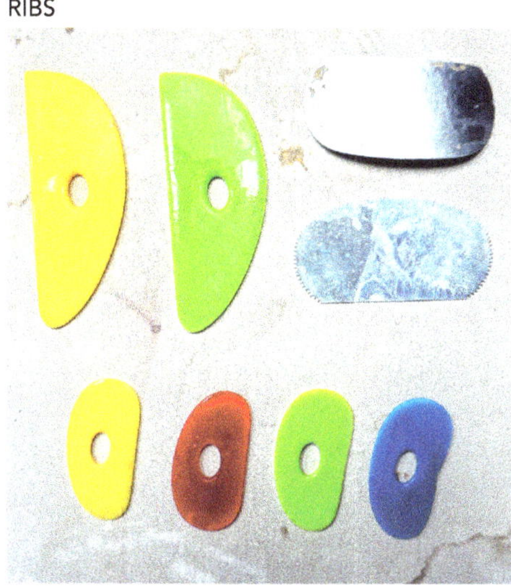

RIBS

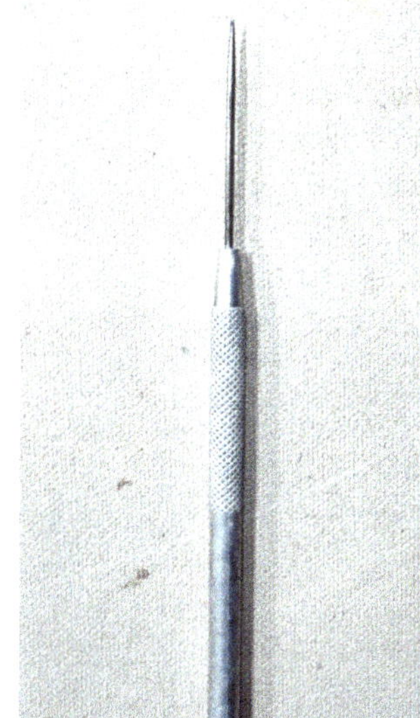

NEEDLE TOOL

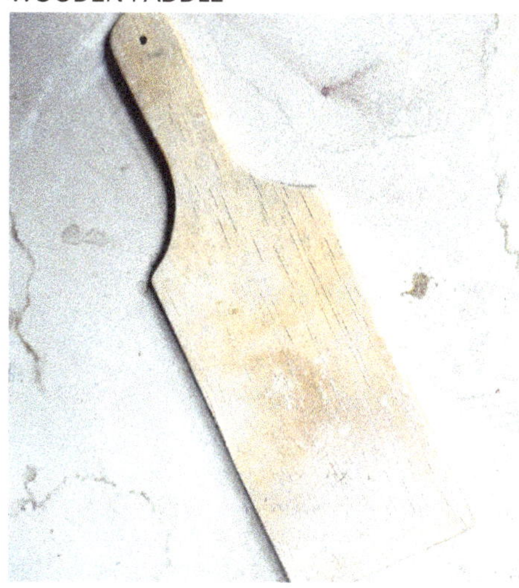

WOODEN PADDLE

WEDGING TABLE | Your work space will need a sturdy table or a board covered in canvas for kneading, cutting, and working on clay. The surface will be alternately wet, scraped, or embedded with clay, so it will need to hold up to rugged use.

WOODEN PADDLE | This small, useful hand tool is used for shaping pots and compressing clay.

OPTIONAL TOOLS

SLAB ROLLER | If you are setting up a professional pottery studio and plan to do a lot of handbuilding, a slab roller is a good investment. It's much like an intaglio printing press that allows large slabs of clay to be rolled out evenly.

BANDING WHEEL | This handy platform is a potter's lazy Susan. You can turn it 360 degrees as you carve or glaze a pot.

CHOP | This is a small stamp with your initials or a symbol that identifies your pots as yours. Make your own chop out of clay and bisque fire it for stamping all of your pots. It's an alternative to literally signing your pot.

WIRE TOOL

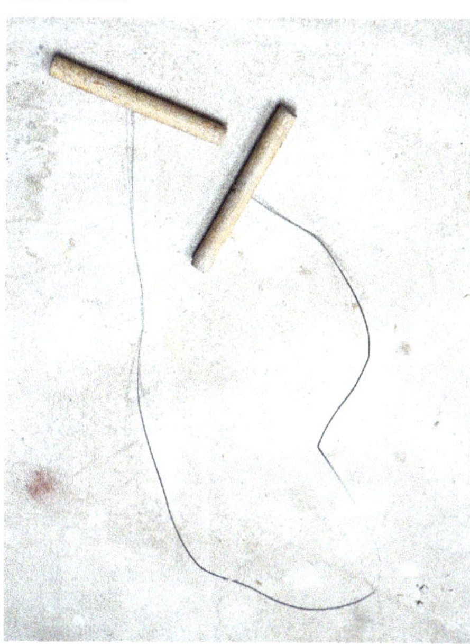

Rules

Although it's true in pottery, as it is elsewhere, that rules are meant to be broken, there are some rules in pottery that prove to be useful. Here are the ones I tend to make pots by:

- All parts of a pot should be of even thickness. The floor of your pot should be the same thickness as the walls. This doesn't mean the walls and floor must be thin—they can be any thickness you prefer, as long as they're even.
- Shaping the base: The foot ring is the circular rim on the bottom of a bowl or vase that provides a base for it to stand on. The foot ring is practical, but the design of the pot is important. If you were to peel off the foot ring there should be a continuous curve from the wall to the base of the pot.
- To make a strong and dependable bond between a handle and a pot, you really do need to score and slip the attachments when you join them.
- Big and thick pots need a long, slow drying time. Don't rush it.
- Clay has a memory. The less you handle your pot, the less it will warp.
- Use a slow bisque schedule.
- Make your cone packs in advance.
- Test new glazes before you use them on your pots.

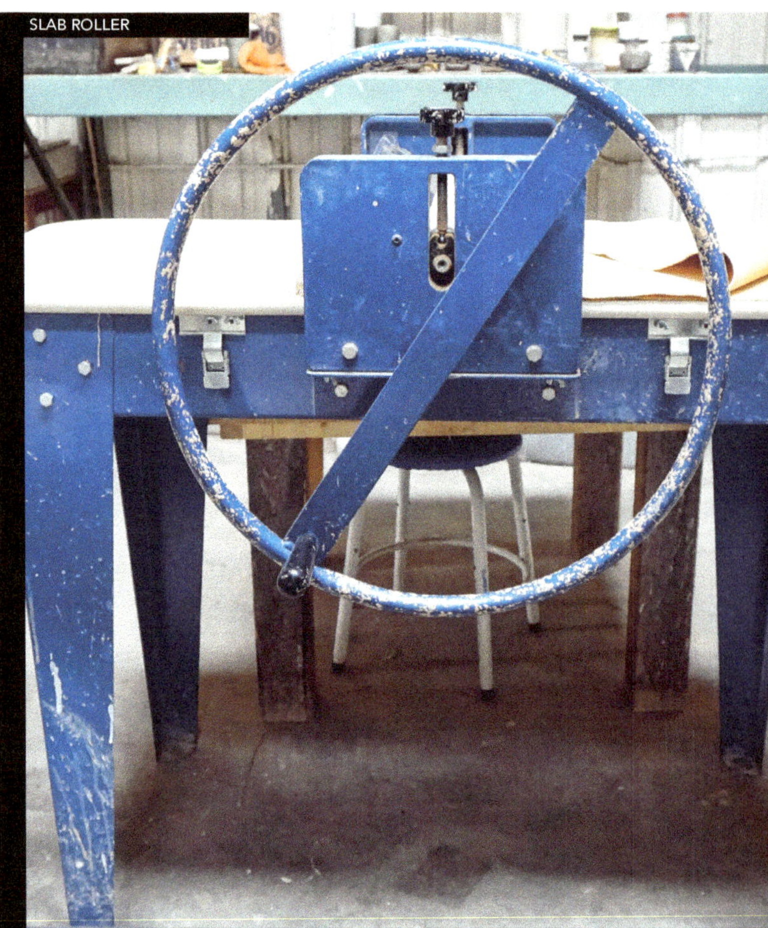

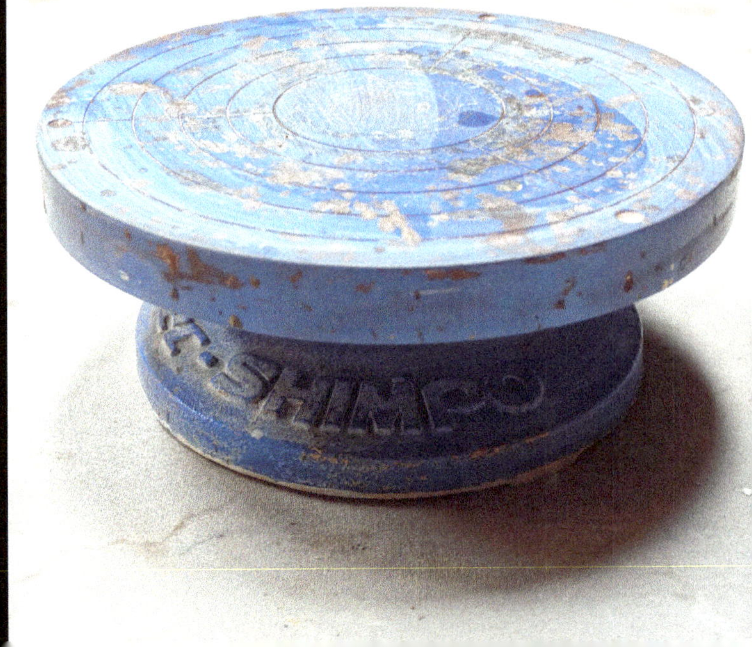

BISQUE | Pots that have been fired to a low temperature, typically 06-04. This dries the pots so they can easily be handled for glazing but are still porous for glaze absorption.

GREENWARE | Refers to unfired pottery.

LEATHER-HARD | The clay has dried to a point where it is visibly damp. It looks dark and feels cool. It is dry enough to trim feet, add handles, and carve into. If you press your finger into it, it shouldn't leave an indention. It will hold its form when handled but will move if squeezed.

SOFT LEATHER-HARD | I refer to pots as a soft leather-hard when they are on the wetter side of leather-hard. You can handle the pot but must be more gentle. If pushed into with a finger, it will leave an indention.

FIRM LEATHER-HARD | I refer to pots as firm leather-hard when they are on the drier side of leather-hard. It is too late to add handles without risk of cracking. Trimming a foot is possible, but not ideal. This stage can be good for carving if you like to use more pressure. Pots are best slipped at this stage.

RECLAIM | This refers to all the old dried clay scraps that are rehydrated with water and mixed. This clay can be used again to make pots.

SCORE AND SLIP | This is the method for attaching two pieces of clay. Scratch the surface where an attachment will go, as well as the attachment, then add the slip on the scratched part and the attachment. Press and smooth the new piece into place.

SLIP | A liquid clay used for decoration or adding color, layers, and texture to a pot.

WAX RESIST | A technique using wax to resist glaze to decorate.

YUNOMI | A Japanese style of teacup in which the cup is taller than it is wide, with a trimmed foot.

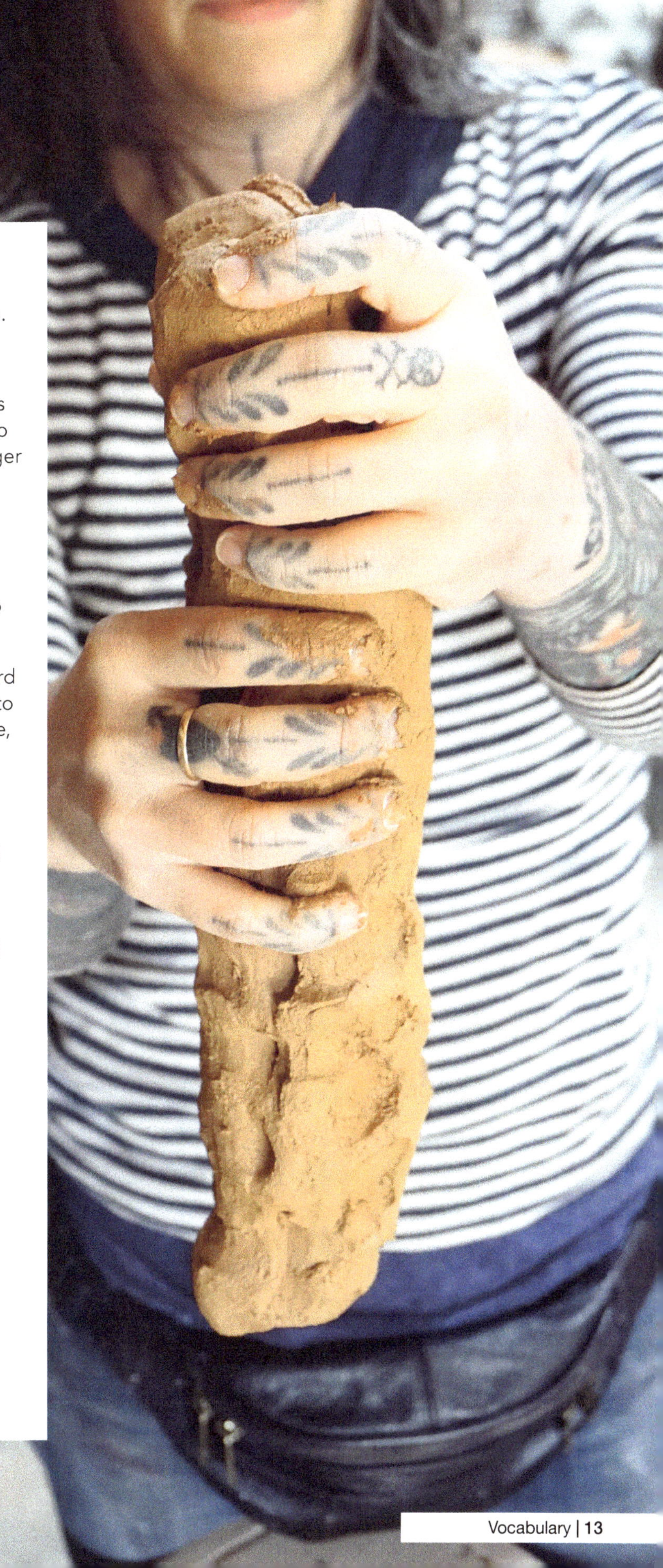

01

In Search
of Wild Clay

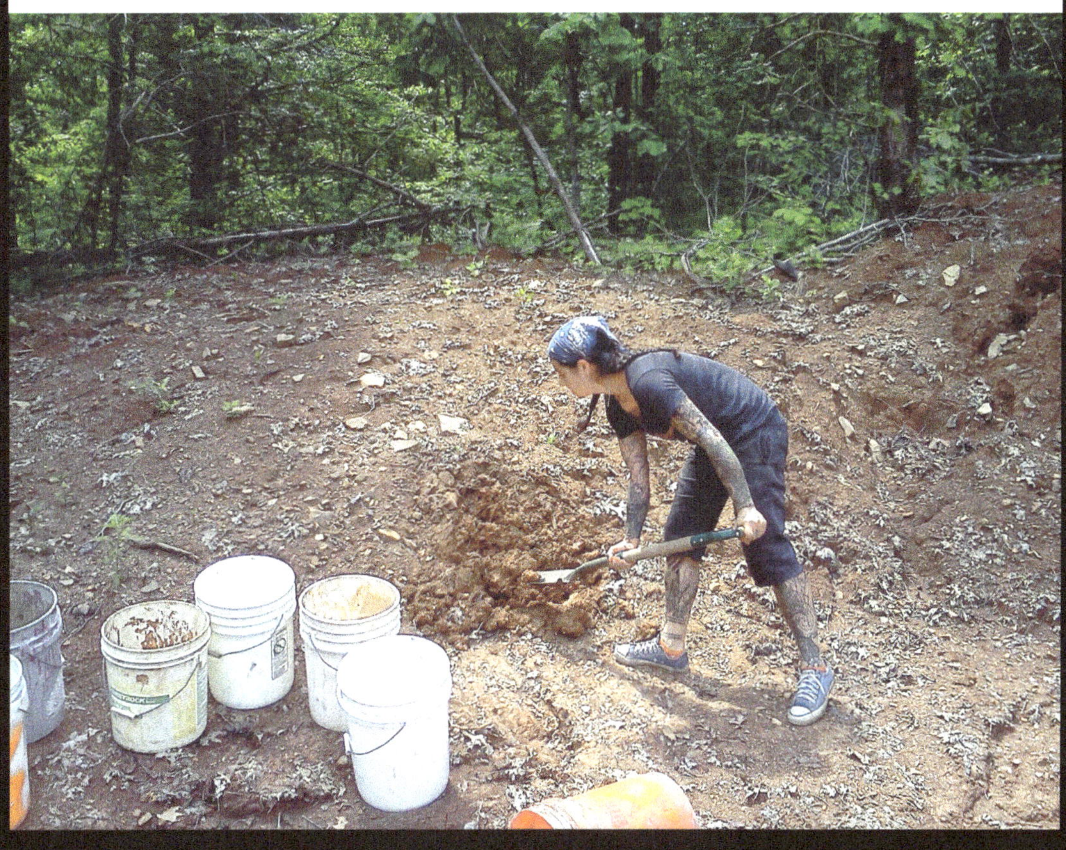

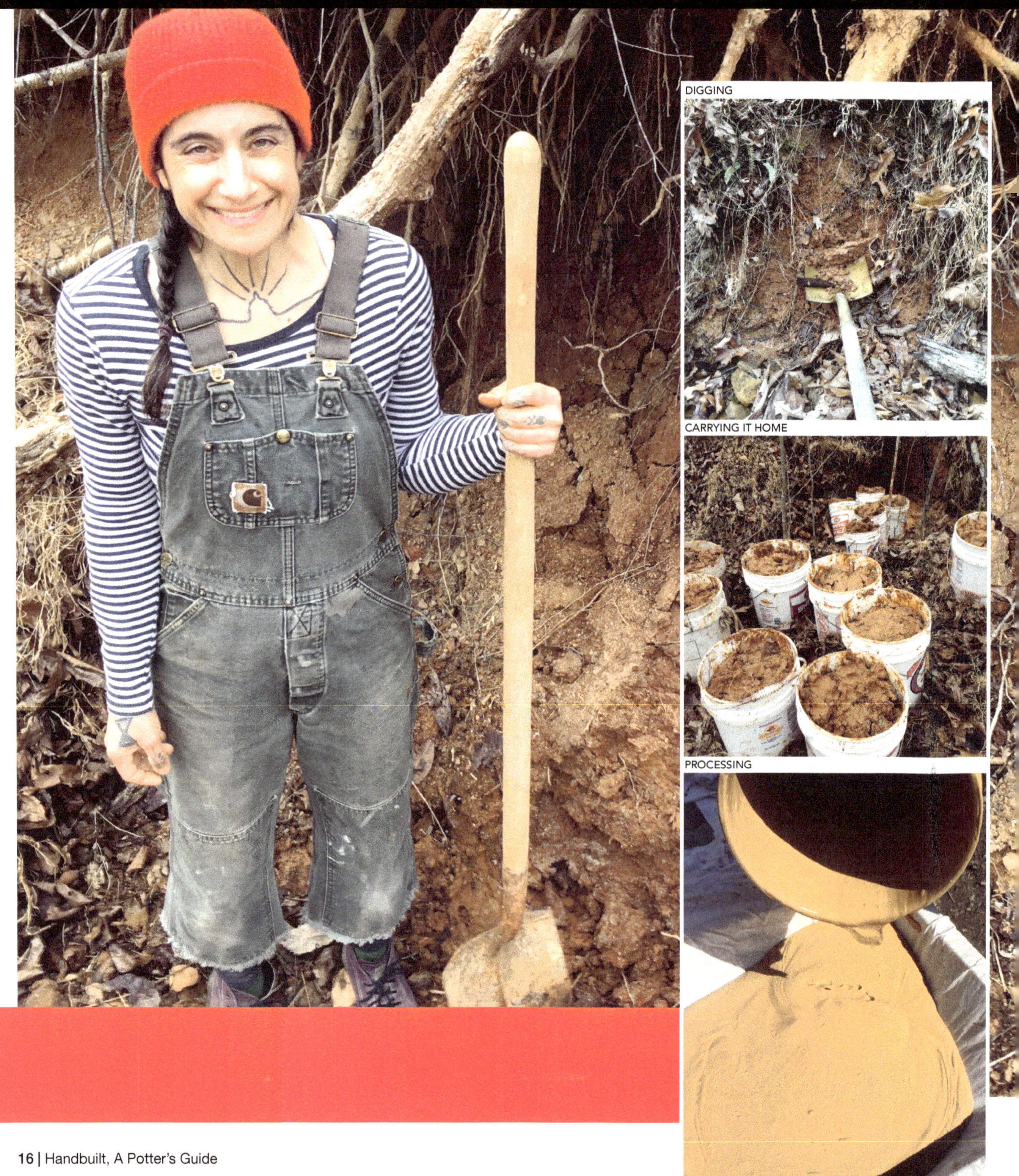

DIGGING
CARRYING IT HOME
PROCESSING

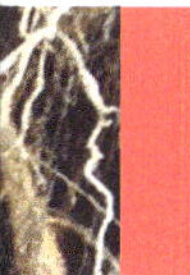

I bought land in the Arkansas Ozarks with friends in 2002 before I was a potter. Little did I know it would become my clay farm. I had no idea what I was doing the first time I dug up a bucket of clay on the land and brought it back to my studio in North Carolina, but I tested it by making a pinch pot. I didn't know what would happen to it in the kiln, so I placed it inside a bowl made of trusted clay and fired it that way. If the pinch pot melted, I would only have sacrificed one bowl. I got LUCKY! The pinch pot survived the cone 10 firing.

Next, I made a wild clay pinch pot to test each glaze I used. When these came out of the firing, the glazes had shriveled and cracked off the pots. This meant my clay was shrinking far more than the glazes. The clay was also hard to use because of its naturally sticky and crumbly qualities. It was too short, not plastic enough. When I rolled a coil and bent it, it broke in half. This is a common issue with wild clay.

TESTING | Now I needed to turn my wild clay into a workable clay body. I had no idea what that entailed, and that's probably what kept me from overthinking and becoming overwhelmed at what to add and how much. I asked friends who'd tried the process where to start and, with their advice, I came up with a basic recipe and tested it. Then I spent the next few months tweaking the recipe, testing ingredients in differing amounts.

When the clay body finally came out the way I wanted it—durable, vitrified at cone 10, rich and beautiful in color, interesting, and workable—I was done. I loved it.

I could never go back to sterile, clean-bag clay. The recipe utilized my wild clay at 25 percent, which seemed a realistic amount to dig and haul all that way. My partner and I make the long drive to Arkansas once a year, get out our shovels, and dig an actual ton— 2,000 pounds—of clay, packing it into 5 gallon plastic buckets. We load this into our van to take back to North Carolina. The clay remains in the buckets and dries out. When we're ready to make a batch of clay, we chip off hunks of it, weigh out the proper amount, and incorporate it into our recipe. Since we use the wild clay at 25 percent, it enables us to make 8,000 pounds of clay a year.

PROCESSING | We make 1,000 pounds of clay at a time—processing it is a labor-intensive task. We modified a 50-gallon food-grade metal drum to work in by cutting a hole in the bottom and fitting it with PVC pipe with a valve. This is what the wild clay goes into. We add water and use a power drill with a paddle attachment to mix it until it is liquid. Then we open the valve and screen the clay through wire mesh into a 300-gallon metal trough. We're ready to add the other ingredients into the screened wild clay slurry, mixing it with enough water until it is the consistency of heavy cream and all the ingredients are fully incorporated.

At this point, the clay must be drained of the excess water. We set up 2'×4' (61x122 cm) racks that we make with 2'×4' boards and ½" (1.25 cm) hardware cloth. Each rack has two 2'×2' (61×61 cm) compartments that we line with old sheets. Then we bucket the liquid clay into the compartments.

When each is full, we stack another rack on top and repeat. And when all the racks are done, we have to wait.

Over a period of weeks (about two weeks in warm, dry weather, longer if it freezes), the water slowly drips through the sheets and wire mesh until the clay, while still soft, is dry enough to remove from the racks. Then we use a pugmill to further mix and incorporate any unevenness in the clay. Now it's ready!

I'm often asked, "Isn't there clay in North Carolina?" Of course there is. There's lots of clay in North Carolina. It's the main reason there's such a rich pottery tradition here. There's even a small clay-making company called STARworks Clay in Star, North Carolina, that makes many beautiful clay bodies from local clays.

WHY DIG? | Then why go all the way to Arkansas just to dig clay? I love my clay. I love its beautiful iron-rich color and its durability and strength. I'm attached to it in a sentimental way too, because it gives me a reason to visit my piece of land every year, to connect with that part of the world and my friends there. If it weren't for my clay recipe, I doubt that I'd always find the time to visit Arkansas every year. So, I am grateful for this process that anchors me to my land.

Everything else in my life has changed since buying the land in 2002, but the clay is the same. I think about that a lot. My clay is a solid, dependable material conveying strength and consistency through all the calm and fury of a human life.

Wood-fired ceramic artist Mitch Iburg grew up surrounded by nature in Wisconsin. He studied art at Coe College in Iowa, spent several years as artist-in-residence at the Cub Creek Foundation in Virginia, and afterward lived, dug clay, and fired his kilns in New York State and Northern California, before settling in Saint Paul, Minnesota. With every move, Iburg's work in ceramics has embraced the natural clays of each region and expressed a deep-rooted appreciation for the landscape it comes from.

MW: YOU MAKE POTS FROM THE CLAY YOU SOURCE IN YOUR IMMEDIATE AREA. HOW DO YOU GO ABOUT FINDING THE CLAY?

MI: My search begins by researching digital or printed maps and publications before actively prospecting. Bedrock geology maps indicate the location of granitic parent rocks, and therefore can lead to sources of primary clays. Soil surveys reveal a closer look at clay levels near the surface. These give a better sense of areas where secondary clays have been transported from their parent source and locally mixed with sand and silt.

These maps and publications point out general areas of interest. Beyond this, the act of finding the clay may require locating cross-sections cut into the landscape. Rivers, road cuts, and construction zones provide a view of the clay's extent and the depth at which a deposit may be located.

MW: WHAT ARE THE INITIAL WORKABILITY TESTS YOU PERFORM? WHAT ARE THE STEPS YOU TAKE, FROM GETTING THE CLAY OUT OF THE GROUND TO MAKING A POT WITH IT?

MI: My current studio practice takes into consideration multiple modes of working through different ideas. Each body of work has its own requirements. With this in mind, I have various approaches to preparing materials to meet the demands of the work.

Functional ware has the most requirements and, therefore, requires the greatest amount of processing. For this line of work, I rigorously test each material by taking into account plasticity, strength, and vitrification at different temperatures.

Certain uncontaminated clays are used right from the ground, while coarse deposits are wet-screened to remove a desired percentage of the aggregate before being dried to leather-hard consistency and foot-wedged. Often, multiple clays are blended together to raise or lower the desired firing temperature based on firing methods available.

Many of my sculptural vessels and objects have opposite requirements. With these, workability is often sacrificed in order to showcase non-plastic materials high in earth, sand, or stone content. For these pieces, clay is either used directly from the source or amended with the aggregate screened from the throwing bodies.

MW: WHAT ARE THE TYPICAL ISSUES YOU ENCOUNTER WHEN USING WILD CLAYS?

MI: Developing a practice that is exclusive to harvesting and processing one's own clay comes with many types of issues. For me, these challenges have manifested themselves in three main ways.

Having pursued this work while living a semi-nomadic lifestyle over the past six years, I have frequently hurdled the problem of land ownership when sourcing materials. Private, state, and federal land restrictions greatly complicate the initial search for a dependable clay source. Acquiring permission to the land and developing a good relationship with the owner is an important first step.

Once the clay is acquired, the availability of storage and processing space can greatly influence the scale of one's operation. Many of the settings in which I have worked involved communal spaces within residency programs.

"There is a deeply ingrained relationship between the objects I make and the landscapes in which I live."

Although their limited spaces created many problems, these settings have given rise to many of my current strategies for storing and efficiently processing large quantities of material.

The biggest challenge has been adapting ideas to meet the properties of local materials in a way that honors them and their origins. The division of my practice into separate bodies of work has been a direct response to this issue and has granted me the freedom to uninhibitedly explore different ideas that make up a material-focused approach. Collectively, I view each mode of working as a unique state of resolution to the tensions between my identity, the properties of the materials, and the greater implications associated with their use.

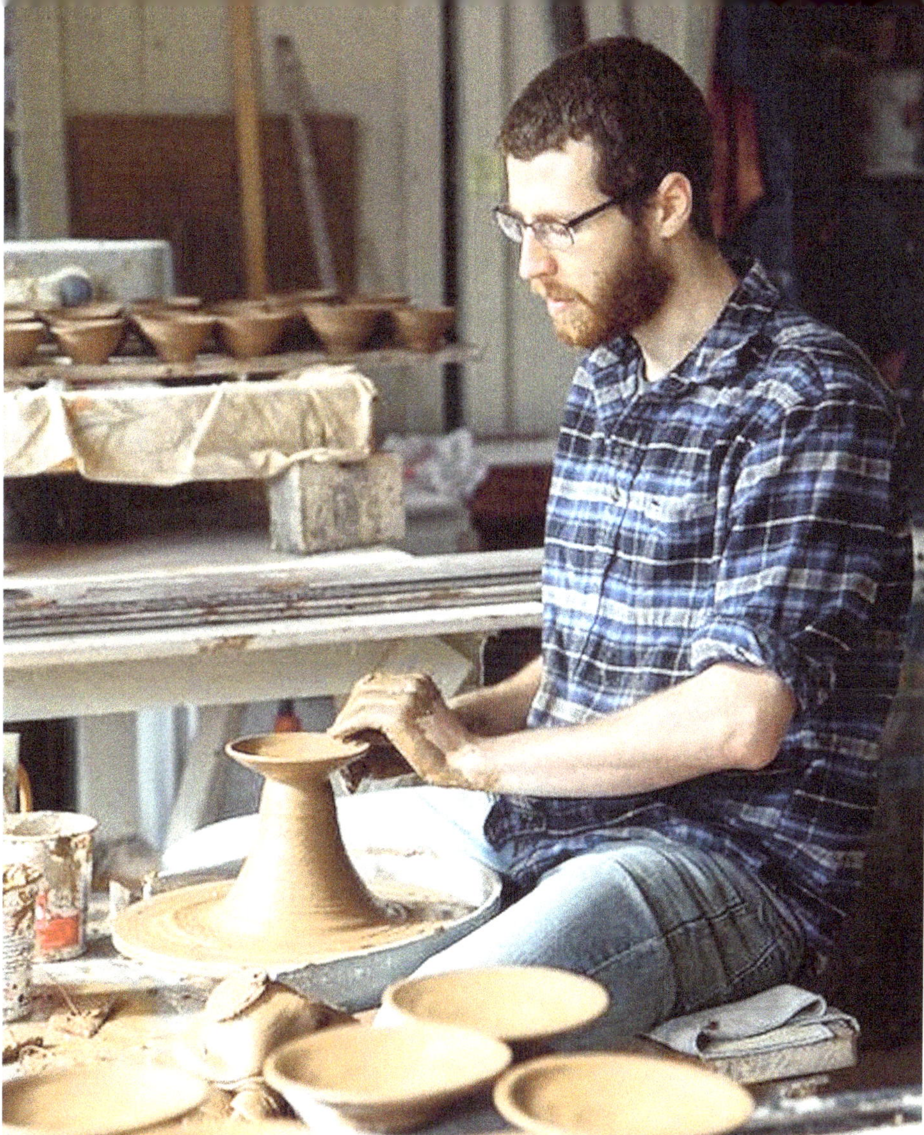

MW: I LOVE HOW YOU SHOW THE POTS YOU MAKE WITH IMAGES OF THE LANDSCAPE WHERE YOU MADE THE POTS. IT LETS THE VIEWER SEE THE NATURAL WORLD AS ART AND VICE VERSA. I IMAGINE YOUR STUDIO FILLED WITH THESE PHOTOS WHILE YOU MAKE POTS. IS THIS THE CASE?

MI: There is a deeply ingrained relationship between the objects I make and the landscapes in which I live. A common theme in my work is how my observations of these places—their behavior through seasonal changes, the expressions of their landforms, and the depth of their history—become manifested in the conceptual and technical considerations of the ceramic process.

To aid the viewer in understanding this relationship, I often pair photos of finished work with selective landscape imagery. My hope is that the two function as different languages in support of a shared dialogue about nature's physicality and ephemerality.

To prevent the risk of mimicking physiological features in clay, I avoid directly looking at these photos during the making cycle. In doing so, I find that the common factors between the two manifest themselves in a subtle and natural way.

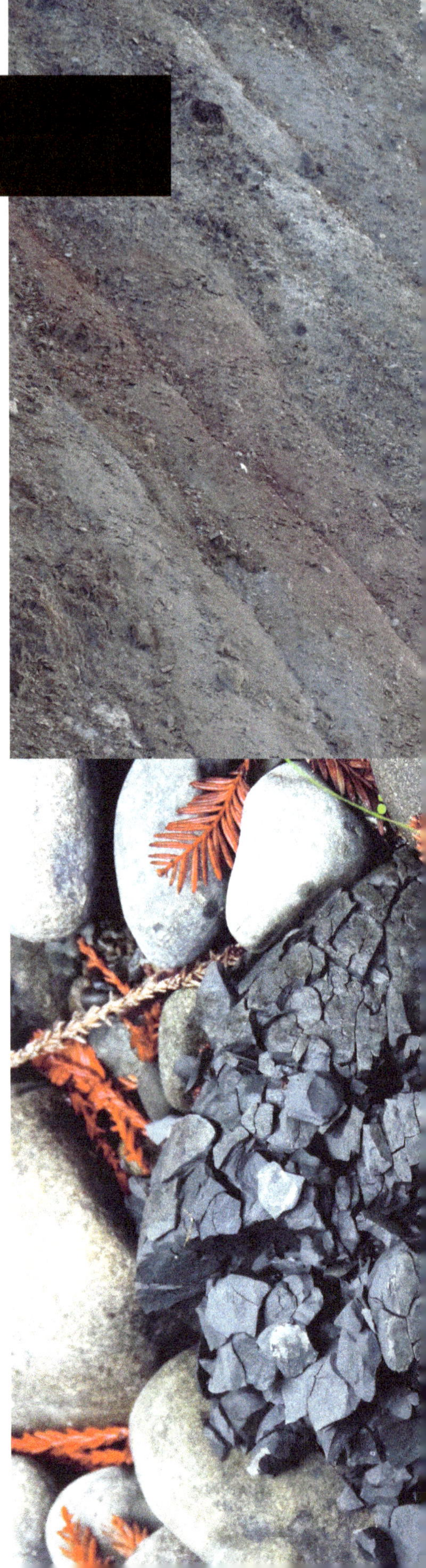

MW: NOW THAT YOU HAVE ESTABLISHED A PERMANENT STUDIO IN MINNESOTA, HOW WILL YOUR WORK CHANGE?

MI: After three years of working in Northern California, I moved to Saint Paul, Minnesota, where I have now established a studio with my partner and fellow ceramic artist, Zoë Powell. While the change from a rural to an urban work environment has greatly challenged my approach to clay harvesting and processing, it has brought about access to new materials and resources that are helping advance my studio practice.

In the coming years, I anticipate new adaptations to previous modes of working that respond to the nuances of Minnesota's geological history, seasons, and glacial topography. By researching these sources of interest through functional ware and sculptural objects, I hope to discover qualities of the region's expressions that span technique and material.

MW: WILL YOU USE A SINGLE CLAY SOURCE? HOW WILL THAT INSPIRE YOUR WORK FOR THE LONG TERM?

MI: Currently, I am using two main clays. The first, a crude kaolin harvested in southwestern Minnesota, contains a high concentration of the decomposed granitic rock, gneiss—some of which has been dated within the region at 3.5 billion years old.

The second is a plastic shale-based clay deposited when much of the state sat below Cretaceous seas. In fall of 2017, I worked with several others to secure 20 tons of this material from the stockpiles of the state's last operating manufacturer of bricks, Ochs Brick & Tile Company.

This collection occurred several weeks before the company was scheduled to close its doors, bulldoze its stockpiles, and sell its land. While it lacks the geological age of the kaolin, this clay holds great historical significance, as Ochs Brick & Tile had been using this stockpile for brickmaking since the late 1800s.

In addition to these clays, I am also looking at non-plastic resources, such as limestone, silica sand, brick grog, and iron ore—all of which have greatly influenced the region's economy, history, and culture. By developing methods of binding and sintering them into sculptural form, I hope to expand the conventional boundaries of using local materials.

MW: IF YOU DIDN'T HAVE ACCESS TO WILD CLAYS, WOULD YOU STILL MAKE POTS? IF YES WHAT WOULD INSPIRE THEM?

MI: I have always been a proponent of the idea that materials, techniques, and firing methods should be used in support of artistic intent. With this in mind, I use wild clays with the intent of exploring the qualities of a landscape through the lens of its material resources.

For bodies of work with different intentions, such as custom restaurant tableware requiring heightened utility, the necessity of using local clay is outweighed by the need for durability and dependability. While I often include some natural component in these clay bodies, I welcome the opportunity to break from the material-focused practice and concentrate on developing forms that showcase food in a creative, yet timeless, way.

"I have always been a proponent of the idea that materials, techniques, and firing methods should be used in support of artistic intent."

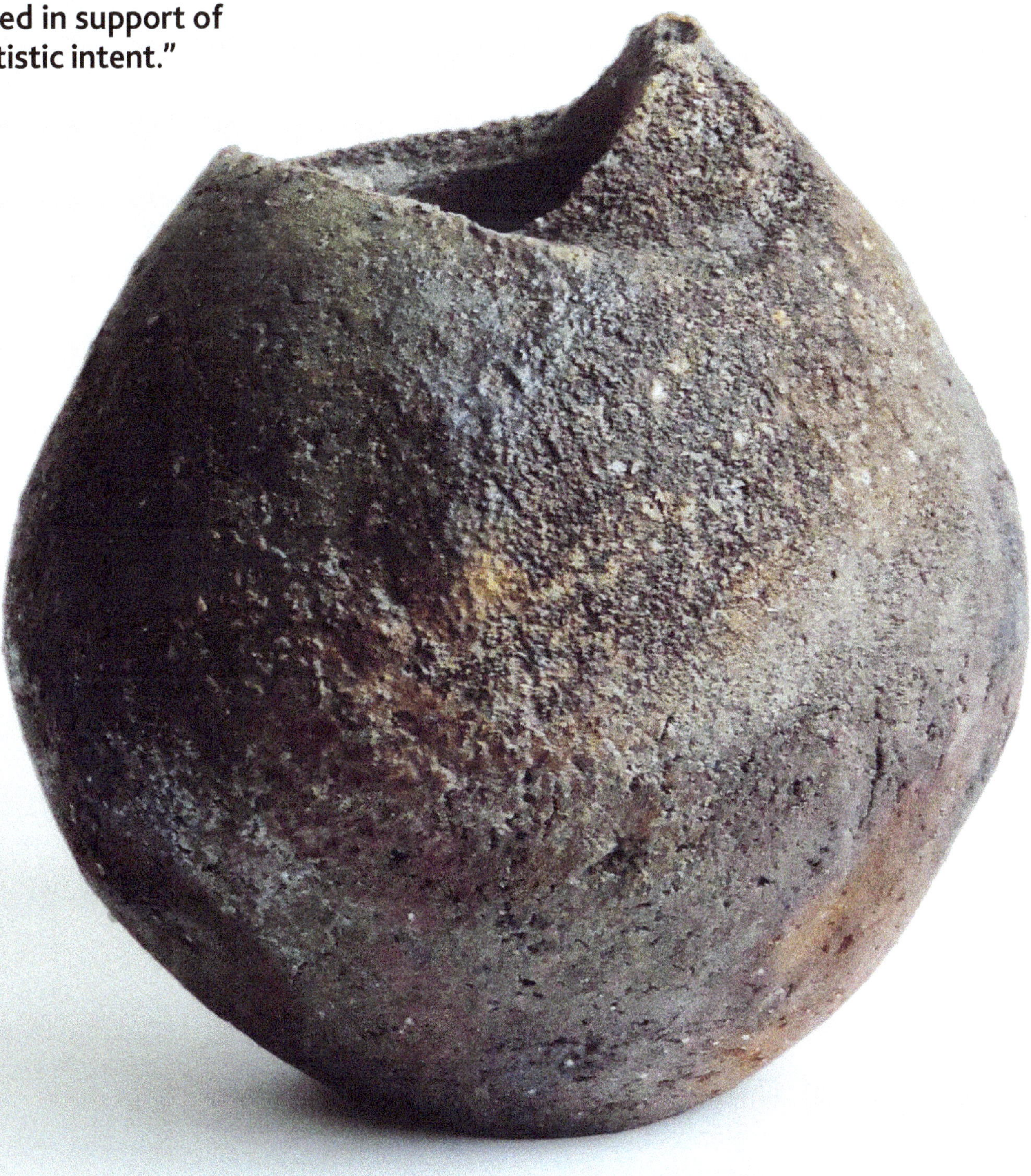

Lindsay Rogers is a potter, educator, and food enthusiast living in the mountains of eastern Tennessee. She studied printmaking at Sarah Lawrence College and received her MFA in ceramics from the University of Florida. Over the years, Lindsay has used her work as a ceramic artist to advocate for a more locally based, sustainable food system. She has participated in collaborations with other artists, chefs, and farmers, and her pottery, writing, and words can be found in a range of publications, from blogs to books and podcasts. She is currently assistant professor of ceramics at East Tennessee State University.

MW: HOW DO YOU GO ABOUT FINDING WILD CLAY?

LR: I am very fortunate that my current home is in the clay-rich mountains of eastern Tennessee. Finding wild clay here is often no more difficult than walking out your back door. However, my access to local clay has not always been so consistent. I was in a very transient moment in my life when I first started to research local clay and clay body development. I did not own my property, and, because of this, I had to learn how to identify the visual signifiers of clay in the landscape. Over time, this task of identification felt almost like a game I would play as I moved through otherwise monotonous daily routines. From afar, I learned how to look for concentrated patches of color, or for the signature cracking that happens when clay dries out. Close up, I would take note of the consistency of the ground that I walked on. Was it slippery? Did it cake up on the side of my boots? If the answer was yes, then I was probably looking at clay.

For several years I would collect small amounts of clay wherever I found it. However, as my curiosity increased, so did my desire to incorporate local clay into my studio work. It was at this point that I leaned more directly on my community. Over the years, people at my local extension agency, farmers, brickmakers, and, of course, other potters have all helped direct my understanding of how and where to find clay locally.

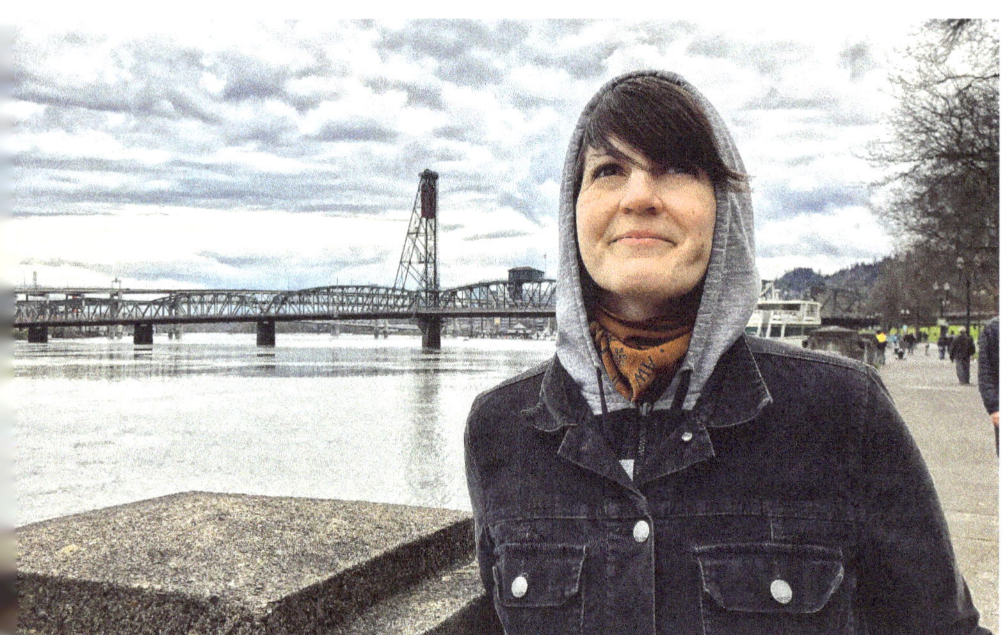

MW: WHAT ARE THE STEPS YOU TAKE TO DETERMINE ITS WORKABILITY?

LR: In the field, the best tools for determining a clay's workability are your hands. A small rolled coil of clay will give you an initial understanding of its character. If the clay is relatively damp and it holds a coil directly from the ground, you are already in good shape. If you wrap the coil around your finger and it does not break or crack, you may be in better shape.

In my studio, testing for workability becomes much more scientific. I always begin by firing a small marble of clay (inside of a pinch pot made out of a known high-fire clay) to both bisque and mid-range temperatures. Once fired, I do a quick "touch" water-absorption test to determine its general firing range. This test is executed by simply touching the fired marble with a drop of water and watching how quickly the water absorbs. If the ceramic marble acts like a sponge at mid-range temperatures, you may have a high-fire clay in your hands. If it melts, or is shiny, nonporous, or sticks to the cup, you are probably dealing with a lower-temperature material. Once I am confident that what I have found is a viable clay, I will move on to making larger round chips that I string on a wire as a record of the clay's fired color, as well as bars to test shrinkage, slumping, and the exact water absorption rate at both temperature ranges.

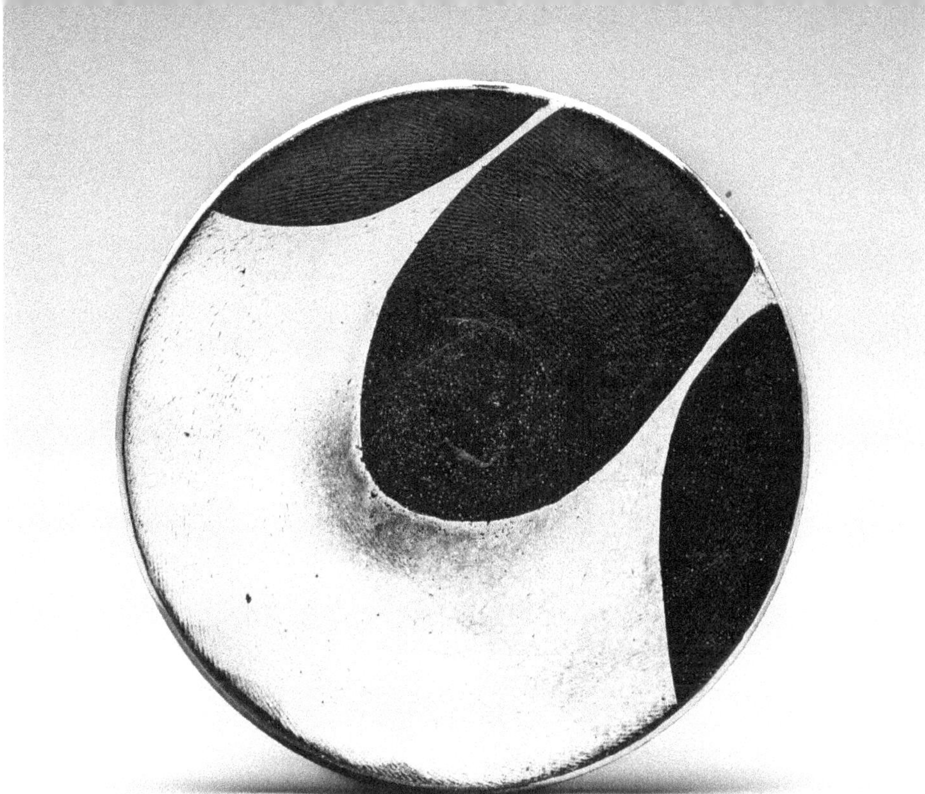

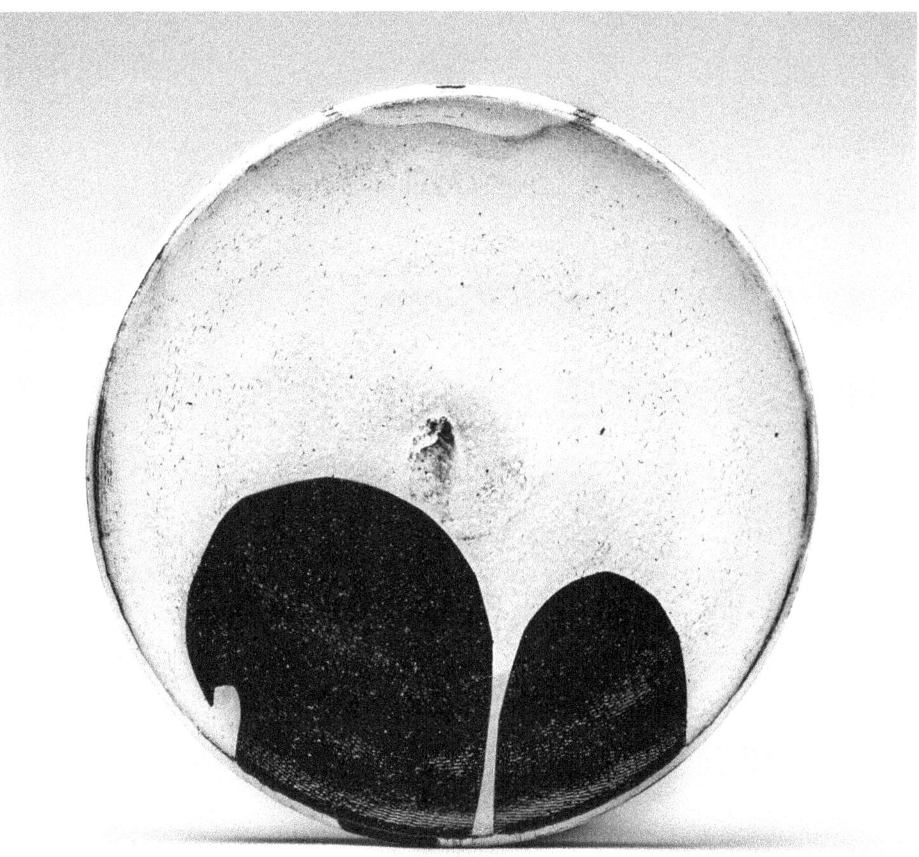

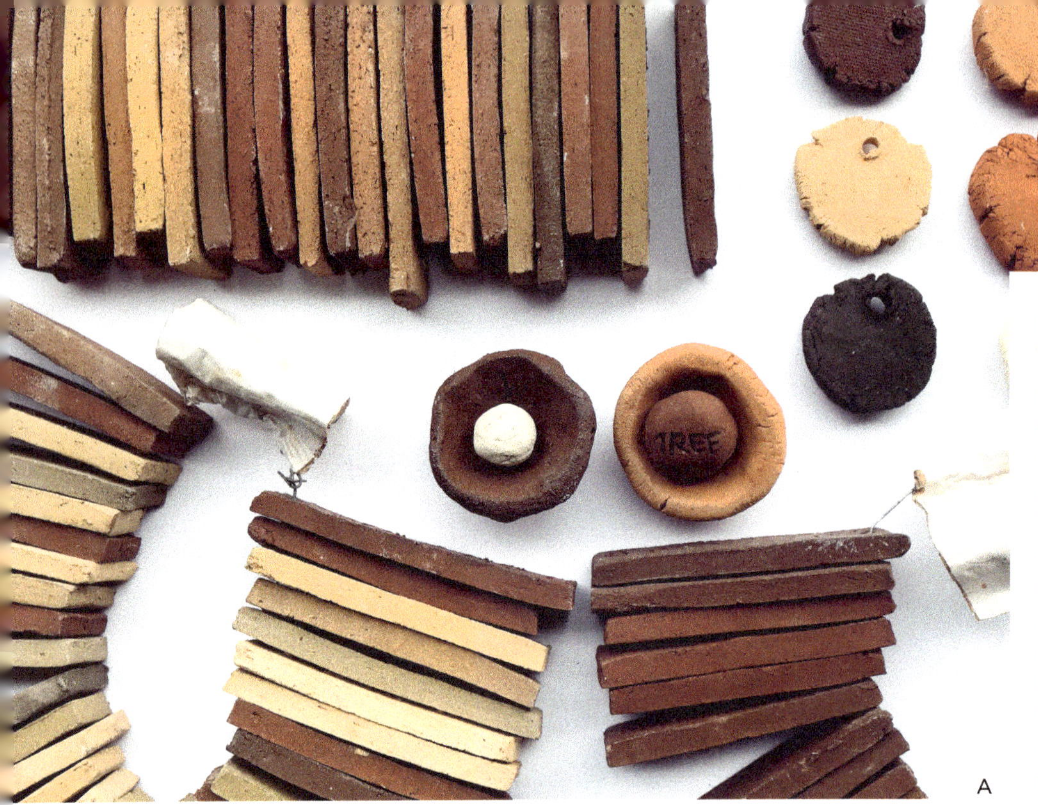

A

MW: HOW DO YOU AMEND THE ISSUES YOU FACE?

LR: The two significant issues that I faced when I first introduced wild clay into my own studio work were reliable access to wild clay and firing temperature. The first issue of access was related to the fact that, due to my living situation, I could only collect small quantities of wild clay at a time. The second issue arose from the fact that the clay that I had recurrent access to had a much higher maturation temperature than my kiln could accommodate. Initial firing tests of this clay showed that it could withstand temperatures over cone 11 in a wood kiln. Since I fire my work in an electric kiln, firing this clay to maturity without any additives would not have been possible. At that point, I had to decide how I was going to use it.

At first, I thought about using industrially mined dry materials to develop a recipe that would use my wild clay as an ingredient. However, I knew my access to this clay would not last forever, and developing a good recipe can be a very long process. Therefore, my solution was to take an already functional, cone 5 commercial clay body and wedge in my local clay in a ratio of 70 percent commercial to 30 percent local. This had the effect of giving the commercial clay body some of the visual and textural flair of the local clay, as well as lowering the temperature of the local clay so that it could be fired to maturity in my electric kiln.

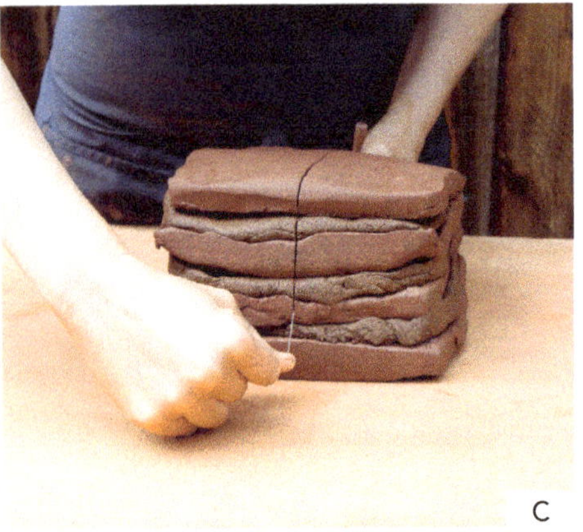

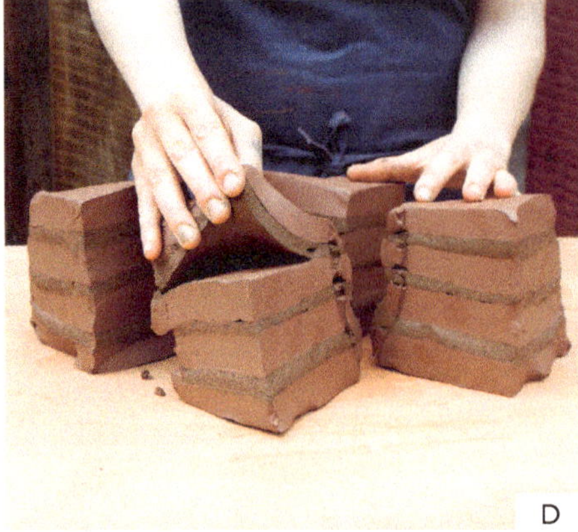

B

C

D

A) FIRST CLAY SAMPLES FOR TESTING POROSITY AND SHRINKAGE.

B, C, D) ALTERNATING LAYERS OF LOCAL AND COMMERCIAL CLAYS ARE CUT WITH A WIRE TOOL BEFORE BEING WEDGED INTO A UNIFORM CLAY BODY

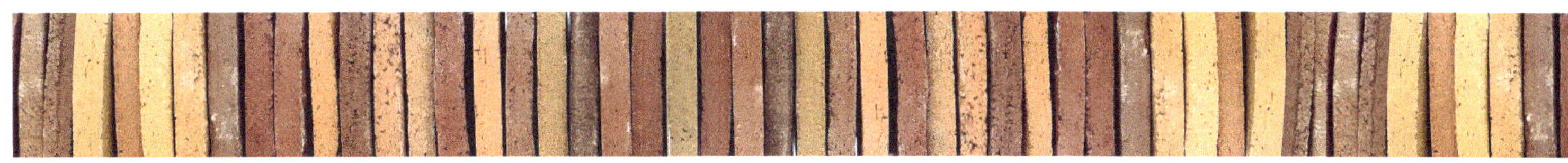

MW: DESCRIBE THE STEPS SOMEONE WOULD TAKE IN BETWEEN FINDING WILD CLAY AND DEVELOPING IT INTO A USABLE BODY.

LR: My current process of digging and preparing local clay for use is pretty rudimentary. First, I dig the clay from the ground with a shovel. Then I haul it to my studio, where I empty it into large bins, cover the clay with water, and let it sit for a couple days. Sitting in water softens and settles the clay. After the clay has slaked down, I remove any organic matter floating on the surface and mix the clay with a drill outfitted with a paddle attachment. Once the clay mixture is a more homogeneous slurry, I place a metal window screen over an empty bin and pour the slurry through the screen. I find that the mesh size of a standard window screen is small enough to block out large rocks, but large enough to let all the beautiful fragments of mica and sand through. Lastly, once my clay is sieved free of rocks, I transfer the slurry into a series of plaster troughs that dehydrate the clay to a workable consistency.

With all of this said, I think the root of this question is based in an individual artist's perception of the word "usability" as it pertains to clay. I suspect there are as many answers to the question of, "What makes a clay body usable?" as there are artists using clay. If you are making functional ware, issues related to workability and fired durability are paramount. In these cases, making wild clay usable would probably include adding other clay and non-clay materials to the local material to adjust for a desired characteristic in the finished ware.

It's just as possible to make your work from wild clay without alteration, but this style of making often requires that you adapt your process instead of adapting your material. In these cases, developing wild clay into a usable material may be as simple as the steps I have outlined above.

MW: WHAT DO YOU THINK IS LOST WHEN WE ARE NOT INVOLVED IN THE FINDING AND MAKING OF OUR CLAY BODIES?

LR: What a great question. Thinking back on it, I'm not sure if I felt a loss of something before I started testing local clays. However, I can truthfully say that, once I did, a new world opened up to me. Learning about clay had the effect of changing the way I moved through my life. Suddenly geology and chemistry were alive, and thrillingly active, all around me. There is a genuine connection to the true nature of the world that you get a glimpse of when you start to understand how clay works.

Next, I found a real connection to my community when I started to research local clays, not only through my research, but also through the objects themselves. As I mentioned earlier, I purposefully leave mica and sand in my clay, and this texture is a visual signature found in many wild clay pots made from my region. So, by digging some of my own clay, I feel a direct connection to my land, but also to my regional community of makers. I am part of a group of artists enthralled by their native materials, and there are frequently some commonalities in aesthetic that appear as part of that devotion.

Lastly, as a potter, clay is and always will be my primary material. It is literally the foundation upon which I built my whole career as an artist and as an educator. I feel that by giving it the respect of understanding its nuance and charm, I have gained a freedom that I did not know I was missing before. In the beginning, everything about the process of making pots felt a little bit like uncontrollable magic. However, when you invest the time it takes to understand your materials, you can transition from being a member of the audience, witnessing what happens, to being the magician. It's thrilling.

"I found a real connection to my community when I started to research local clays…"

02

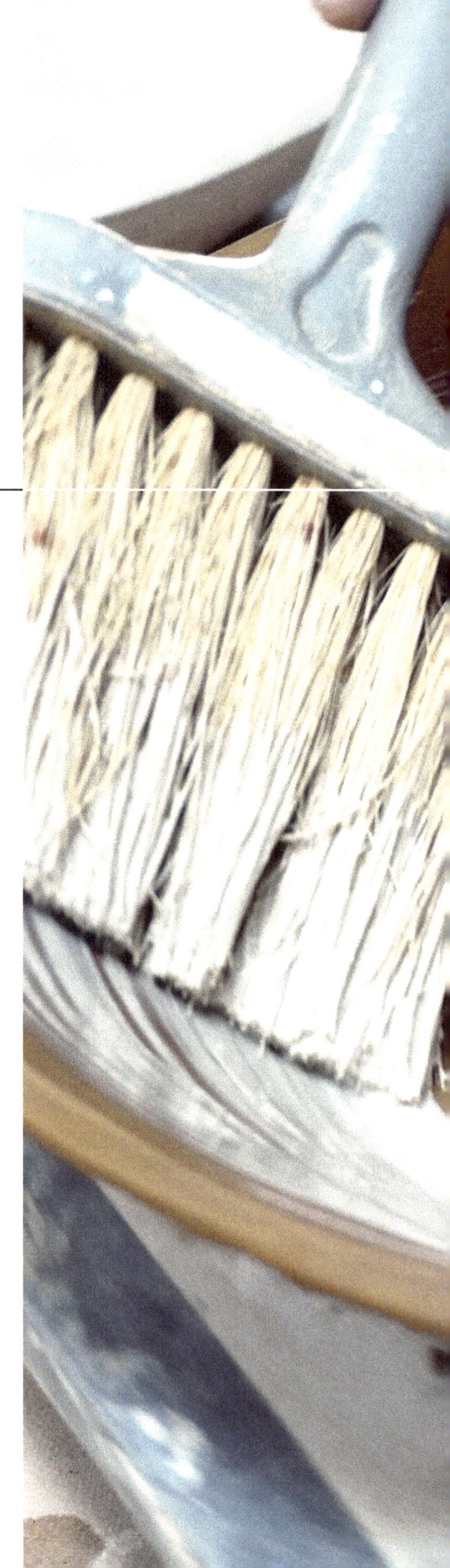

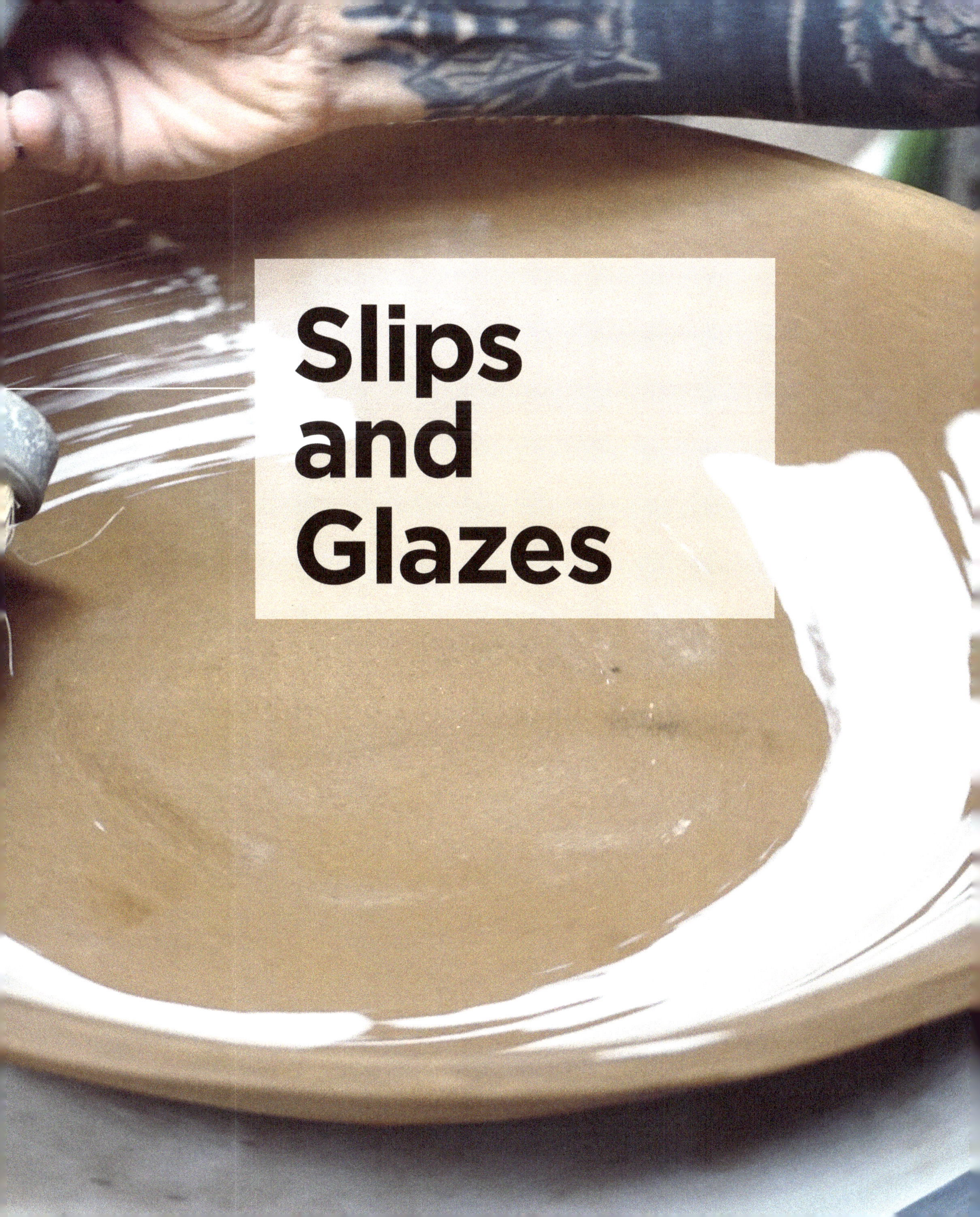
Slips
and
Glazes

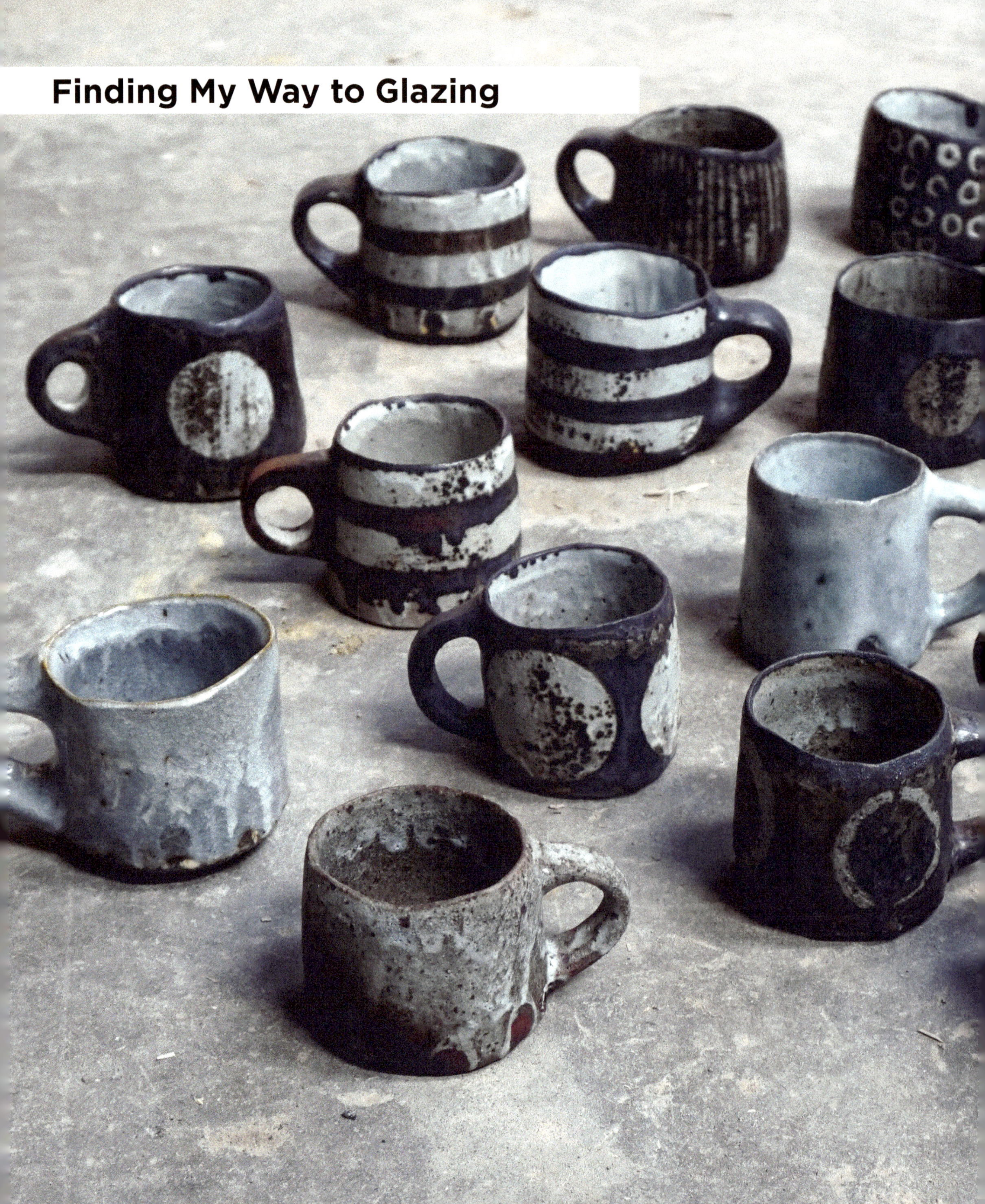
Finding My Way to Glazing

When I first started making pottery, I didn't think too much about glazing. I was taking classes at a community college and a local ceramic center. I wasn't afforded much of a voice in the glazing realm, aside from choosing my color. As for the firing, it was a mystery I had no part of. This was okay for the first couple of years: I was learning how to make pots and that consumed me. But I got to a point where it dawned on me that I loved making pots, but I didn't love pottery. The glazes finished the process but left me with a shiny, coated form that smothered the life out of it: a thick, opaque frosting that erased any marks or voice in the clay.

About that time, when I had begun looking for more control in how my finished pots looked, my teacher, Becca Floyd, gave me the opportunity to take a wood firing workshop taught by Michael Hunt and Naomi Dalglish. She knew how much the experience of an intense workshop would benefit me and evolve my making process. This week-long workshop at the John C. Campbell Folk School has proved to be the most defining moment in my pottery career. It opened the door to a whole new world of making pots. It was what I was looking for but didn't know it.

I learned about wood firing, wild clay, Hamada, Korean pottery, ash glazes, rocks, imperfections, crazing, and pots that look alive. I discovered I did like pottery. In fact, I loved it. I went down the rabbit holes of glazing, firing, and clay. I assisted Shawn Ireland and Bandana Pottery in wood firing and clay making. I joined a small studio with interesting working potters who generously answered my never-ending questions and encouraged and critiqued my work. I made as many pots as I could every chance I got. Life became what I imagined it would be when I was a kid—when you find the thing that gives you purpose, you matter.

I experimented constantly. I made and tested countless glazes, slips, and washes. Slowly, my voice started to emerge through my pots and they started to look and feel like me. I still experiment regularly.

Pottery is exciting and the more I learn, the more motivated I get. It is a cavernous craft with no limits. The explorations in form, method, firing, and glaze have no end. The more I make and learn, the more I feel inspired and full of ideas. I feel grateful and lucky that such a fire has been lit inside of me, marrying heart, head, and hands. As I work, I tend to this flame and it lights every aspect of my life.

I approach glazing as I do every other part of the process. Glazing is as important as the choice of clay and the type of kiln firing. Each of these aspects that go into making a pot are equally deserving of attention. I think of glazing as a contributing layer that enhances and showcases the slip and/or the clay underneath. The materials have a symbiotic relationship, all working together to let their individual qualities shine and become one finished piece.

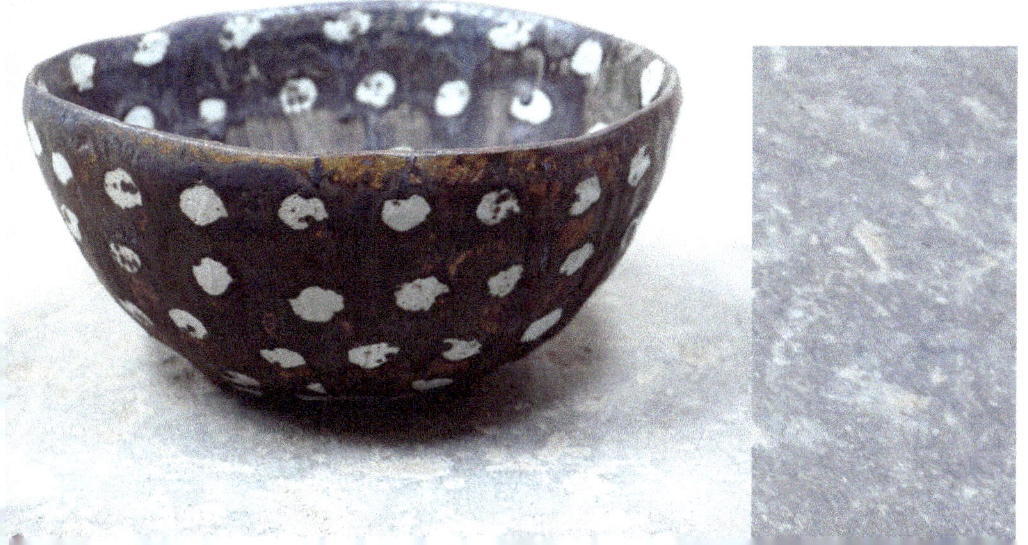

"Pottery is exciting and the more I learn, the more motivated I get."

Making and Using Slips and Glazes

YOU'LL NEED

- ✓ Talisman rotary sieve or sieve with 60 and 80 mesh screens
- ✓ Empty 5-gallon (19 liter) buckets with lids
- ✓ Quart mason jar, Tupperware, or other equivalent container with lid
- ✓ Electric drill with a mixer attachment
- ✓ Assorted bamboo brushes
- ✓ Assorted hake brushes
- ✓ Oil-based wax, such as Aftosa blue wax
- ✓ Water-based wax, such as Amaco or Forbes
- ✓ Sponge
- ✓ Large whisk or wooden spoon for stirring glazes, slips, and iron wash dry ingredients, according to desired recipes
- ✓ Digital scale
- ✓ 4-cup (1 liter) plastic measuring cup scoop
- ✓ Respirator

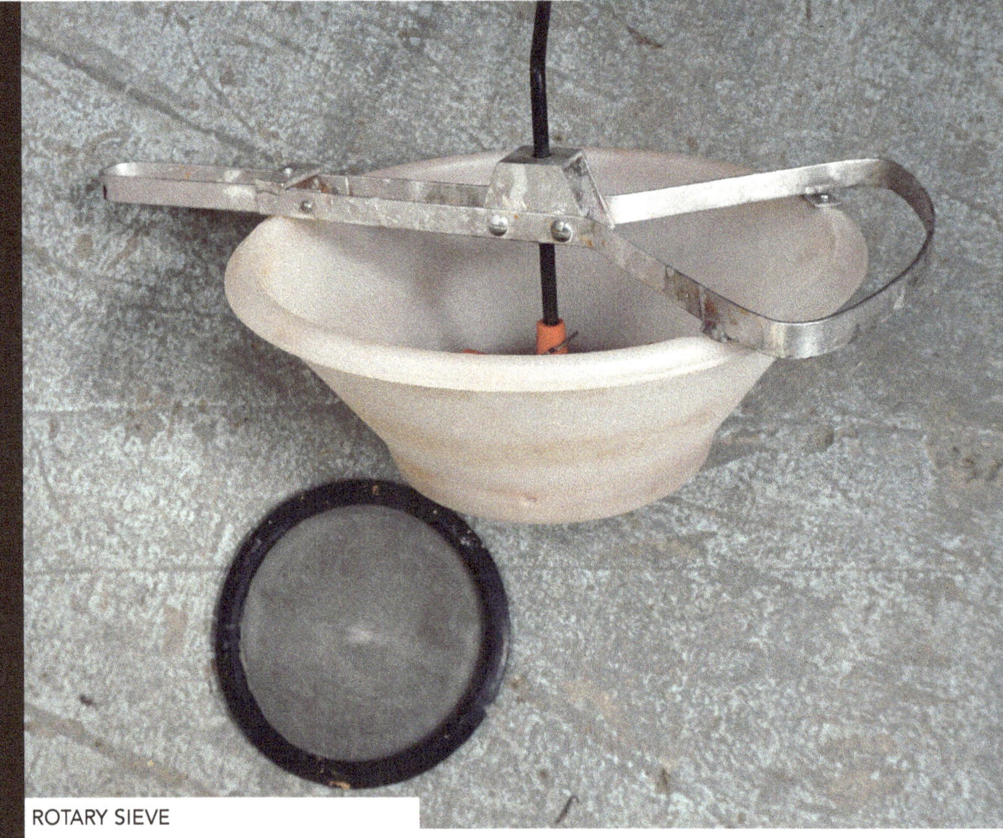

ROTARY SIEVE
IRON- AND ASH-GLAZED VASE

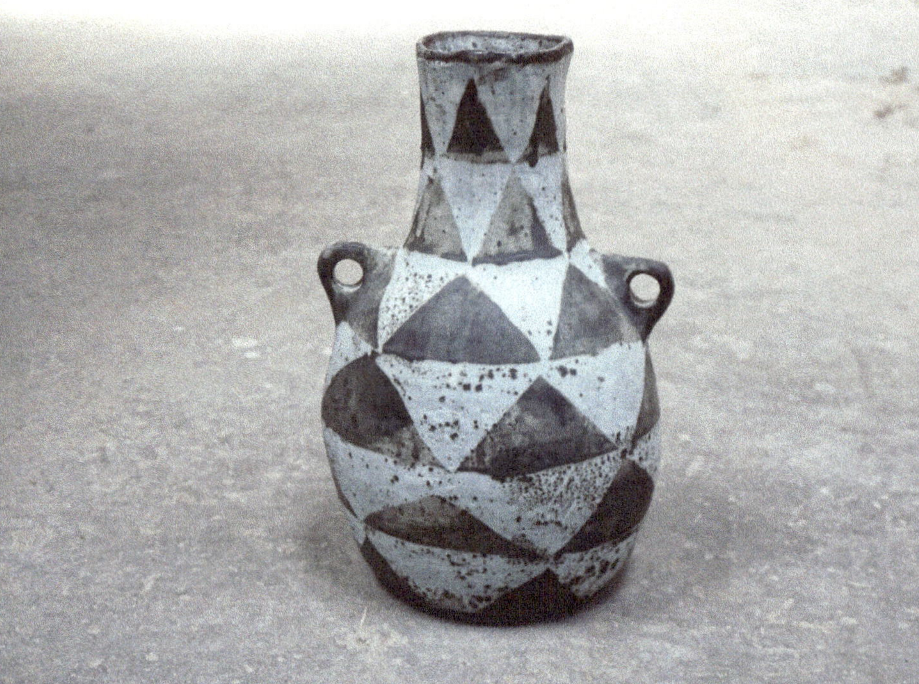

ABOUT ASH GLAZE

My main choice is a simple ash glaze made with ash, kaolin, and feldspar. I got the basic recipe from a Japanese potter on the Internet who informed me that the feldspar in Japan is much different than the feldspar in the United States. The type of wood burned for the ash is important, as is the type of kaolin. It's a simple recipe of three ingredients, but the variance in the materials can completely change the look and feel of the glaze.

I did a lot of testing and, depending on the type of materials I used, the glaze came out shiny, matte, dry, yellow, or pink—that's how much it can vary. The way you apply the glaze also matters greatly: thin to thick make almost entirely different glazes.

I honed in on the ingredients that imparted the qualities I was looking for—a matte finish with a satin feel and a slightly bright white color. Every batch of glaze varies slightly because the ash is not a controlled ingredient—I like that about it. This glaze is very versatile, which is important to me. I use it over slip for a warm white, over slip with iron for a spooky and nuanced black, and over slip decorated with wax and iron for a contrast of black and white. I use it over raw clay and it varies from a finish reminiscent of stucco to concrete to metal to rock.

Essentially, I'm able to get many glazes from my single ash glaze, and they relate one to another. This is important to me because I don't want a bunch of colored glazes complicating things and sending my pots all over the place visually. I want the work to be cohesive, with neutral tones so the wild clay looks at home. Here are some of my glaze recipes. The processes for mixing them follows.

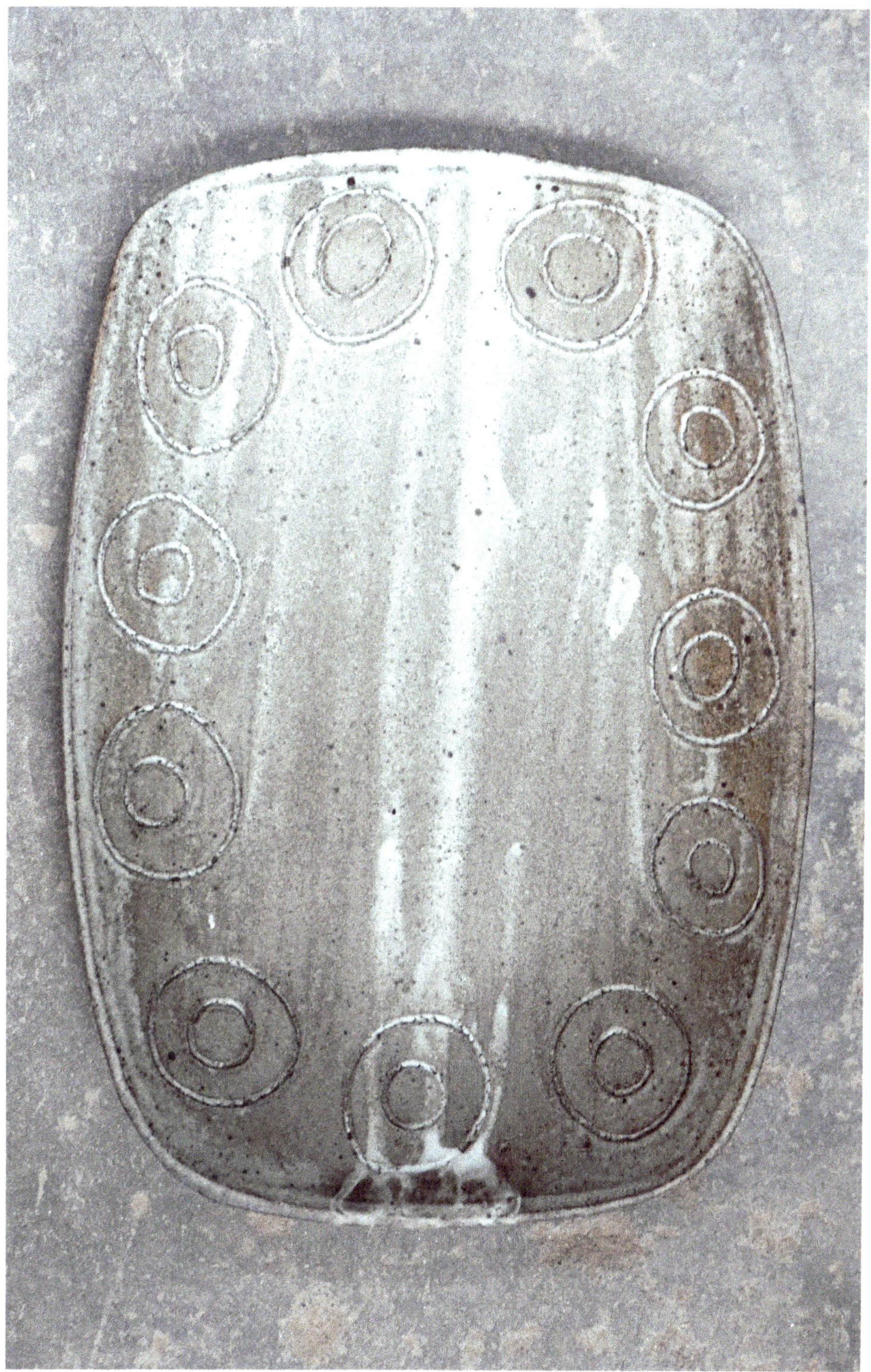

SERVING DISH WITH ASH GLAZE AND CARVING

My recipes are formulated for cone 10 reduction fired pots.

Cone 10 Ash Glaze

10,000 grams makes roughly a 5-gallon bucket of glaze

- ☐ 30 grams ash
- ☐ 30 grams kaolin
- ☐ 40 grams feldspar

Please experiment with different types of ash, kaolin, and feldspar, as they will significantly alter your glaze.

SLIP

Slip is a clay in liquid form. I use it to brighten my glazes because my clay is very iron-rich and dark. The use of the slip adds another layer of movement to the pot. I use it thin to enhance the marks and character of the clay, rather than masking them. This gives the glaze a lighter backdrop to make it appear white. I use this slip before bisque on leather-hard pots.

Silica Slip for Bisque

- ☐ 25 grams Grolleg
- ☐ 25 grams EPK
- ☐ 15 grams XX saggar
- ☐ 5 grams bentonite
- ☐ 35 grams 200 mesh silica

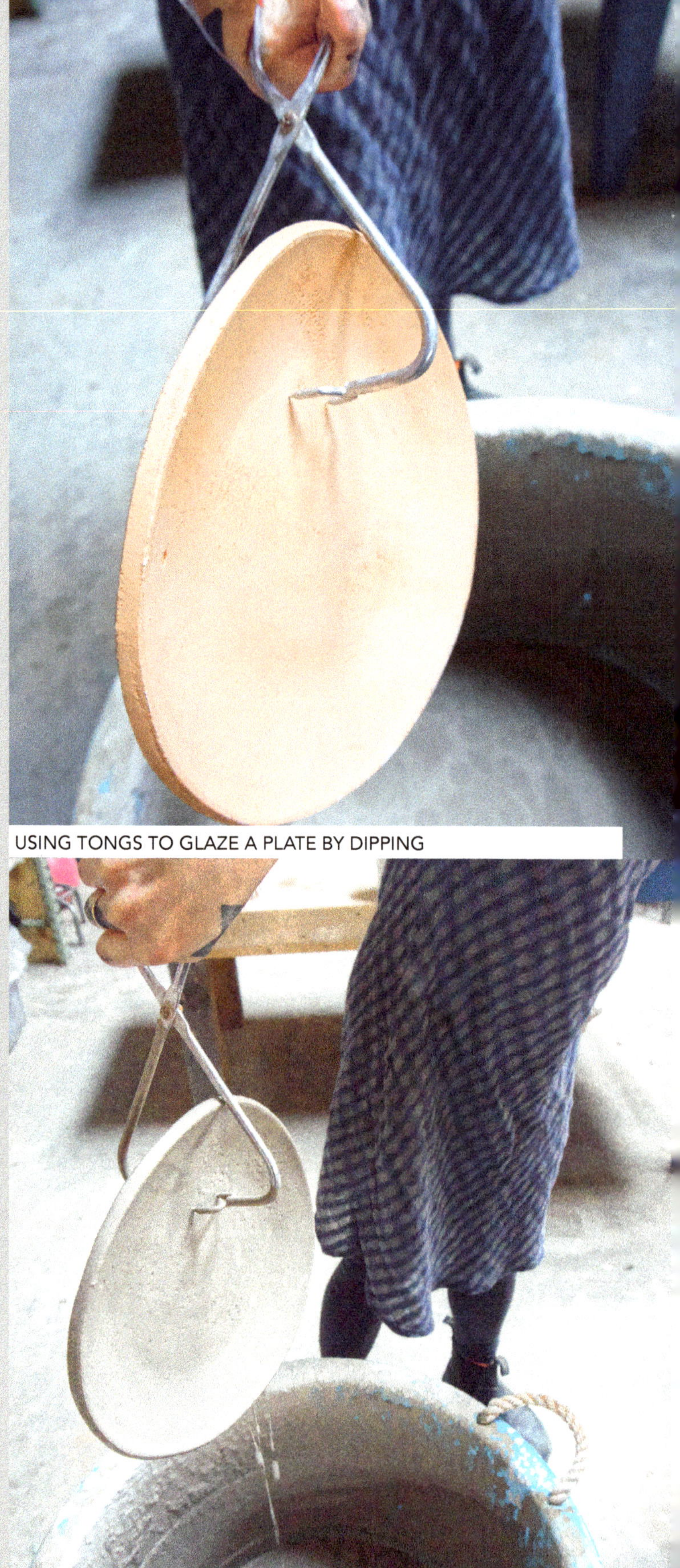

USING TONGS TO GLAZE A PLATE BY DIPPING

Basic Process for Making Glaze and Slip

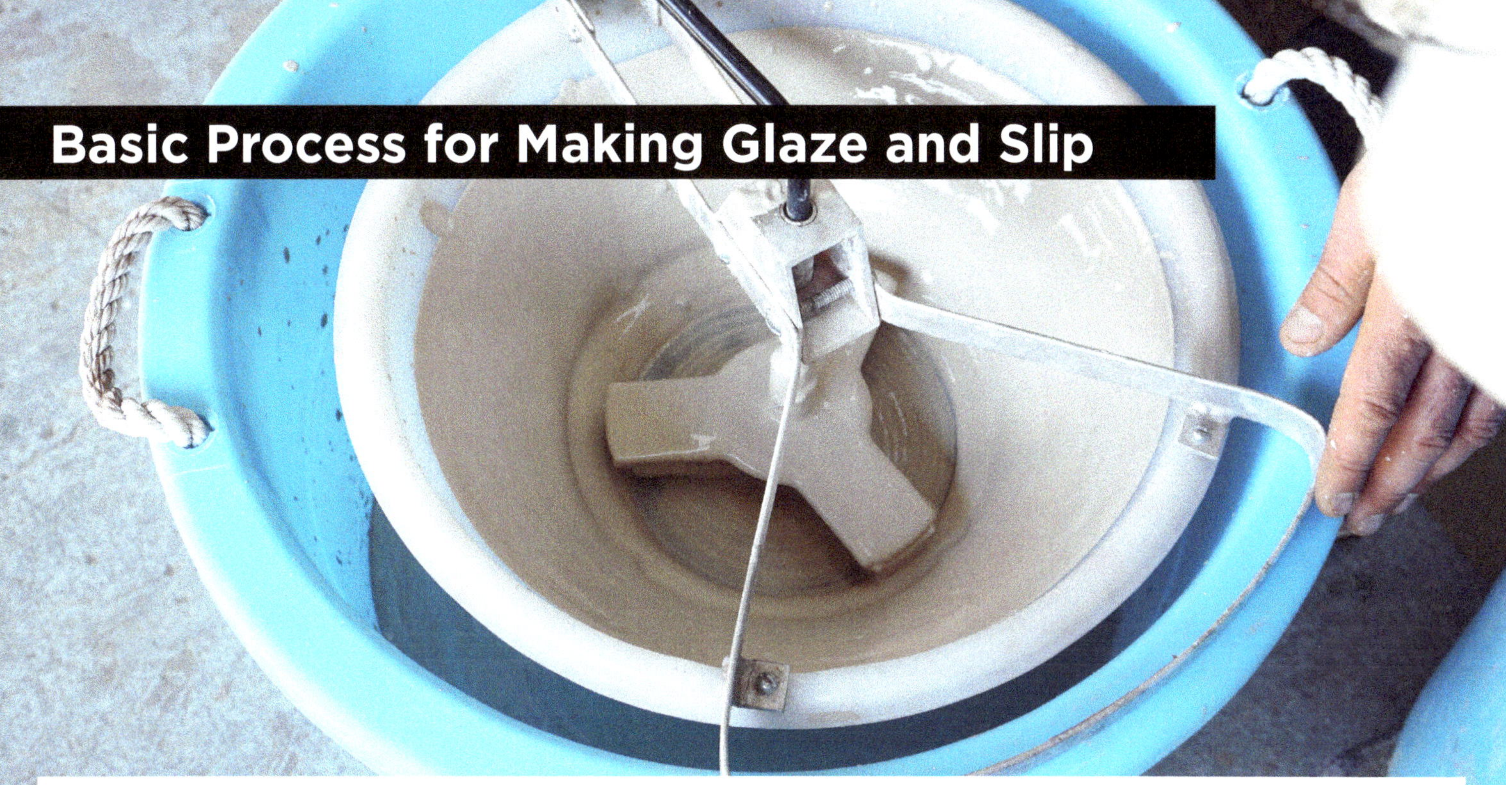

TIPS TO START WITH

☐ Making glaze and slip follows the same process, except that you generally use a 60-mesh sieve for straining slip and an 80-mesh sieve for glaze. Slip usually needs to be sieved more times.

☐ I always make a test batch of glaze to see how it's going to work with my clay and firing technique. A test batch should be no less than 500 grams.

☐ Once the test is done, I generally make batches of glaze in 10,000 grams, which is about a 5-gallon (19 liter) bucket's worth. The exception is my ash glaze. Because I use so much of that, I make 30,000 grams and store it in a 20-gallon (75.7 liter) tub. I can also easily dip large pieces in the bigger bucket, instead of having to pour out the glaze into a wider trough.

Note: If you add too much water and your glaze becomes too thin, set it aside for a day to let it settle. Pour off the excess water and mix again to a heavy cream consistency.

MIX A BATCH

Make your glaze outdoors or in a well-ventilated area and wear a respirator. For a 10,000-gram batch, you'll need:

☐ Your dry ingredients

☐ Respirator

☐ Digital scale

☐ Scoop measuring cup

☐ Two 5-gallon (19 liter) buckets

☐ Water

☐ Drill with mixer attachment

☐ Sieve

Note: An easy way to convert your recipe to 10,000 grams is to move the decimal point twice to the right— 20 grams becomes 2,000. Important: Write down your conversion, and after you weigh and add each ingredient to the bucket, cross it off the list. A mistake could cost you an entire kiln load of pots, and perhaps kiln shelves too. Glaze mistakes can be costly and ruin months of hard work. If I get interrupted while making a glaze, I can be sure of what has been added so far because I have crossed it off my list.

1. Carefully weigh the glaze ingredients one at a time and add them to a 5-gallon bucket.

2. When you have added all the dry ingredients, add enough water to mix the glaze easily with the drill. It should be on the thick side of a heavy cream consistency.

3. When thoroughly mixed, pour the bucket of glaze through a sieve into an empty bucket. Use an 80-mesh sieve for glaze and a 60-mesh for slip. If you are not using a Talisman (rotary) sieve, you will need to use your hand or a rubber spatula to push the glaze through the sieve.

4. Use a small amount of water to rinse out the original bucket. Repeat step 3, pouring the glaze back into the original bucket. Check to make sure the glaze is smooth and free of small, chunky particles. If it's not, sieve it again. You can add more water at this point and mix it in if the glaze is too thick.

5. Label your glaze and keep it in a bucket with a secure lid. Stir or mix the glaze with the drill prior to use.

Steps for Making Ash Glaze

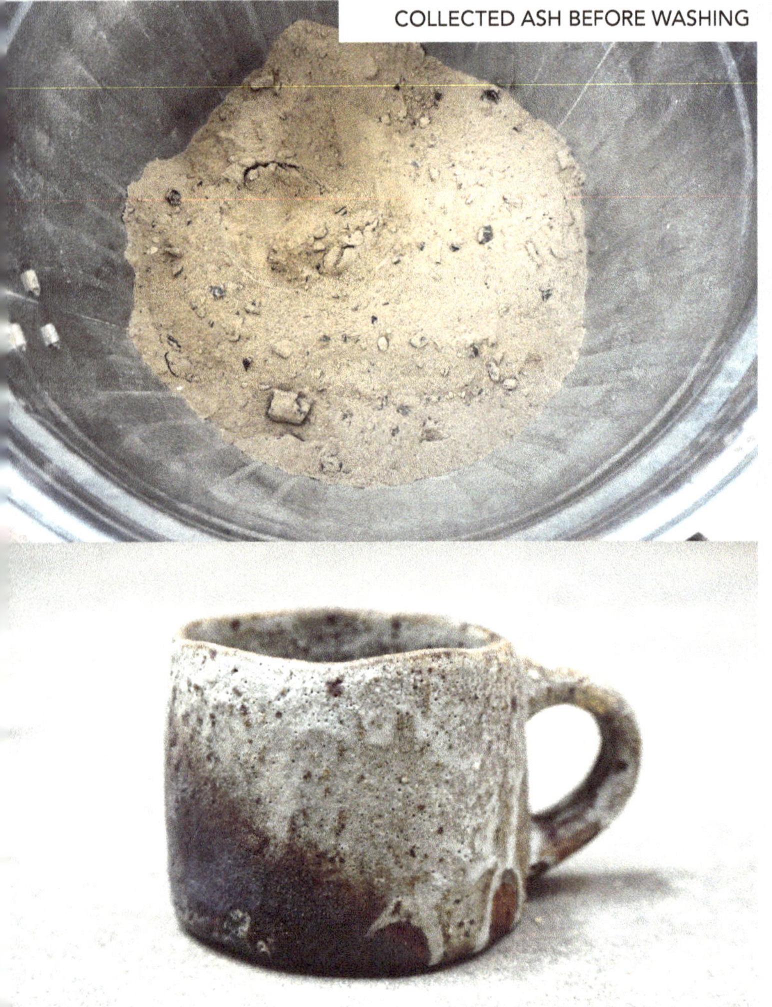

COLLECTED ASH BEFORE WASHING

ASH-GLAZED MUG

WASHING ASH

Washing ash before using it in a glaze is not a requirement, but it's important for a couple of reasons. First, ash is caustic and can give you chemical burns. Washing the ash minimizes this risk significantly. If you don't wash the ash, you will need to wear gloves or use glaze tongs as you work with it. And if you do wash the ash, you will still need to be careful with it when washing the glaze off your hands, especially if you have sensitive skin.

The other reason for washing it is that glaze made with washed ash will keep for many months. If you don't wash it, you will need to make a new batch for each kiln load.

For my recipe, I weigh the ash dry, then wash it. The weight from chunks and unburned pieces isn't significant enough to matter for my purposes. If you need a more exact amount, you will need to wash your ash first, let it dry, sieve it, and then weigh it.

To wash ash, put the amount needed in a 5-gallon (19 liter) bucket and fill it with water. Make sure there is room for half to one-third of the bucket to be filled with water. Let the ash sit in the water for 12 to 24 hours. A stinky, yellow liquid will rise to the top; carefully dump this water off without losing the ash particles. Refill with clean water and repeat three to four times, or until the water stays clear. You can leave this water once it's clear, to make your glaze.

MIXING THE ASH GLAZE

1. Add the weighed-out feldspar and kaolin to the bucket of washed ash.
2. Add enough water to give it a thick cream consistency. Use a drill with a mixer attachment to fully incorporate your ingredients.
3. When fully mixed, pour the glaze through an 80-mesh or higher sieve into a clean bucket. If you need to add a small amount of water for the glaze to pour and sieve, that's okay. Just keep your glaze at least as thick as heavy cream.

Note: If you add too much water and your glaze becomes too thin, set it aside for a day to let it settle. Pour off the excess water and mix again to heavy cream consistency.

4. Sieve the glaze twice, then test for chunks or unabsorbed particles. You will need to sieve until the glaze is completely smooth.
5. Test your glaze at different thicknesses.

Iron Wash

☐ 80% red iron oxide

☐ 20% ball clay

☐ water

I generally make 1,000 grams of iron wash at a time, and it goes a long way.

Mix the wash in a container that has a lid. A Tupperware container or glass jar works well.

1. Mix the iron oxide and ball clay. Add water for a 50/50 ratio. I use a stick blender to mix this.

2. Strain the mixture through an 80-mesh sieve.

Note: The iron lasts indefinitely, but it becomes more concentrated over time and you will need to add water to maintain the 50/50 ratio.

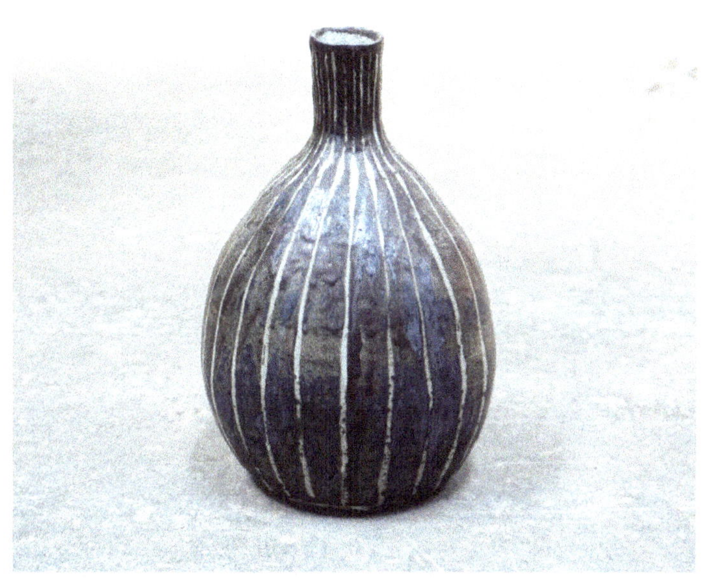

VASE WITH ASH GLAZE AND AN IRON WASH

The Glazing Process

Pots are ready for glazing after they've been bisque fired. When the pots are bisqued, I wipe them down with a damp sponge to clean off any dust that might interfere with the glaze adhering. I brush on a water-based wax called Forbes wax on the bottoms of the pots and anywhere else I do not want glaze.

Ash Glaze by Itself

My ash glaze is formulated for bisque ware. I apply it by dipping a pot in the glaze. Whether I use the glaze thick or thin depends on the desired outcome. By thick I mean heavy cream consistency —any thicker and it may crawl, or shrivel, when it's fired. By thin I mean milk consistency. Typically, when it's applied, the glaze appears darker where it's thinner.

Ash Glaze with Iron Wash

I use a thin ash glaze when I'm combining it with iron wash.

1. After dipping the pot in the ash glaze, I wait a few minutes for it to dry.

2. I decorate the surface with a wax resist technique, using an oil-based wax such as Mobil or Aftosa. I pour the wax into a cup and add about a fifth of the volume in hot water. This helps the wax flow and prevents it from gumming up.

3. I paint the wax on with a brush and let it dry. This generally dries in about 10 minutes if it's not too thick. If I don't like my wax design, I can wash off the glaze and wait a day for the pot to dry and start over.

4. The iron wash needs to be stirred after decorating each pot because the iron particles sink to the bottom. I use a wide soft-haired brush to apply the wash, being careful not to brush over the same area too many times, add thicker layers, or let it pool up. If the iron is too thick it can bubble, crust, and run, ruining the pot.

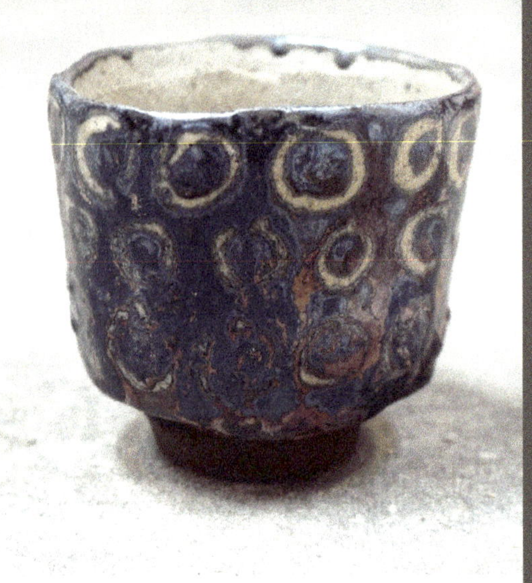

CIRCLE DESIGN CUP WITH
IRON AND ASH GLAZE

> I typically glaze a kiln load of pots, decorate them with wax, and then apply the iron all at once. This takes me two to three days. The ash glaze and the iron can be tricky. I've been using them together for years and I still encounter issues. If the ash glaze is too thick it can be a problem. If the iron is too thin or too thick it can be a problem. If the reduction is too much or not enough it can be a problem.

I've put years of testing, adjusting materials and firing schedules, and continued tweaking, into the process to figure out how to make the pots come out the way I want, with interesting and exciting surfaces. Each kiln load can differ dramatically. The iron might come out gray, brown, red, purple, black, shiny, matte, or with other differences in color and texture. I choose to control this to a point, but so many factors are involved that it is not in my interest to subject my work to a rigid, tightly controlled environment where the results are the same each time.

The slip, glaze, iron application, kiln load, and oxygen reduction during the firing and cooling in the kiln are all contributing factors. I enjoy opening the kiln and not knowing exactly what I will see. I like discovering the variation in each kiln load, with some pots shiny and black and some matte and red, and all the colors and surfaces in between. Each pot is significant and interesting on its own, and as a group, the pots display all of the variance of their materials and process.

SHINY GLAZE

I use a couple of shiny glazes to break up the surface decoration and create contrast. These pots tend to be elegant and quiet on their own but fit in nicely with the majority of matte and darker ash-glazed pots. The shiny glazes I use regularly are a celadon and a shino. Celadon glazes originated in China and are known for their subtle green tones that range from a pale gray-green to jade. Shino is a satiny, white feldspar-based glaze that originated in Japan in the sixteenth century. Both glazes have vast categories on their own.

SHINO

The shino recipe I use is named Sprague Shino. I got the recipe from a potter named Steve Lloyd. I bought a beautiful tea bowl from him made from a local clay that he had dug. The glaze was what I was looking for, lending itself beautifully to the imperfections in wild clay. He generously shared the recipe. Sadly, he died a few months after I met him. Every time I use this shino, I think of him and the moment of buying the tea bowl and talking about wild clay.

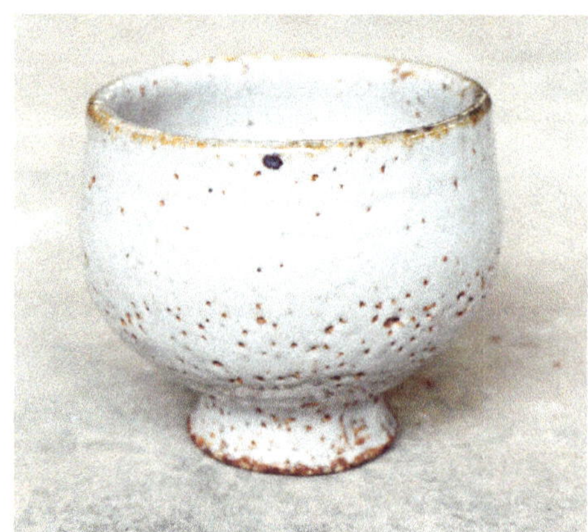

CUP WITH SHINO GLAZE BY STEVE LLOYD

Cone 10 Sprague Shino

- ☐ 4.04 grams soda ash
- ☐ 15.35 grams spodumene
- ☐ 45.45 grams nepheline syenite
- ☐ 16.57 grams OM4
- ☐ 18.59 grams minspar NC4

Cone 10 RU Celadon

- ☐ 34.5 grams Custer Feldspar
- ☐ 19 grams Grolleg
- ☐ 18 grams silica
- ☐ 15 grams whiting
- ☐ 9.5 grams dolomite
- ☐ 1.7 grams red iron oxide
- ☐ 1.5 grams bone ash
- ☐ 3 grams bentonite

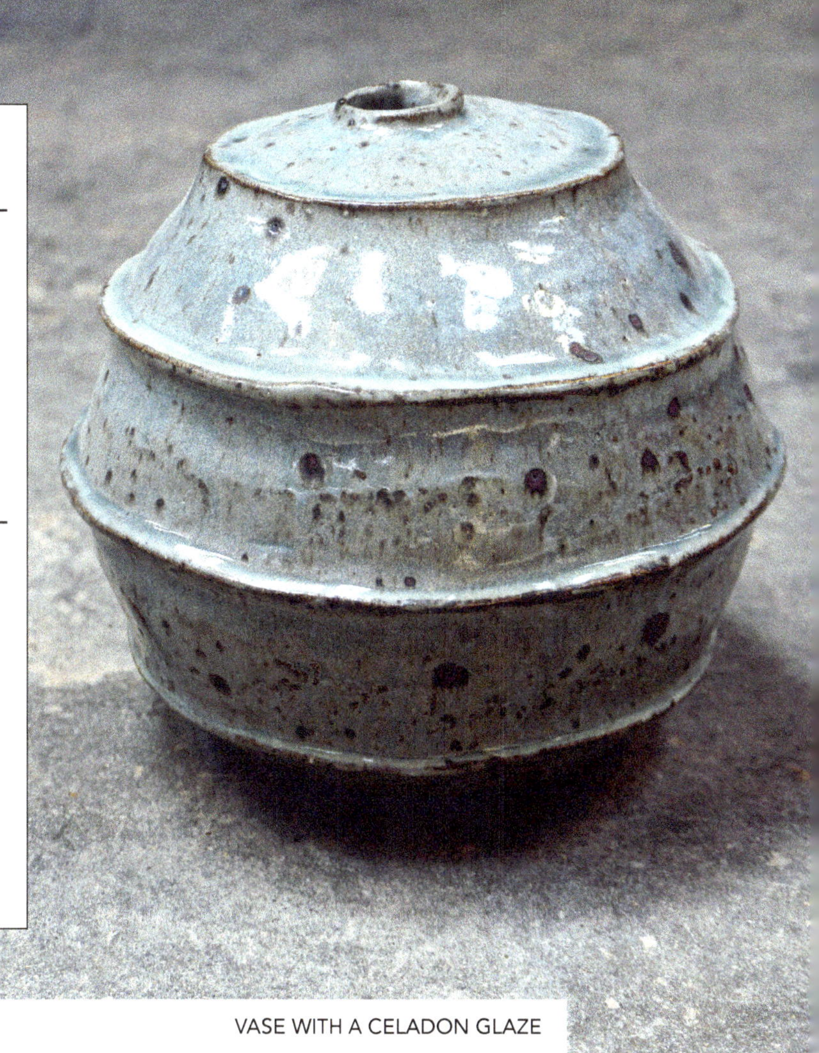

VASE WITH A CELADON GLAZE

CELADON

The celadon recipe I use is called Ru Celadon. Ru ware is a famous category of Chinese pottery from the Song Dynasty. This glaze has been reformulated with modern ingredients to evoke the original Ru glaze. The glaze is a greenish-blue color, and has a shiny texture when it comes out in gas reduction. When I first tried this glaze, it didn't resemble Ru ware. It wasn't until I started reduction cooling that the glaze took on the palest and richest shade of blue and a satin-to-matte surface. This was closer to the colors of Ru ware pottery, but really not even that close! Regardless, the glaze evokes a calm and fragile utilitarian feel in the finished pot—simultaneously ancient and new.

Guest Potter Interview: Michael Hunt and Naomi Dalglish of Bandana Pottery

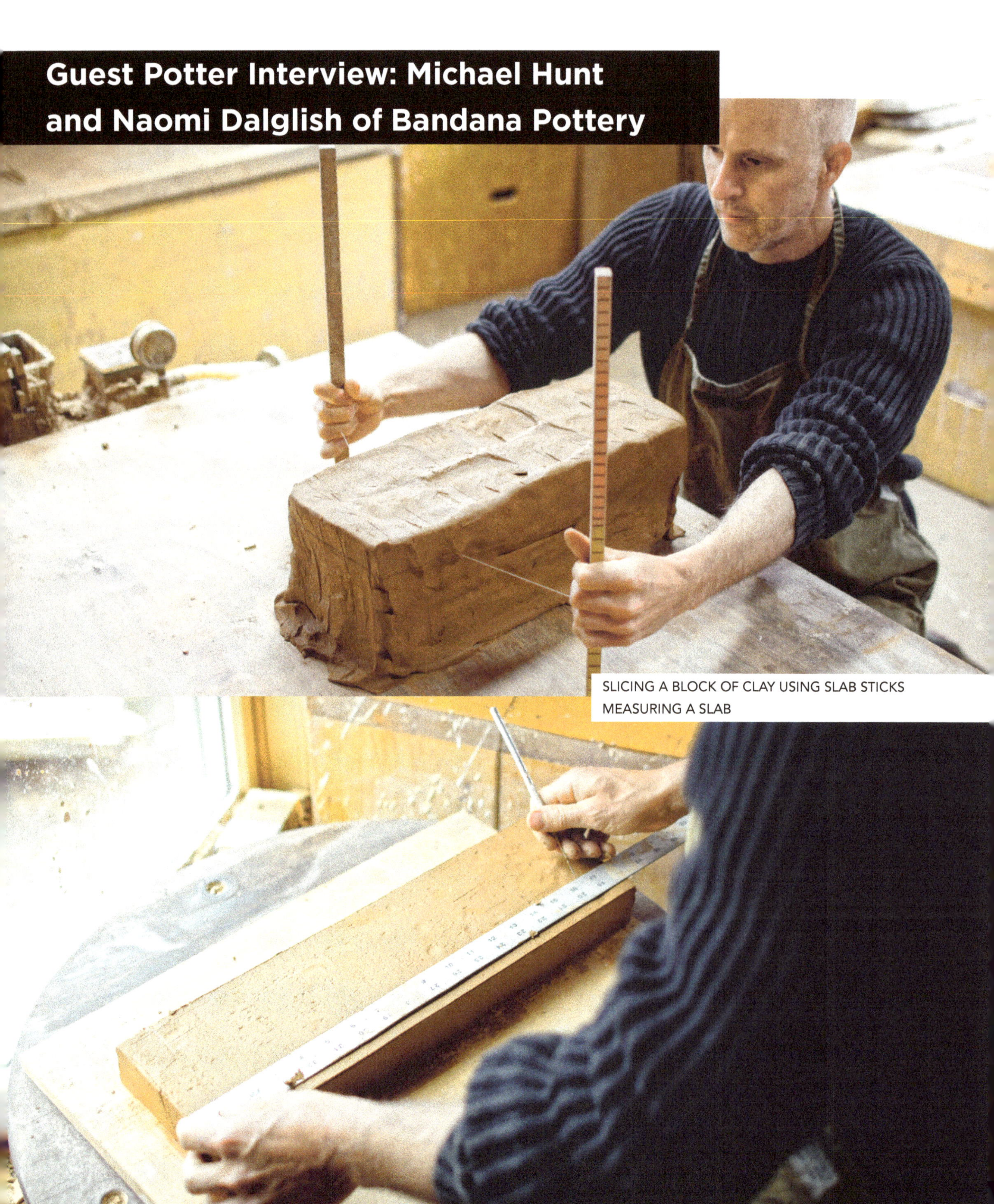

SLICING A BLOCK OF CLAY USING SLAB STICKS

MEASURING A SLAB

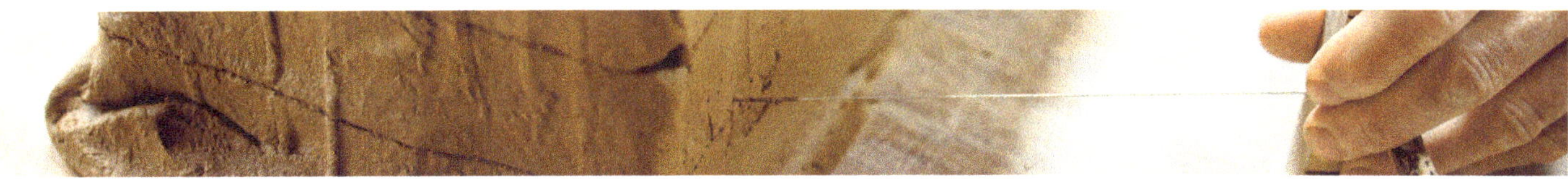

MW: WHO WERE YOUR MENTORS? HOW DID THEY INFORM YOUR POTS?

MH AND ND: Will Ruggles and Douglass Rankin were longtime mentors. We were deeply influenced by their process: using soft clay on a slow-turning kick wheel, layering slips, and wood firing. Every part of this process was all about communicating the feeling of wet clay.

They impressed on us the importance and expressiveness of the clay wall itself—it's not merely a line drawn in clay, but something with substance and depth. Whether in the pottery or around the dining room table, we were welcomed into searching conversations around life and clay that propelled the two of us onto the path we are on today.

Michael Simon was also a mentor who taught throwing and altering as a way to combine wheel- and handbuilding techniques. All three of these potters were masters at integrating pattern with the form of the pot—something for which we continue to strive.

MW: YOU HAVE AN APPRECIATION FOR MATERIALS THAT IS VERY EVIDENT IN ALL OF YOUR POTS. WHAT IS YOUR PROCESS? WHY USE LOCAL CLAYS?

MH AND ND: We have always been in love with the way funky, impure materials give life to the historical work that we admire, so we spend a lot of time exploring local materials for our clays, slips, and glazes. These materials can have their limitations, but as in any creative endeavor, those limitations can help give you a framework to explore an idea. Perhaps a clay isn't plastic enough to throw a pitcher, but it reveals a beautiful texture when it's carved at the foot or faceted. Each clay, with its own character, is teaching us to listen and respond, influencing not only the pots themselves but ourselves as makers.

We make our clay by mixing the raw local clay into a slip and pouring it through a screen into a feed trough. We consider the screening process to be one of the first aesthetic choices in making the pots—the size of rocks and sand that are allowed through will determine the final landscape of clay. To this slurry, we add a relatively small percentage of commercial powdered materials, and then pump it all into fabric-lined racks where it will dry out to working consistency.

Our pots are fired in a large, Thai-style wood kiln. Since our pots are mostly glazed, our firings aren't aiming for intense ash buildup, but for moderate amounts of ash melting into the glaze, as well as the subtle fluctuations of atmosphere that happen within each stoke of the kiln.

MW: DESCRIBE YOUR MAKING CYCLE.

MH AND ND: Because we mostly fire in a large kiln that holds 600 to 700 pots, our making cycle usually lasts about two months. We often enjoy making a large run of similar pots at one time. This can lead to a freedom of expression that might not be as easy if each pot feels precious.

It also creates an environment where you can respond in the moment to what is happening—small details of one pot lead us to explore something new on the next pot.

Bandana Pottery

MW: HOW DO YOU EXPERIMENT WITH THE NATURAL MATERIALS YOU USE?

MH AND ND: When we find a new wild clay, we conduct a variety of tests to determine its shrinkage, porosity, and working properties. A clay might have a gorgeous bright color in its pure state, but not hold water that well. When we vitrify the clay, suddenly it becomes a duller brown. Thus, we are always trying to find the right balance between the beautiful wild qualities of the clay that inspire us and the functional demands of tableware.

MW: YOU USE A VARIETY OF HANDBUILDING TECHNIQUES TO MAKE YOUR POTS. CAN YOU LIST AND DESCRIBE THEM?

MH AND ND: Hump molding: Forming a soft slab over a bisque mold.

Carving off from solid clay: Sometimes we make a rough form, wait for it to become leather-hard, and then carve the outside and inside (e.g., for boxes). Other times, we make very thick slabs in the shape of the pot and scoop out the soft clay right away and then do more finishing of certain details, like the foot, after it is leather-hard (e.g., for triple trays or triangle bowls).

Press molding: We press a soft slab into a plaster mold to make plates and trays. After they come out, we carve the foot out of the generous amount of clay we had in the mold.

Constructing with hump-molded forms: Some vases are made by taking two hump-molded forms and sticking them together.

Coil building: Some vases are finished with coil building, and Naomi uses coil building for her sculptures.

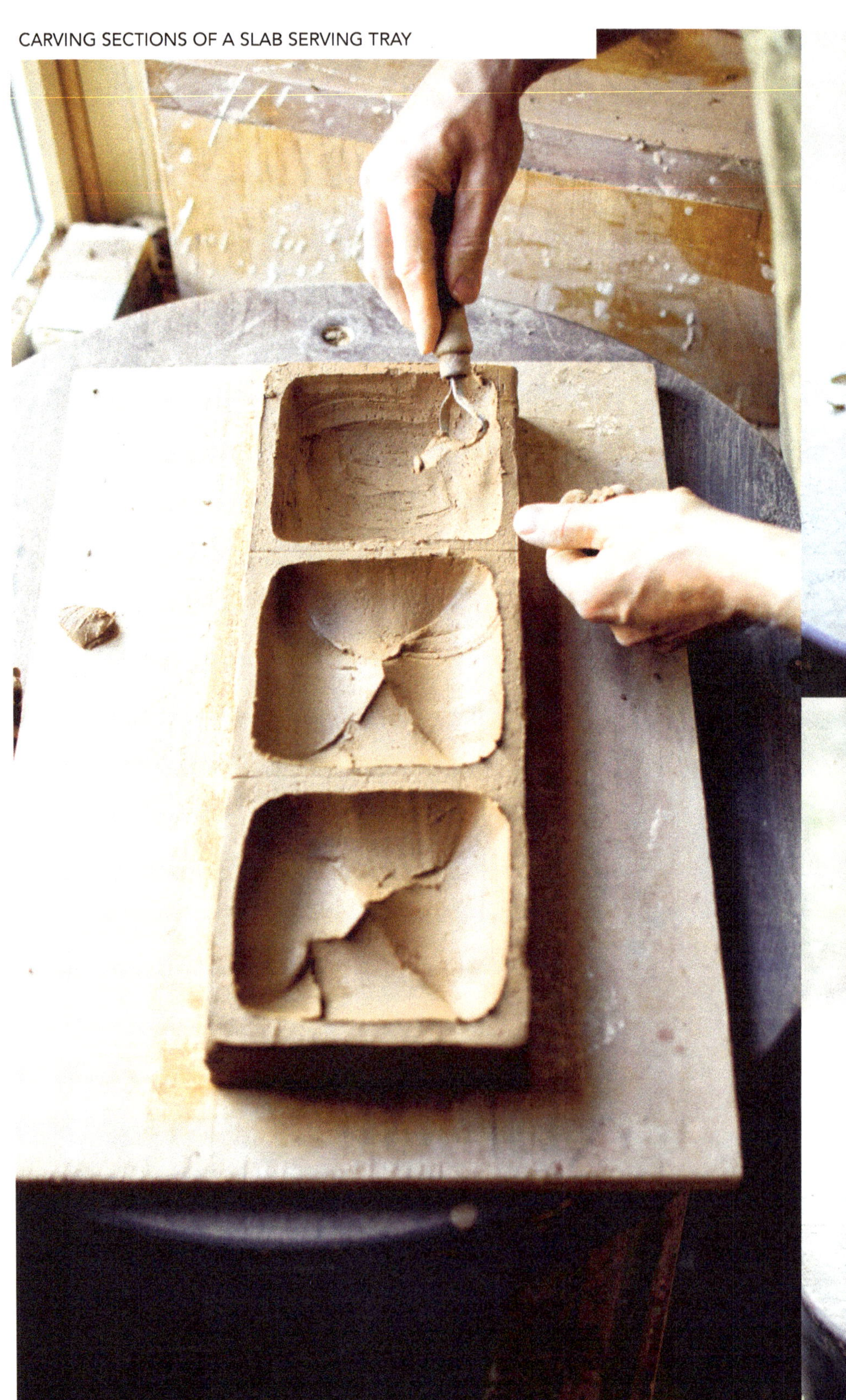

CARVING SECTIONS OF A SLAB SERVING TRAY

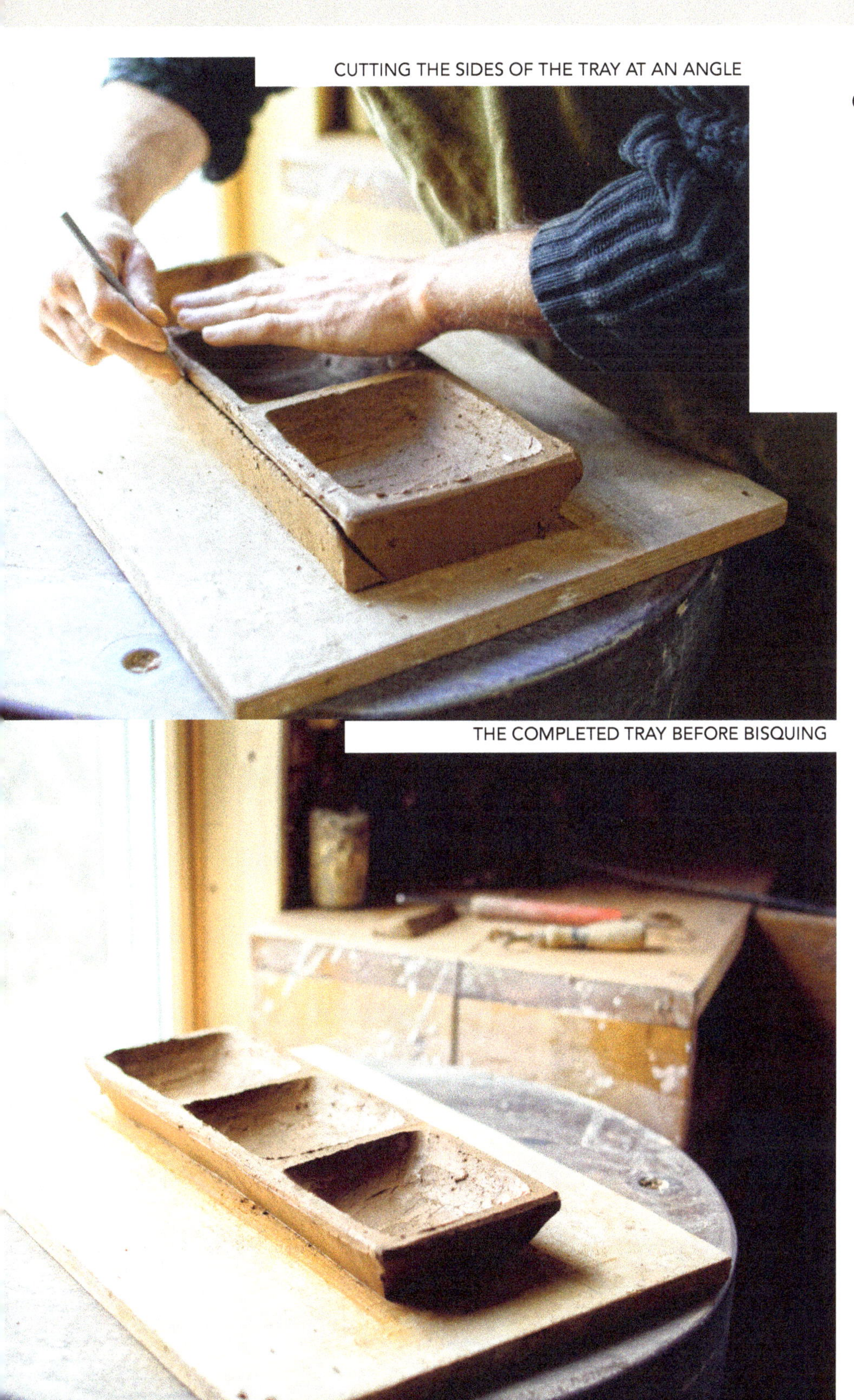

CUTTING THE SIDES OF THE TRAY AT AN ANGLE

THE COMPLETED TRAY BEFORE BISQUING

"We have always been in love with the way funky, impure materials give life to the historical work that we admire."

03

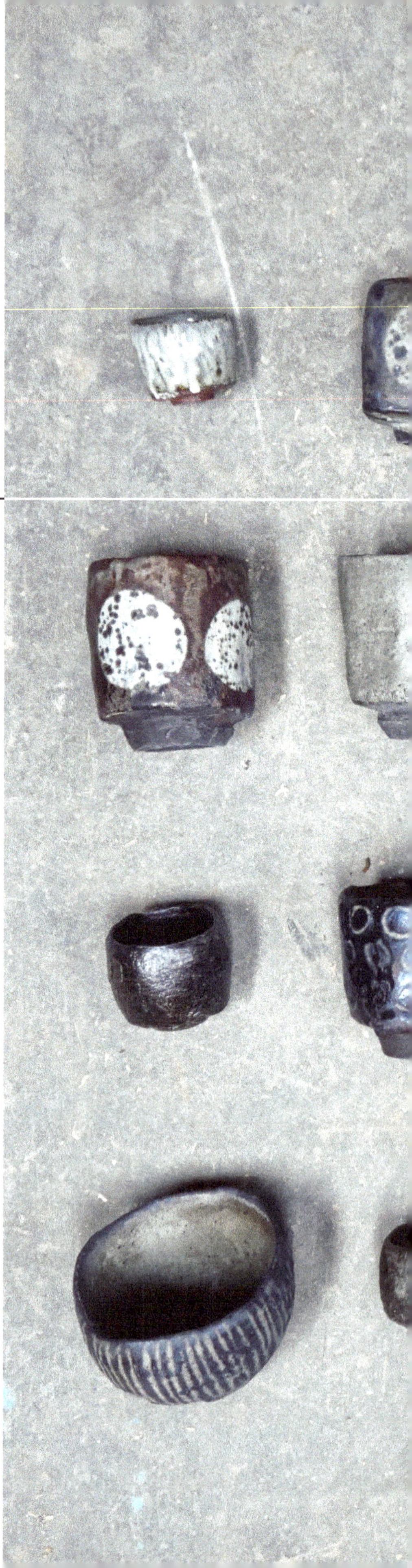

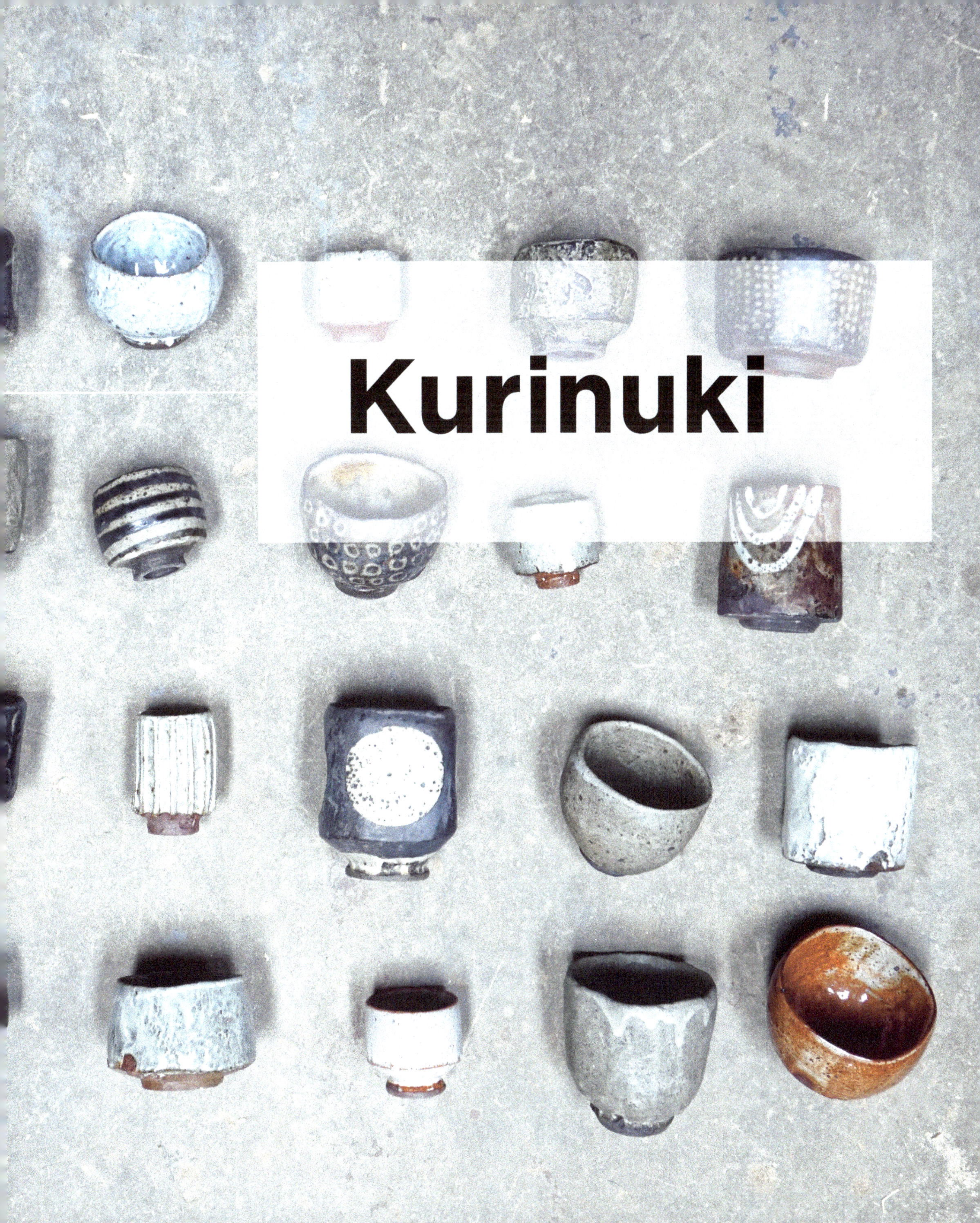
Kurinuki

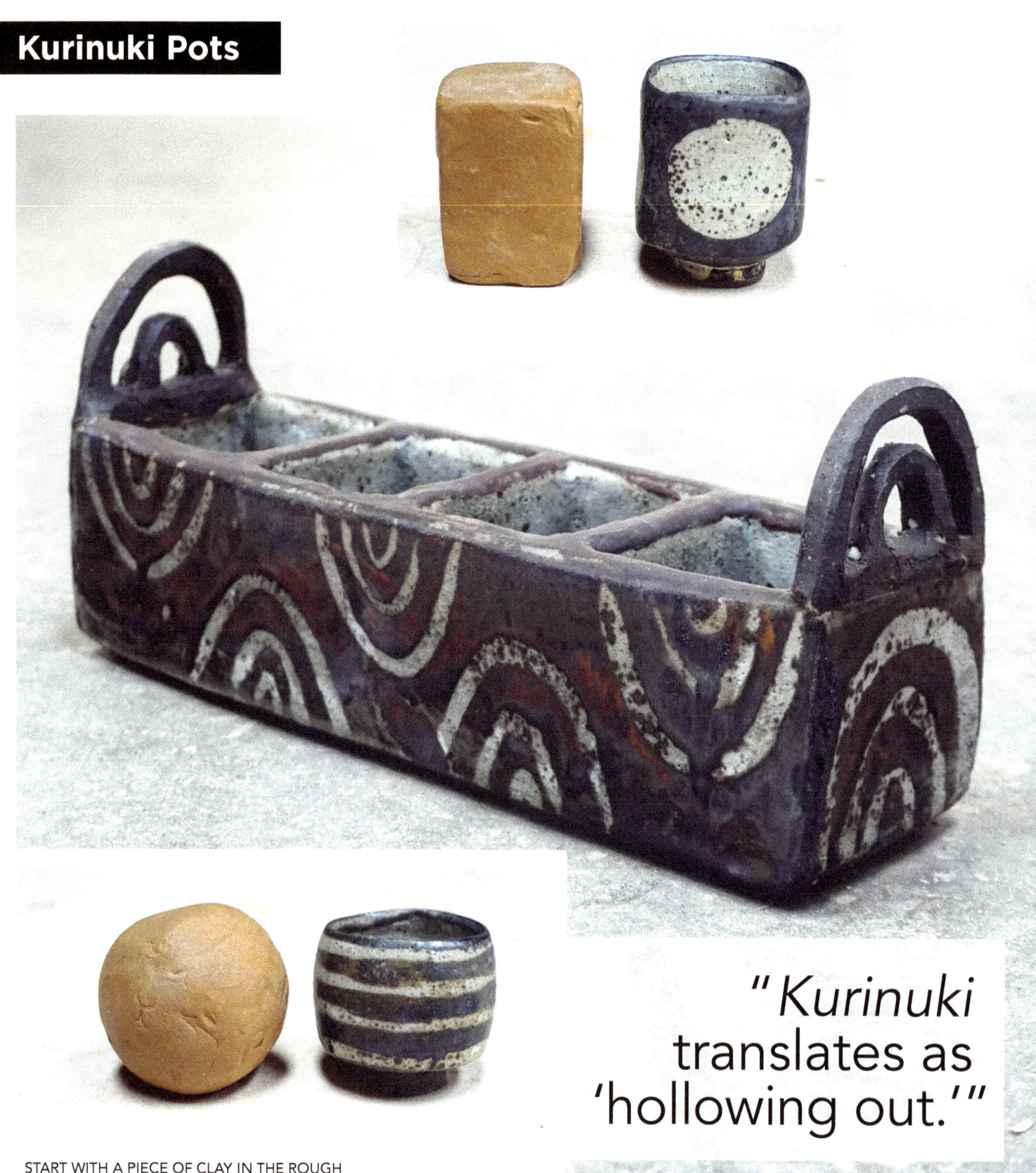

"*Kurinuki* translates as 'hollowing out.'"

START WITH A PIECE OF CLAY IN THE ROUGH
SHAPE OF THE POT YOU WANT TO MAKE.

Kurinuki is a Japanese method of carving a pot from a solid block of clay. It's a slow, contemplative process that takes shape as you carve. It takes a bit of forethought so that you know where you are going when you begin to carve.

Kurinuki translates as "hollowing out." You start with a solid shape of clay and hollow out the middle using carving tools. The technique seems to work best when your hunk of clay is leather-hard. But it's also possible to hollow out the bulk of the clay while it is soft, and then allow the clay to become leather-hard before continuing to thin the walls and finish the pot.

Every method of working has its own requirements for the clay's hardness or softness. For kurinuki, if the clay is too soft, you'll find it impossible to maintain the shape of the pot without squishing it. If it is too hard, it is apt to crack during carving, and it will dull the blades of your carving tools prematurely.

I started making kurinuki pots as a break from making fast, production-style forms. I'd collect all the scraps that were too hard to use, pounding out many different shapes of clay and carving them into cups, bowls, trays, and boxes.

My kurinuki practice started out as simple cups and rectangle trays. My steady exploration and love for this technique has evolved into adding handles to make mugs, handled trays, and wall shelving. It is fun to think about the world in shapes and the functionality of those shapes. The kurinuki trays in all their different sizes and shapes lend themselves to serving and displaying food in a particular and fitting way that a plate and bowl do not. The narrow, long rectangle kurinuki tray is perfect for olives. The taller rectangle form holds crackers upright in a visually pleasing presentation. The many-segmented trays are a natural for nuts and candies or dips, cheeses, and grapes. The cups— from tiny sake forms to a larger yunomi tea bowl—feel like a carved-out and polished stone, a gutted rock. They all have such personality and character in their undulating rims and carved feet.

I like to set them out after they are fired and look at them closely, taking notice of their differences in textures and form. It's a little like gathering seashells or pretty rocks and looking at them all, appreciating them individually and as a whole. There is something satisfying and real about a collection of natural, imperfect things. You can understand the beauty, subtlety, and tiny wonders of the world this way, by holding them. These kurinuki pots allow me to feel even more connected to the clay through this intimate and primal process.

Kurinuki

The day before you plan to make a kurinuki pot, prepare your clay. Using your wire tool, cut a hunk of clay to the size of the pot you wish to make. Then use your hands to pound the clay into the rough shape of the pot: If you intend to make a square pot, start with a square block; for a round pot, start with a sphere.

Make a Kurinuki Footed Cup

For a sake cup use a ½-to ¾-pound (227 to 340 g) ball of clay

For a yunomi (tea cup) use a 2-pound (900 g) ball of clay

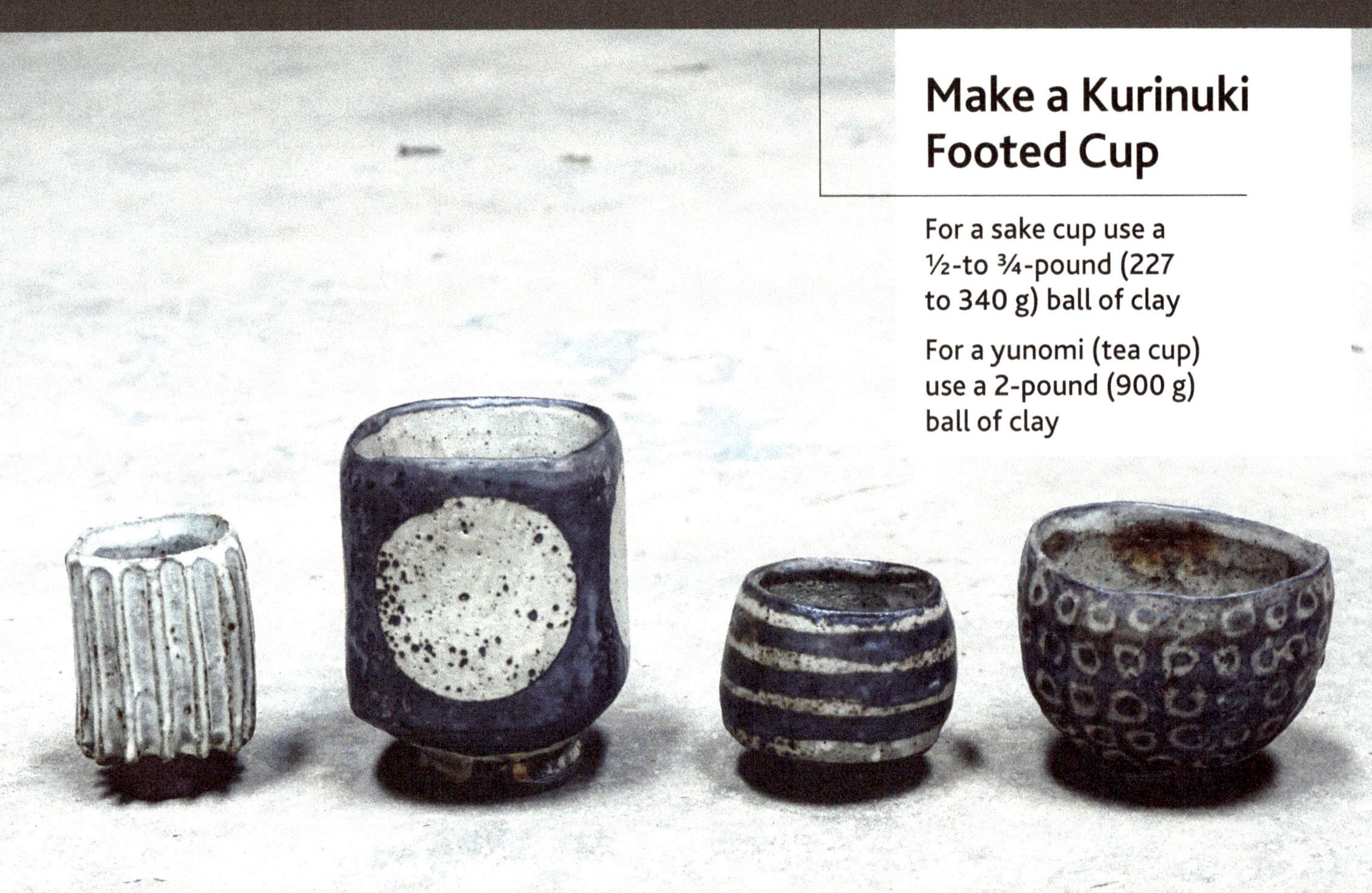

FOOT NOTES | The foot is an important part of a cup because it determines so much of its character. Do you want a tall foot that puts your cup on a pedestal? Do you want a humble, short foot? Should the walls of the pot coming up from the foot be rounded, or should there be an angled plane? Should the sides be flat as if your cup is floating on the table? These are all things to think about ahead of time. You'll find it useful to make some sketches to help you determine the shape and style of your cup so that you'll know where you're going when you start to carve. And, of course, the best way to know is to make many cups and try a different style of foot on all of them.

1 | Hold the ball of clay with one hand and the teardrop carving tool in the other. Use the tool to dig out the clay from the inside of the cup, leaving no less than a ½" (1.25 cm) on all sides. Think of hollowing out a pumpkin.

2 | When you are nearing the bottom of the cup and have removed the bulk of the clay from inside—stop! This is the time to get started on the foot. At this point, because you haven't removed too much clay, you will have more choices as to how tall or short the foot should be.

3 | Turn the cup over. (You can hold it in your hand as you work on the foot, or you can place it on a piece of foam or on a banding wheel.) Establish the foot by outlining its outermost ring with your needle tool.

4 | Decide how wide you would like the foot to be and make another circle inside the first ring.

5 | Move to the outside edge of the foot and carve outward, away from the foot. You can either carve straight out, squaring the angle where the wall of the cup turns to meet the bottom, or you can curve the line, giving the bottom of the cup a rounded form.

6 | Go back to the center of the foot and carve away the material inside the second ring, establishing the depth of the foot. The inside depth of your foot should match the outside depth your foot ring, so if you were to peel off the foot ring you would have a continuous curve.

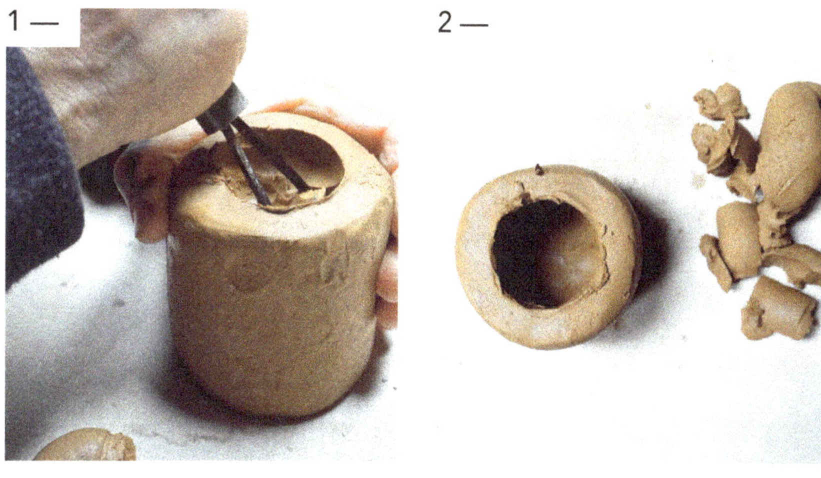

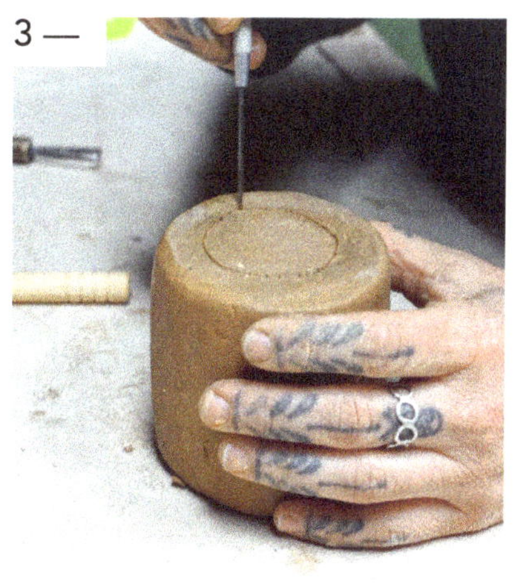

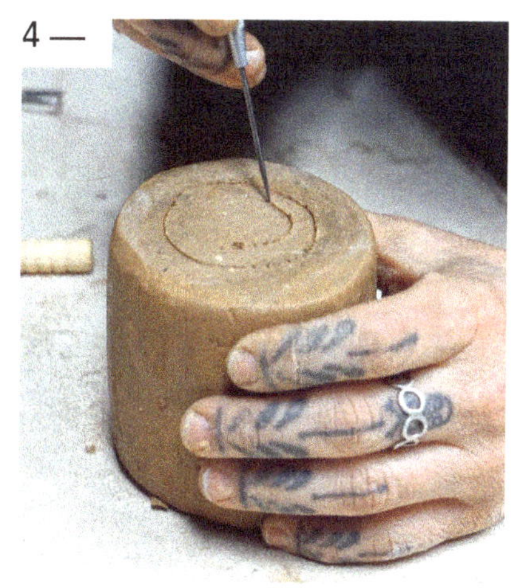

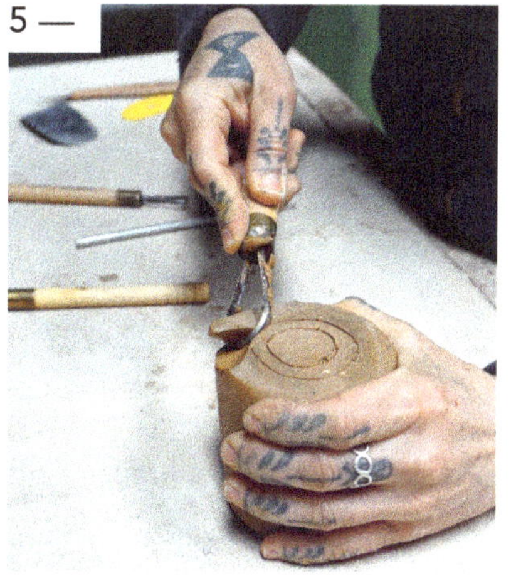

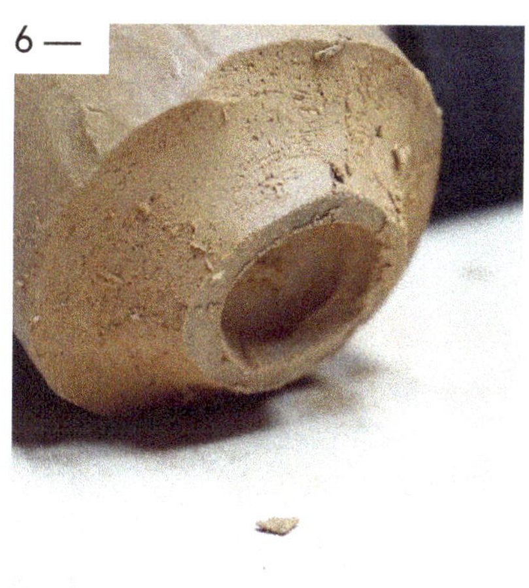

Kurinuki

7 | Turn the cup upright again and carefully carve layers from the walls to thin them. Before the walls get too thin, put the cup down and take a look at the foot.

8 | Does it look the way you want? Does the foot need any refining? More of an angle? Less? This is the time to decide. Once the walls of your cup reach the desired even thickness of about ¼" (6 mm) it will be too late to remove any more clay to further change your foot.

9 | Check to see if your cup has excess clay inside, in the angle where the cup walls meet the bottom surface. Clay tends to hide there and makes the cup too heavy. Use the teardrop carving tool and angle it to remove any excess clay as you turn the cup. It will come out as a ring of clay. Continue carving until the inside has no deep pits or cuts. Use your fingers and thumb to gently smooth the inside of the cup to your liking.

10 | Use a rib tool to smooth or create texture on the outside of the cup to finish it.

11 | Trim the lip. At this point the cup probably has a squared-off lip. If you put this to your mouth as if to drink, it will feel awkward. The lip of your cup will feel more natural and comfortable if it is tapered. To do this, hold your knife at an angle, and with the cup in the other hand, trim away the inside edge of the lip.

12 | Trim the outside edge of the lip to meet the inside edge at an angle. If the angle is crisp and sharp, smooth it slightly with your finger. You don't want the lip to be too sharp or it will chip easily. Sign your cup or mark it with your chop.

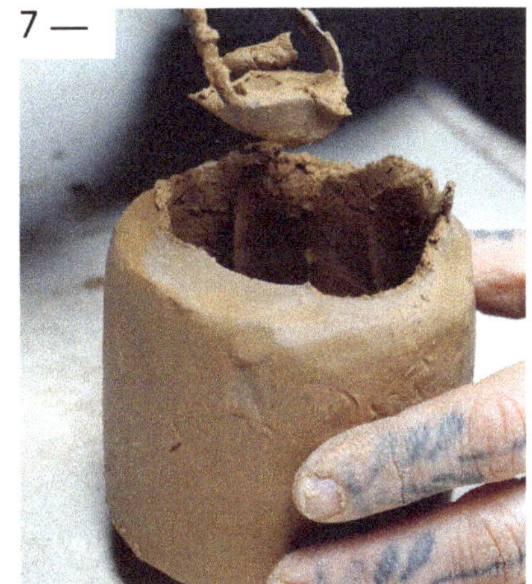
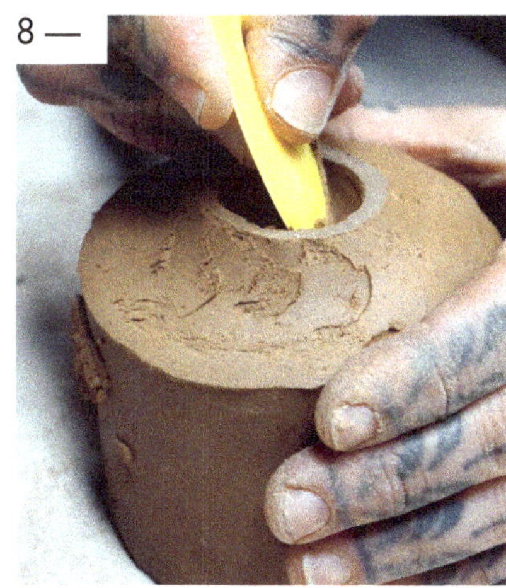
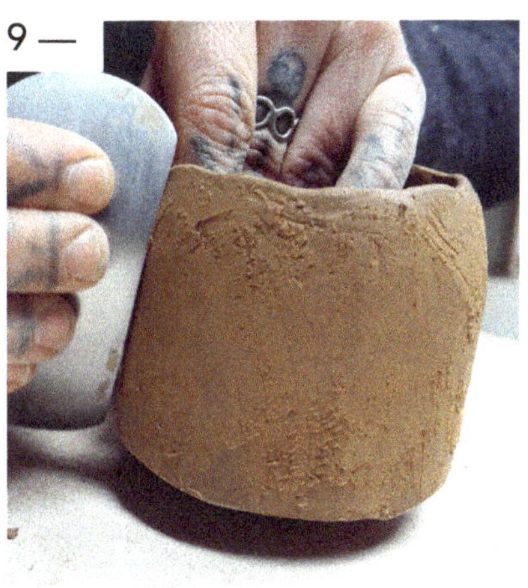
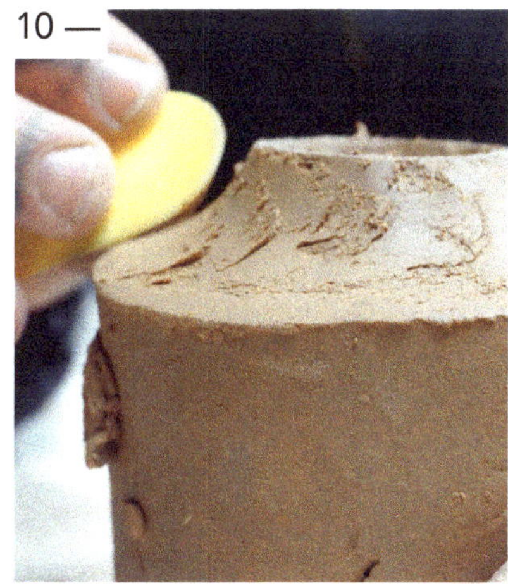
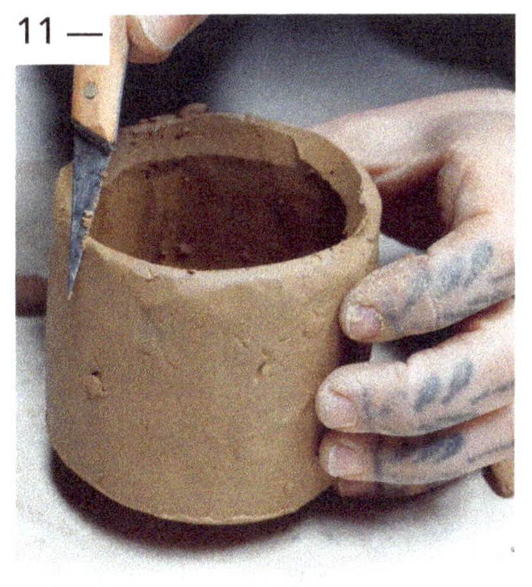
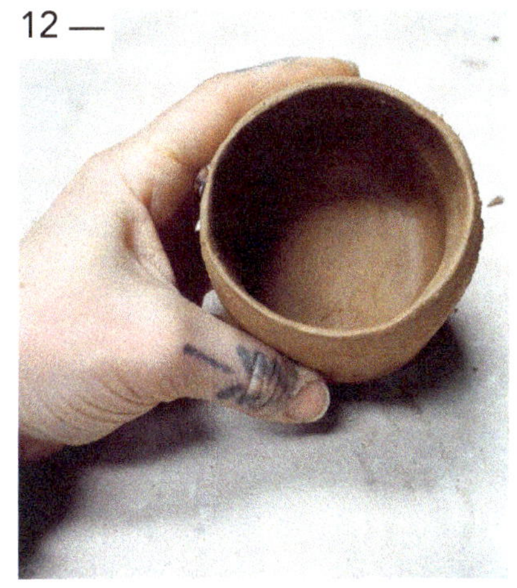

Trimming a Shallow Foot

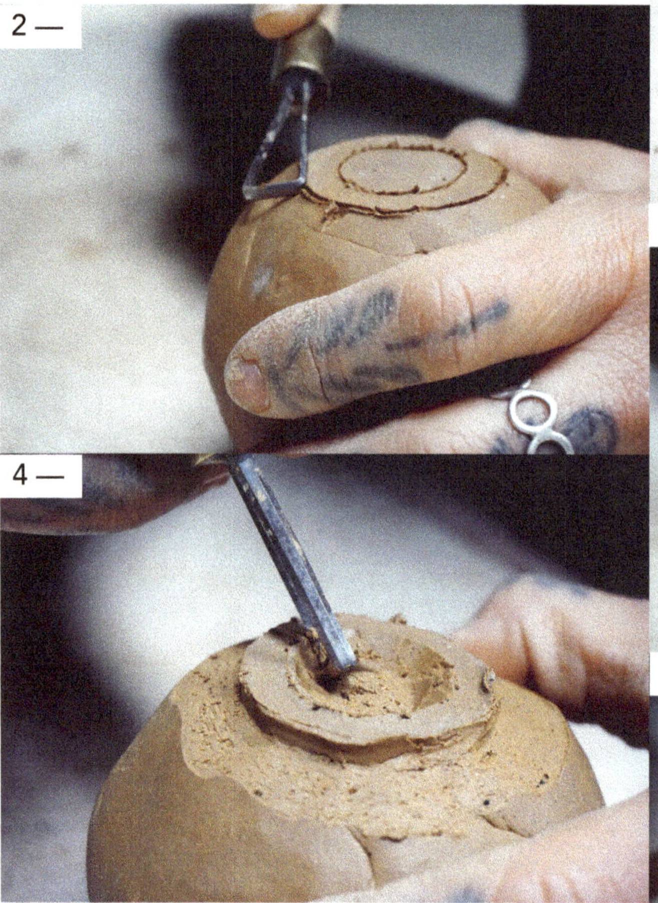

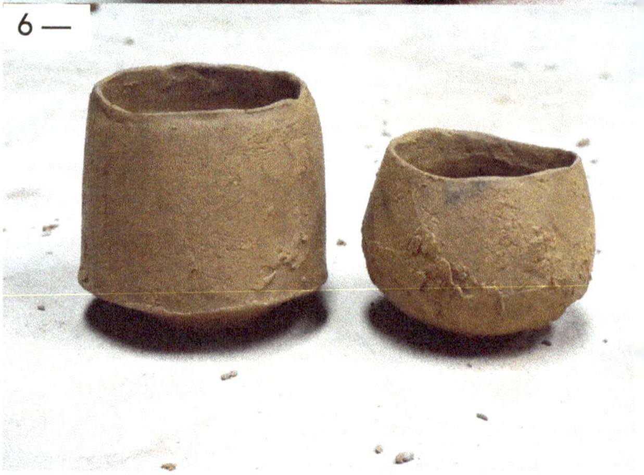

1 | Start by drawing an outer and an inner ring with your needle tool to designate the foot ring.

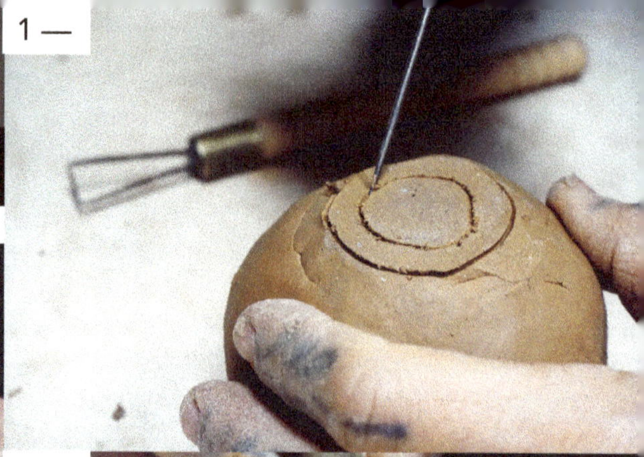

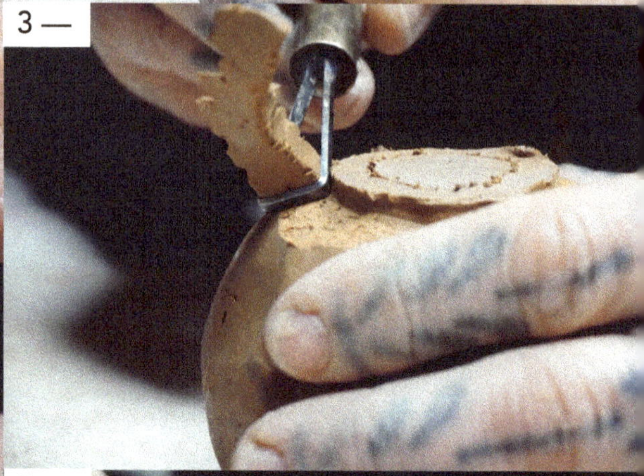

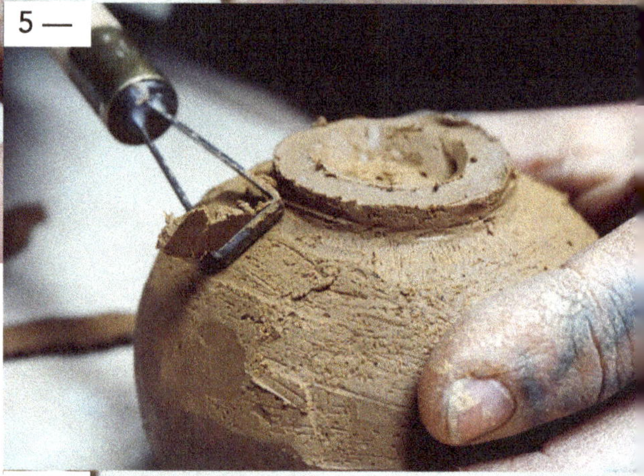

2 | Using a carving tool (I prefer one with an edge), begin to cut away the clay on the outside of the ring.

3 | The outer carving will raise the foot into existence.

4 | Next, remove the clay from the inside of the foot ring. You now have a fully emerged ring.

5 | Turn the cup over and feel how thick the bottom and sides are. This will tell you how much more clay you need to remove so that the entire cup is of even thickness. Keep cutting away clay until the bottom thickness is the same as the sides and top.

6 | Here are examples of cups with shallow foot rings, with a squared and curved bottom edge.

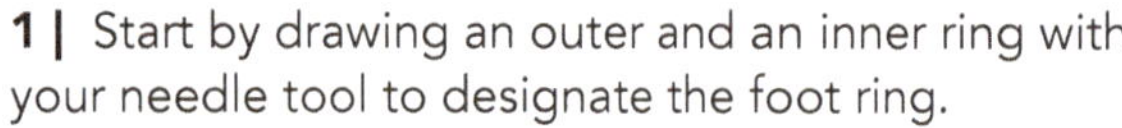

A ceramic box is beautiful and useful. It can sit on your dining table, holding salt. It can live next to your sink, holding soap, or it might fit in nicely on your dresser, holding rings or other precious things.

YOU'LL NEED

- ☑ Carving tools
- ☑ Flexible knife
- ☑ Plastic ribs
- ☑ Wire tool
- ☑ Serrated rib
- ☑ Slip
- ☑ Soft clay for making a coil

Note: Read through the steps for the preceding kurinuki pot to familiarize yourself with the carving process. For this project, you'll start with a block of clay the size of the complete box with its lid. Carve the decoration on the outside of the box, then slice off the lid and carve the interiors.

- ☐ For a small box, pound a solid block using 1 pound (450 g) of clay.
- ☐ For a medium box, pound a solid block using 2 pounds (900 g) of clay.

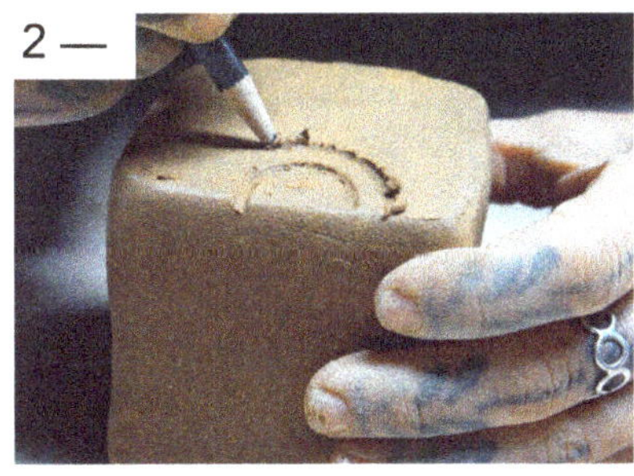

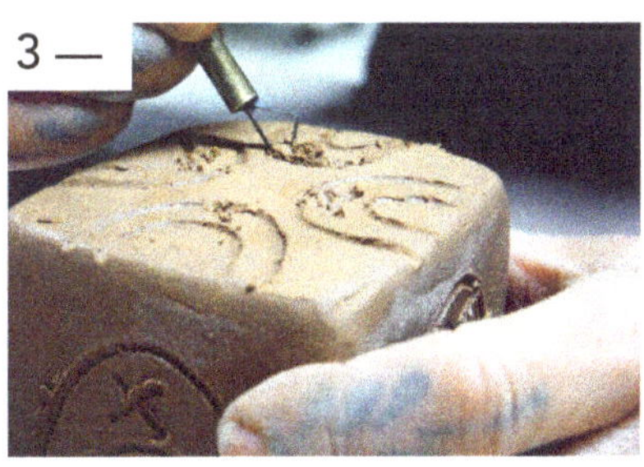

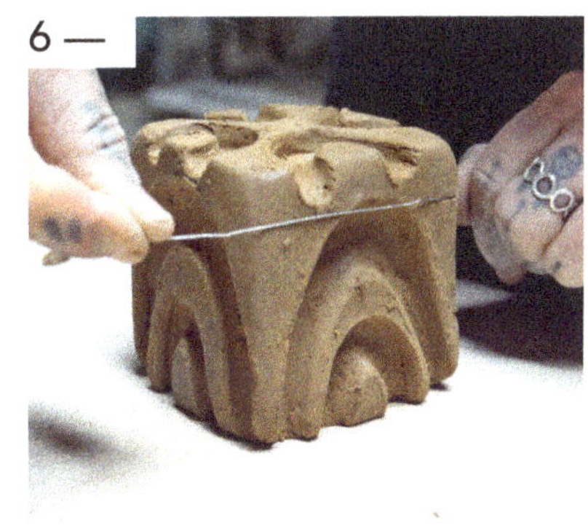

1 | Using a tool with a blunt point, or a dull pencil, draw your design on the outside of your box. You will be carving in relief, so think of your design as being raised from the background. You will achieve this effect by carving away the negative space—the background that surrounds your design. Try not to make the lines of your design too thin. Skinny, fragile, raised lines in your design could easily break off the box.

2 | Start drawing on the top of the box, etching your drawing into the clay deep enough to see it but not so deep that you can't erase the lines with a flexible rib or your finger if you make a mistake.

3 | Moving downward, continue etching your design into each side of the box. I find it best to leave the bottom plain so the box will sit flat. When you have finished laying out your design, you'll be ready to carve it into relief. It can help to put "x's" or other marks on the areas of clay that you'll be carving away, to help prevent mistakes.

4 | Carve away all of the negative space to a depth of about ¼" (6 mm). The small angled carving tools are great for getting into tight corners and small spaces. Turn them sideways to go in and clean up the edges of your design.

5 | When you have finished carving the relief design and cleaned up any unwanted marks, you're ready to slice off the lid. Decide how thick you want the lid to be. For example, if my box is 3" (7.5 cm) tall, I might want my lid to be ½" (1.25 cm) thick. Measure or simply eyeball where you want to cut into the box.

6 | With your wire tool in hand, pick a corner of the box at lid depth. Notch the wire into the corner deep enough so that it won't fall out. Pull the wire across to the next corner and notch it there in alignment with the first. Repeat this with the other two corners, so that the wire is wrapped around the box, notched into all four corners at the same height.

7 | Bring the two ends of the wire together in front of you and simultaneously, with firm pressure, pull up on one end of the wire tool and down on the other end as you pull toward yourself. Try to keep the two ends of the wire meeting and slicing on the same plane. The wire will eventually straighten out as it cuts through the clay, slicing off the top of your box.

8 | With the top separated from the bottom, you can now hollow out each part. Start with the lid. Place the lid upside down on a piece of foam to protect the carved design. Use the dull pencil or tool you used for starting your design to create a border about ½" (1.25 cm) inside the perimeter of the lid. This line will serve as your guide for carving.

9 | Carve out the clay from the inside of the lid until each surface has an even thickness of about ½" (1.25 cm).

10 | In order for your lid to stay in place on your box, it must have a flange. Start the flange by rolling out a coil of clay about a ½" (1.25 cm) thick, and long enough to wrap around the edge of the hollowed-out space on the inside of the lid.

11 | Score the inside edge of the lid, and brush on some slip. Score the coil.

12 | Gently press the scored surface of the coil onto the prepared edge of the lid. Smooth the coil to join it to the lid, leaving the bulk of the coil raised up.

13 | Pinch the coil to make an edge all around, until it is squared and angled in slightly. Set the lid aside and cover it with plastic to keep it from drying out.

14 | Draw a line around the edge of the box about ¼" (6 mm) in from the perimeter. Use this line as your guide to carve away the clay inside the line.

15 | Carve out the clay to hollow out the box. Be mindful not to carve too much or make your box too thin. Leave about ¼" (6 mm) thickness on all surfaces.

16 | When the box is of an even thickness, smooth out any unwanted marks or rough spots.

17 | Take the lid from the plastic wrap and place it on the bottom section of the box. Press down on it gently to push the coil into the bottom section. Remove the lid and place it upside down on your work surface. Using the marks created in the coil to guide you, remove any clay that is in the way with your fingers or a flexible rib.

18 | You also might need to gently push the coil flange inward or outward to get it in the right place. Go back and forth, trying the lid on the bottom each time, to determine the right place for a tight fit. You will have achieved this when your lid fits snugly onto the bottom and doesn't shift or have a big gap.

19 | Your carving is done. Sign your box or use your chop to mark it as yours.

7 —
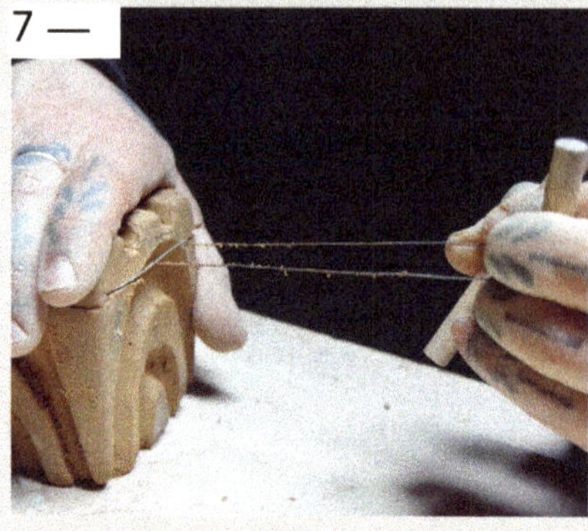

8 —
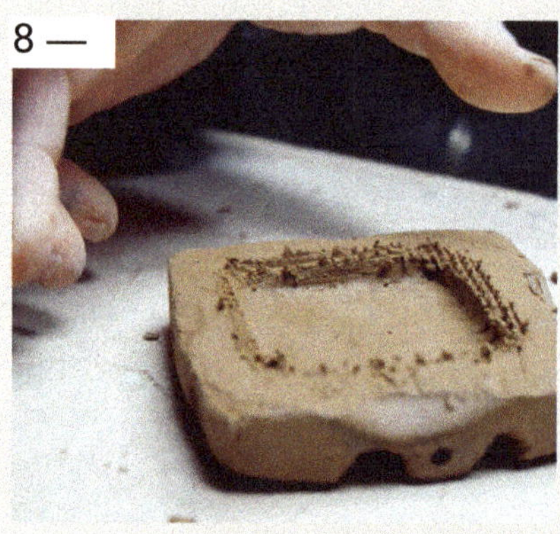

11 —
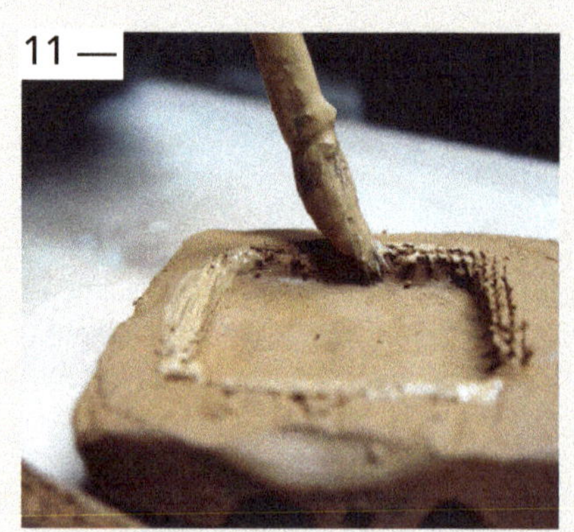

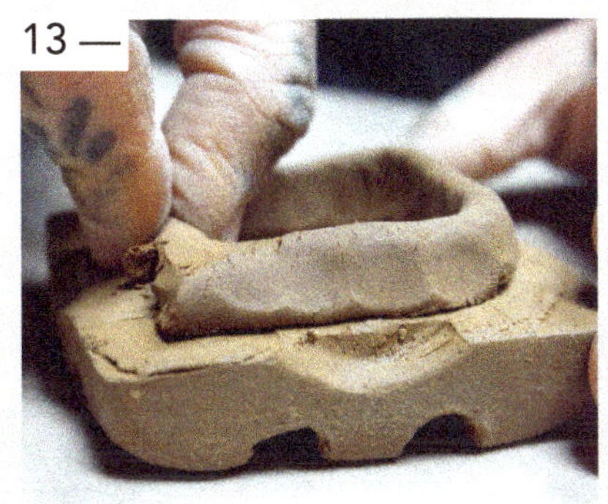

13 —

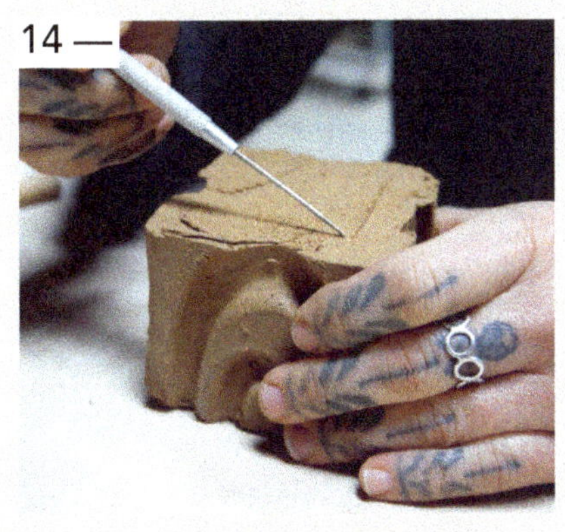

14 —

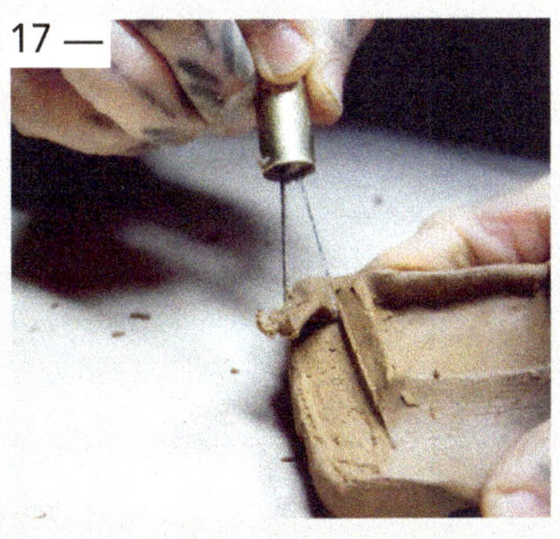

17 —

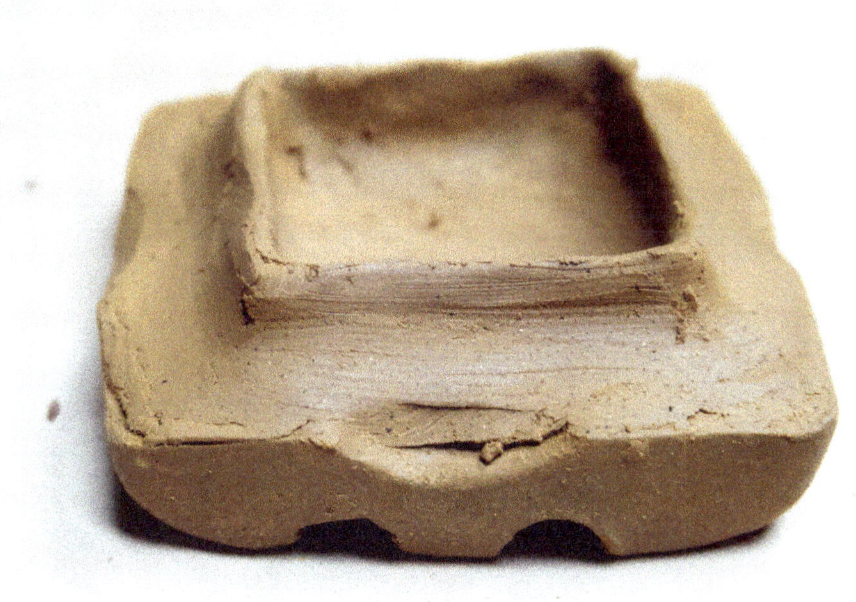

Make Kurinuki Snack Serving Dishes

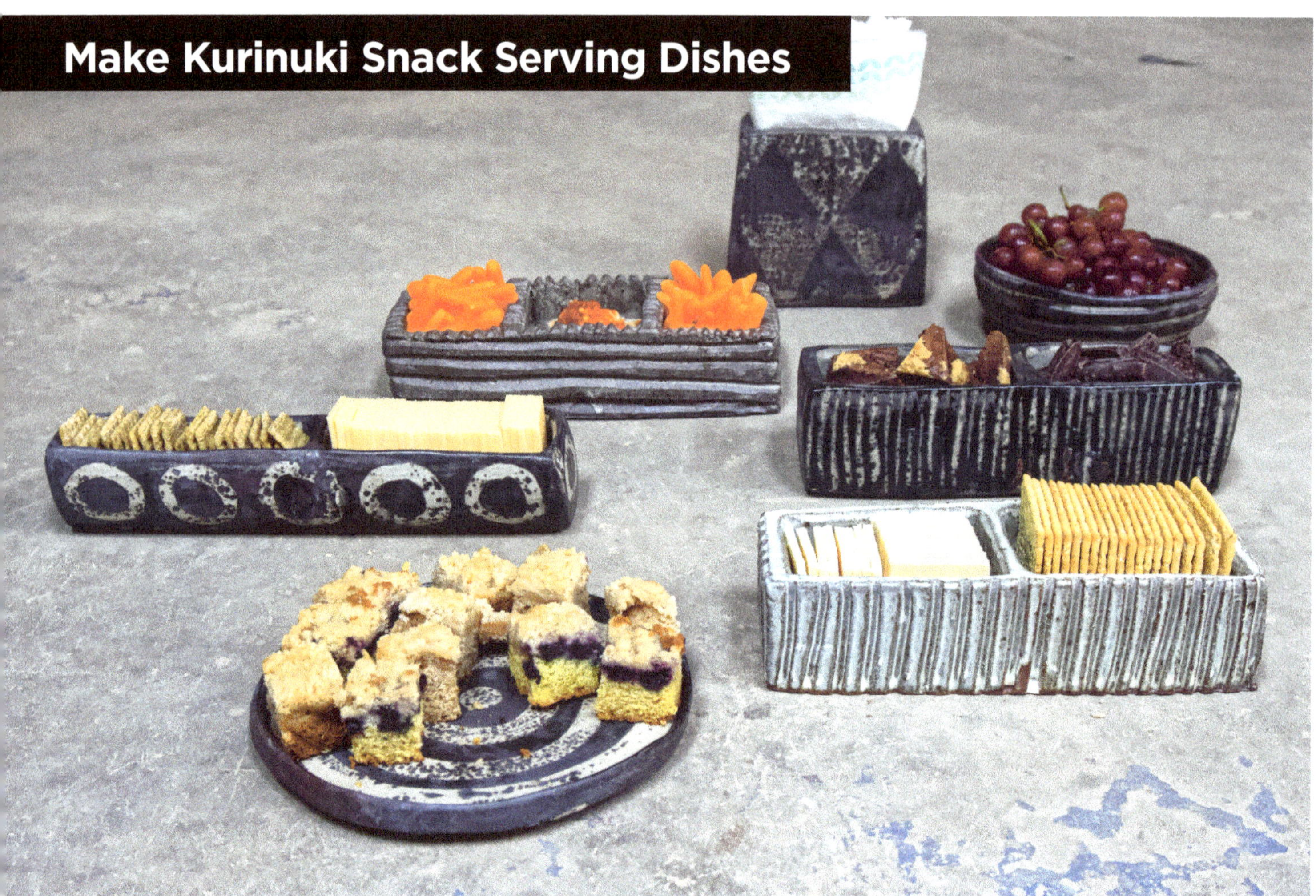

YOU'LL NEED

- ☑ Ware board
- ☑ Angled carving tools
- ☑ Flexible knife
- ☑ Surform
- ☑ Plastic ribs (yellow and green, small and large)
- ☑ Ruler

It's so nice to offer snacks in dishes designed specifically for the purpose. The dividers in these serving dishes let you keep crackers, dips, and sliced vegetables separated and your presentation creative. The shapes and sizes of serving dishes have endless possibilities, but I've focused here on a rectangular dish, with and without dividers. Feel free to apply this method to any shape you wish.

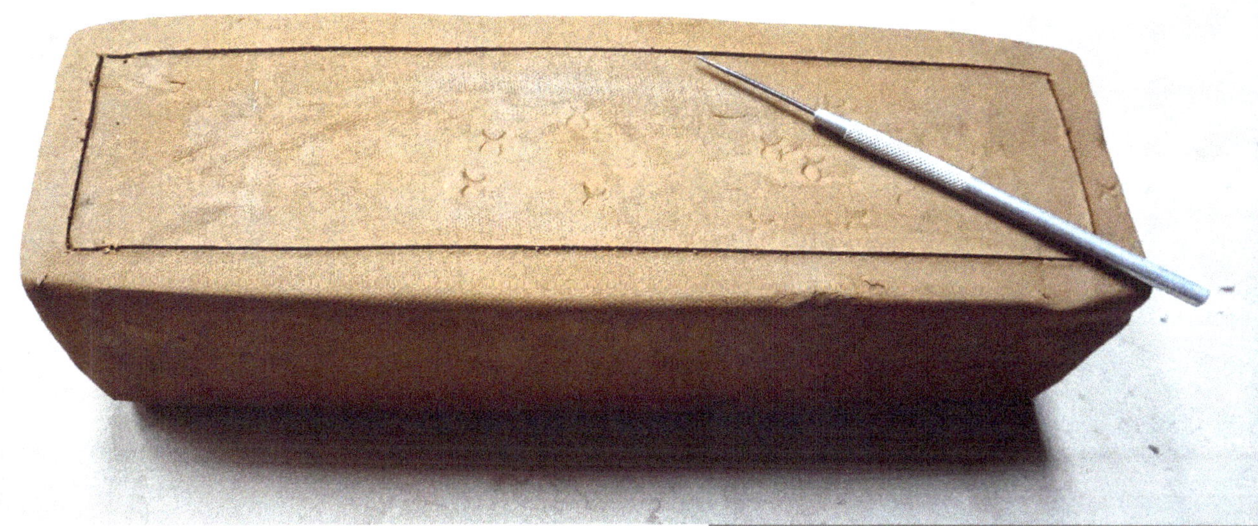

1 | Pound a block of clay into a solid rectangle about 3" × 8" ×3" (7.5 × 20.3 × 7.5 cm). Let this set up until firm but still soft enough (soft side of leather-hard) for your carving tool to hollow out the inside with minimal effort.

2 | Leaving a ½" (1.25 cm) thickness on each surface, use your angled carving tool to hollow out the clay from inside the block.

3 | When the bulk of the clay is removed, start thinning each surface, beginning with the floor. Use your carving tool to remove thin layers of clay until each surface is even and roughly $\frac{3}{8}$" (1 cm) thick. Set the dish aside until leather-hard.

4 | At the leather-hard stage, use the surform to gently remove a thin layer from each surface of the dish to even out any lumps and bumps. Then even out the rim of the dish by placing the surform flat on the rim and moving it with gentle downward pressure.

5 | When the tray is even and free of lumps, use the yellow or green plastic rib to smooth the surform lines and compress the inner floor.

6 | Sign your dish or use your chop to mark it as your own.

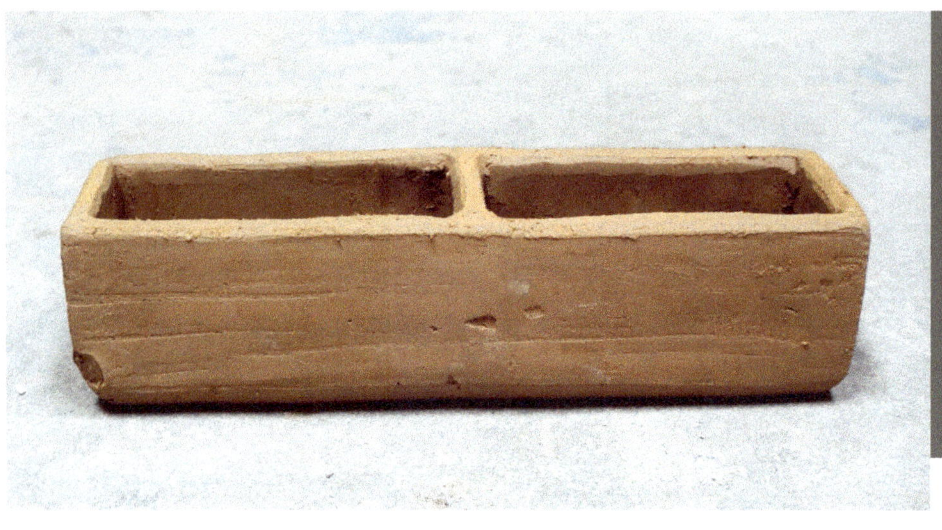

SERVING DISH WITH TWO SECTIONS

1 | Pound a block of clay into a solid rectangle about 3" × 10" × 3" (7.5 × 25.5 × 7.5 cm).

2 | Set the block aside until firm but still soft enough (soft side of leather-hard) for your carving tool to hollow out the inside with minimal effort.

3 | Measure the length of the dish along the top and find the center. Mark a line down the center to create two even sections.

4 | Leaving a ½" (1.25 cm) thickness on each surface, use your angled carving tool to hollow out the clay from both sections of your dish.

5 | When the bulk of the clay is removed, beginning with the floor of the dish, use your carving tool to remove thin layers of clay until each surface is roughly ³⁄₈" (1 cm) thick. Allow the dish to sit until leather-hard.

6 | At the leather-hard stage, use the surform to gently remove a thin layer from each surface of the dish to even out any lumps and bumps. Then even out the rim of the dish by placing the surform flat on the rim and moving it with gentle downward pressure.

7 | When the tray is even and free of lumps, use the yellow or green plastic rib to smooth the surform lines and compress the inner floor.

8 | Sign your dish or use your chop to mark it as your own.

4 —

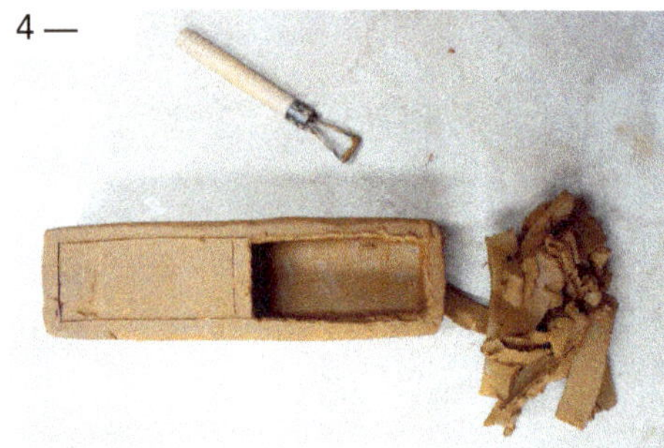

5 —

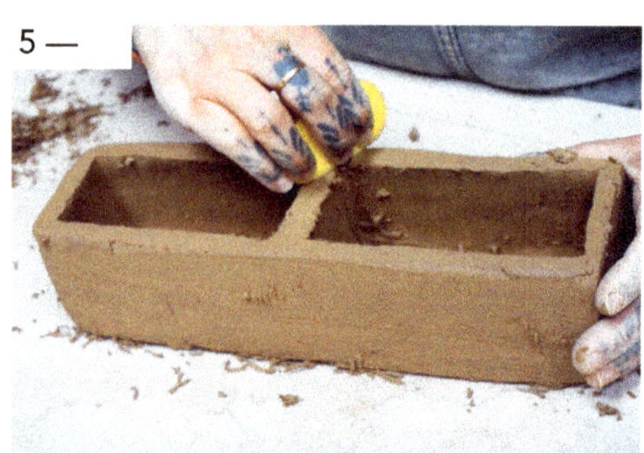

6 —

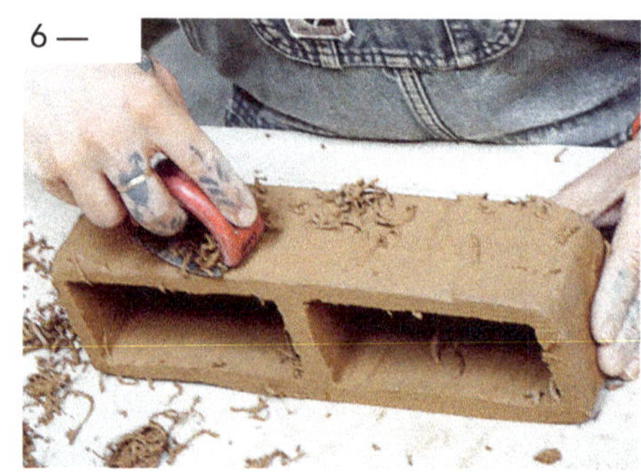

SERVING DISH WITH FOUR SECTIONS

1 | Pound a block of clay into a solid rectangle about 3" × 12" × 3" (7.5 × 30.5 × 7.5 cm).

2 | Set the block aside until firm but still soft enough (soft side of leather-hard) for your carving tool to hollow out the inside with minimal effort.

3 | Measure the length of the dish along the top and find the center. Mark a line down the center, then find the center of each half and mark with a line for four equal sections.

4 | Follow steps 4 through 8 of the "Serving Dish with Two Sections" to complete your dish.

5 | For all of your kurinuki pots, if you wish, finish them by carving the outside of the pot when the clay is leather-hard.

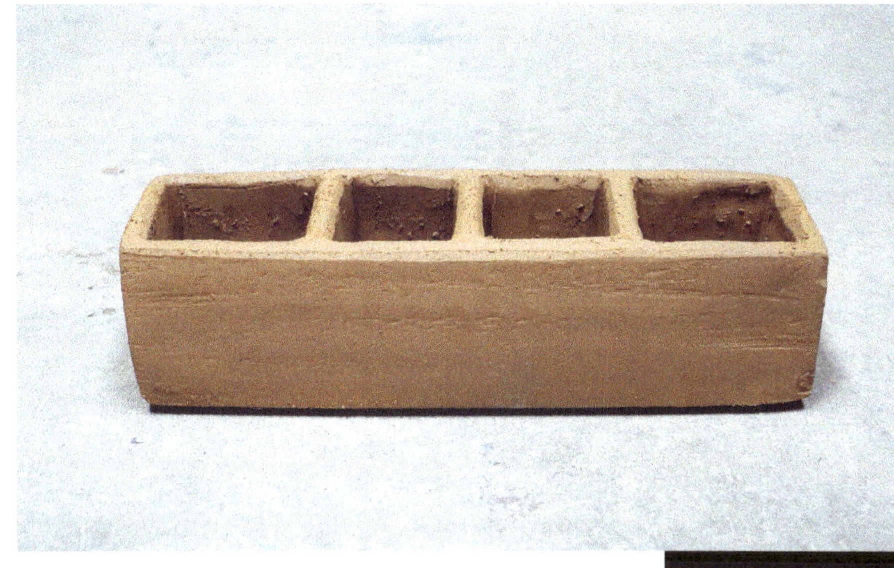

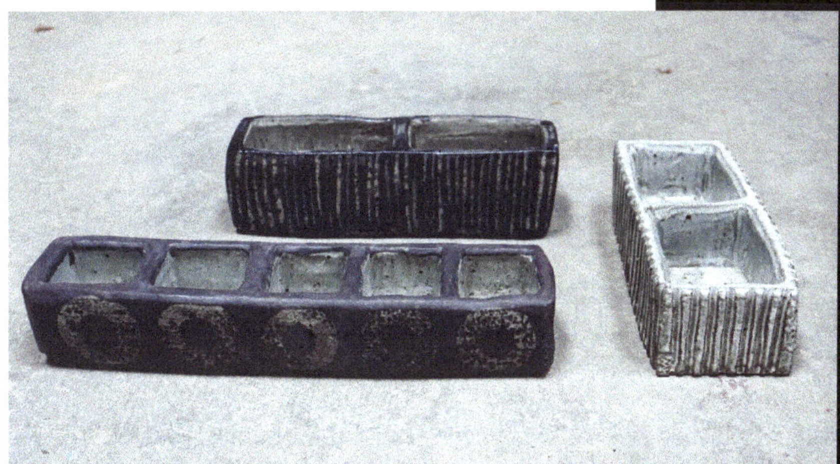

5 —

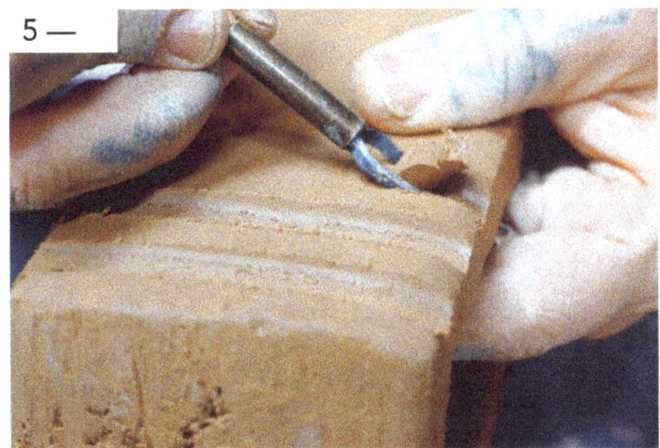

5 —

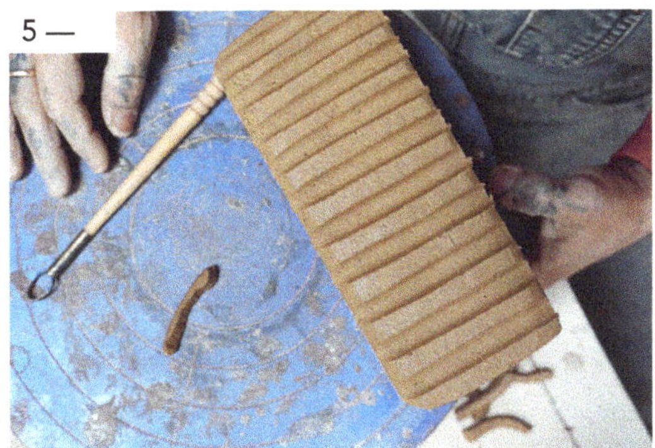

5 —

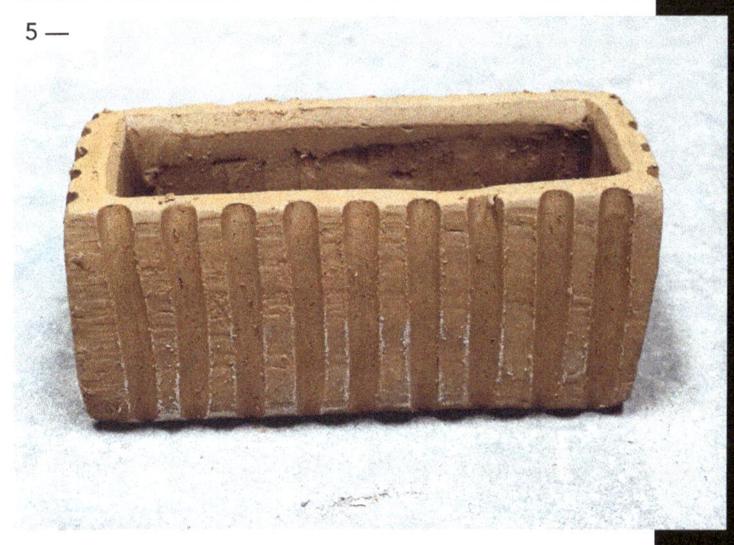

Guest Potter Interview: Nicholas Danielson
Incorporating 3-D Modeling into Slab Building

Nicholas Danielson was born and raised in the suburbs of Chicago, Illinois. After twenty years there, he moved west to Montana, where he completed his BFA in ceramics at Montana State University in 2012. He went on to earn his MFA from Utah State University. While a graduate student, he completed a study abroad program at Hongik University in Seoul, South Korea. Most recently, he was chosen as a 2016 Long-Term Resident at the Archie Bray Foundation in Helena, Montana.

MW: YOU ARE CURRENTLY A LONG-TERM RESIDENT AT THE ARCHIE BRAY FOUNDATION IN HELENA, MONTANA. HOW HAS THIS ENVIRONMENT INFORMED YOUR WORK?

ND: Presently, the Archie Bray studio is strongly diverse. I enjoy being surrounded by numerous approaches in the ceramic field. The studio environment has allowed me to question my use of color, design, and concept. I came to the Archie Bray right after graduate school, and I couldn't have asked for a better place to transition from a student researcher to a professional practitioner. Another benefit of being a resident is time—the one and only thing you never have enough of and can never get back.

MW: YOUR POTS ARE LIKE FUNCTIONAL LANDSCAPE PAINTINGS. FOR ME, THEY EVOKE THE SAME SORT OF SENSE THAT I HAVE WHEN I LOOK AT A PAINTING OF CÉZANNE PEACHES. THERE IS NO END; IT'S AS IF LOOKING INTO A LONG TUNNEL. IT'S SUBLIME. HOW DO YOU ACHIEVE THIS SURFACE?

ND: Currently, I am consumed by surface. I have been experimenting with colors and textures, along with slips, glazes, and terra sigillata. Ultimately, I am searching for balance and composition. For the last few years I have been using slip on top of my work. I use a Korean technique called *buncheong* as a reference point. Buncheong came into existence in the fourteenth century and was created to replicate porcelain. For my purposes, I am interested in irregularity, how the surface creates depth, while also complementing the interactions with sections of flat textures and color. During the firing, the pieces are deeply affected by the reduction atmosphere, allowing the clay, slip, and glaze interface to deteriorate, creating depth. I am deeply interested in materials and their interaction with one another to create a complex visual experience.

MW: YOUR POTS ARE VERY ARCHITECTURAL. I SEE STAIRS, COLUMNS, AND BALCONIES. IS THIS INTENTIONAL?

ND: I have always wanted my work to have a monolithic quality, from my mugs to my largest vessels. I'm sure this is influenced by my own introduction to art and craft in museums. Pieces in a museum almost always have an unspoken impact. I often think about German conceptual artist Wolfgang Laib, who has spoken about his relationship to form and how you can make or do something today that has a connection to 4,000 years ago. I am also searching for that connection, and I believe clay inherently links us to history. So, I see these architectural elements as physical and visual representations of objects that are synonymous with being human.

MW: YOUR FORMS SEEM TO PUSH THE BOUNDARIES OF CLAY. HAVE YOU HAD TO DEAL WITH ISSUES OF CRACKING, WARPING, AND SLUMPING? AND IF SO, HOW HAVE YOU DEALT WITH THESE PROBLEMS?

ND: I think of these issues often in my studio. To start, I design my clay body to withstand the particular types of pressure that I put it though. That means that I incorporate different ball clays for plasticity, and iron-rich clays for tooth and color, while also using mullite and sand to help with clay strength and drying. Although these ingredients can help with cracking and other issues, I think practicing and getting to know the process you're working on really will help alleviate problems.

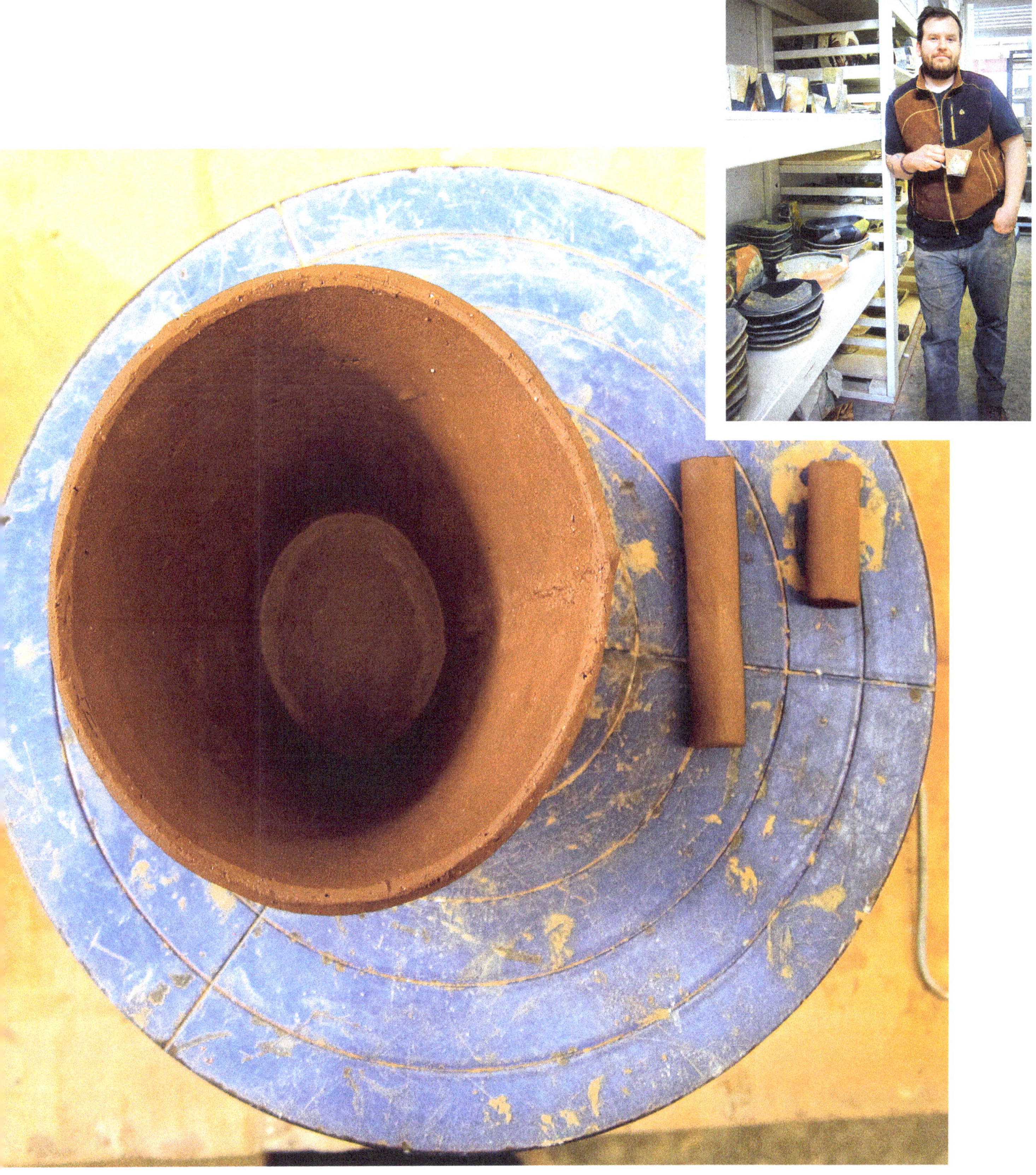

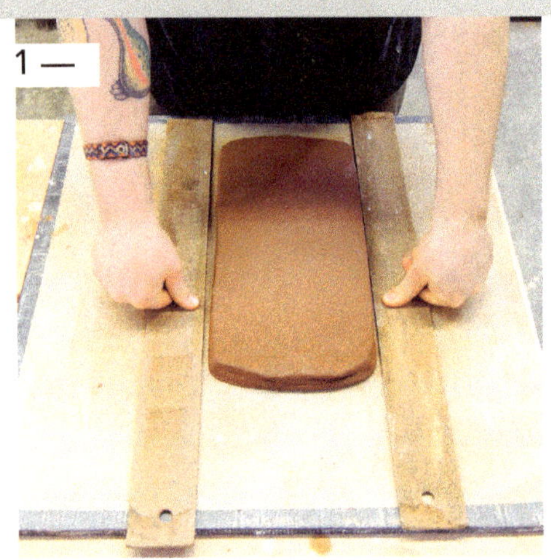

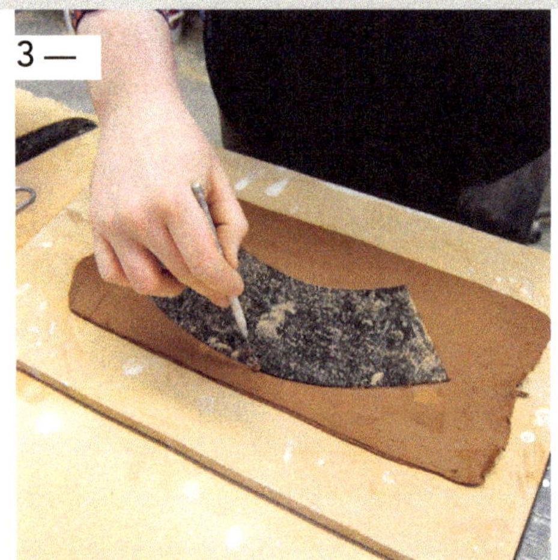

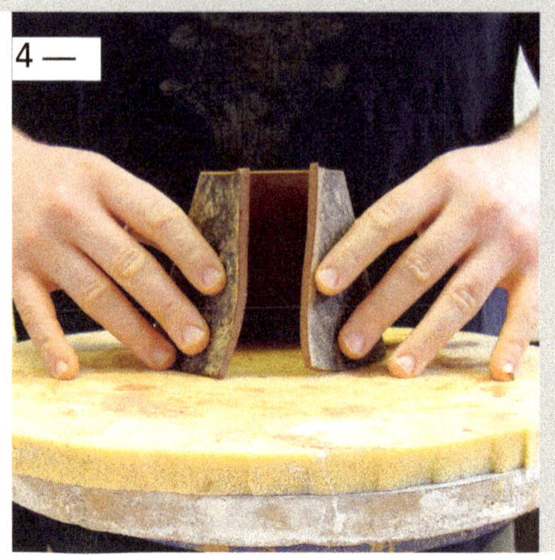

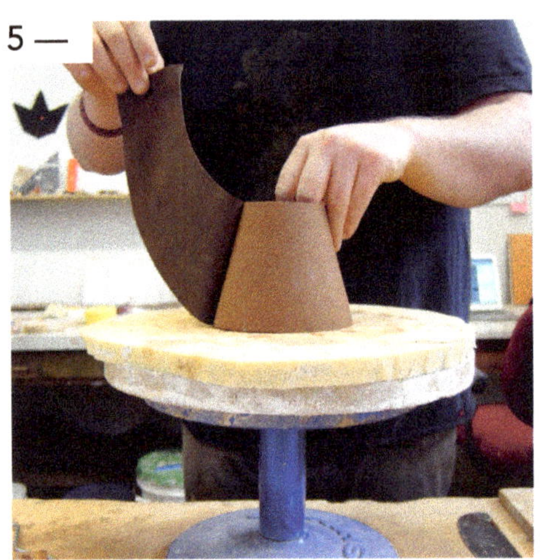

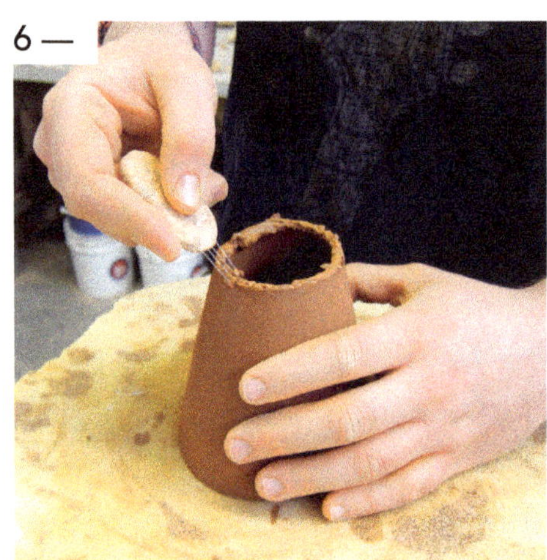

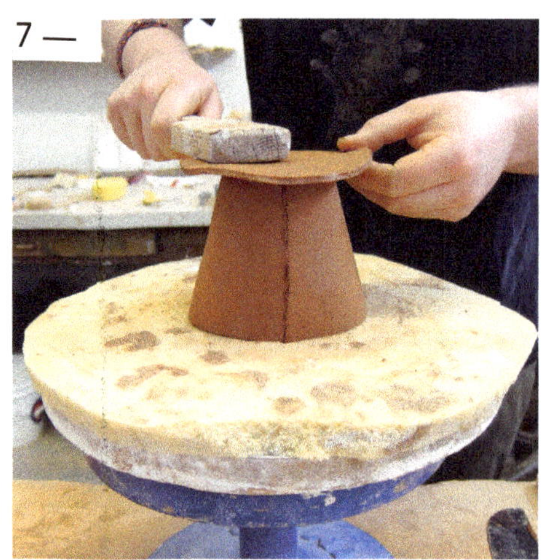

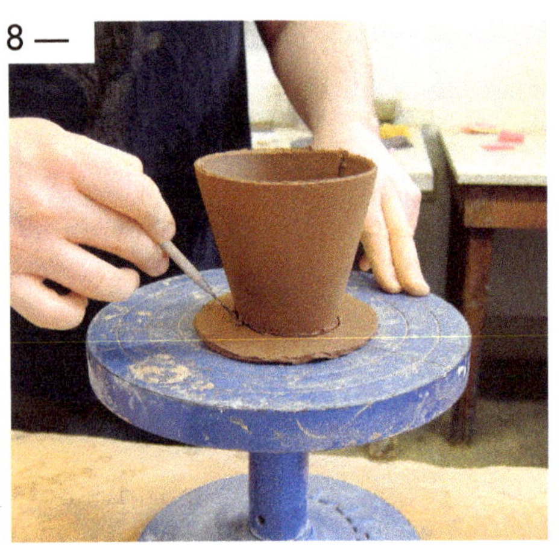

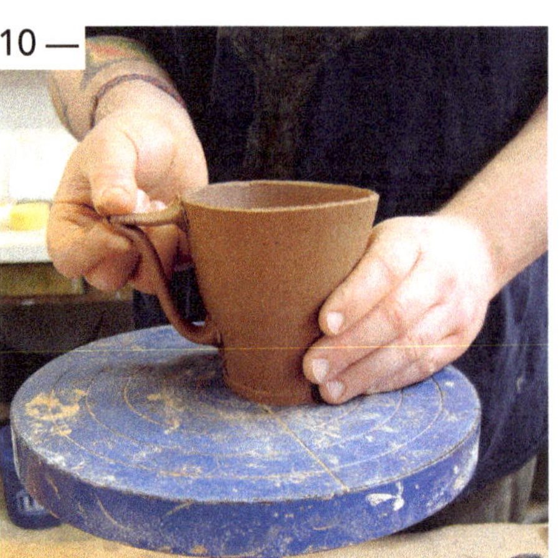

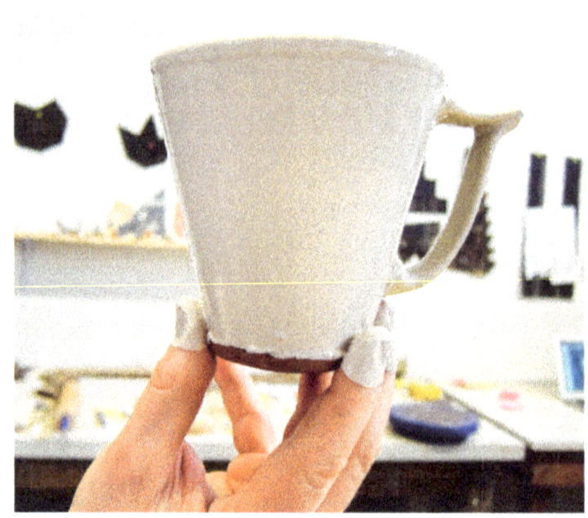

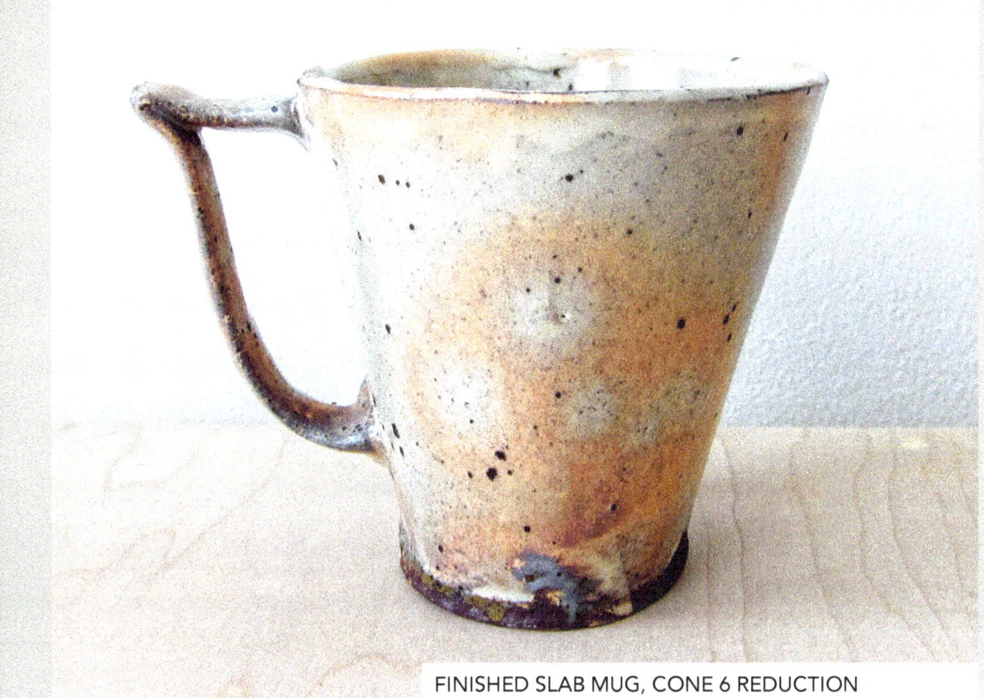

FINISHED SLAB MUG, CONE 6 REDUCTION

MW: **WHAT IS YOUR PROCESS?**

ND: I have always been inspired by historical ceramics and use photos as starting points for different forms. I look for ways to reprise certain forms or functions while combining cultures and time periods. When researching ceramic history, I found there was really no way for me to be completely original. The phrase, "Nothing comes from nothing," helps me in conceptualizing my ideas through clay.

Recently, through grant funding, I was able to purchase 3-D modeling software and a vinyl cutter. These two tools have really changed my process, whether designing a mug or a sculptural vase. When starting a piece, I begin rapid prototyping of a new design in the 3-D software. Once I arrive at a form and proportion that strikes my curiosity, I flatten the 3-D object into a 2-D template. Then I cut out the template from tar paper with my vinyl cutter, or by hand, depending on the scale of the object. Once I have the template, I compress it onto soft slab clay, and from there begin the construction.

MAKE A SLAB MUG

1 | Position a solid block of clay in between two level "slats." Now, with a wire tool, press down with your thumbs to cut a level slab. This will be the mug wall. Following this cut, cut another slab. This will be your "base" or bottom. This ensures even dryness when attaching the wall and bottom.

2 | After compressing both sides of the slab, spray the tar paper template with water and press onto the slab. Use a small roller to help evenly adhere the template to the clay.

3 | Use a needle tool or knife to cut around the template.

TIP: I like using a needle tool to cut slabs because it has a rounded shaft, unlike the edge of a knife.

4 | After cutting out the template, move the mug body to a cushioned bat. Keeping the mug level, meet both ends together. Allow the slab to harden for 20 to 45 minutes, depending on the studio's humidity.

5 | After the slab is firm, bevel each end and slip and score the joint. Then, while holding the joint, pull the tar paper away.

6 | Now, while holding the mug upside down, slip and score the bottom joint. I use very thick slip, which allows excess slip to seep inside the mug after compression. I use this excess slip to help connect the interior seam.

7 | With a slab that is of equal dryness, lightly paddle or roll the bottom slab to the mug wall.

8 | Using a needle tool or knife, cut along the wall into the bottom slab.

9 | Now that the mug wall and bottom are attached, pinch a two-part handle.

10 | With the connecting side down, pinch upward in a diamond shape, creating a taper from the outside of the handle to the center. Pinch both segments, attaching the smaller portion to the lip, parallel to the table. Then attach the second segment three-quarters of the way down the mug.

11 | Lightly pinch where the two segments meet, creating a slight recurve, which relates to the curvature of the oval mug.

12 | After the mug is leather-hard, dip it in a thin layer of deflocculated slip.

04

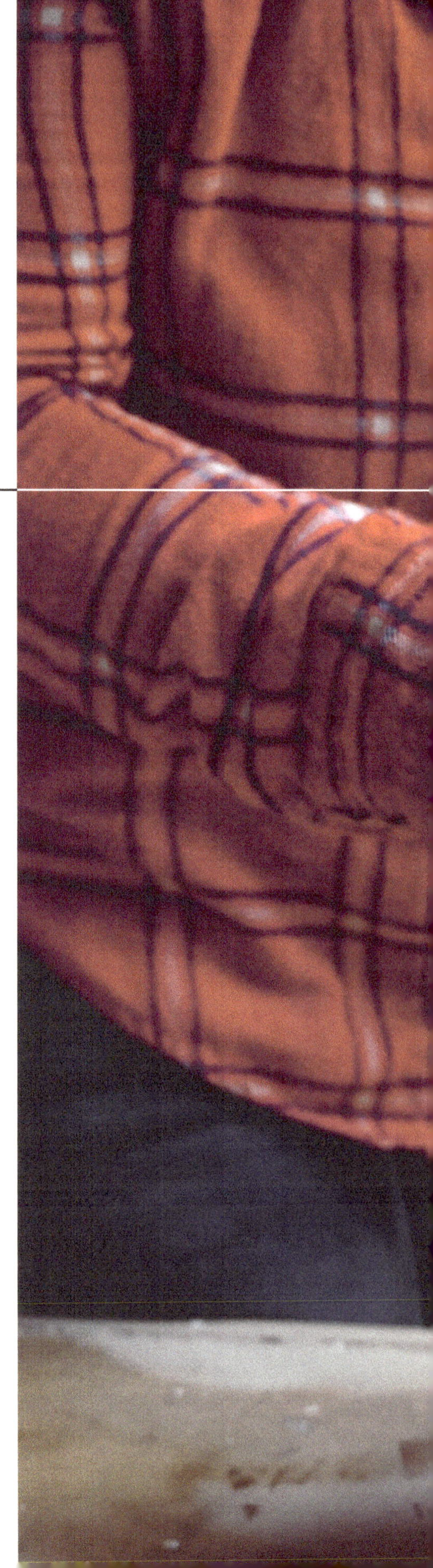

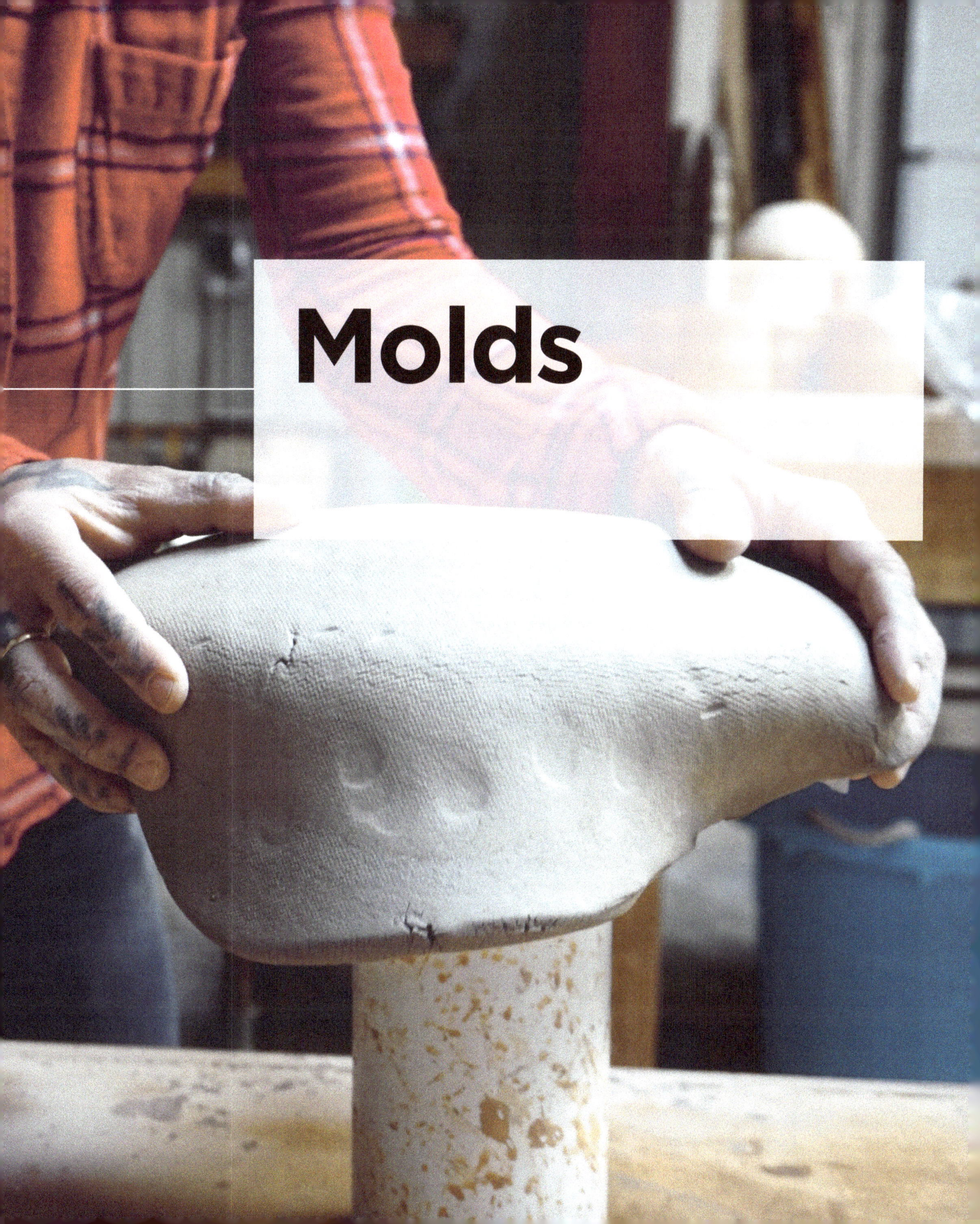
Molds

Steps for Making Hump Molds

There's a lot of flexibility with handbuilding, particularly with slab work. When you combine slab with molds, for instance, it can take endless forms. If you've hit on a style of bowl, or dish, or platter, or vase that you like to make over and again, using a mold is a great way to go.

Hump molds, also known as drape molds, are made when a slab of clay is draped over a form. The form, or mold, is typically made from plaster or clay. Personally, I don't use plaster molds because they're less durable and more complicated to make. I make my molds from clay because, after they're bisque fired, I can use them indefinitely.

You can also make a mold from found objects, such as wooden and plastic dishes. To do this, you'll need to either coat the dish with cornstarch or oil or cover it in fabric to prevent the clay from sticking. Roll out a slab of clay ½" (1.25 cm) thick and drape it over the prepared dish. When the slab becomes leather-hard, remove it and let it dry. Bisque it, and that is your mold.

To make a custom mold, I use a clay called Purge from a local ceramic supplier. This is a very cheap clay body guaranteed to fire just to cone 04. Since the mold only needs to be in bisque form, cone 04 is fine. Check with your ceramic suppliers to see what they have available for a cheap, low-fire clay body.

In making a mold, I start with a block of clay about the size of the dish I ultimately want to create, taking the depth, the slope of the sides, and the shape into consideration.

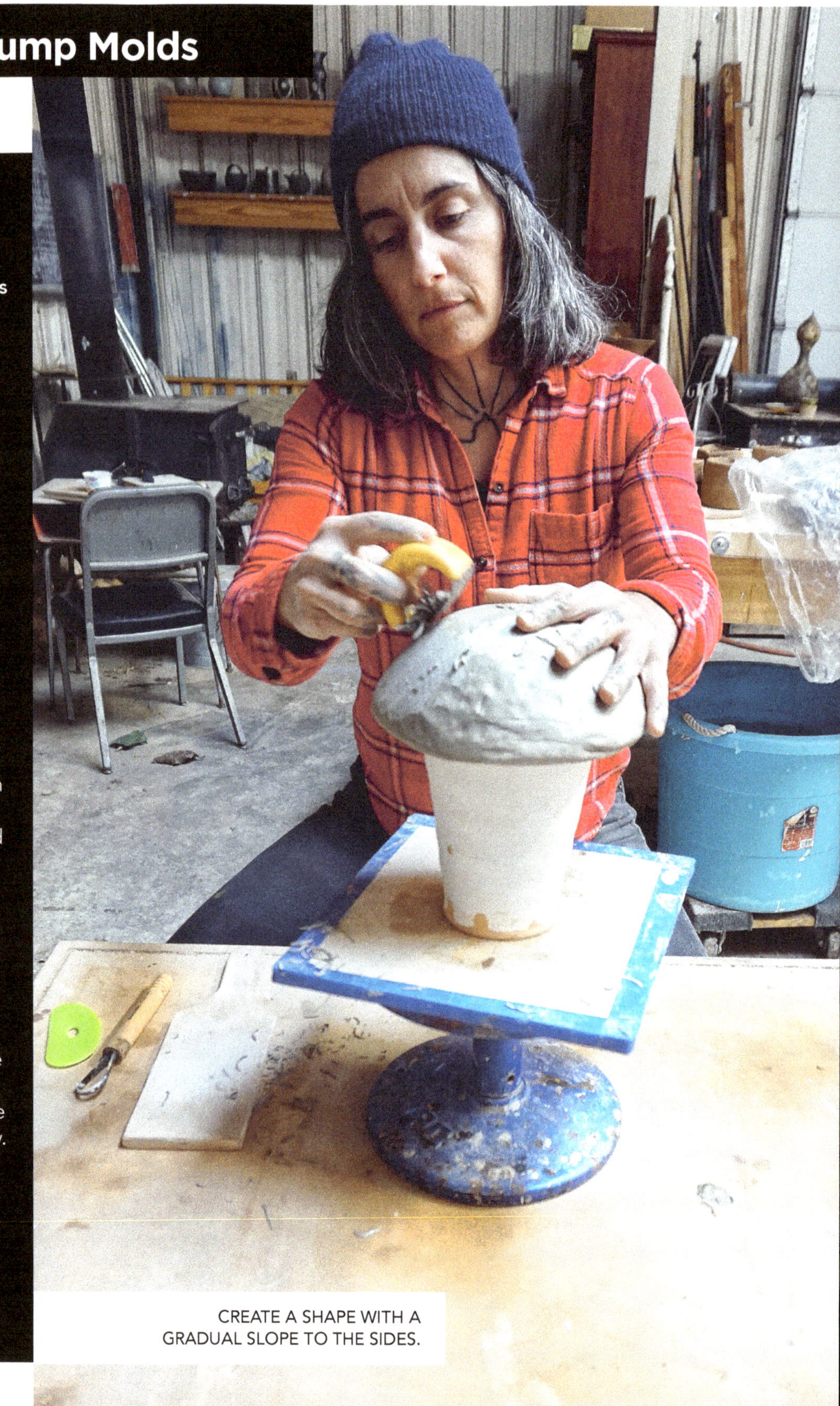

CREATE A SHAPE WITH A GRADUAL SLOPE TO THE SIDES.

Start with the shape of dish you want to make—square, round, oval, etc. Using your hands, pound and roll the clay into the rough shape. Hump molds tend to be most successful when they don't have steep sides, so I try to create a mold with sides that slope gently, without creating an angled transition from the bottom to the sides. Think of a gradual slope, as opposed to a sharp turn. The degree of the slope will determine the shape of the sides of your dish and the size of the flat bottom. When you get the shape of the mold where you want it, set it aside, and let dry to leather-hard.

When the mold is leather-hard, use a surform to refine and hone the shape. Look at it from different angles to make sure it's even.

"You can make molds from found shapes."

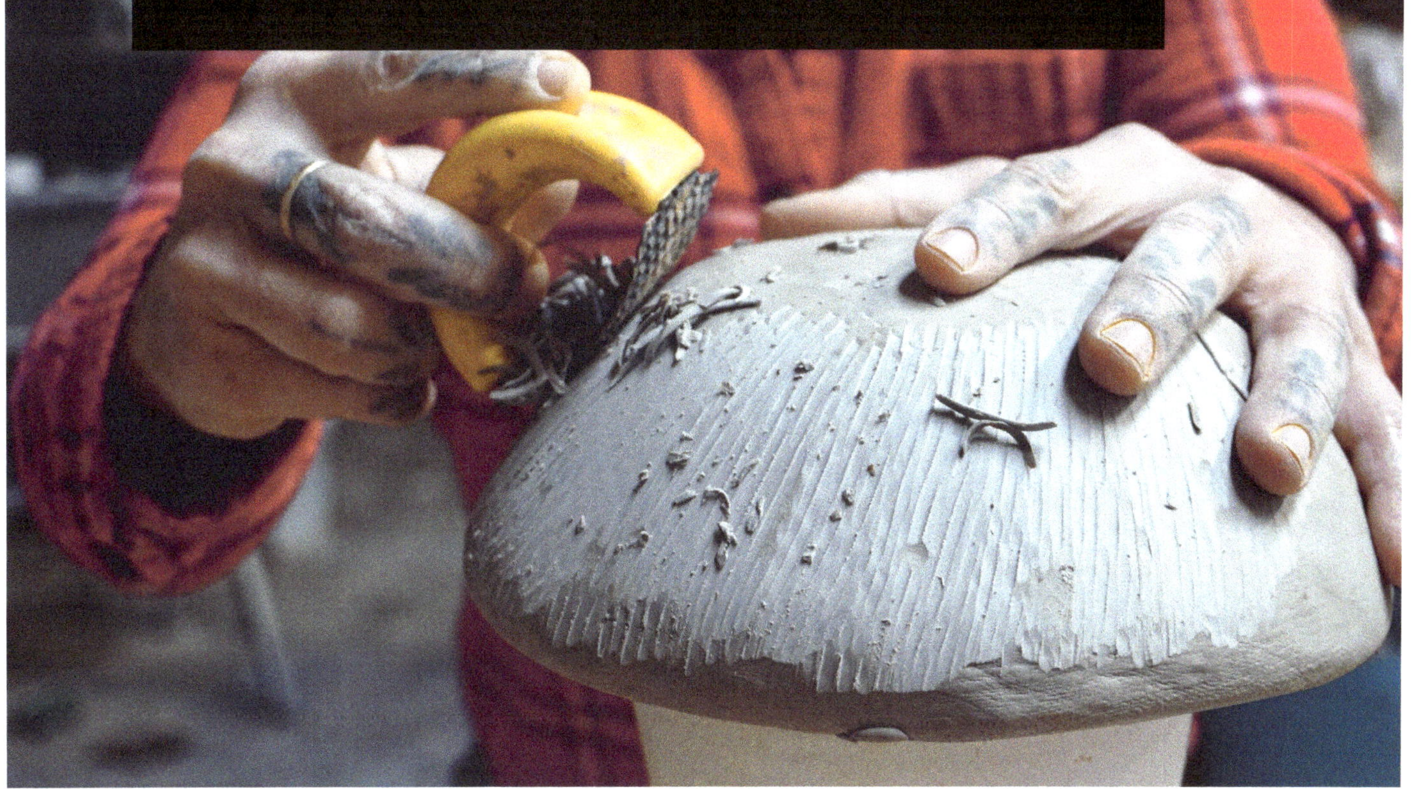

USE THE SURFORM TO REFINE THE SIDES WHEN THE THE CLAY IS LEATHER-HARD.

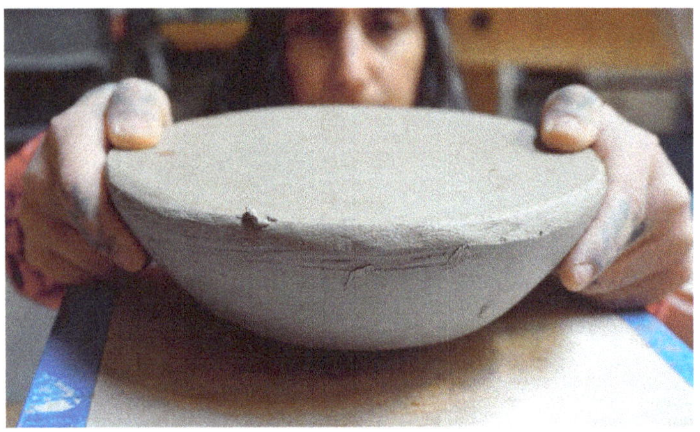

Every dish you pull from this mold will be the same shape, so if something bothers you about it, or isn't just right, this is the time to fix it.

When it's just the way you want it, flip it over and hollow it out with your carving tool. The sides and bottom of the mold should be no less than ½" (1.25 cm), preferably closer to 1" (2.5 cm) in thickness.

Flip it back over and remove all the carving marks with a rib. I like to hollow the mold right after finishing the shape, because you can apply a lot of pressure on the mold then. Every single mark will show up on every pot you make with this mold, so make it as clean as possible.

Remember that the outside of your mold will be the interior of your dishes. Let your finished mold dry slowly to prevent cracking. Fire to bisque temperature 04–06. Your mold is now ready to use and can be used indefinitely.

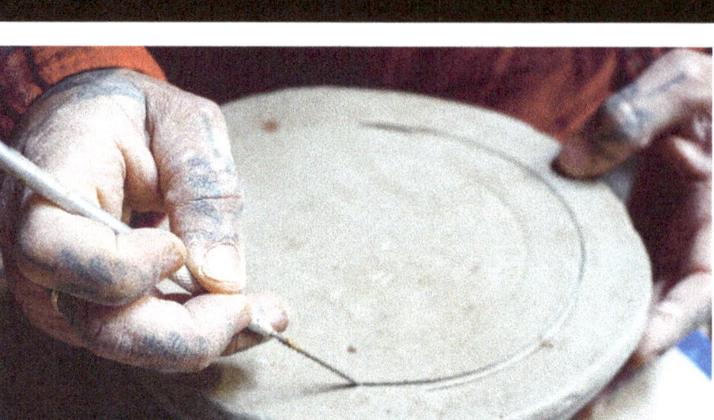

THE SIDES AND BOTTOM SHOULD BE NO LESS THAN ½"(1.25 cm), PREFERABLY CLOSER TO 1"(2.5 cm)

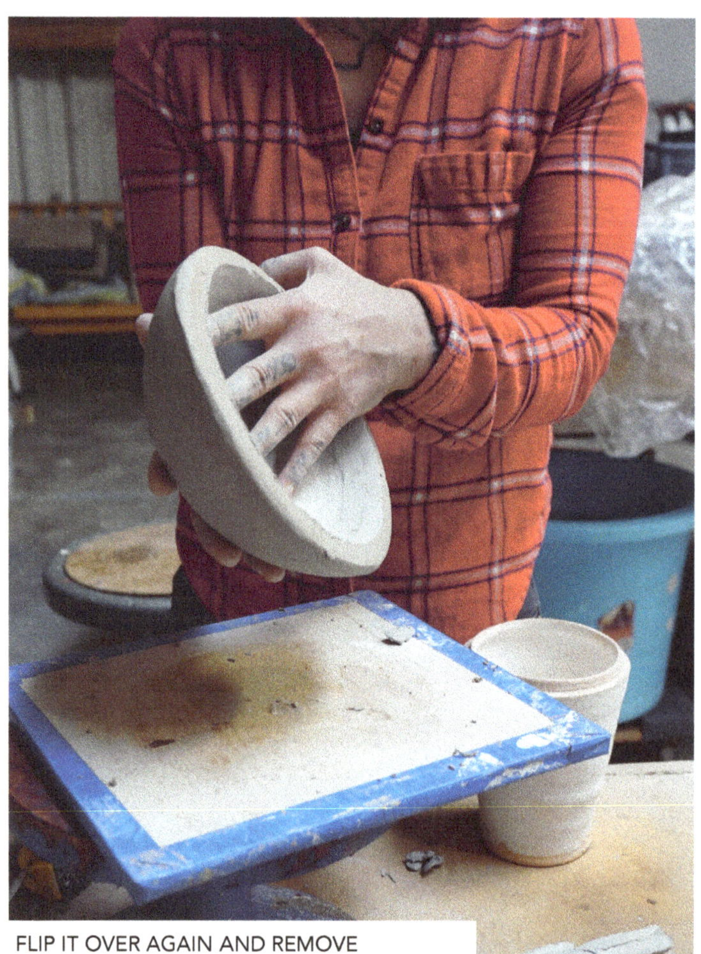

FLIP IT OVER AGAIN AND REMOVE ALL THE CARVING MARKS WITH A RIB.

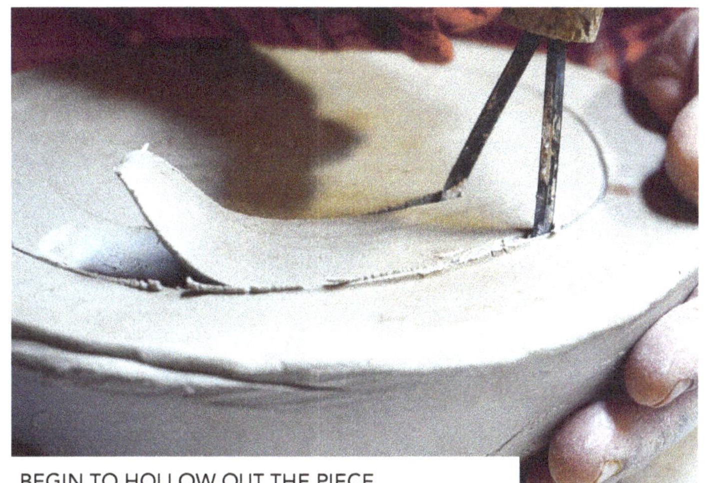
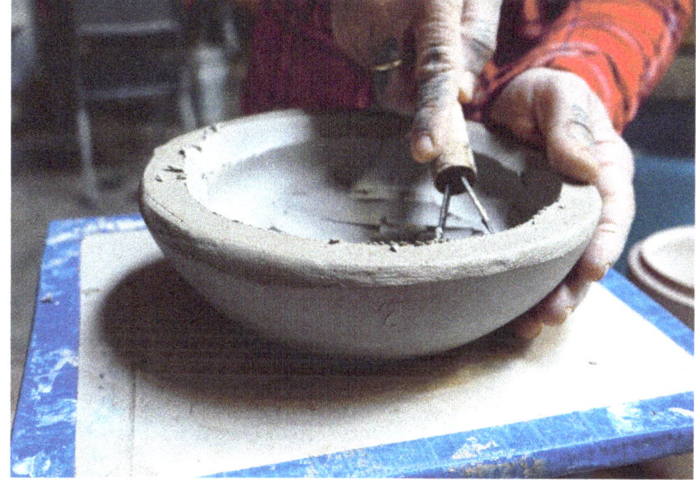

BEGIN TO HOLLOW OUT THE PIECE

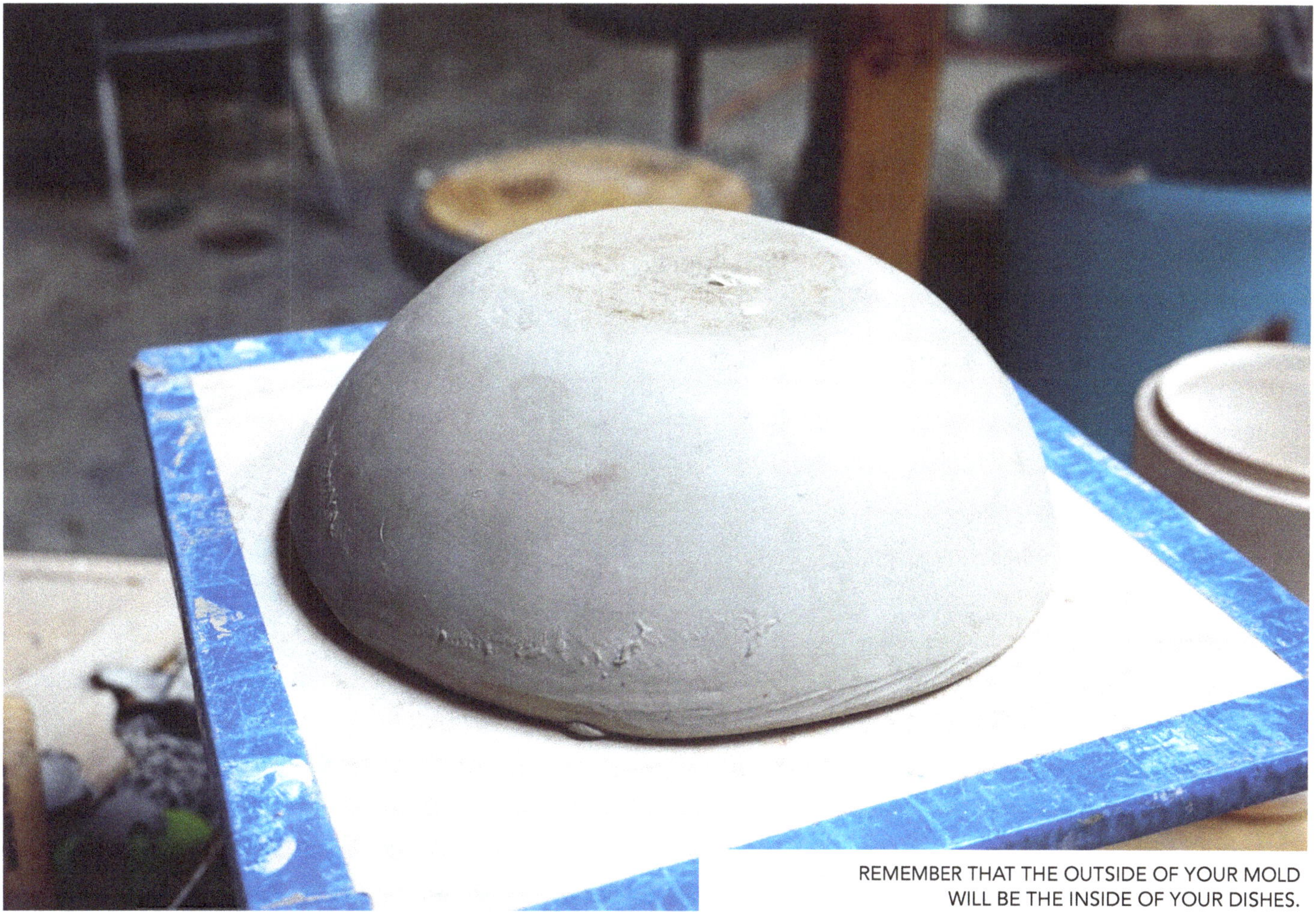

REMEMBER THAT THE OUTSIDE OF YOUR MOLD
WILL BE THE INSIDE OF YOUR DISHES.

Guest Potter Interview: Nancy Green
Casual, Comfortable, Elegant, Quiet Clay

MW: HOW DID YOU GET STARTED IN CLAY?

NG: My start in clay came from a casual exchange with a neighbor and friend. She asked me if I had ever been to one of Liz Lurie's sales. I said, "No, why would I want to go and what does she sell?" She said, "Liz makes pottery, and I think that you would like her work." Long story short, I started going, and after two years of attending Liz's studio sales, Liz said to me "You know, Nancy, you could make pots." Within weeks I was taking classes at a local ceramic center.

MW: WHAT ARE YOUR MOST ESSENTIAL TOOLS?

NG: I have a few favorites. In no particular order, these are the things I always have around: Thick backing material; 4" (10 cm) diameter tube about 18" (45.7 cm) long; Sherrill wire-cutting Mudtool; a big, heavy rolling pin; wood slats; a Sherrill red flexible rib; a fine-toothed scoring rib; a banding wheel; bats; and a fettling knife.

MW: YOUR POTS EXPRESS COMFORT AND FAMILIARITY AND SPEAK OF THE LIFE OF A STUDIO POTTER AS A SIMPLE, PRACTICAL LIFE. IS THAT YOUR LIFE?

NG: My pots, like my life, are simple, minimal, unadorned, casual, and comfortable. They are quiet but elegant, in a nonfussy kind of way. They mirror the practicality of how I move through life.

MW: WHAT IS YOUR FAVORITE FORM TO MAKE?

NG: Hollow forms—trays and vases. I like to make walls by throwing a bottomless cylinder—change the cylinder's shape while it is still flexible but not tacky— cut portions of the wall away, and add a textured slab to the top and bottom. Some forms are turned up on a side into a vertical orientation and an opening is cut in the top to make a vase. Forms that remain horizontal are either round, square, wedge-shaped, or boat-shaped.

MW: DO YOU MAKE POTS WITH SPECIFIC FOODS IN MIND?

NG: I don't consciously make forms to serve particular foods, but I am aware of what size tray is necessary for various courses of food one might serve. Serving pieces vary in size depending on their intent for appetizers, main dish, or dessert. A lunchtime plate is smaller than a dinner plate. Bowls vary in size and shape depending on their intent. A larger bowl would be made for a main-meal stir-fry; a smaller bowl for a side of soup, salad, or ice cream.

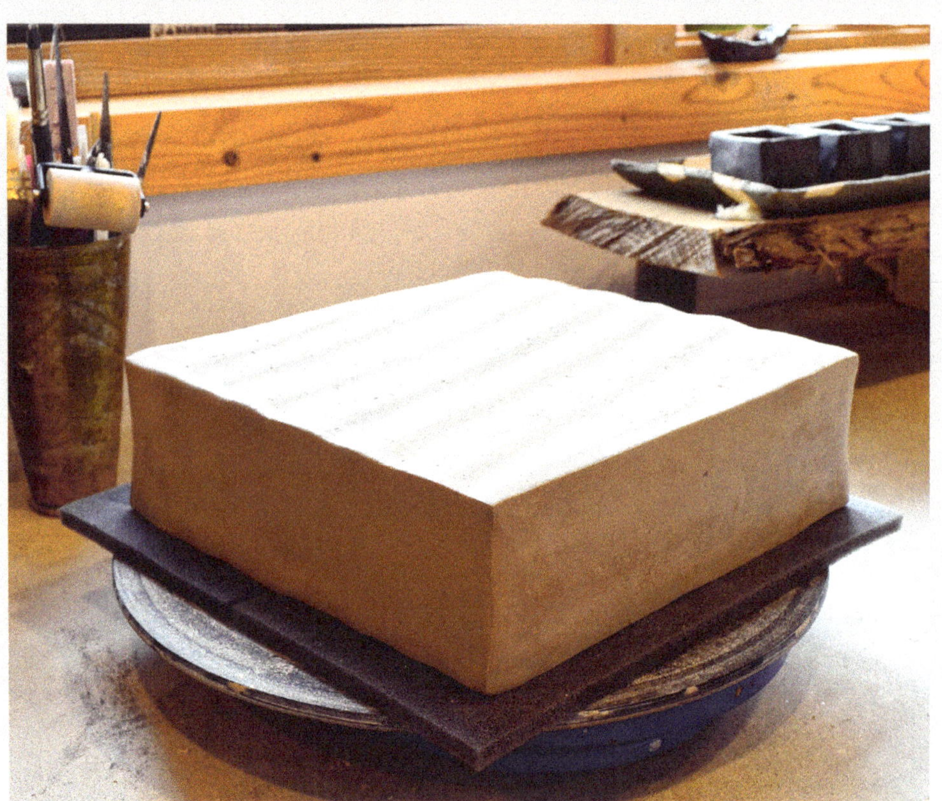

THE VASE ON ITS SIDE, READY FOR FINISHING

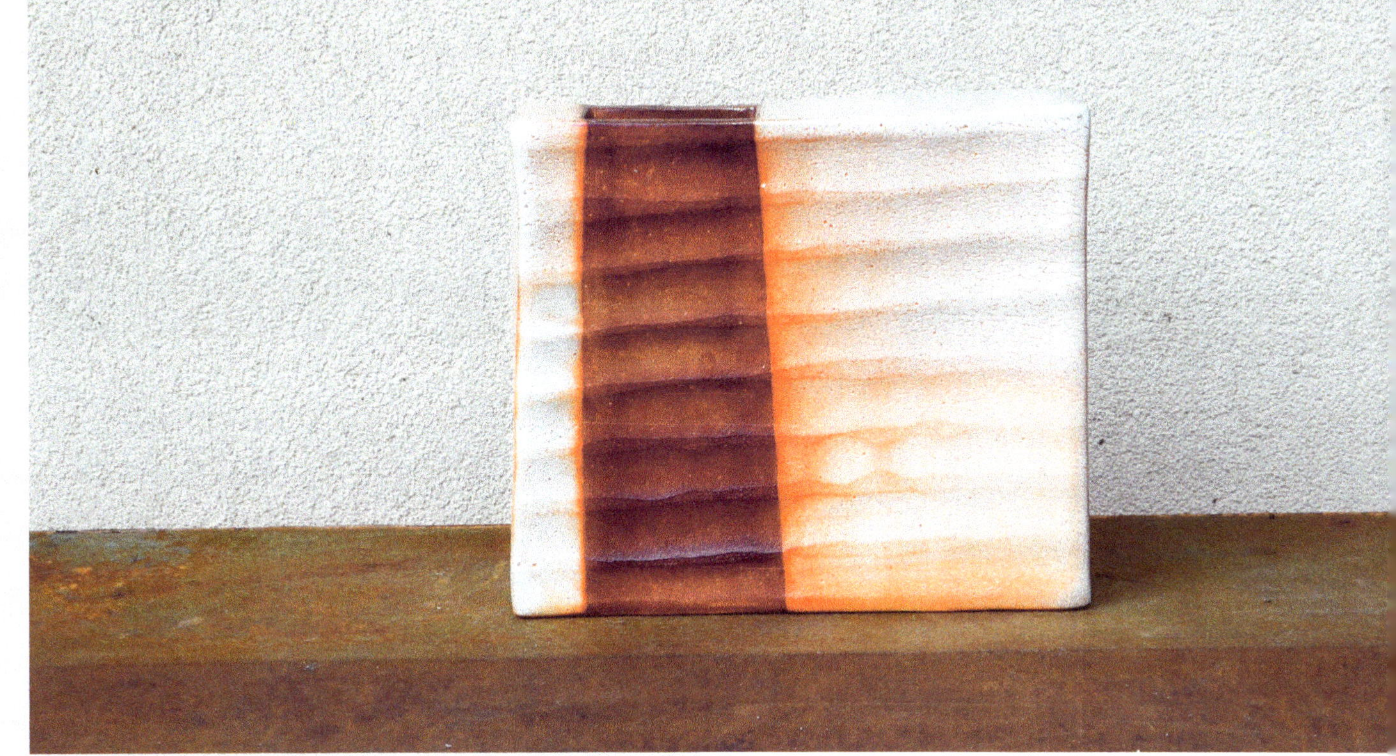

"My pots,
like my life, are
simple, minimal,
unadorned,
casual, and
comfortable."

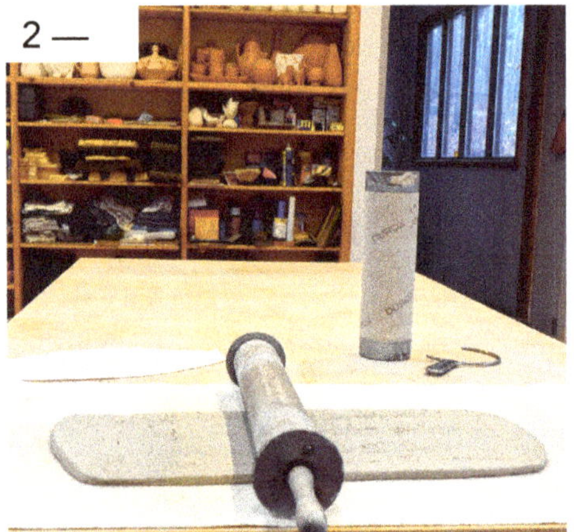

ROLLING THE SLAB

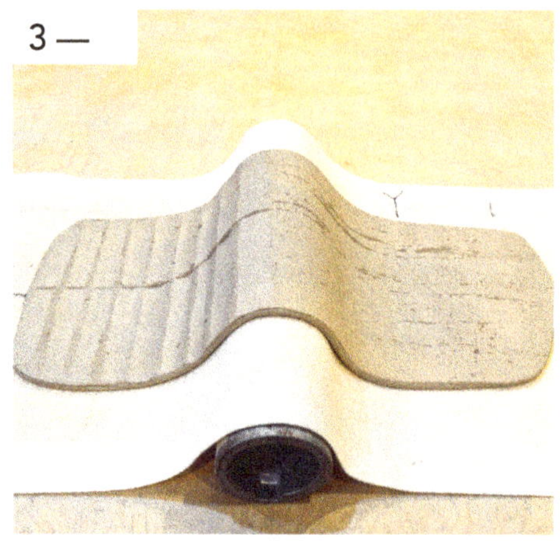

FACETING THE SLAB

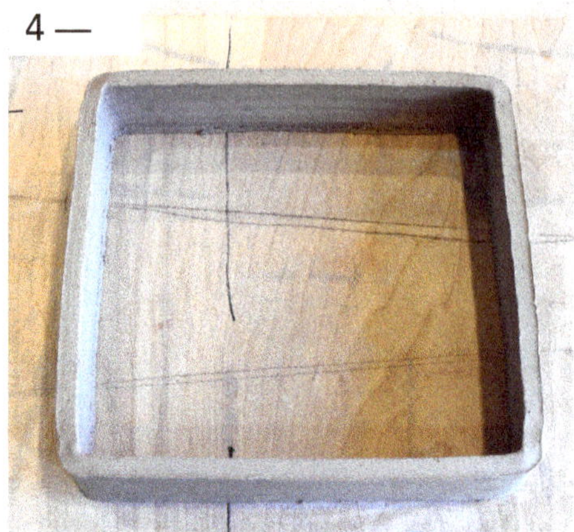

SLABS CREATING THE WALLS FOR THE VASE

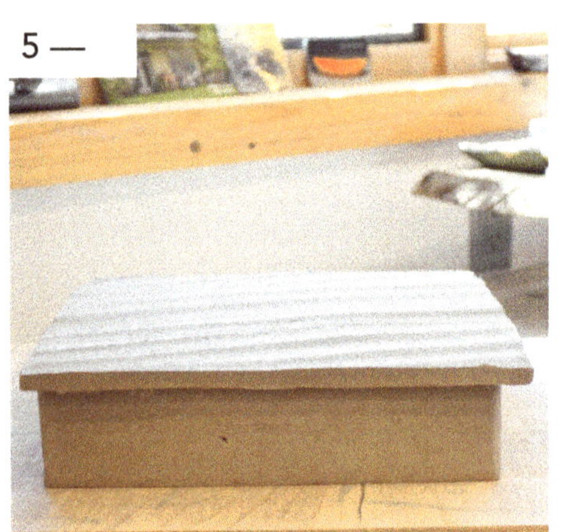

PUTTING A SIDE IN PLACE

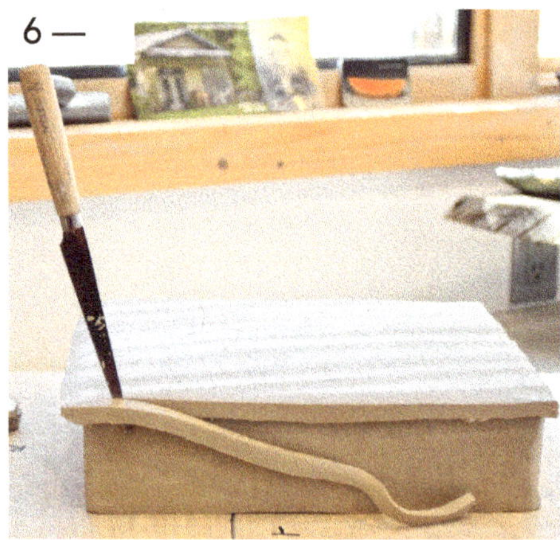

TRIMMING TO FIT

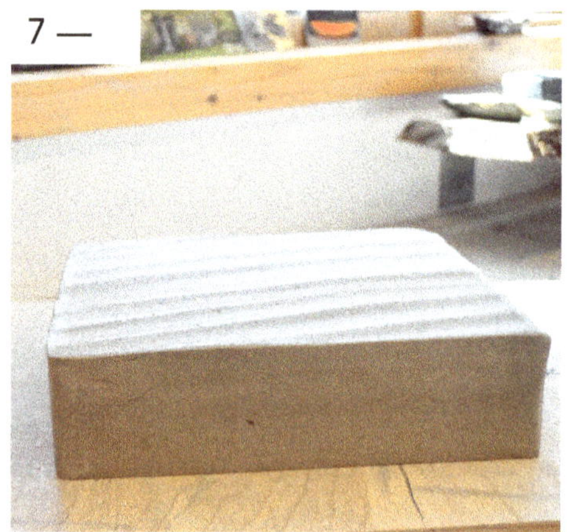

THE SIDE JOINED WITH THE WALLS

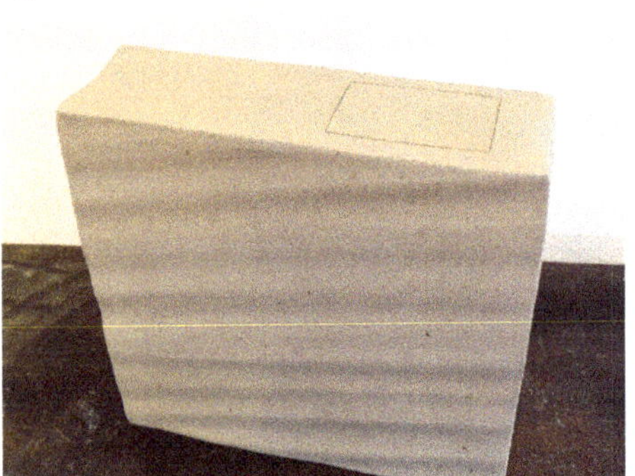

MARKED HOLE FOR CREATING
THE OPENING

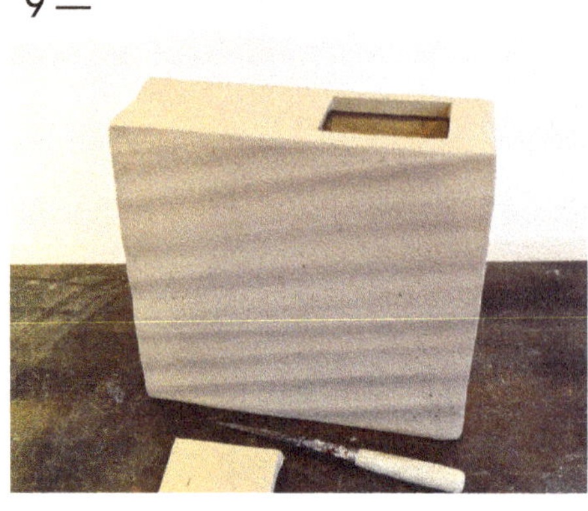

THE PIECE REMOVED FROM THE OPENING

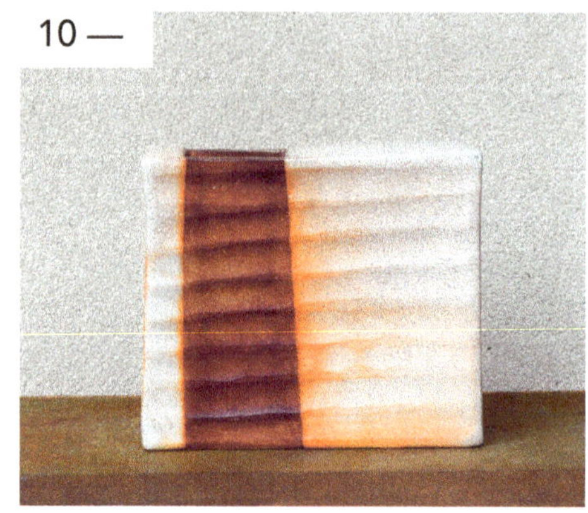

COMPLETED VASE

CONSTRUCTION OF AN ASYMMETRICAL VASE FORM

1 | SLAB WALL

While I start this form with a thrown bottomless cylinder, it can just as easily be started with a handbuilt wall. If handbuilding the wall, I encourage you to start with a handbuilt bottomless cylinder so you can play around with the shape you want to morph it into.

2 | GETTING READY TO ROLL A SLAB AND SLAB ROLLING

I roll out a slab by using a rolling pin and slats. The slab can be made with a slab roller, cut with a wire and cutting sticks, or thrown by hand on a hard surface. Choose the process that you like. You have to enjoy the process, and I like using a rolling pin and slats.

3 | FACETING

I like to use a textured slab that I make by faceting. The facet texture can be replaced by a design that could be anything from sprigging, slip design, drawing, wax resist patterns, decals, or stamping.

4 | ROUND WALL INTO A SQUARE BY GENTLE MANIPULATION

I changed the walls from round to square while the walls were no longer tacky to the touch and still flexible.

5 | SECURING THE SLAB

The slab is securely attached by first putting slip on the upper wall edge and then ribbing the outer edges of the slab onto the wall of the form.

6 | TRIMMING TO FIT

I used a paper pattern to figure out how big to cut the slab. I cut the slab about ½" (1.25 cm) larger on each side than the periphery of the walls. Then I trim off the excess and smooth the slab to the walls.

7 | A CLOSED HOLLOW FORM

I outline marks on top of the piece for guidelines to cut an opening for the vase. After I finish cutting, I smooth the edges of the opening.

8 | *VOILA:* MY FIRED ASYMMETRICAL VASE.

> "I encourage you to start with a handbuilt bottomless cylinder so you can play around with the shape you want to morph it into."

05

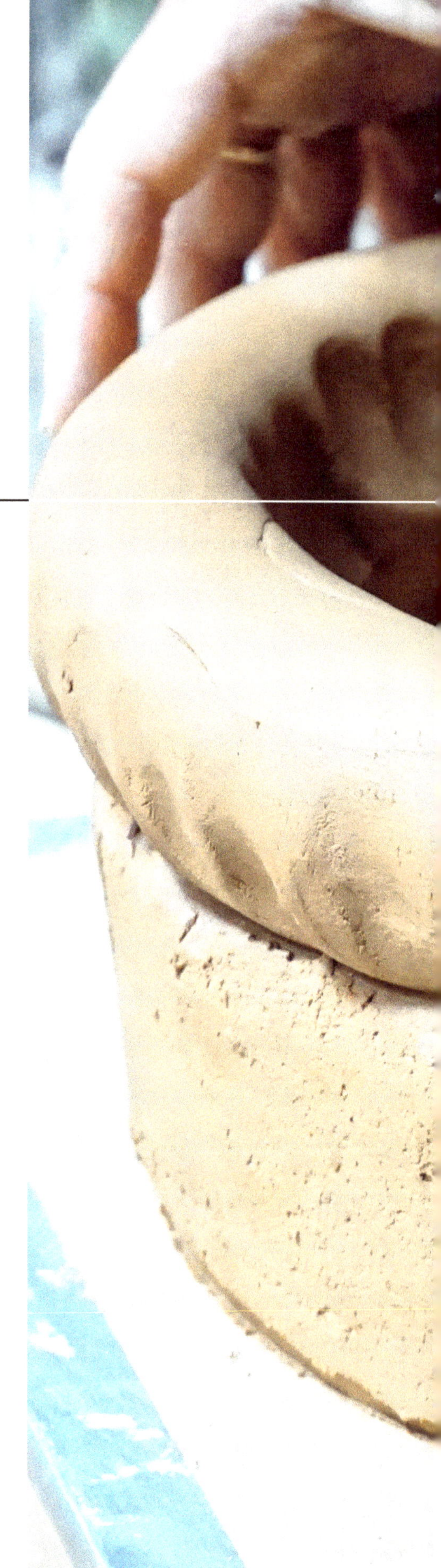

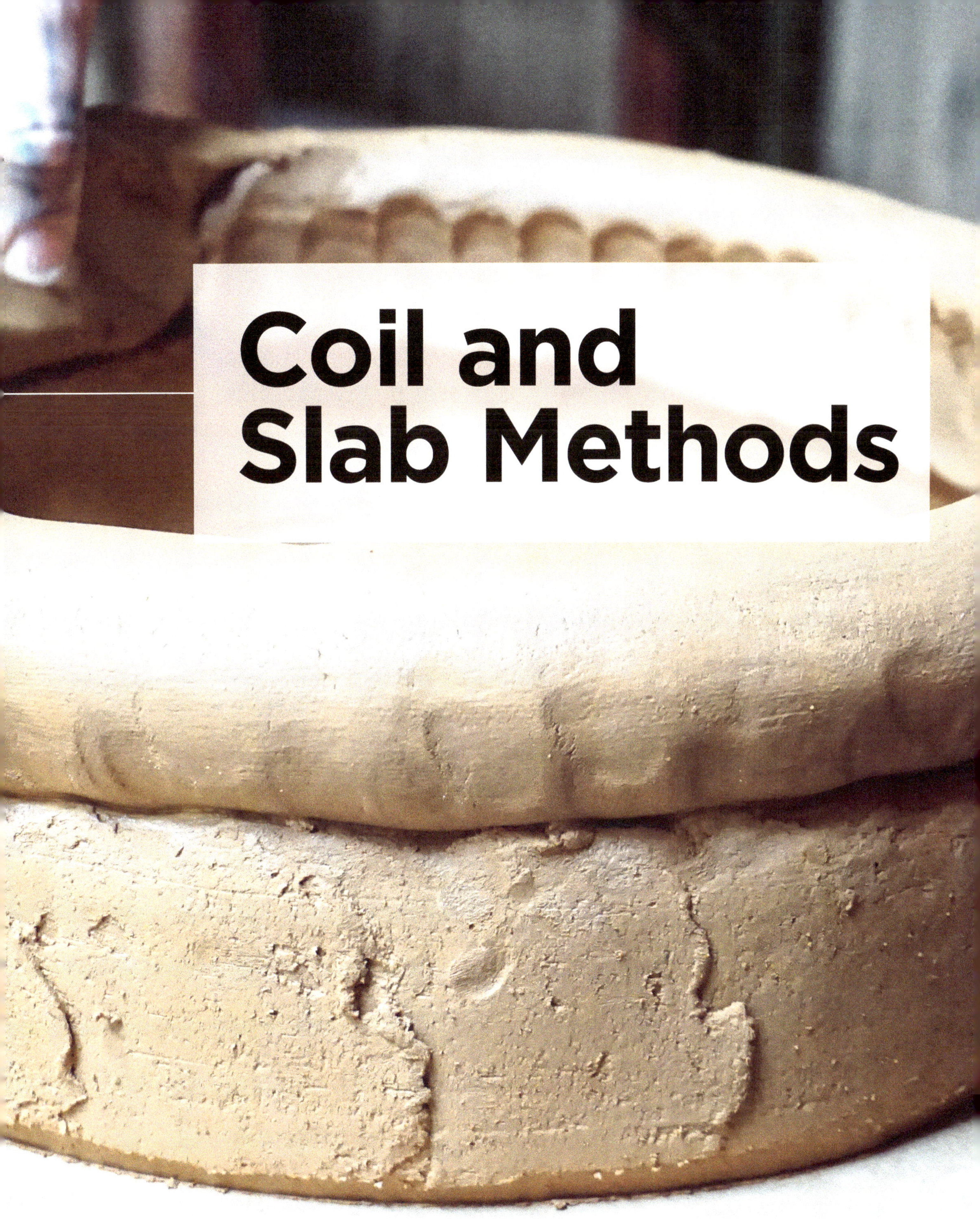
Coil and
Slab Methods

Slab Sticks Method

YOU'LL NEED

- ☑ 2 slab sticks
- ☑ Wire tool
- ☑ Plastic rib

For this technique, you'll use slab sticks combined with a wire tool to create slabs of even thickness. Slab sticks have notches carved into them at even intervals along their length. Tightening the wire tool around the two sticks allows the wire to slice slabs of identical thickness (see page 11).

Making slabs is essential for creating dishes from hump molds and as a base for coil pots. There are a few techniques for making slabs that I have used. I use a rolling pin if I just want a single slab. For multiples, the first way I did it was by using slab sticks. I didn't have a slab roller, and this simple technique is an easy and inexpensive way to work. It is also a great way to make a stack of slabs of identical size and thickness. I now have a slab roller, and it is my preferred way to roll slabs, as it is quick and it gives me the ability to roll out large slabs.

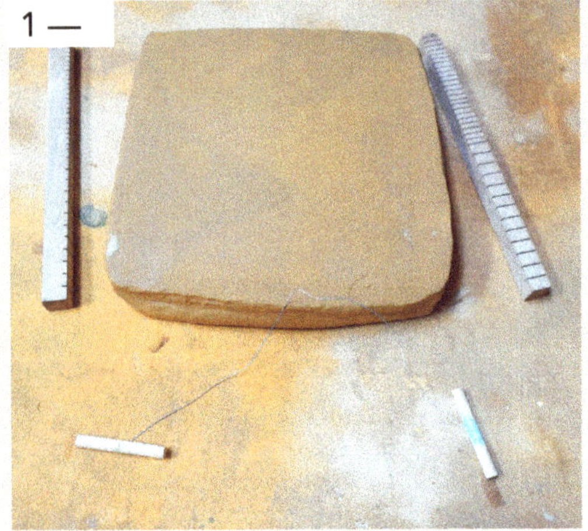

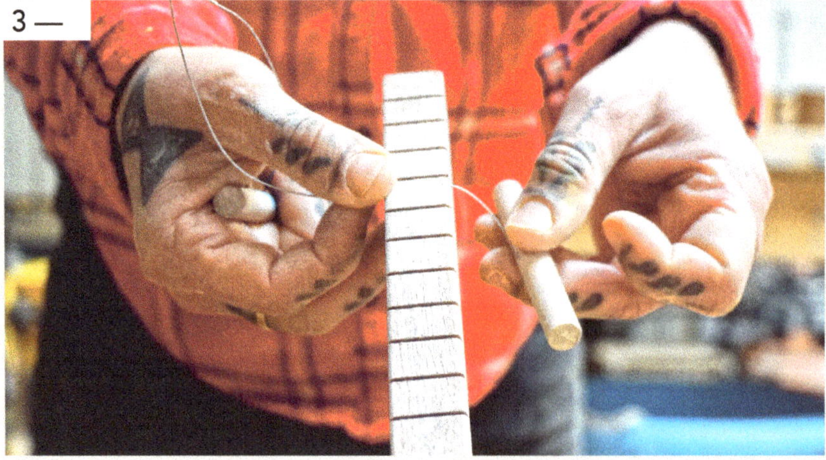

1 | Pound out a hunk of clay slightly larger than the mold or template you will be using. If you start with a big hunk of clay, you can slice many slabs from the one piece.

2 | Hold one of the slab sticks up to the hunk of clay and note the notch just below the top of the hunk of clay.

3 | Wrap one end of the wire tool around the stick at that notch, allowing for a firm grip. Pull the wire tool across and attach in the other end at the corresponding notch in the other stick.

4 | Hold the sticks upright on either side, just behind the hunk of clay. You'll be slicing it horizontally, from the top down. Keep the wire taut and the sticks perpendicular by gripping the ends of the wire tools and keeping the bottoms of the sticks flush with the table as you slowly pull the sticks toward you.

5 | The first slab that is removed won't be even. Ball it up and use it later.

6 | Move the wire tool down one notch on each side and line up the sticks on each side, behind the slab of clay again. With the wire stretched taut, pull it toward you. This time you will have an even slice.

7 | Repeat, moving the wire tool down a notch each time, until the whole mound of clay has been sliced. You should now have a stack of even slabs.

8 | Remove each slab from the stack by lifting and sliding one hand underneath it and the other hand on top so that you sandwich the slab between your hands.

9 | Carefully lift the slab with even pressure and place on your work surface. You can smooth the slab with a rib or leave it. It is now ready to use.

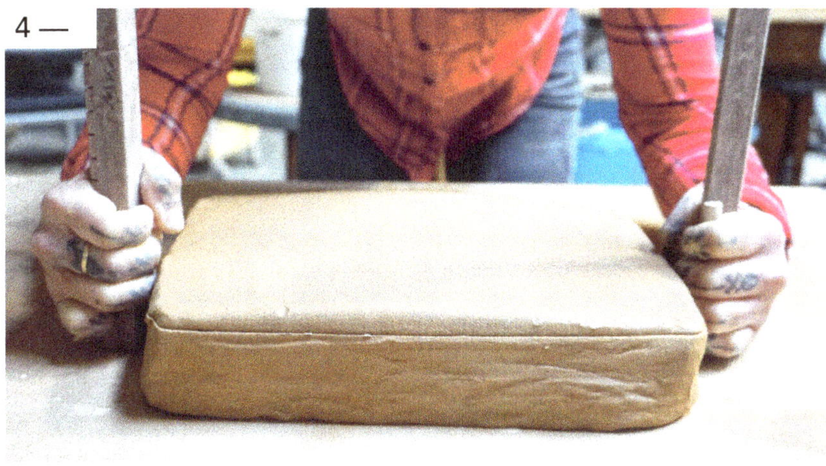

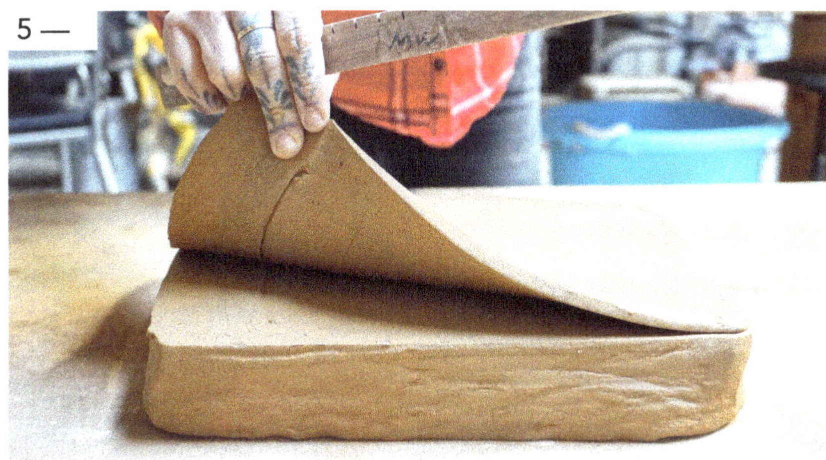

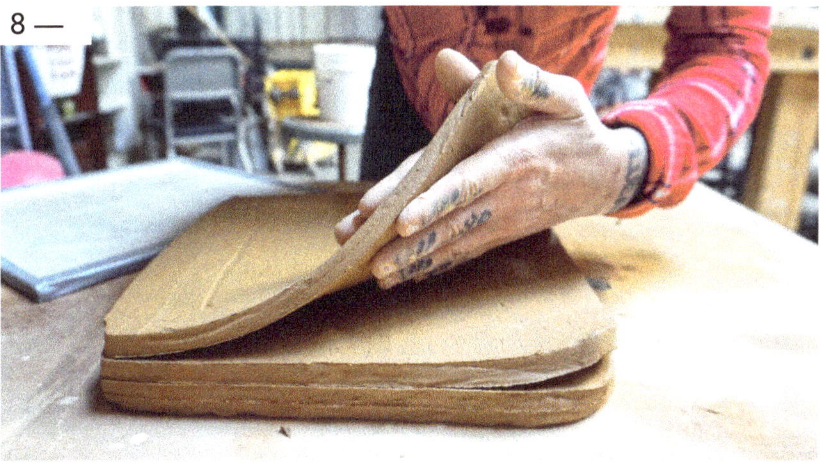

Rolling Pin Method

YOU'LL NEED

- ☑ Wooden slats, such as paint stirrers
- ☑ Rolling pin
- ☑ Plastic or rubber rib

1 | Pound out a piece of clay slightly thicker than your desired slab thickness. This should be as big as your final slab size.

2 | Align the slats on either side of the clay. The handles of the rolling pin should rest on the slats, with the clay under the rolling pin.

3 | Roll the rolling pin back and forth, stretching the clay to the thickness dictated by the slats. When the rolling pin rolls with little effort, the slab should be to the desired thickness and ready to use.

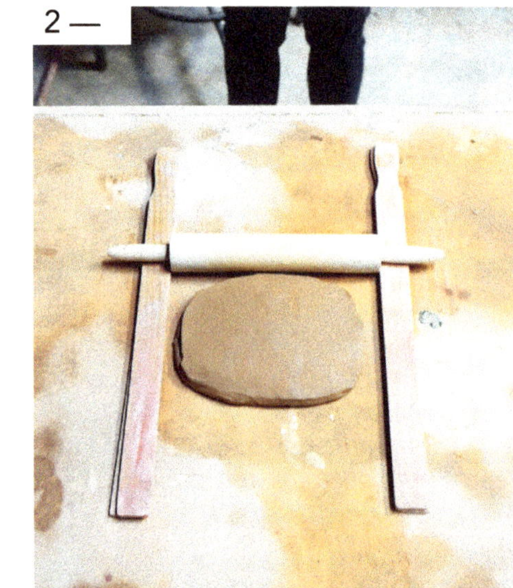

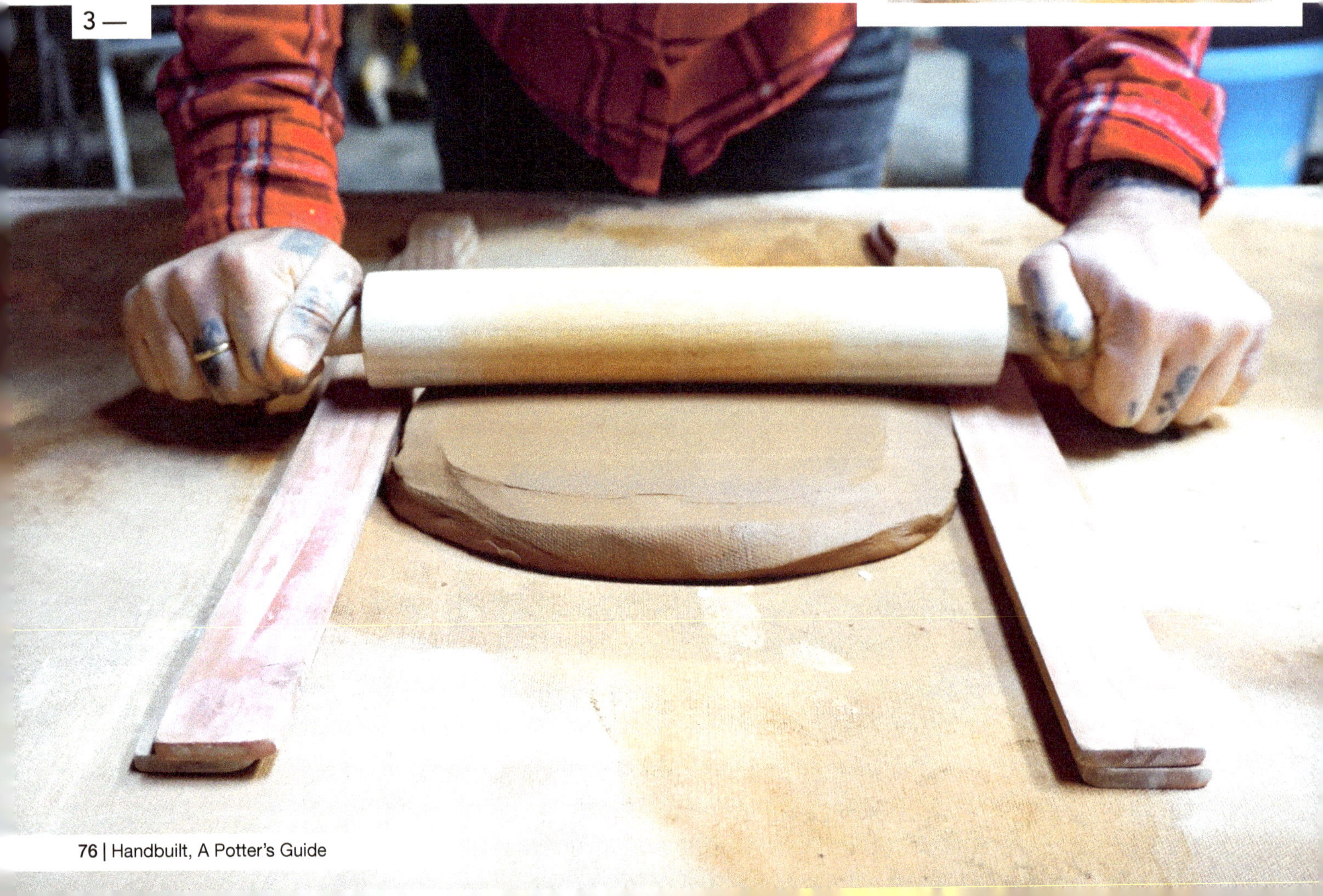

Slab Roller Method

1 | Adjust the roller by raising it up or down to your desired slab thickness.

2 | Pound out a piece of clay that is as wide as, or slightly wider than, your desired final slab. This piece of clay will be thicker than your final slab and will roll out longer but not wider.

3 | Sandwich the pounded piece of clay between two pieces of canvas and place it on the bed of the roller.

4 | As you turn the wheel, tug the canvas to start feeding it under the roller. As it starts to feed through and come out on the other side, you can let go and turn the wheel until the slab has completely rolled through.

5 | Lift the canvas with the slab from the roller bed onto your work surface.

6 | Use a rib to remove the canvas texture from the slab. It is ready to use.

There are a variety of mechanical slab rollers out there. They come in a variety of widths, and they're very simple to use, with the turn of a wheel. Some slab rollers are tabletop models and others are freestanding. I use one by North Star that I purchased secondhand.

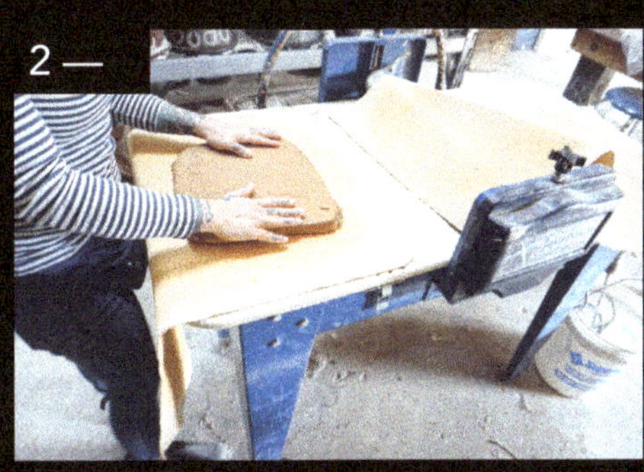

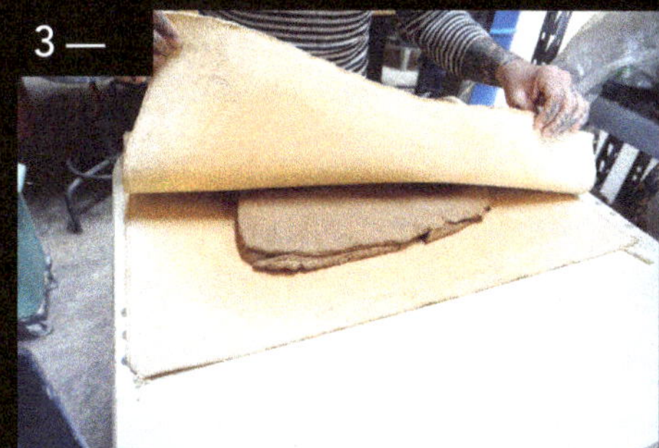

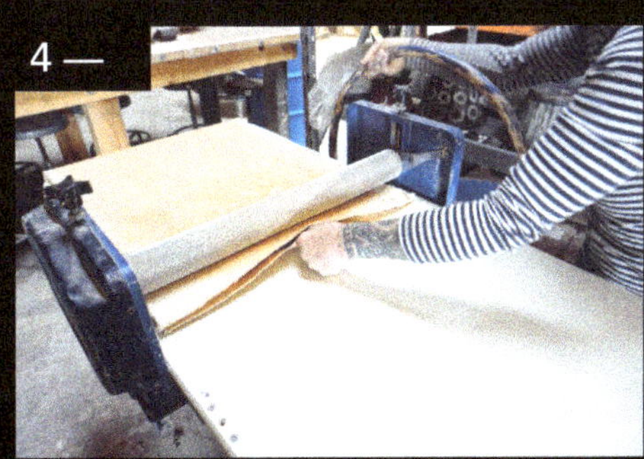

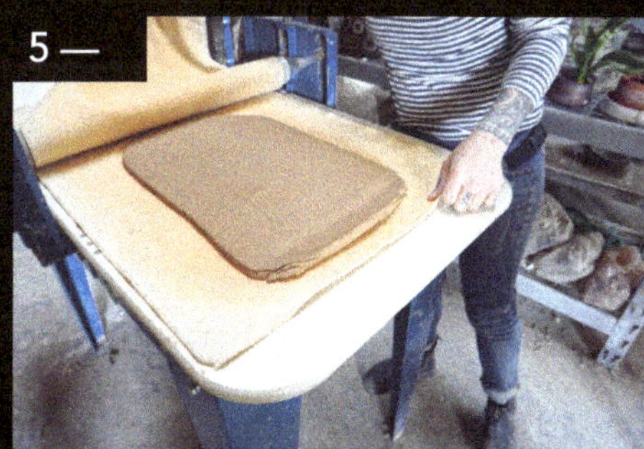

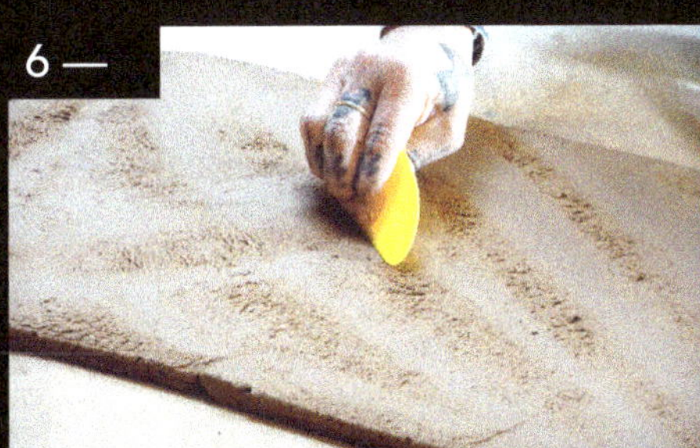

Slab Dishes from a Bisque Mold

All my plates, platters, and bowls are made from drape molds. These are called slab dishes, as they are made from draping a slab over the mold. It is a simple way to make dishes of the same size. I prefer slab dishes to wheel-thrown because they are simple and I can make the same form over and over once I make the mold. I usually keep my platters and bowls plain, but you can add handles and feet to them if you wish.

YOU'LL NEED

- ☑ Surform knife
- ☑ Plastic ribs
- ☑ Mason Jar
- ☑ Cut PVC pipe, or other prop to raise your mold off the work surface
- ☑ Slab sticks, rolling pin, or slab roller
- ☑ Ware board

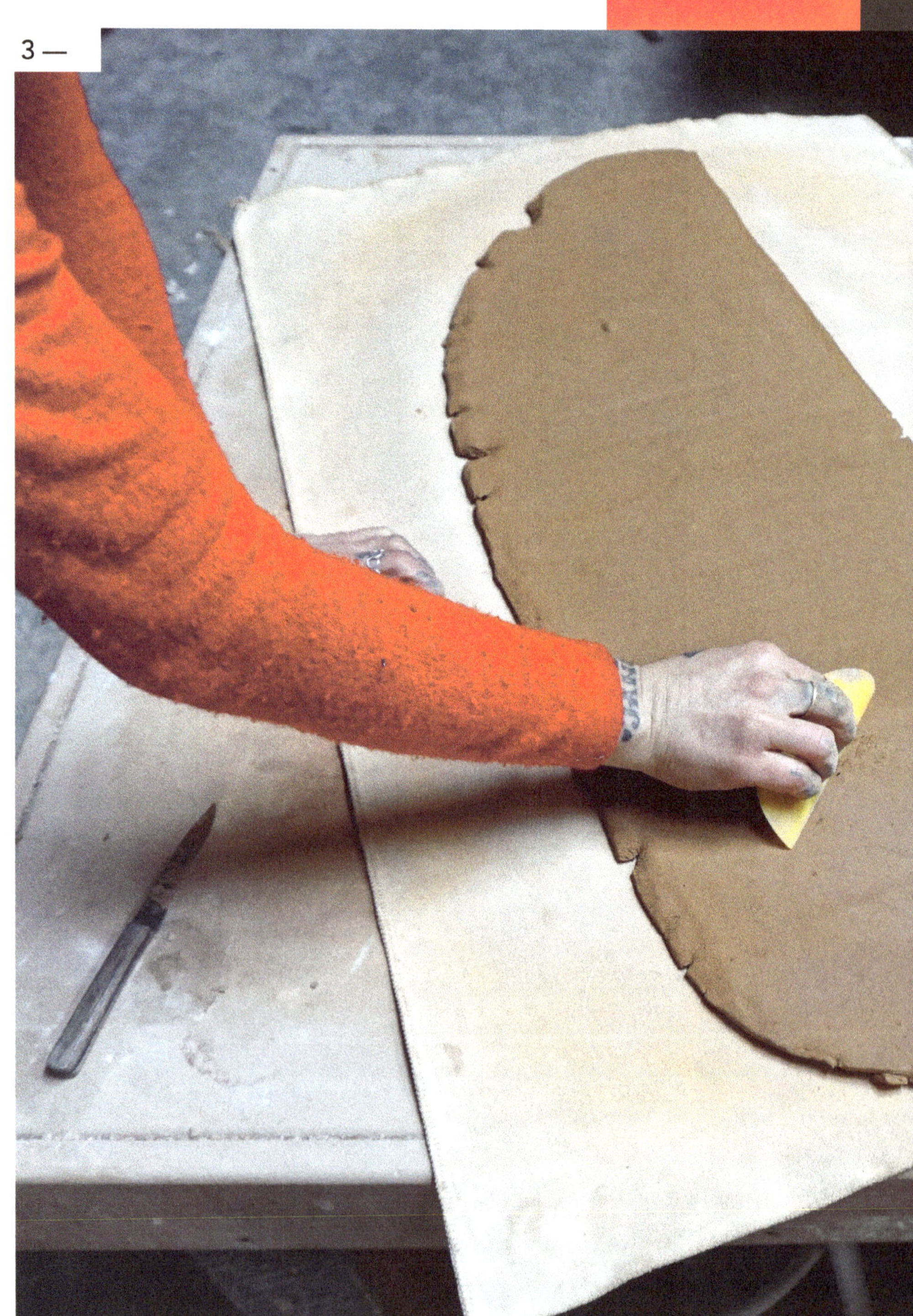

3 —

ROLL OUT YOUR SLAB AND USE A FIRM BUT FLEXIBLE RIB TO SMOOTH IT

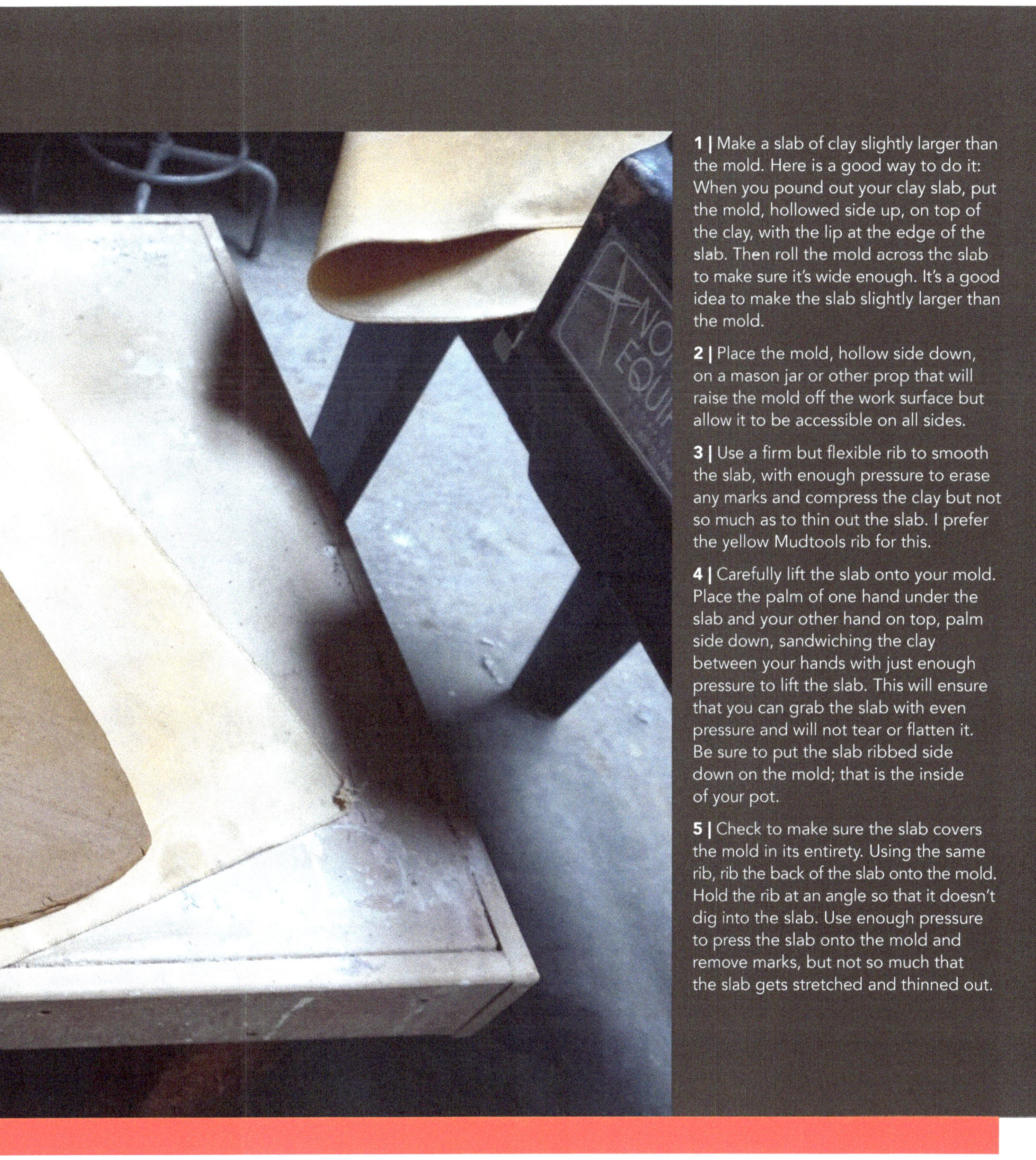

1 | Make a slab of clay slightly larger than the mold. Here is a good way to do it: When you pound out your clay slab, put the mold, hollowed side up, on top of the clay, with the lip at the edge of the slab. Then roll the mold across the slab to make sure it's wide enough. It's a good idea to make the slab slightly larger than the mold.

2 | Place the mold, hollow side down, on a mason jar or other prop that will raise the mold off the work surface but allow it to be accessible on all sides.

3 | Use a firm but flexible rib to smooth the slab, with enough pressure to erase any marks and compress the clay but not so much as to thin out the slab. I prefer the yellow Mudtools rib for this.

4 | Carefully lift the slab onto your mold. Place the palm of one hand under the slab and your other hand on top, palm side down, sandwiching the clay between your hands with just enough pressure to lift the slab. This will ensure that you can grab the slab with even pressure and will not tear or flatten it. Be sure to put the slab ribbed side down on the mold; that is the inside of your pot.

5 | Check to make sure the slab covers the mold in its entirety. Using the same rib, rib the back of the slab onto the mold. Hold the rib at an angle so that it doesn't dig into the slab. Use enough pressure to press the slab onto the mold and remove marks, but not so much that the slab gets stretched and thinned out.

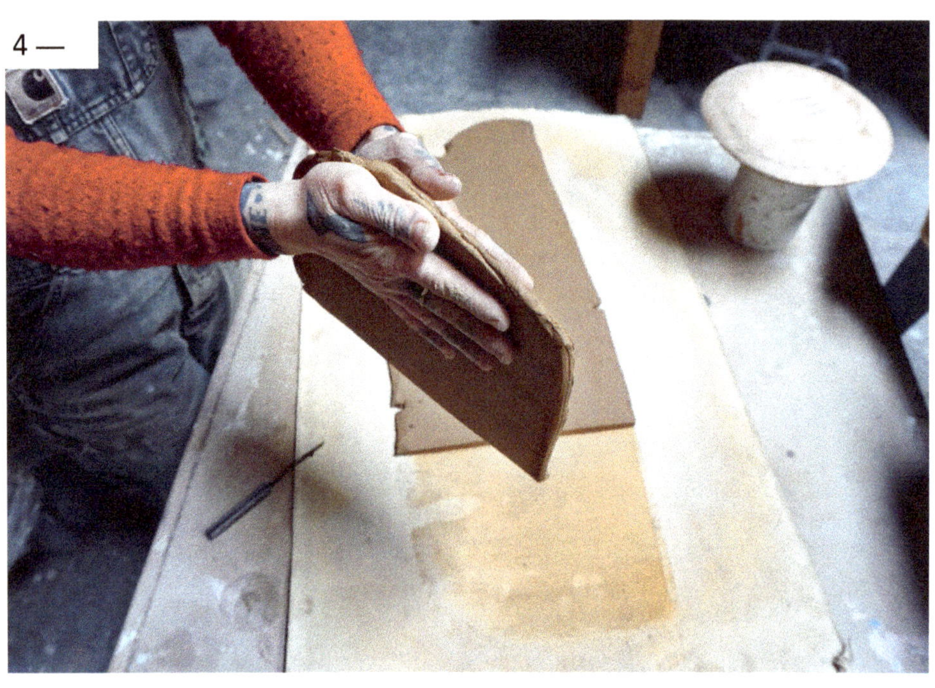

4 —

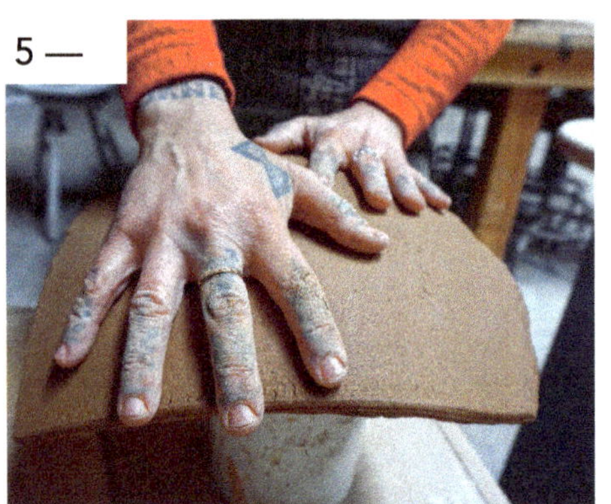

5 —

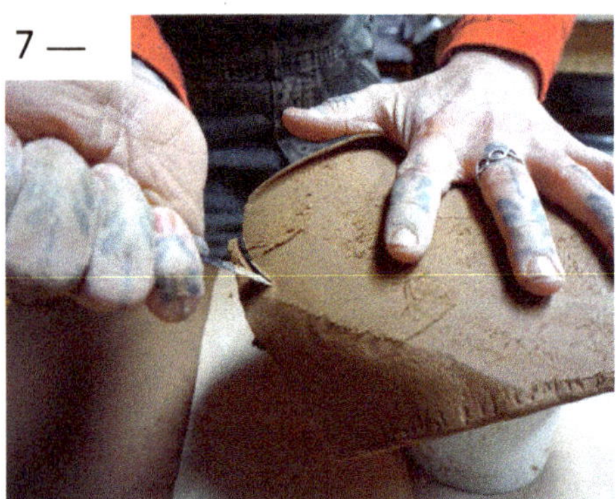

7 —

6 | Pay careful attention to the rim, as it can easily get thinned out. I like to ease off on pressure just before the edge of the mold and then go around the mold, ribbing that last inch around the rim sideways.

7 | When the slab has been ribbed to the mold, use a long knife to cut off the overhang around the rim. You can do this by placing the mold and mason jar on a banding wheel and turning it. Or you can do it simply by turning the mold by hand while you keep the side of the knife flush with the edge. To do this, cut up through the overhang until the knife hits the rim of the mold. Then turn the blade sideways and use the rim of the mold as your guide to cut off the excess around the rim.

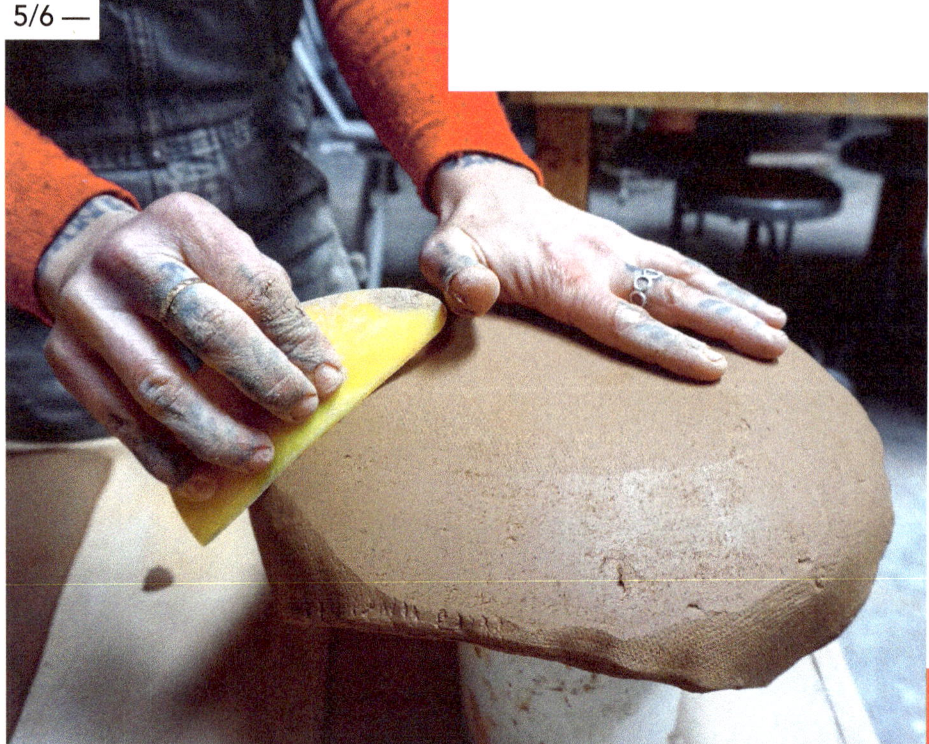

5/6 —

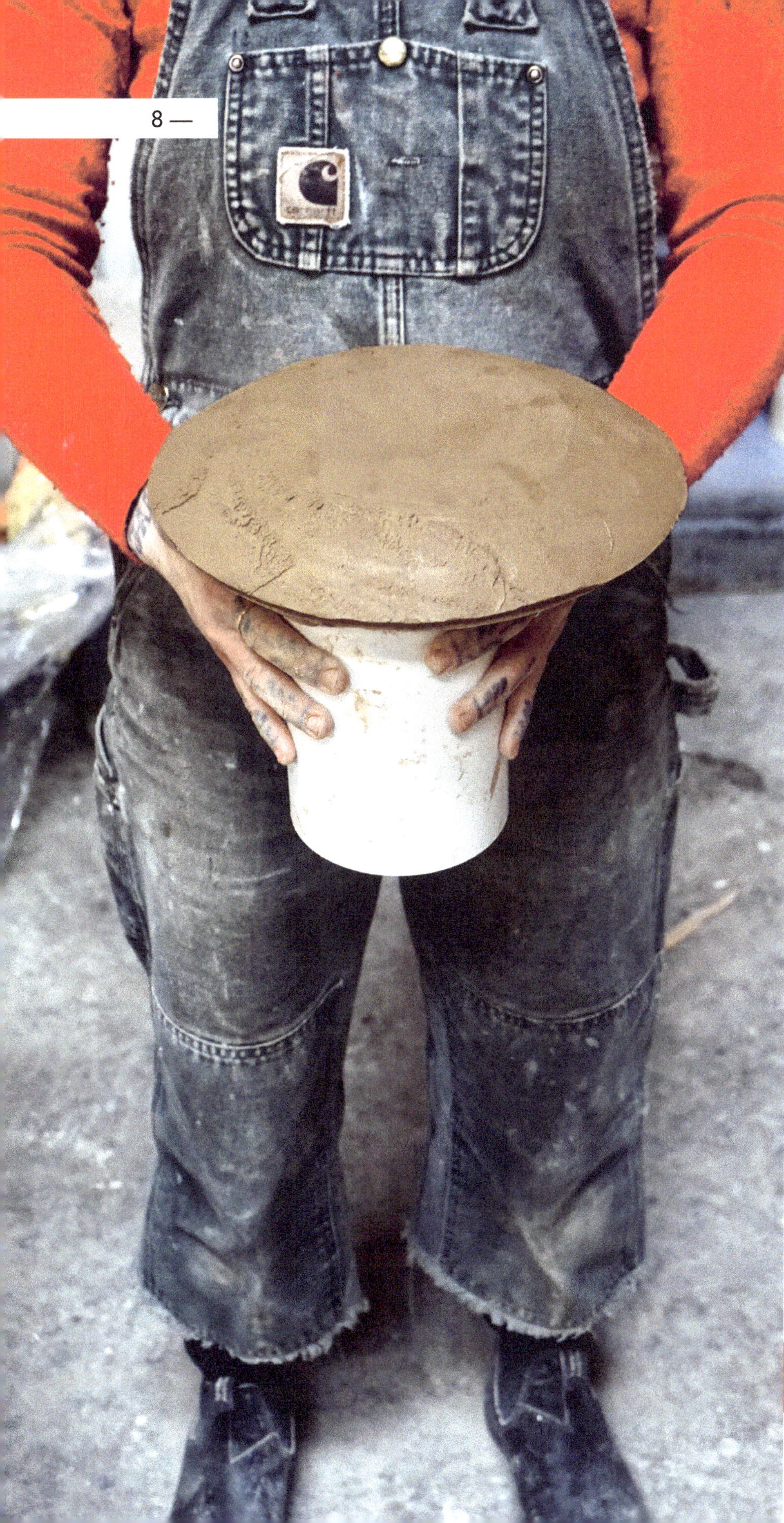

8 | Remove the mason jar and let the slab firm up on the mold until leather-hard. You will know when it is ready to lift off the mold because it will have shrunk from the edge and will easily pop off.

9 | To take the slab off the mold, place a ware board or square of drywall on top of the slab. Put one hand flat on the board and use the other hand to lift the mold from underneath. With the mold, slab, and board sandwiched between your hands, flip them over and set the board on the table. Your mold will be upside down and on top of the slab.

10 | Carefully grab the mold with your fingers opposite each other and lift straight up and off the slab. Your mold can be used again to make another dish.

11 | Let your slab dish firm up to a hard leather-hard. When the rim is firm, use a surform to trim it. Use it flat for a flat rim or angled for a beveled rim. When the rim is as you like it, clean it up with a rib. Your slab dish is done. You can now apply slip and any slip decorating techniques.

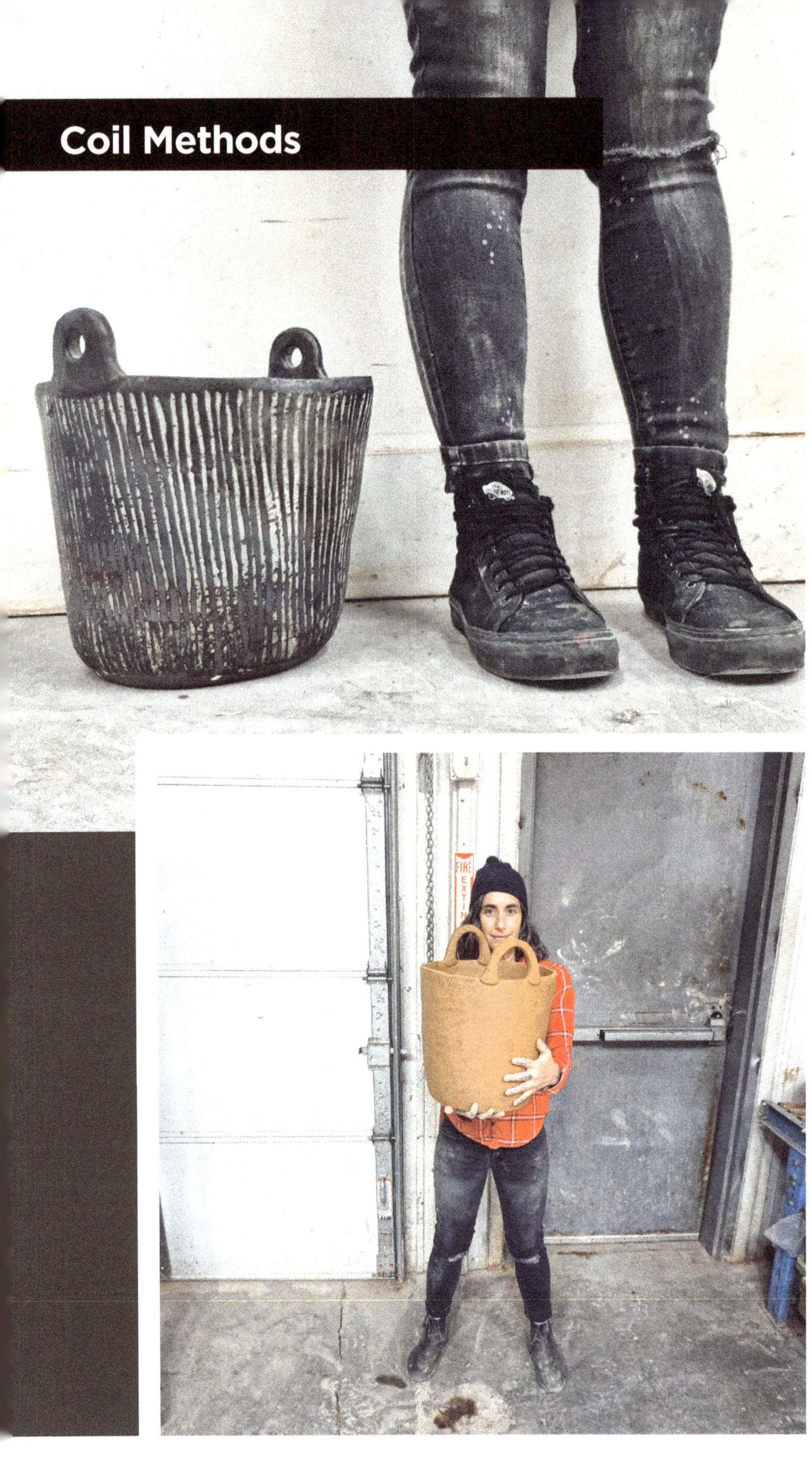

An Ancient Means for Making Pots

Coil building is a method of making pottery that has been used for thousands of years in cultures throughout the world. For many people, learning to make a coiled pot is their first introduction to clay in elementary school. Not me. I never had ceramics in school when I was a kid. I made my first coil pot ever as an adult in 2017.

When I had started making pots twelve years earlier, I jumped right on the wheel and didn't consider handbuilding as interesting or as something I wanted to investigate. Aside from making slab dishes from hump molds, I made everything on the wheel.

By the time I started to make coil pots, I already had such a deep understanding of clay that the coil method made it easy for me to build what was in my head. I may have done my learning backward, but I think that timing allowed me to respond to this method positively, and it enabled me to make the larger works I had been wanting to try.

My process of learning reminds me a little of those bikes for small children that are available now. Instead of training wheels, kids start on bikes with no pedals that are low to the ground—they use their feet for momentum. This teaches them balance first, then they naturally learn to ride. I did not learn anything in ceramics in the linear way it's normally taught. I learned how to wood fire before I could operate an electric kiln. I took a class making bottle forms before I had mastered cylinders. In some ways, I made it hard for myself, but in the long run, I made it easier.

I love the coil-building method and have only just begun my journey into this method of creating pots.

Make a Coil Bucket

YOU'LL NEED

- ☑ Knife
- ☑ Serrated rib
- ☑ Plastic rib (yellow Mudtool)
- ☑ Ware board
- ☑ Slip
- ☑ Banding wheel (optional, but highly recommended)
- ☑ Tools for rolling a slab
- ☑ Needle tool
- ☑ Surform

Buckets are one of my favorite utilitarian things. I use buckets so much in my studio that I have become a little obsessed with them. I "hunt them in the wild" out of dumpsters: empty frosting buckets from grocery stores, empty soy sauce buckets from the Chinese buffet, empty peanut butter buckets from the co-op. I have even been known to pull over on the interstate to rescue an abandoned bucket from the side of the road, as if I were saving a lost puppy.

The first thing I made with coils was a bucket. I had been wanting to make one, but I'd never been able to throw large enough forms and didn't like the method of adding multiple wheel-thrown forms together to create a bigger one. I tried making a mold, but the transition from the bottom to the wall of the bucket was too steep and the body too round. I had more failures than successes, and it seemed like there had to be a better way. Coil building this form was the better way.

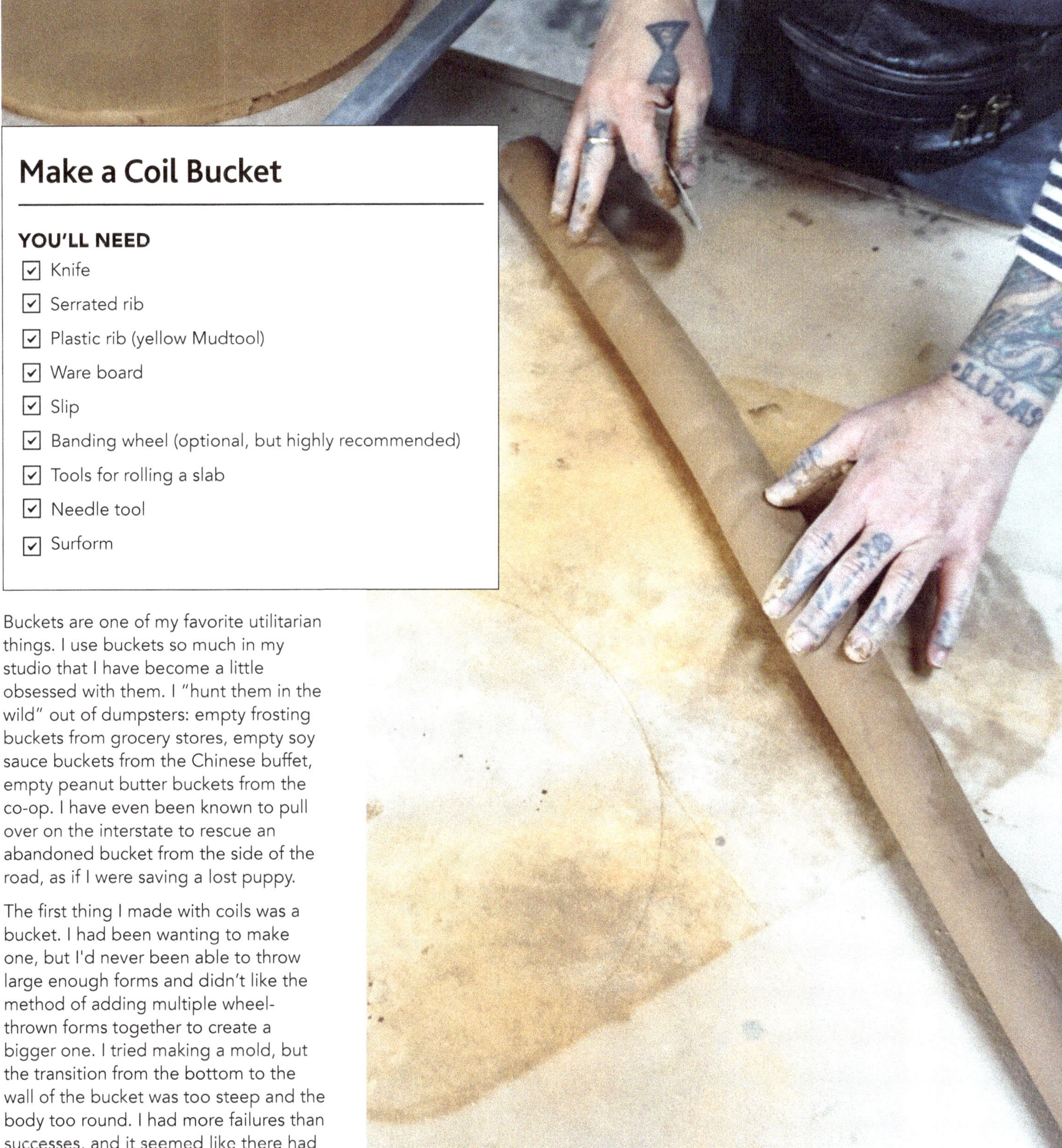

1 | Start by finding something circular to use as a template for the bottom of your bucket.

2 | Roll out a slab slightly larger than the diameter of your template. I use a ½" (1.25 cm) slab. Measure. Rib the slab smooth.

3 | Place the template on the slab and trace it. Cut out the bottom and carefully lift it onto a ware board. I find that working on a banding wheel is very helpful when making coil pots. If you don't have one, you can turn the ware board by hand.

4 | Score and slip the outer top ½" (1.25 cm) circumference of your slab.

5 | Roll out a coil long enough to wrap around the entire circumference of the bottom of the bucket. Your coil can be any thickness you want to work with. I tend to use large coils because it takes fewer of them to build the pot. I work with about 1"(2.5 cm) thick coils when I'm making bigger coil pots.

6 | Score the coil and press it onto the scored edge of the slab. When it's adhered, use your thumb to blend the seam where the slab and coil join, inside and outside. Once the seam has disappeared, you can use a plastic rib (I prefer the yellow Mudtools rib) to further blend it.

7 | Pinch the coil evenly all around to the relative thickness you want for the walls. Try to get them about the same thickness as the bottom. This process thins out the coil and stretches it upward.

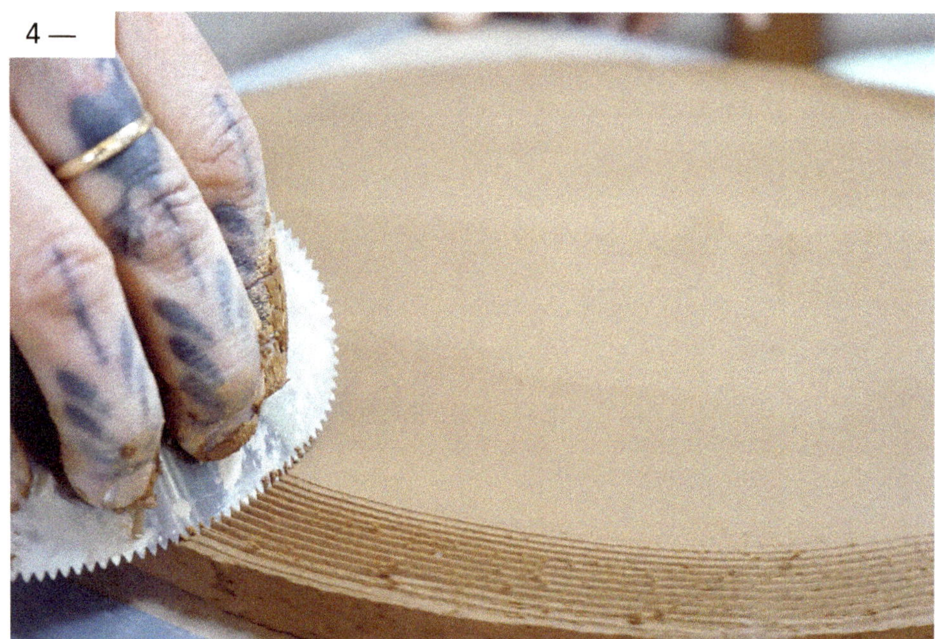

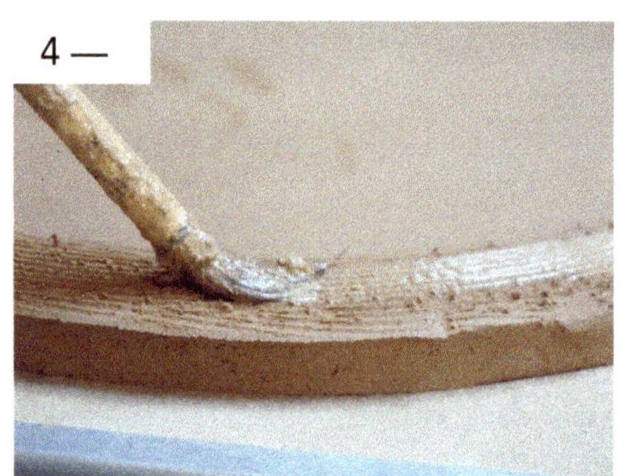

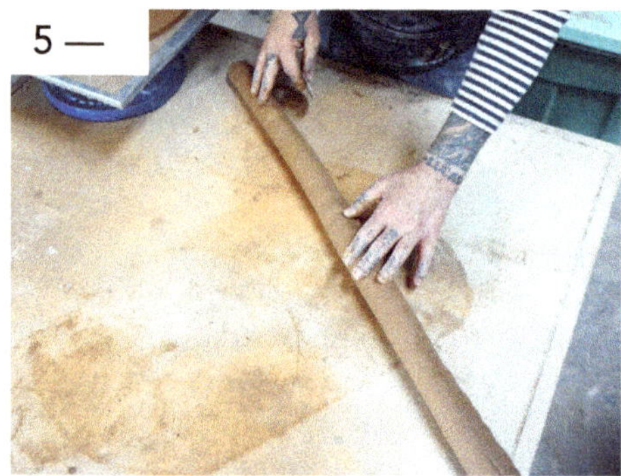

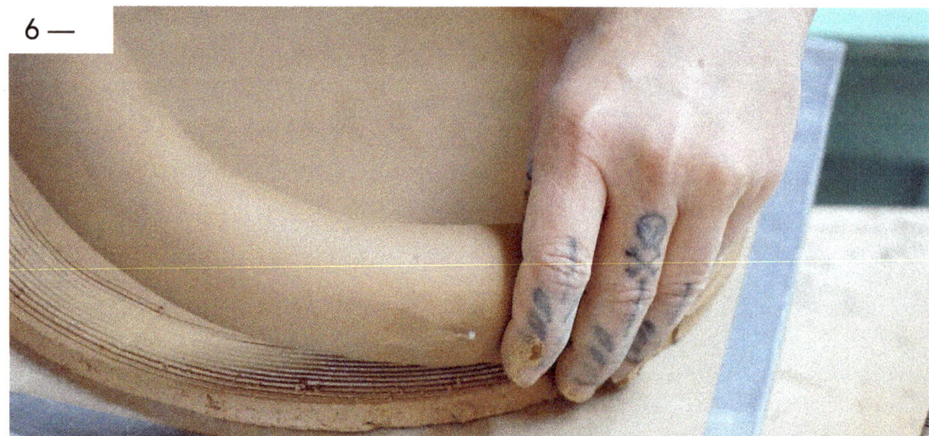

8 | When building coils upward, if you add the next coil directly on top of the one before it, your walls should go straight up. If you add the next coil slightly to the outer edge of the previous one, the wall will start to flare out. Add the next coil slightly to the inner edge, and the wall will angle in. For the bucket, I want my walls to go straight up and down, so I add my successive coils directly on top of the previous.

9 | Keep adding coils in the same way as the first one, blending the seams between them. When you reach the desired height, stop adding the coils. It doesn't matter if the top is uneven, you will fix this later.

10 | Use a rib on the sides to even out any thick places, applying some pressure on the rib to move the clay from a thick part upward.

11 | Let the bucket dry to leather-hard. When it's leather-hard, you can even out the thickness with your surform by grating away the clay in the thick parts. You can also use the surform to remove any lumps and bumps to create a smooth, even surface.

12 | Use the surform or knife to even out the top edge and create a flat or beveled lip.

13 | While supporting the wall of the bucket from the inside, use a rib with enough pressure to smooth away any marks and create or remove texture in the clay.

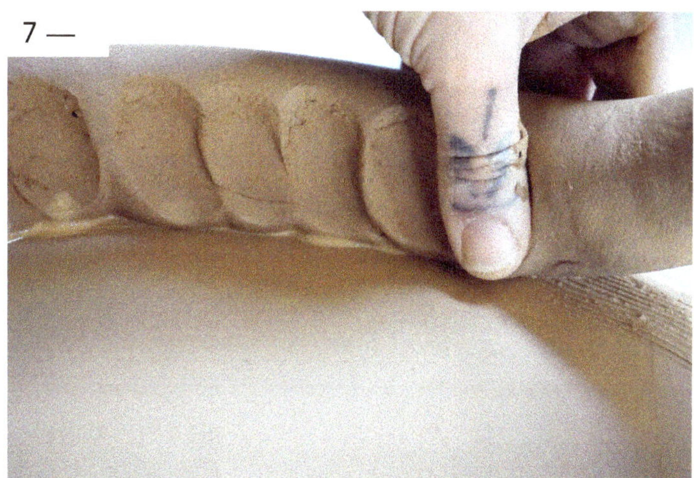

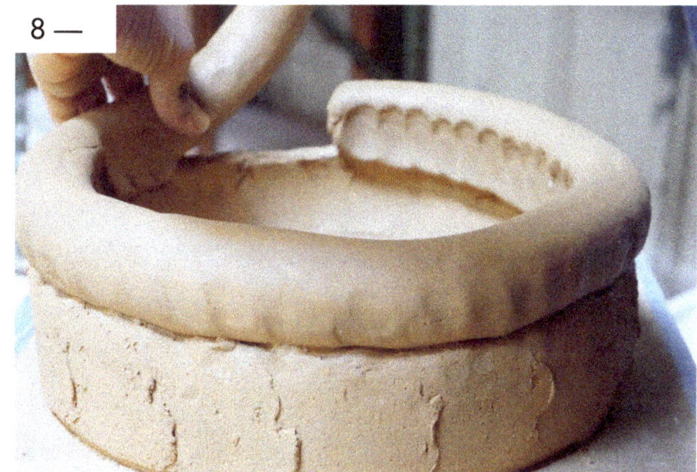

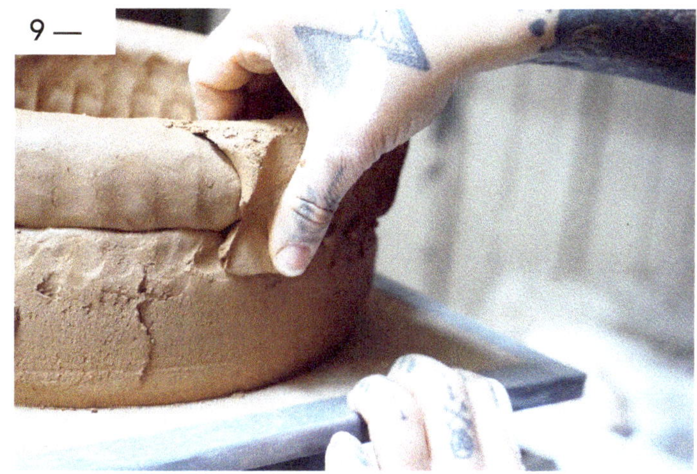

14 | Decide what kind of handles you want and where you want to attach them. Mark the spots. I decided to make disc handles and attach them to the top of the lip. (The steps for disc and other handles begin on page 118.) You'll be adding them as wet clay to the leather-hard clay.

15 | Score and slip the spots, and add the handles gently, pressing all around the attachment seam. I do not blend these handles into the form; instead, I accentuate the attachment seam, using the corner of the rib to create a small channel all the way around the seam.

16 | Let the handles get to leather-hard and use a knife or a hole punch tool to make a hole in each handle. This can be decorative or, after it's fired, you could add a handle of a different material, such as an actual bucket handle or rope.

17 | Further refine the handle with a knife and/or a rib, removing any lumps and cleaning up the edges.

10 —

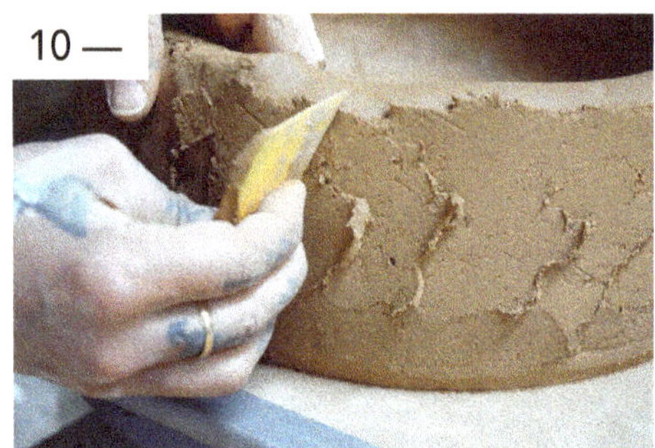

11 —

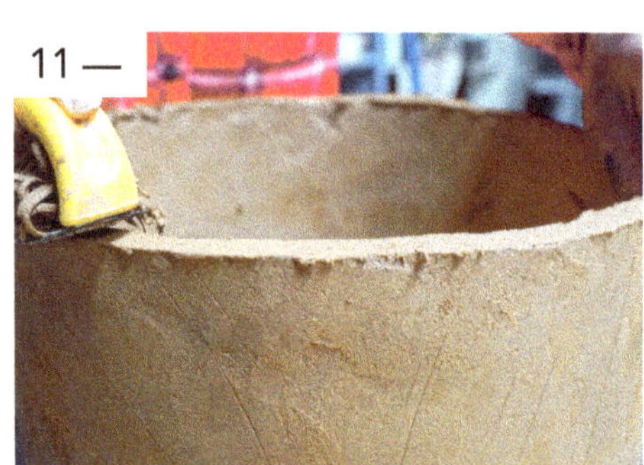

13 —

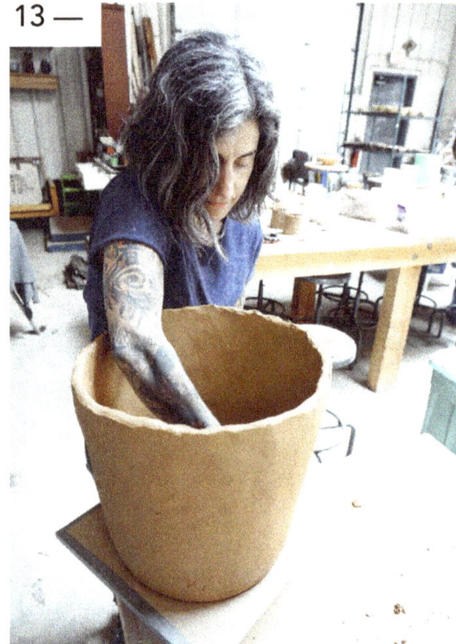

15 —

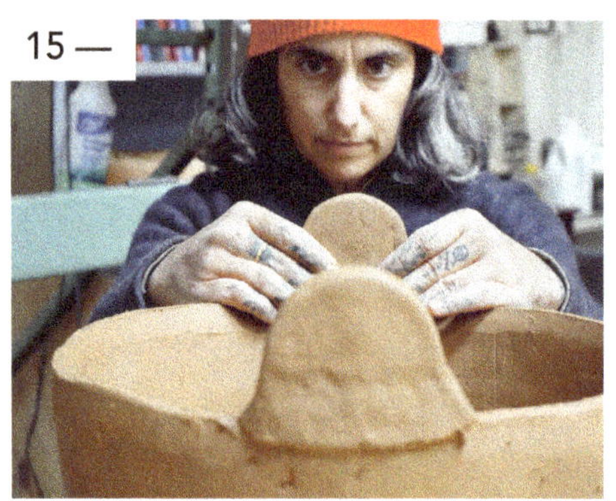

16 —

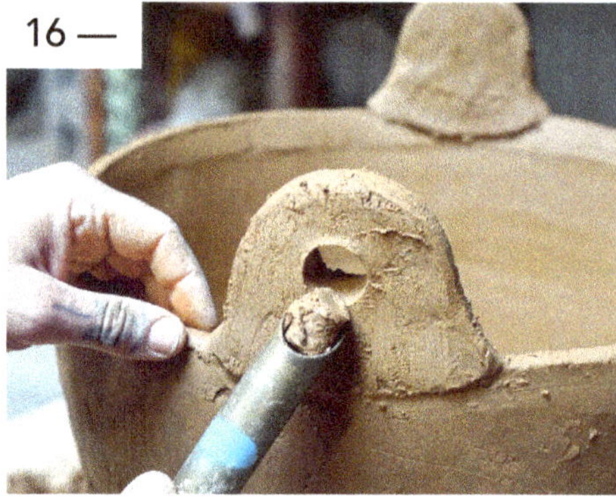

12 —

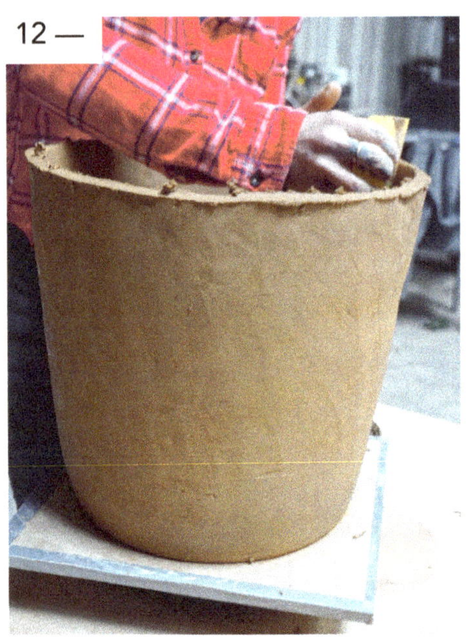

17 —

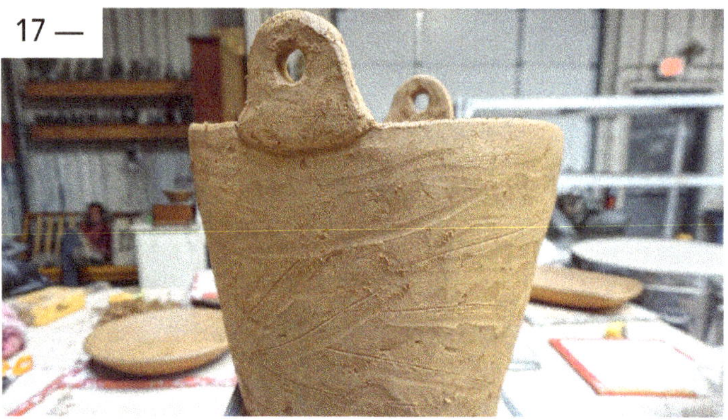

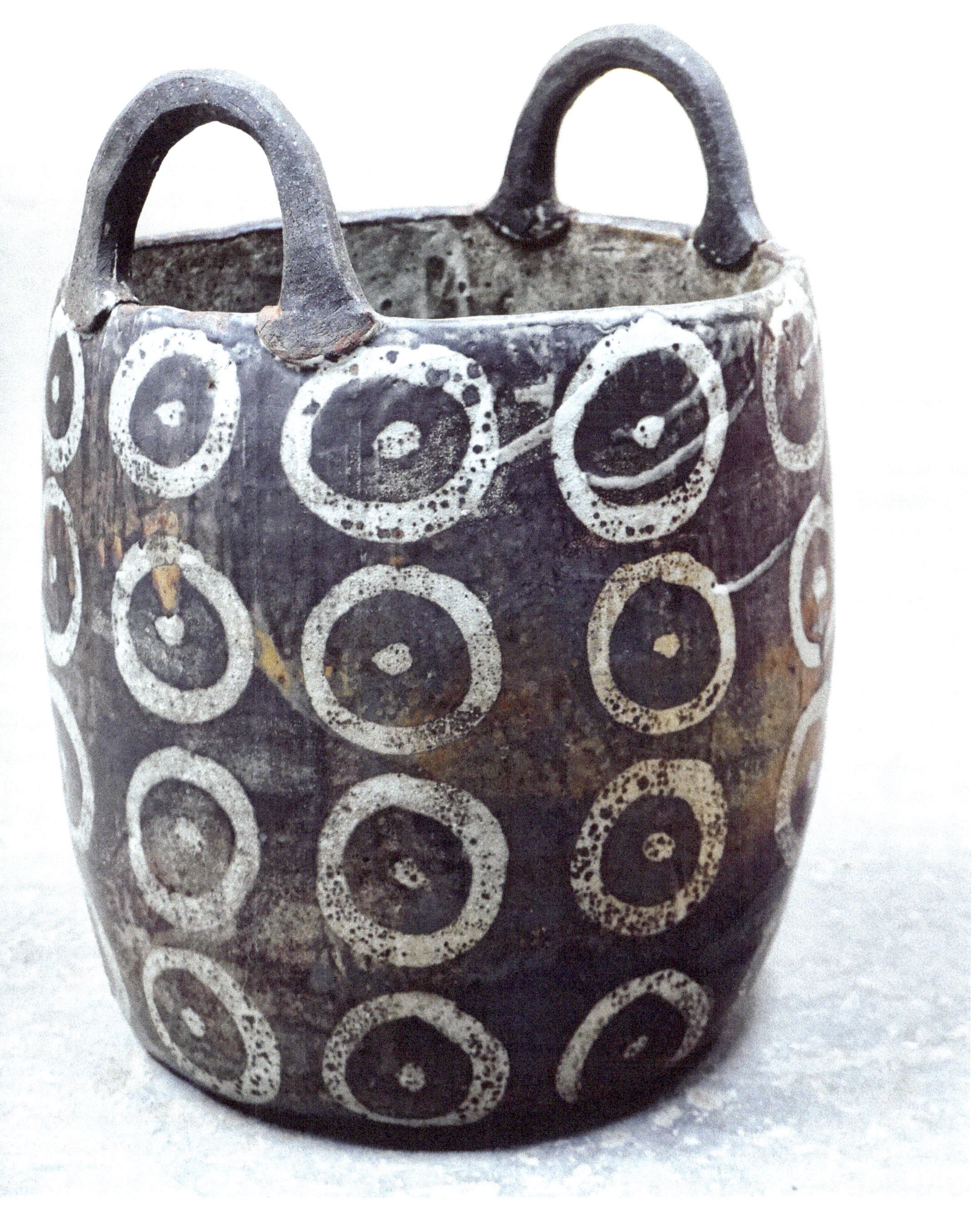

Make a Serving Tray

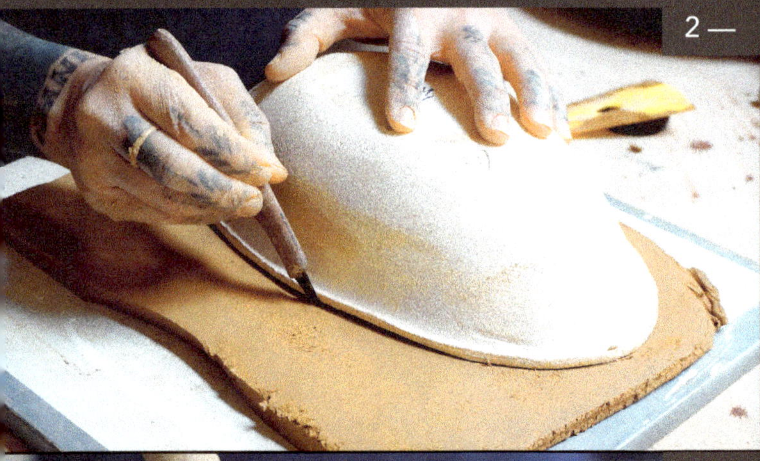

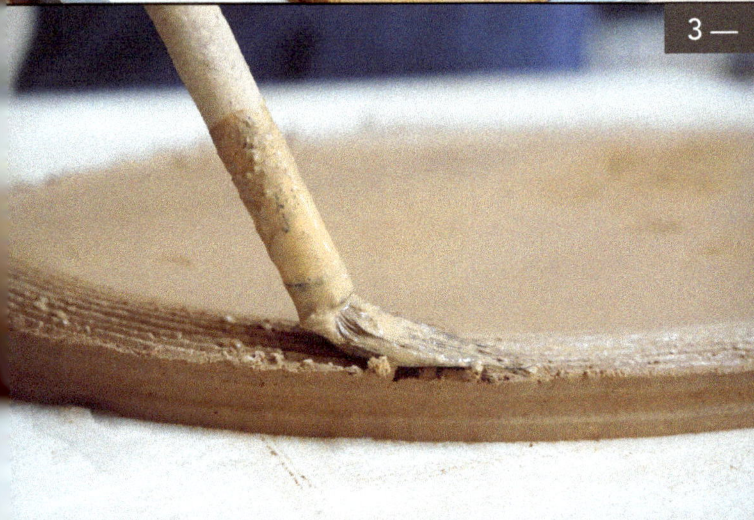

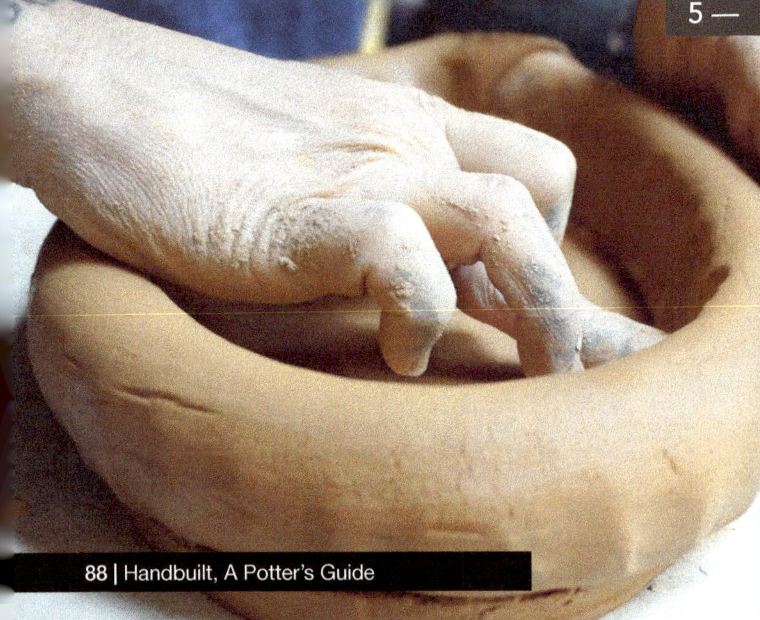

1 | Start by making a template for the size and shape you'd like for your tray. I often use an oval shape.

2 | Roll out a slab slightly larger than the diameter of your template. I use a ½" (1.25 cm) slab. Rib the slab smooth. Place the template on the slab and trace it. Cut out the bottom and carefully lift it onto a ware board. Put the ware board on your banding wheel.

3 | Score and slip the ½" (1.25 cm) edge around the top surface of the slab.

4 | Roll out a coil long enough to wrap around the entire circumference. Your coil can be any thickness you want to work with. I tend to use large coils because it takes fewer of them to build the pot. I work with coils about 1" (2.5 cm) thick when I'm making bigger coil pots.

5 | Score the coil and press it onto the prepared edge. When it is adhered, use your thumb to smooth the seam, inside and outside.

6 | Once the seam has disappeared, you can use a plastic rib (I prefer the yellow Mudtools rib) to further blend it.

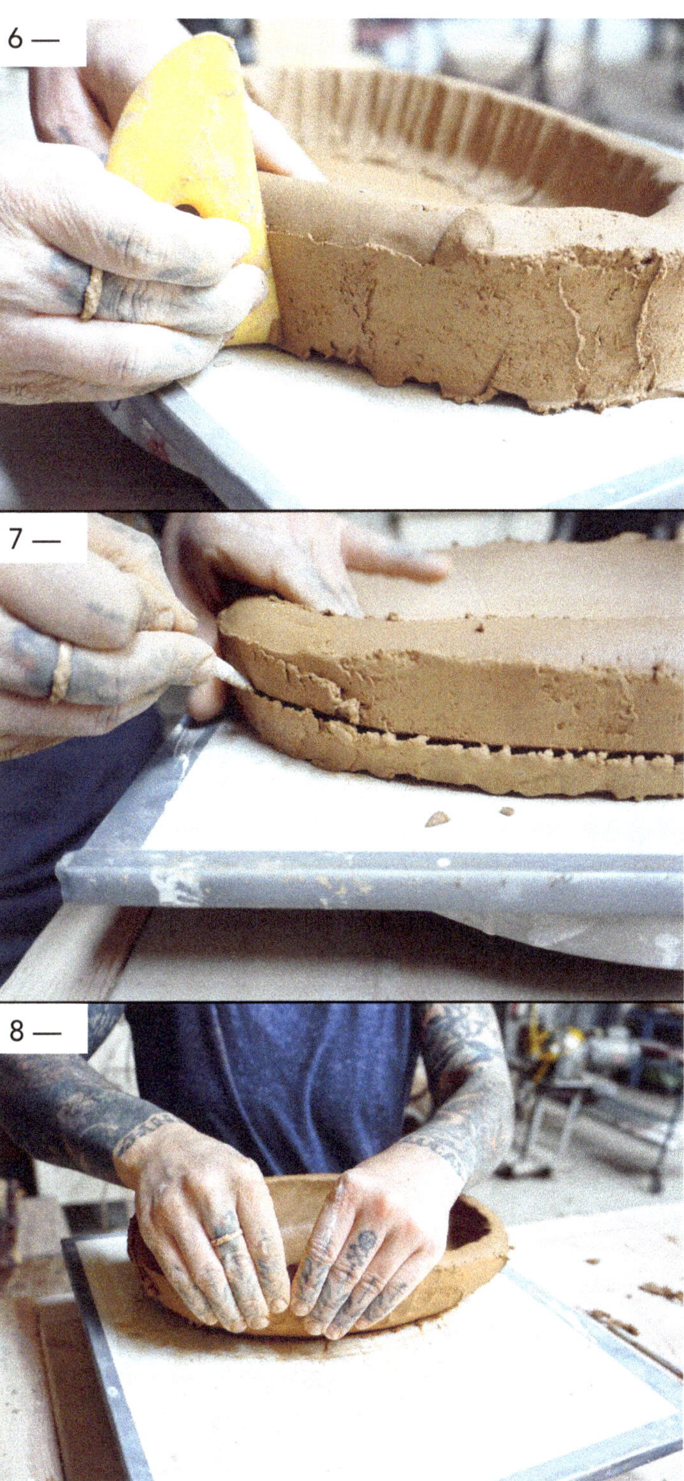

7 | Use your needle tool to remove the excess clay where the bottom meets the wall on the outer side. To do this, hold the needle tool at an angle that will remove the clay, but don't make that transition too thin. This will be dictated by the inside floor-to-wall angle. Insert your needle tool at that angle and hold it steady. The needle tip should remain in contact with the ware board while you turn the pot, cutting away a ribbon of clay.

8 | Pinch the coils evenly all around, to the thickness you want your walls, trying to make them about the same thickness as the bottom of the pot. Doing this thins the coil and stretches it upward. Add as many coils as you want to create the height of your form. If you want to add a divider to create a sectioned tray, this is the time to do that.

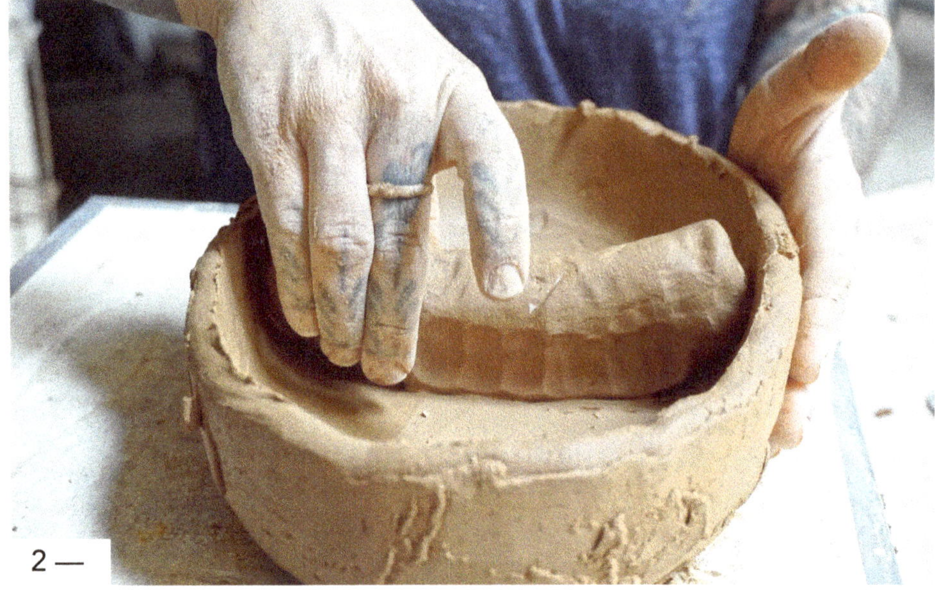

2 —

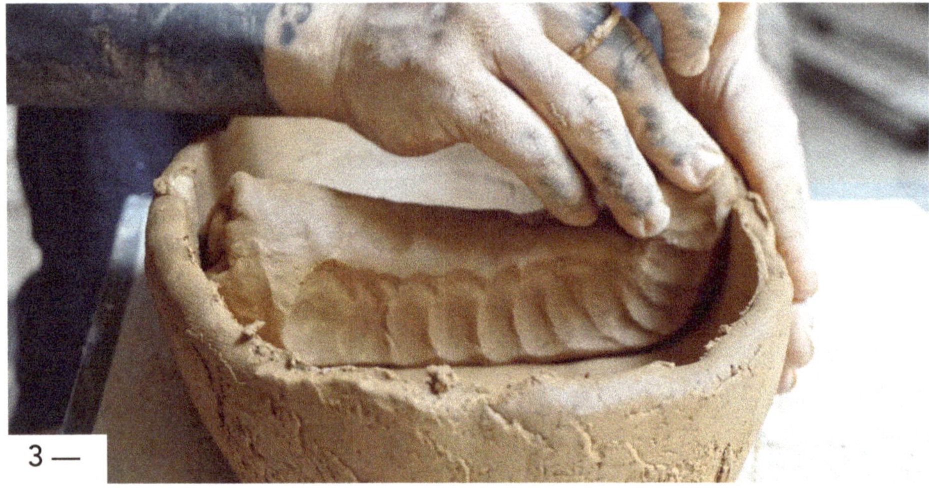

3 —

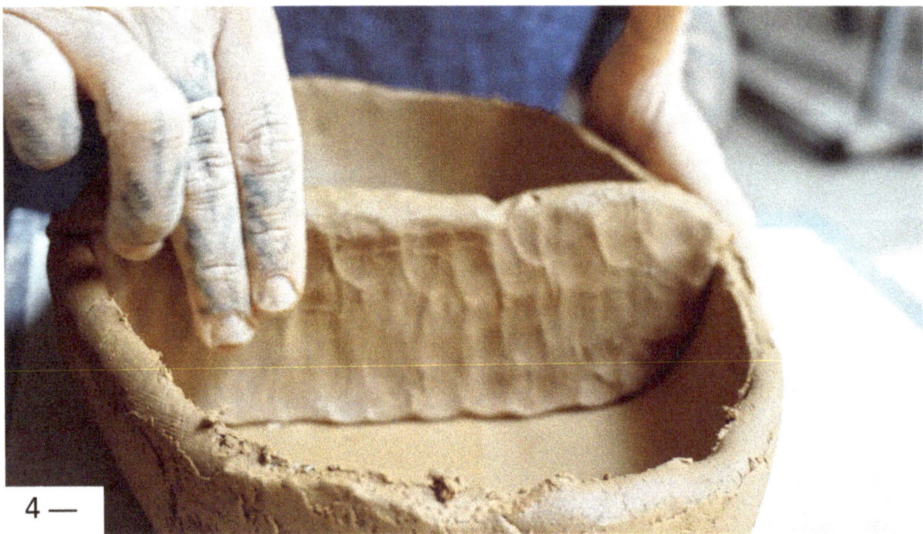

4 —

Add a Divider

1 | Follow the instructions on the previous pages until the desired height of coils is achieved.

2 | Measure the halfway point of your tray and score the bottom and sides. Roll a coil that spans from one side to the other.

3 | Attach the coil by pushing it into the bottom of the pot on each side.

4 | Carefully pinch the coil to raise and thin it.

5 | If you want higher walls, score the top of the coil and add another, smoothing the seam. Pinch to raise and thin it. Repeat until the divider is the height of the outside walls.

6 | When you've reached the desired height, let the tray dry to leather-hard. Then even out the thickness with the surform, grating away the clay in the thick parts.

7 | Use the surform or a knife to even out the top edge and create a flat or beveled lip.

8 | Supporting the wall from the inside, use the rib with enough pressure to smooth away any marks and create or remove texture in the clay. You can now add handles and/or feet, if you desire. I like to add feet to this form.

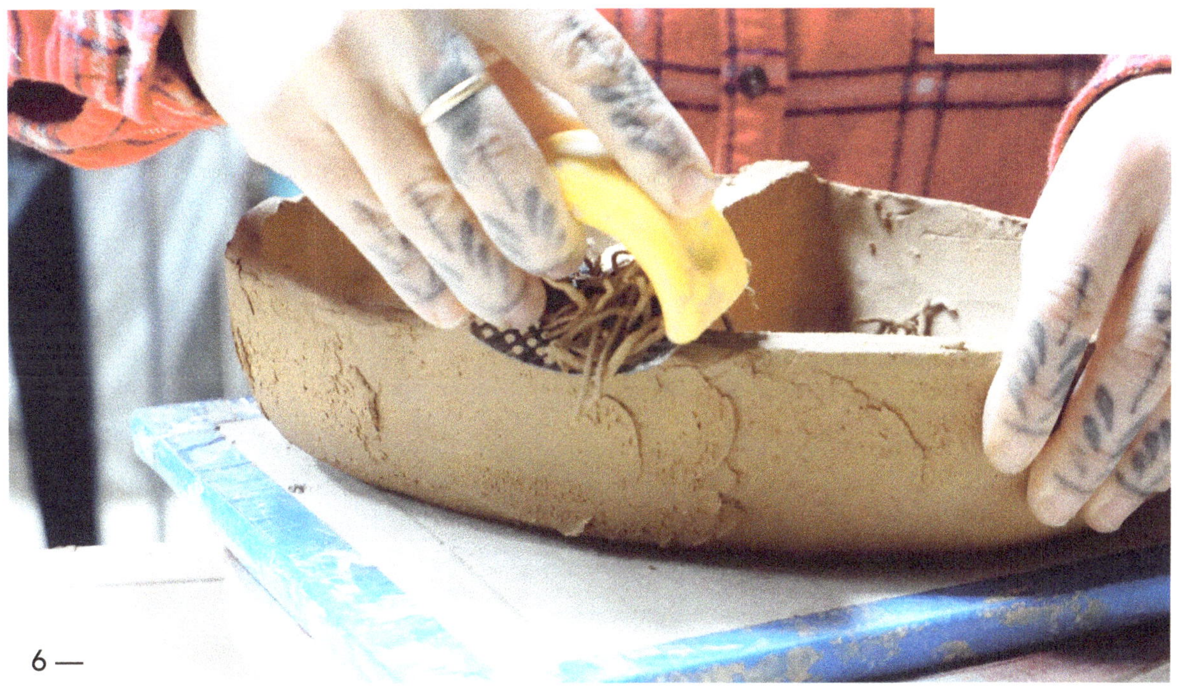

6 —

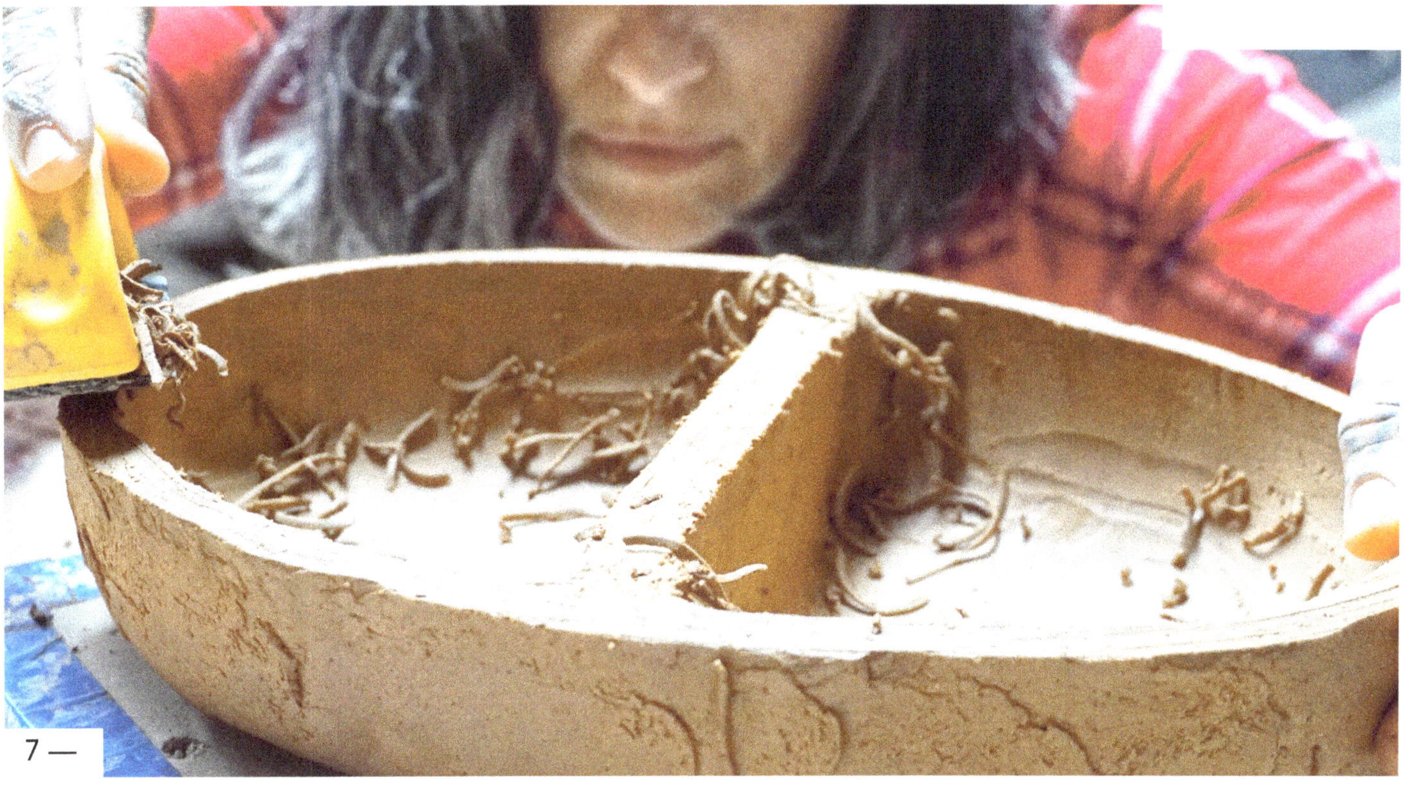

7 —

Add a Foot

1 | Turn the tray over onto a piece of ware board.

2 | Surform the sides to a unifrom thickness with even bevel lines.

3 | Roll out two coils about 1" (2.5 cm) thick.

4 | Score the coils and put them in place at either end of the tray.

5 | Blend in the seams with your thumb and a rib.

6 | Turn the tray over and tap it to slightly flatten the coils until the tray stands even. Flip it back over again.

7 | Refine the rim using a Surform and rib.

8 | Allow the coils to get leather-hard and then use your knife, rib, and surform to refine and shape the feet. I like to angle the side edges of the feet inward, so when looking at the tray from the ends, there is a diagonal line from the lip to the bottom of the foot.

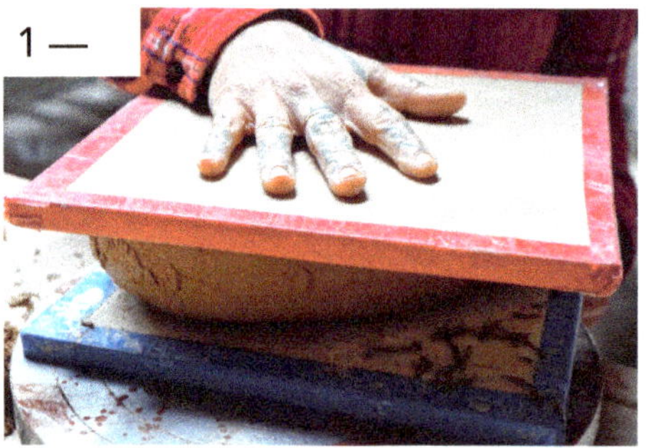

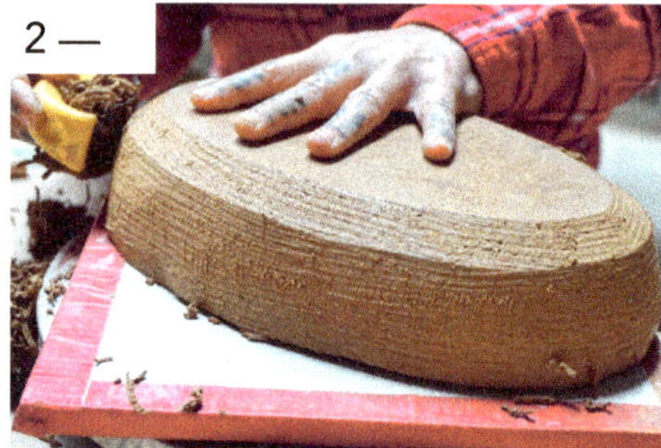

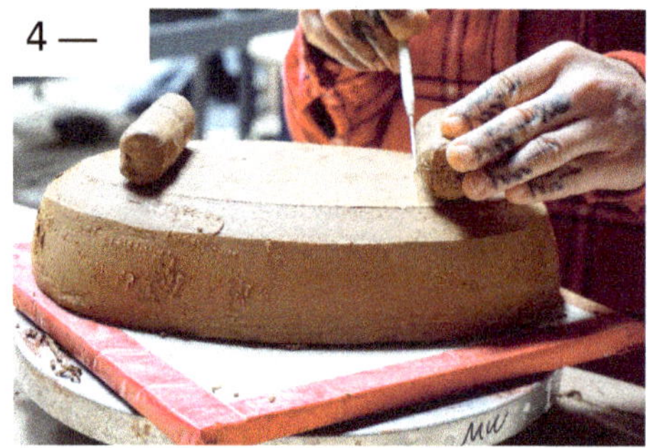

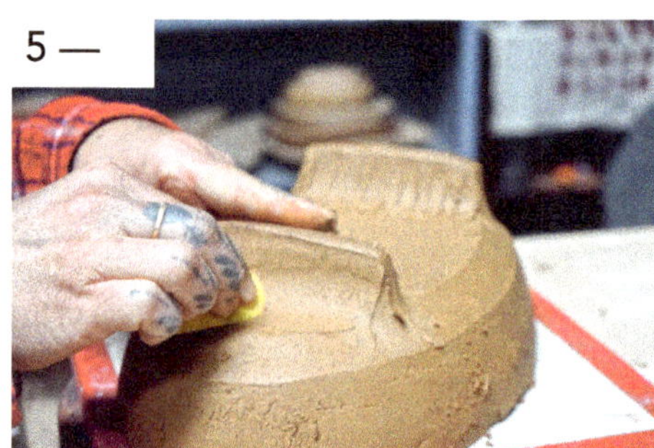

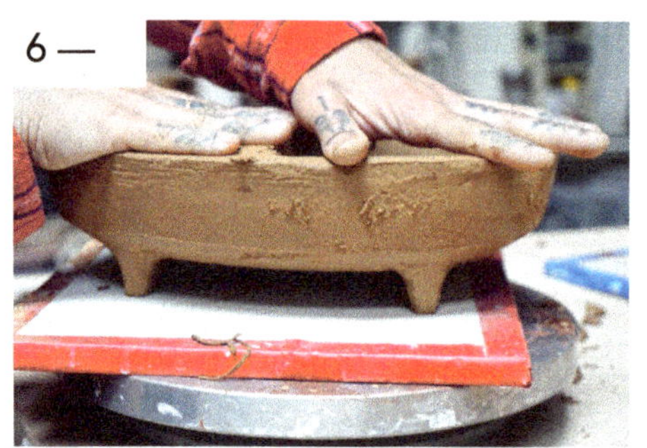

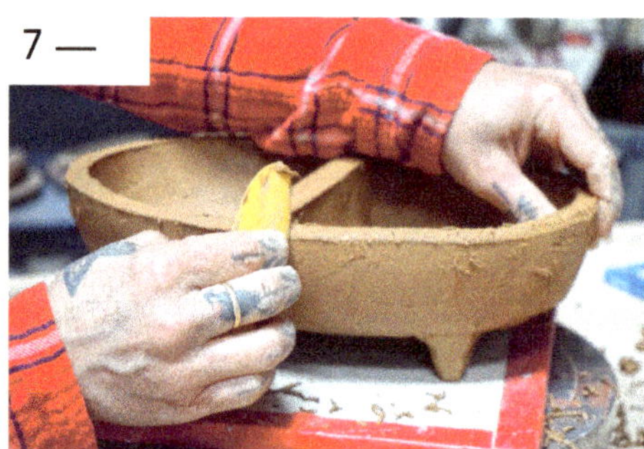

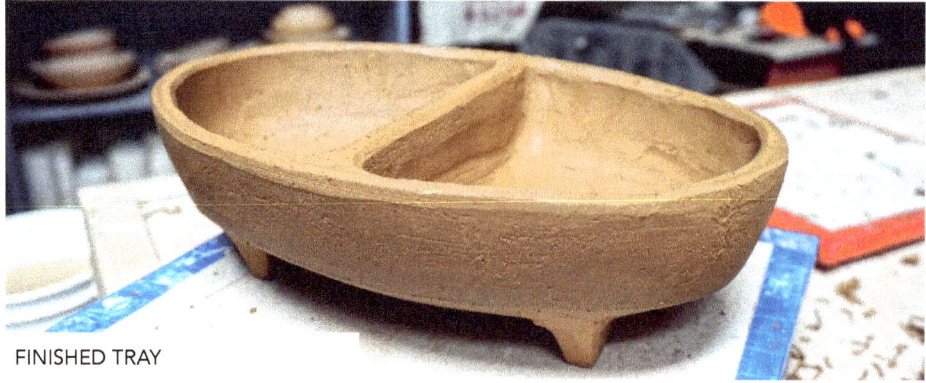

FINISHED TRAY

WITH FEET

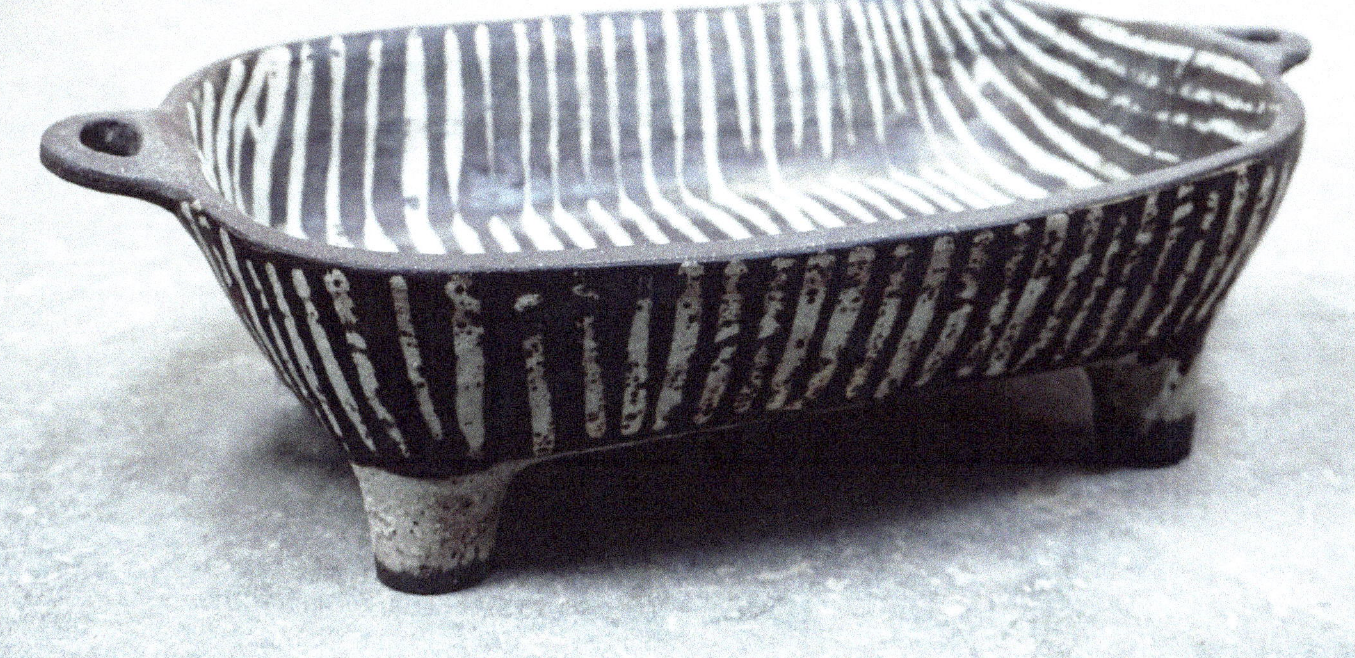

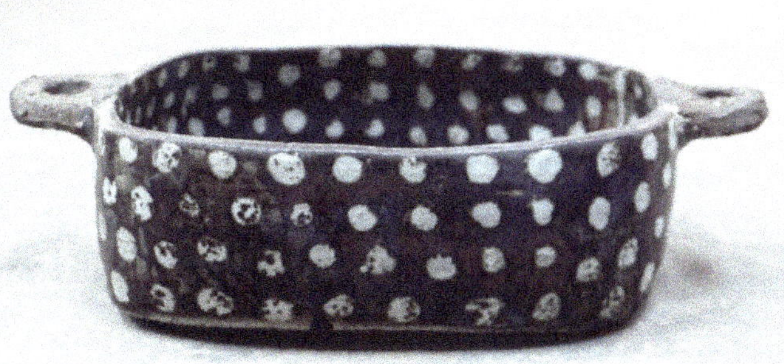

WITHOUT FEET

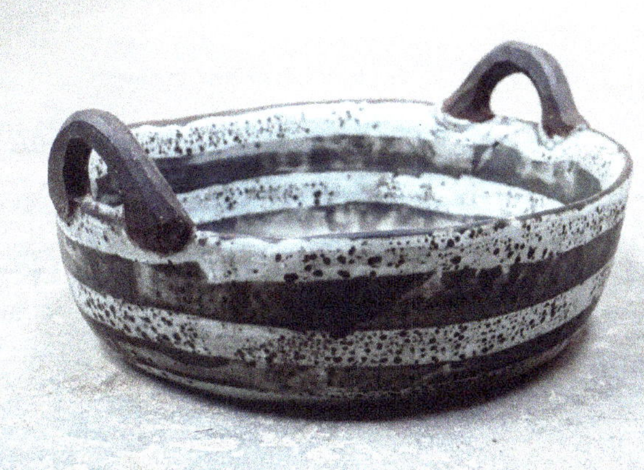

WITHOUT FEET

Lindsay Oesterritter works in her studio in Manassas, Virginia. She first started working with clay in her home state of Kentucky. And then, while studying ceramics at the University of Louisville, Utah State University, and traveling abroad in China and Australia, she was able to experiment with a wide range of raw materials and clay bodies. The surfaces in her current line of work are achieved by reduction cooling with a wood kiln. The majority of her wares are unglazed, letting the clay play a large role in the finished wood-fired surfaces.

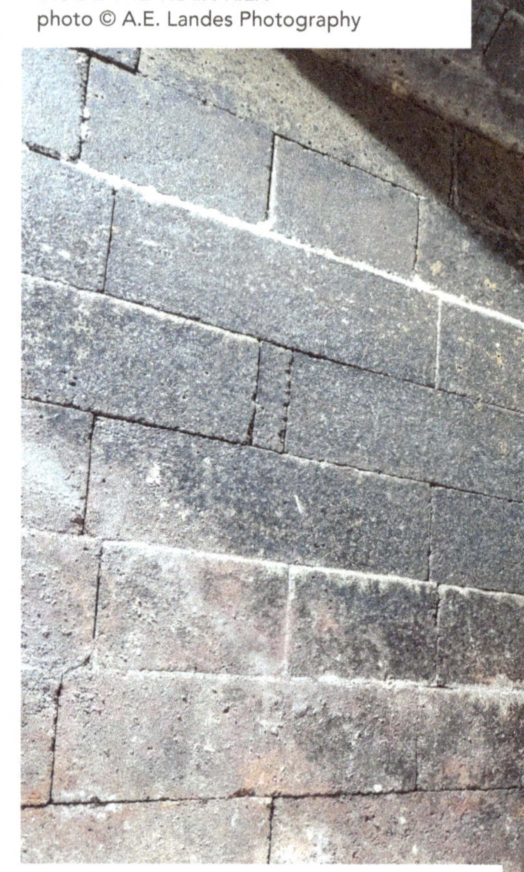

INSIDE THE TRAIN KILN
photo © A.E. Landes Photography

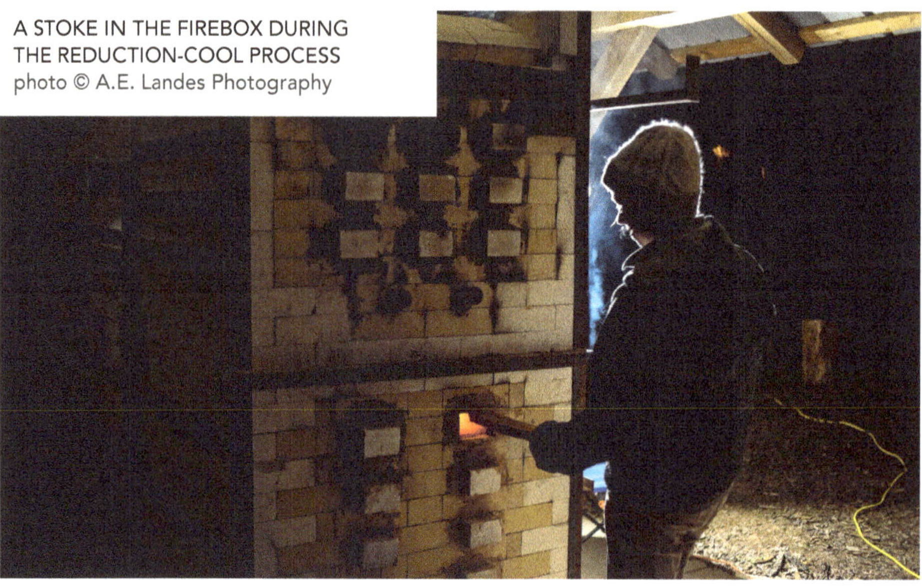

A STOKE IN THE FIREBOX DURING THE REDUCTION-COOL PROCESS
photo © A.E. Landes Photography

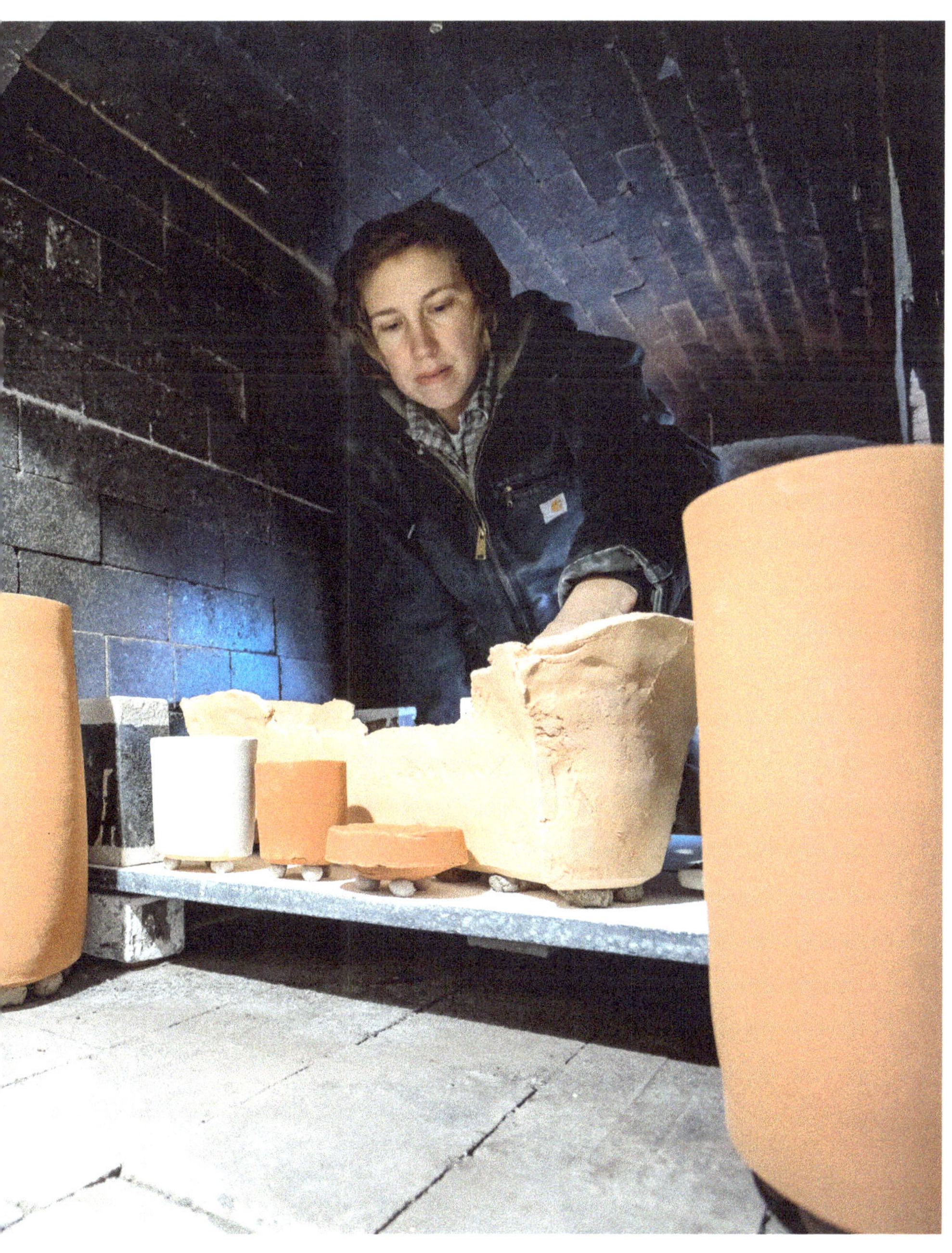

MW: DESCRIBE ONE OF THE HANDBUILDING METHODS YOU RELY ON AND WHY.

LO: I regularly use one-piece and two-piece press molds. I started using press molds because I liked the idea that while the contours of the form were standardized, the surface of the clay could be changed, depending on how you prepare and press the clay into the press mold form.

Part of my goal as a maker is to relay the process of how a piece is made by the process marks left behind. With molds, I leave the seams where the mold comes together and leave the lines where the clay is pressed into the mold, using both in the final surface and design.

MW: REDUCTION COOLING IS A PROCESS WHERE YOU CONTROL THE COOLING OF THE KILN BY KEEPING IT IN A REDUCED ATMOSPHERE AS IT COMES DOWN IN TEMPERATURE. WHY DOES THIS TECHNIQUE APPEAL TO YOU?

LO: Reduction cooling appeals to me because of the darker, often subtle, more matte surfaces that it yields. The first time I reduction cooled in a wood kiln, it was only my second wood firing. The palette and surface rang true, and that was the beginning of my reduction-cooling path. I was a beginner at wood firing, and learned how to wood fire while also learning how to reduction cool. I also appreciate how the darker surfaces support and interact with the colors of fresh food and flowers.

MW: **SINCE I STARTED REDUCTION COOLING A COUPLE OF YEARS AGO, I'VE HAD A LOT OF TROUBLE FINDING INFORMATION. IT SEEMS AS IF IT'S NOT VERY COMMON, ESPECIALLY IN GAS KILNS. WHY DO YOU THINK THIS IS? DID YOU LEARN IN SCHOOL?**

LO: I started researching reduction cooling in graduate school at Utah State University (USU) in Logan, Utah, with John Neely, Dan Murphy, and Ted Neal. I learned how to reduction cool with gas and wood with the help of my professors and other students. In investigating the process, I looked to historical pots from Tamba and Echizen in Japan, and the Silla wares from Korea. I read the archived research from USU graduates and referenced what few articles I could find written by John Neely, Owen Rye, and Arthur Rosser. When I started this research back in 2006, it seemed that, while there were a lot of historical examples, reduction cooling was still a very new idea, actively being explored in the United States. Today it seems there are many more potters investigating reduction cooling with both gas and wood, and there is a better network of shared information from which to glean.

MW: **I AM DRAWN TO YOUR POTS BECAUSE OF THEIR PERFECT BALANCE OF ANCIENT AND MODERN. YOUR POTS REMIND ME OF THE JAPANESE SHOU SUGI BAN TECHNIQUE OF CHARRING WOOD. WHAT INSPIRES YOU?**

LO: I am inspired by the inseparable relationship between time and place, and form and surface. I look to my everyday surroundings for visual inspiration, referencing everything from worn leather and river stones to retired industrial objects. I love strong geometric shapes and patterns and clean contour lines.

MW: **TELL ME ABOUT BEING A WOOD-FIRED POTTER. WHY WOOD?**

LO: Wood firing allows me to be able to focus more on form. A lot of my creative process goes into thinking about how I am going to make something: wheel thrown, press mold, slab, coil, carve, or a combination of processes. The building process is reflected in the surface of the finished piece. In deciding the ideal weight and size relationship, I imagine how the piece will be used and what I can do to improve its function while staying true to what I find to be aesthetically interesting and beautiful.

Most of my wares do not get glazed, leaving the process marks and relying on the wood firing to finish the surface. While I have a pretty good idea of what to expect coming out of the kiln, I could never plan the variety of surfaces the kiln is able to yield. One of the things I really like about the reduction-cool, wood-fired surface is how the darker, drier, more subtle results imply a history to the piece, even though it is brand new. This directly relates to some of the materials and objects I am inspired by.

MW: **YOUR POTS SEEM PLANNED IN AN ARCHITECTURAL WAY—MAPPED, SKETCHED, CONSIDERED FROM ALL ANGLES. THEY ARE COMPLICATED IN A WAY THAT ISN'T OBVIOUS. HOW DO YOU ACHIEVE THIS?**

LO: I aim to achieve depth through simplicity. Before starting any new form, I do, in fact, sketch it from all sides: top, bottom, left, right, and in cross section. Doing this helps me answer basic formal questions before I start in clay. Then I tend to make a short series of three to six initial 3-D sketches in clay, and play around with how I might build something, or resolve an element of the form that bothers me. Developing new forms, and that critical dialogue and tinkering creative process from initial idea to first successful finished piece, is the most gratifying and my favorite part of the process of making in general.

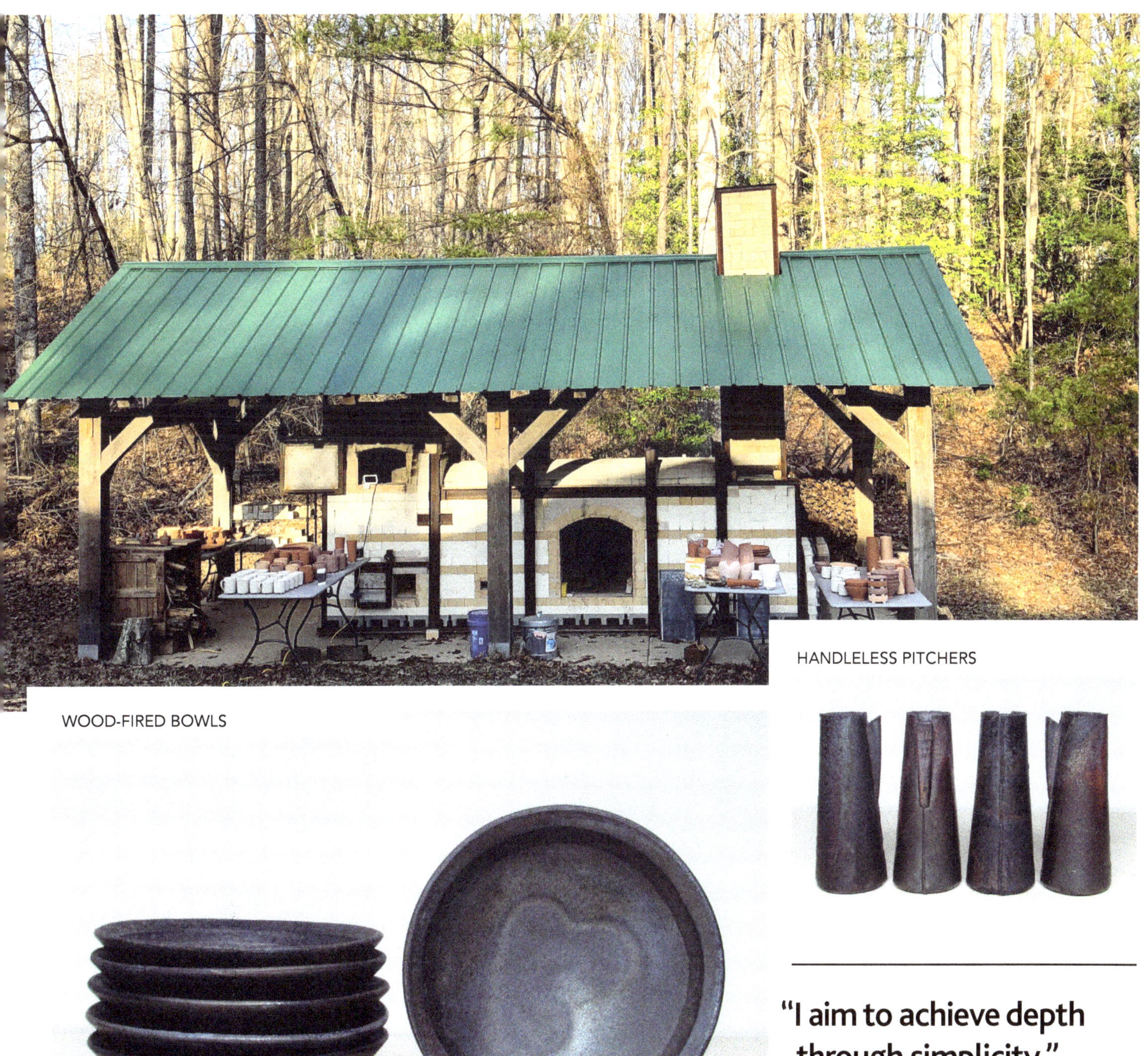

WOOD-FIRED BOWLS

HANDLELESS PITCHERS

"I aim to achieve depth
through simplicity."

06

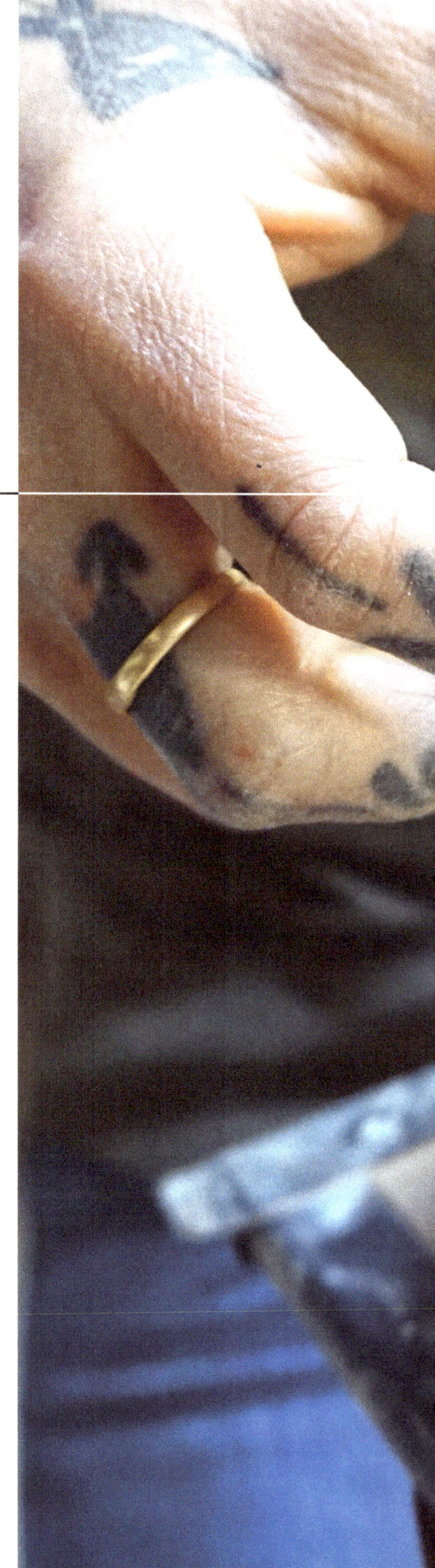

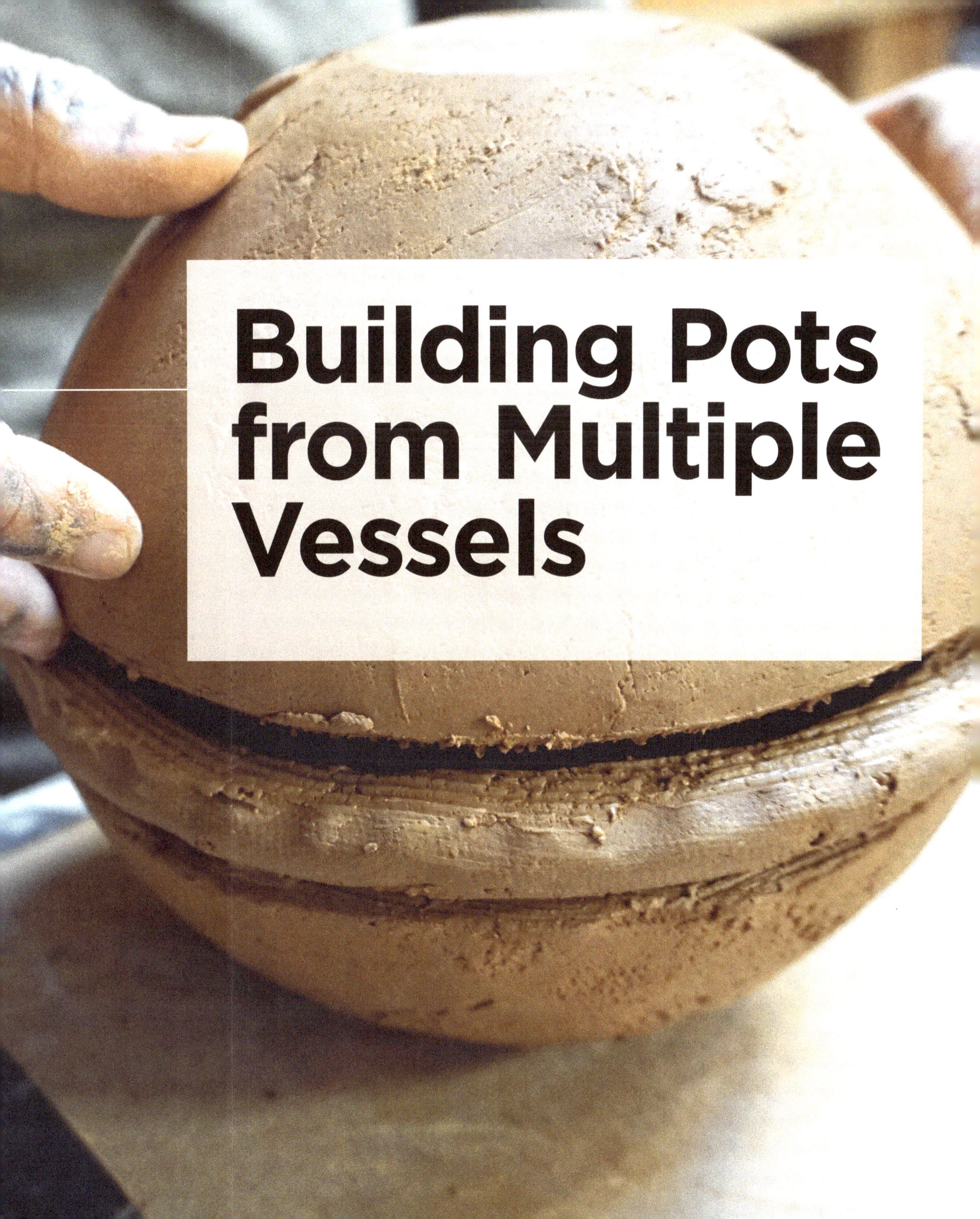
Building Pots
from Multiple
Vessels

Make a Moon Vase

WORKING LARGER WITH MULTIPLE POTS

By using a single joining technique and then varying the size of the opening, you can make the pot a vase or a pitcher. By adding coils to the opening you can create a neck at any height you wish. You can add handles and spouts. Putting two pots together is a fun way to make larger forms without struggling on the wheel. And it's a great way to experiment and find unconventional and interesting shapes for new pots.

YOU'LL NEED

- ☑ Surform
- ☑ Flexible knife
- ☑ Plastic ribs
- ☑ Mason jar or other tall prop
- ☑ Slab roller, rolling pin, or slab sticks
- ☑ Ware board
- ☑ Serrated rib
- ☑ Slip

I got to a place where I wanted to make larger forms, but I just didn't have the strength to throw them. There is a way to throw multiple forms and put them together on the wheel, but I didn't love that technique. So, I tried making two bowls from the same mold and attaching them and it worked really well: It was a fun form to leave as is or expand upon.

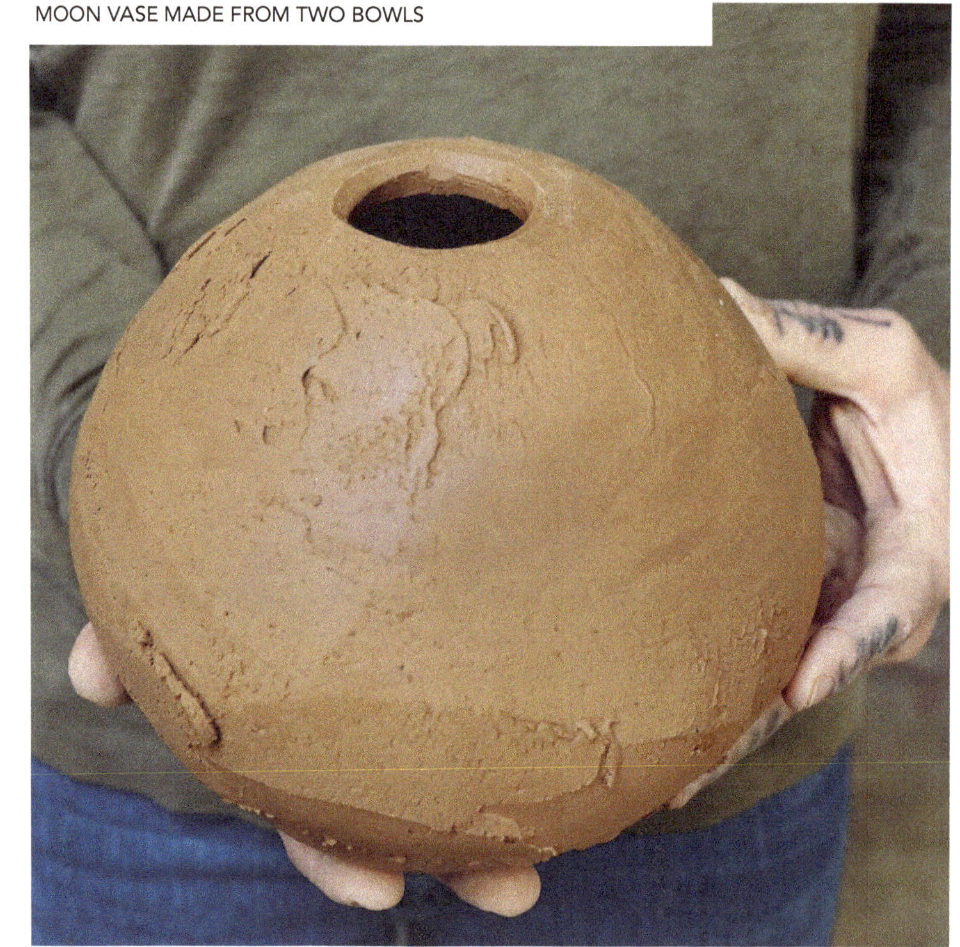

MOON VASE MADE FROM TWO BOWLS

1 | Make two slab bowls from the same mold. Use the directions for making a slab dish from a hump mold on page 66.

2 | Take the bowls off the mold at soft leather-hard. If you have a banding wheel, place one bowl right side up on the wheel.

3 | Roll out a coil about the width of a pencil and long enough to go around the rim of the bowl. Score the coil.

4 | Score and slip the rim of the bowl and attach the coil to the rim.

5 | Score the top of the coil you just added. Score and slip the lip of the other bowl. Place this bowl upside down so the lip is on the coil. You now have the two bowls resting lip to lip with a coil between them.

6 | Gently tap the top bowl with your hand to help attach it to the coil. Score around the seam of the coil.

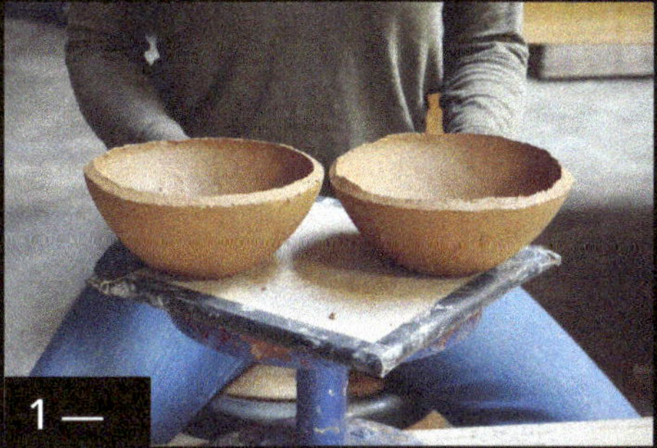

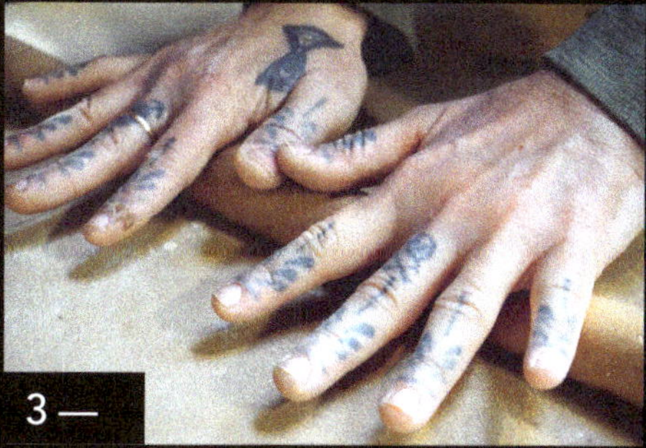

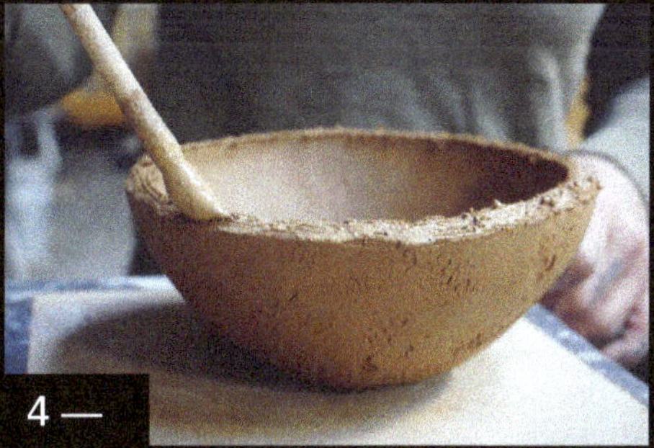

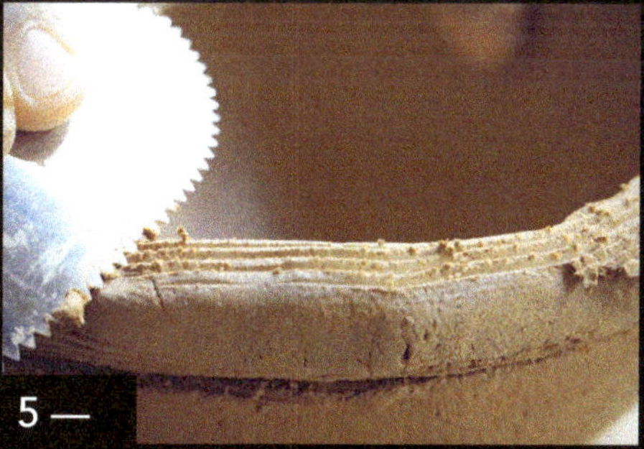

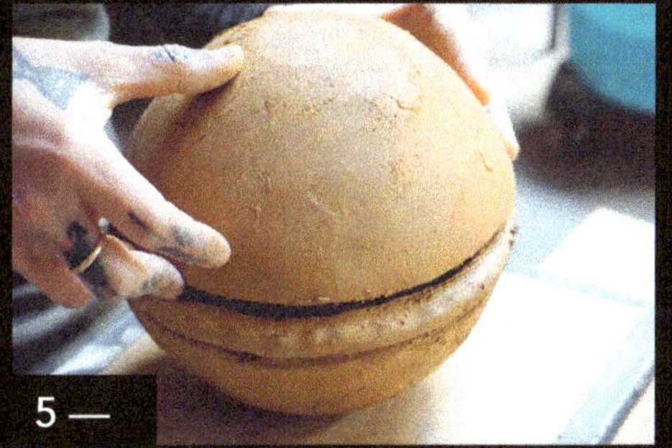

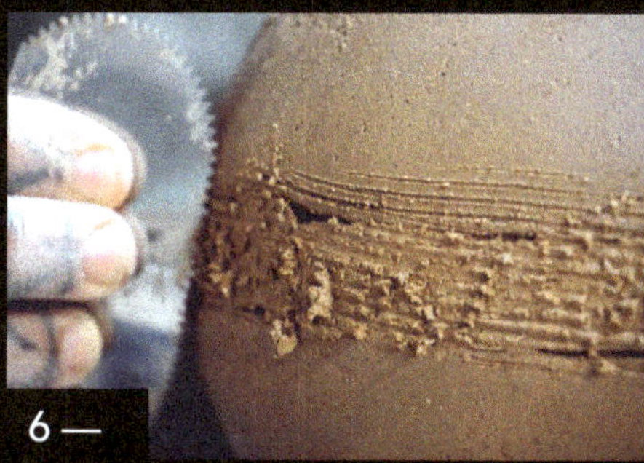

7 | Roll out another coil, about twice as thick as the first, and long enough to wrap around the entire form.

8 | Score and slip the coil and wrap it around the bowls at the seam.

9 | Use your fingers to smooth this coil, blending it into the bottom half of the coil downward, and the top half upward.

10 | Use a rib to further blend the attachment, eliminating the seam.

11 | Stick the needle tool into the center top of the form to make a hole.

12 | Decide how large you want the opening and cut around it, keeping the hole in the center. I think these look beautiful with about a 1" (2.5 cm) wide opening. Use your knife or rib to refine the opening by beveling or just smoothing the cut.

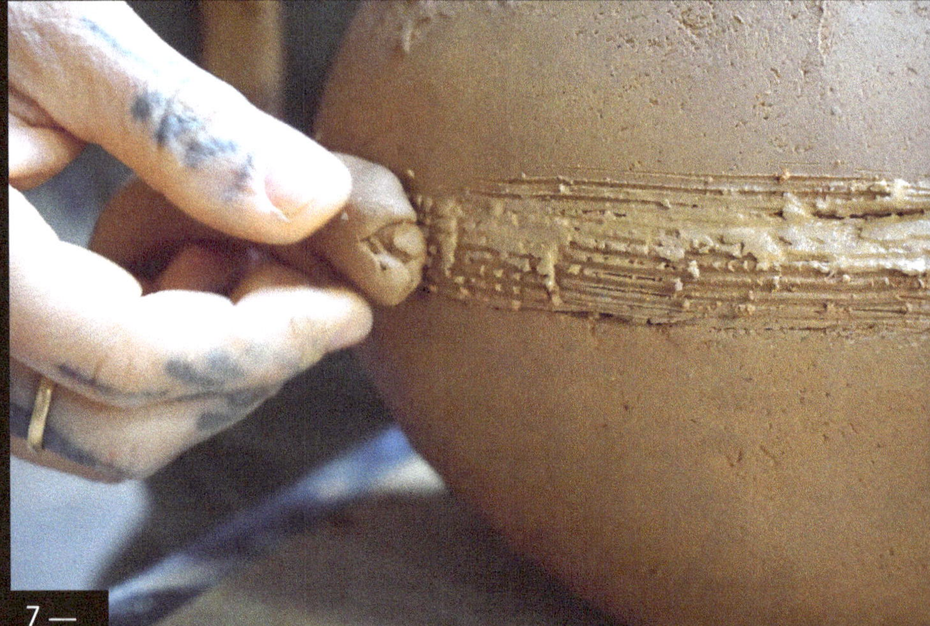

7 —

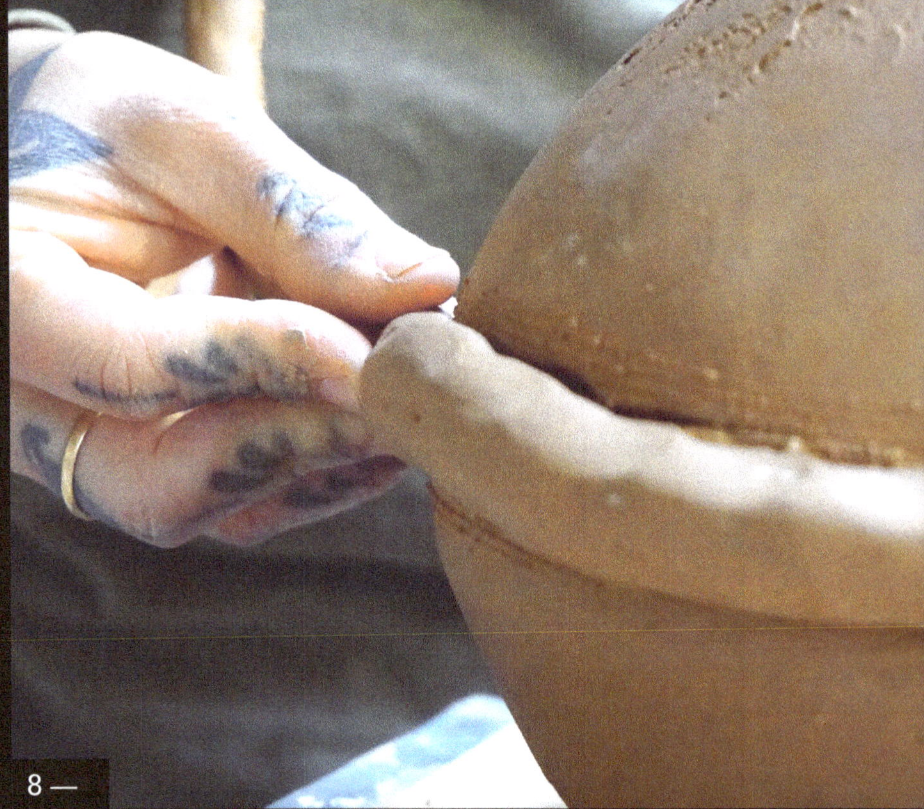

8 —

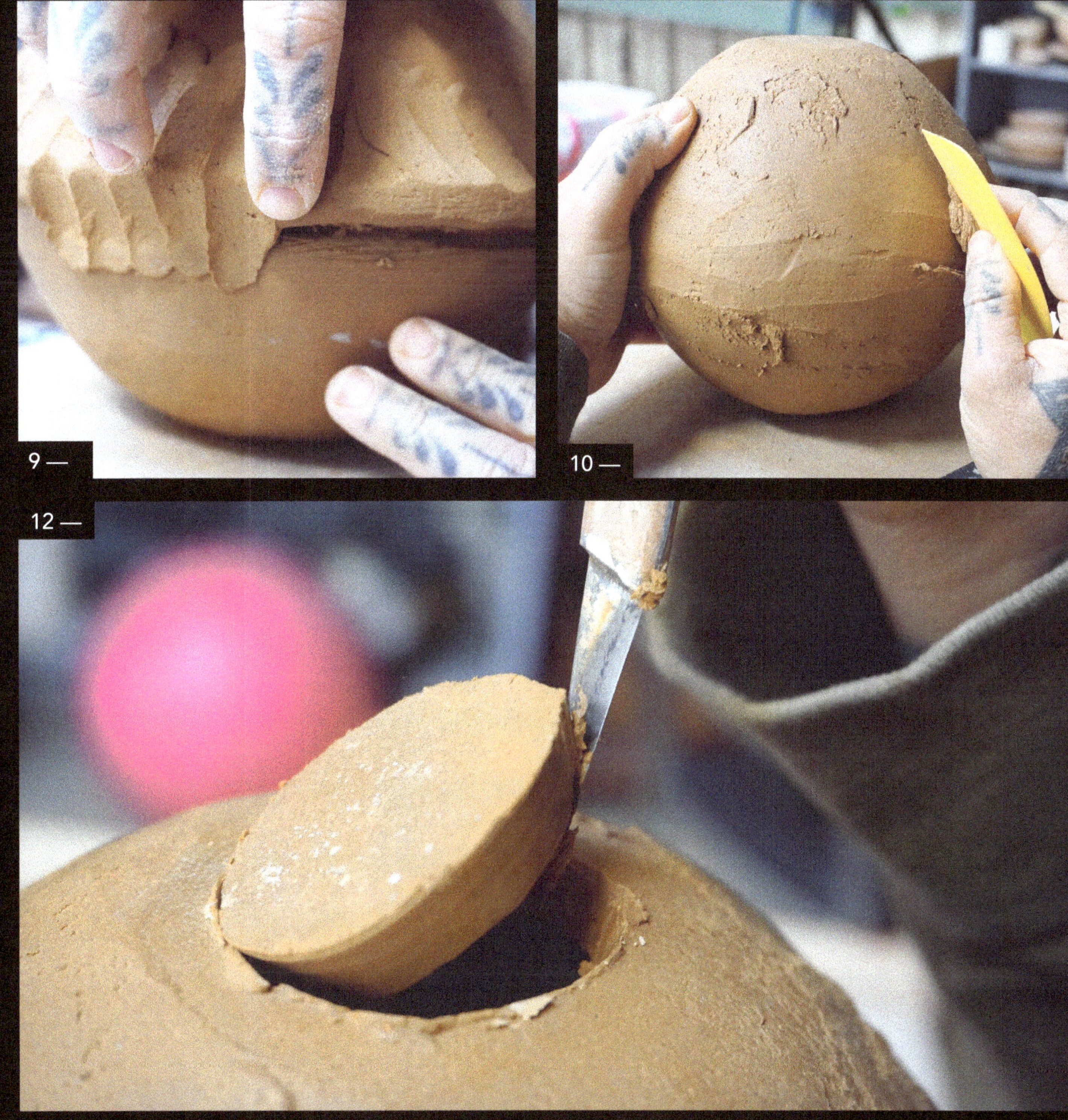

Make a Vase with a Coil Neck

1 | Follow the directions for making a moon vase until the cutting of the opening, step 11.

2 | Decide what size neck you want and cut the opening to that size.

3 | Roll out a coil long enough to wrap around the opening. Score and slip the rim of the opening and coil.

4 | Apply the coil around the opening, blending it at the seam. Pinch the coil to thin it out as you go.

5 | Add as many coils as you need to reach the desired length of the neck. Score, slip, and attach each new coil to the previous one.

6 | Let the neck dry to leather-hard. Use a rib to refine, smooth, and shape the neck. Use a flexible knife and/or rib to refine and shape the edge of the neck.

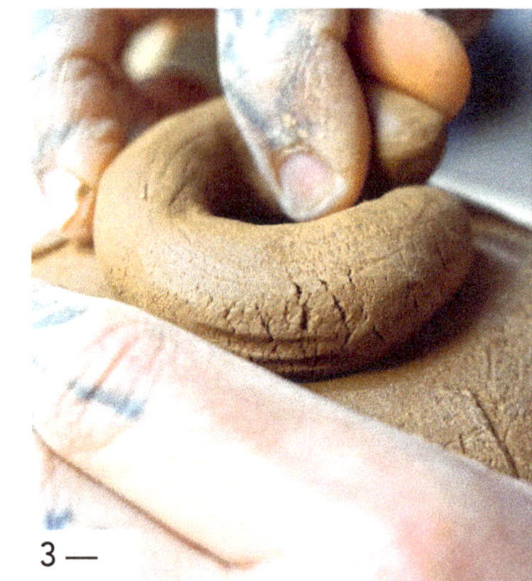

3 —

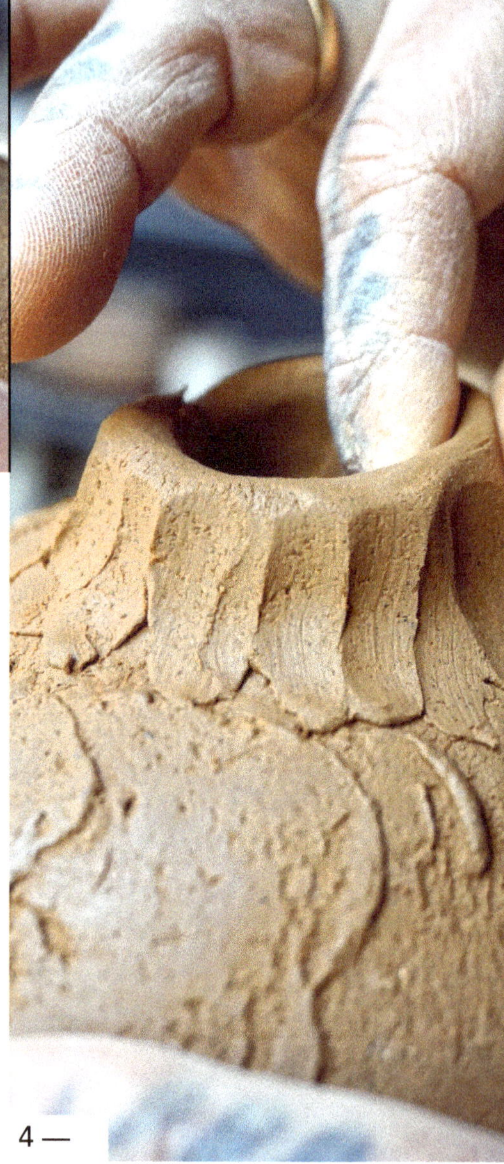

4 —

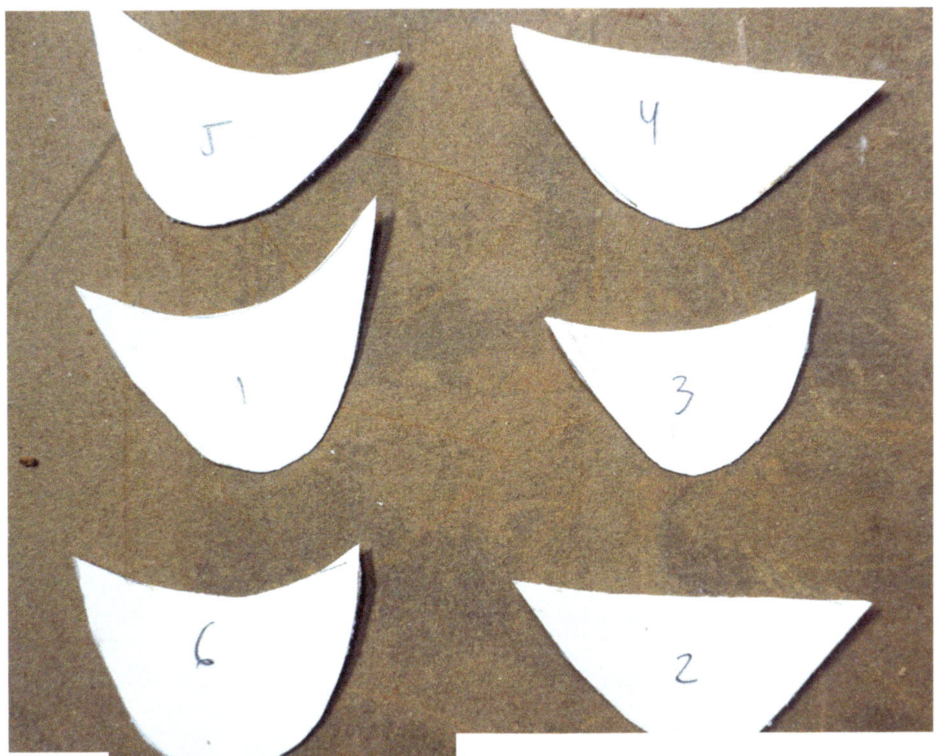

2 —

MAKE A SPOUT TEMPLATE

1 | Roll out a piece of clay to experiment with making spout templates.

2 | Gently mark a few triangular shapes with a rounded bottom and soft curve at the top point. Try some about 2" (5 cm) across, some slightly bigger, and some smaller.

3 | When you have a few mapped out, cut them out of the clay. Gently curve them and hold them up to your pitcher.

4 | Make adjustments and cut out more samples until you find one or more that you like. Take those and lay them on a piece of cardstock. Trace around the clay and cut out the shapes. Keep the templates to use for future spouts.

YOU'LL NEED

- ☑ Cardstock
- ☑ Scissors
- ☑ Pencil

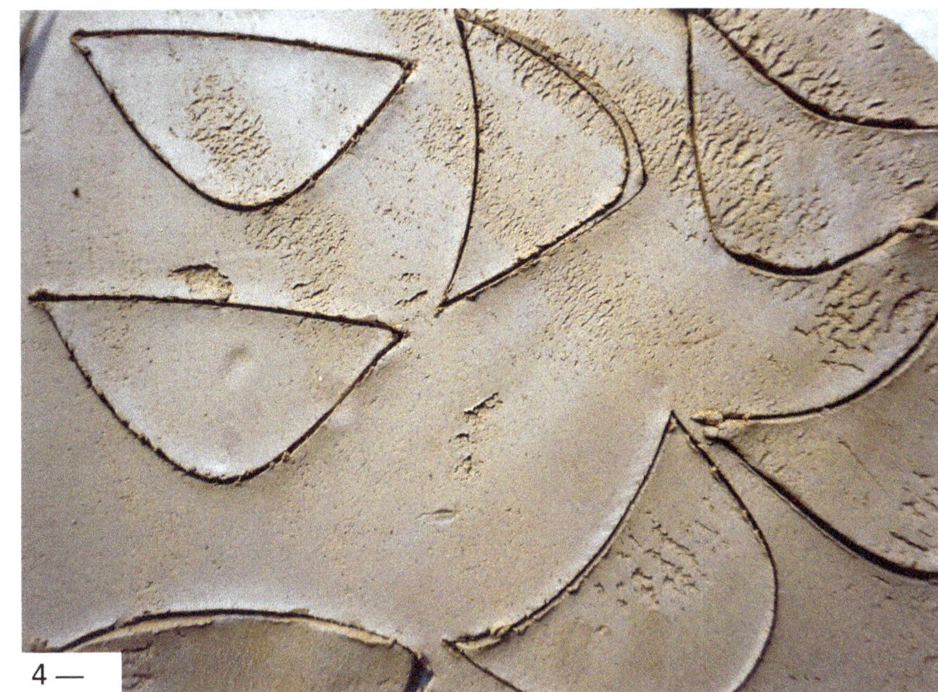

4 —

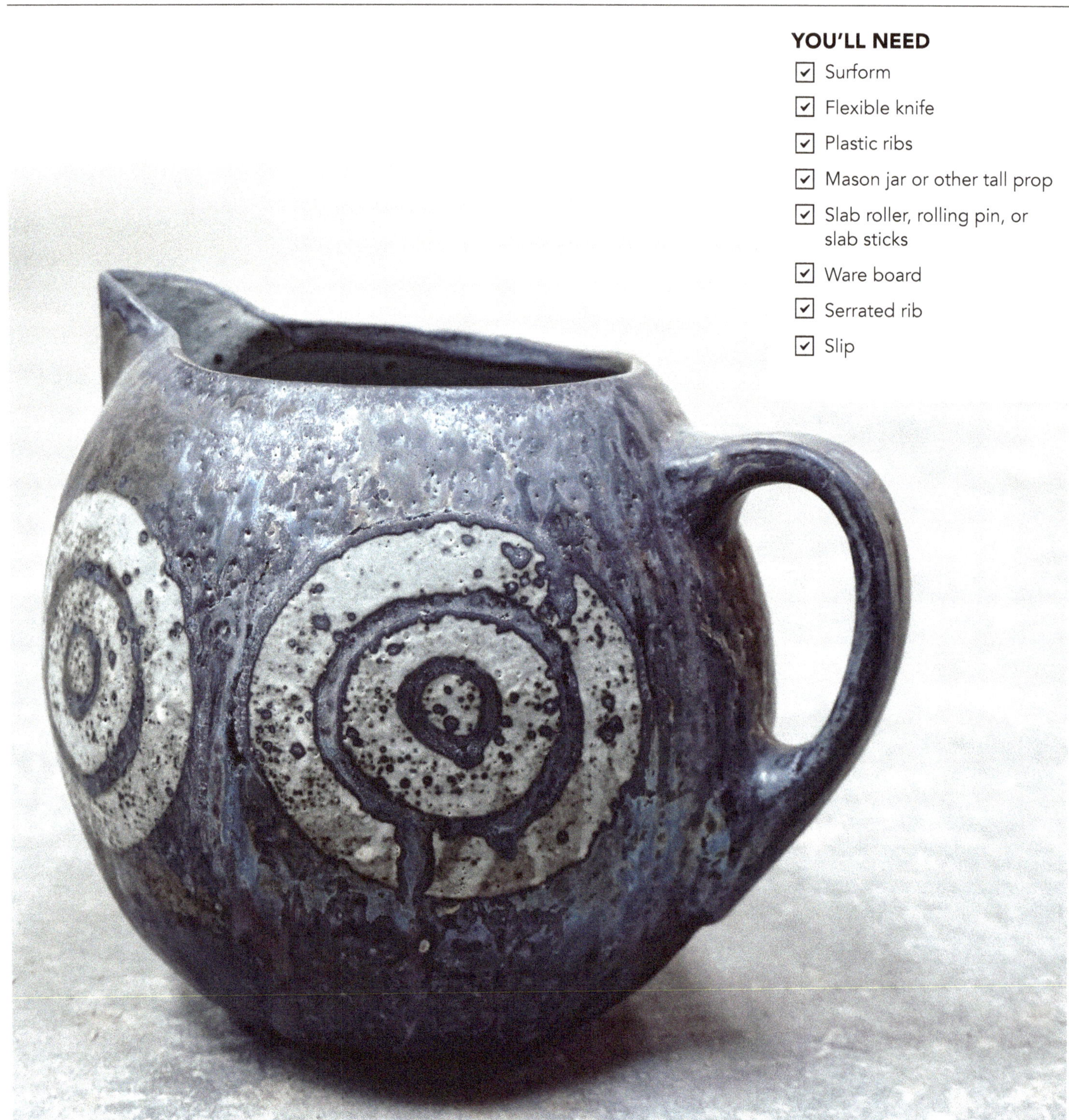

YOU'LL NEED

- ☑ Surform
- ☑ Flexible knife
- ☑ Plastic ribs
- ☑ Mason jar or other tall prop
- ☑ Slab roller, rolling pin, or slab sticks
- ☑ Ware board
- ☑ Serrated rib
- ☑ Slip

1 | Follow steps 1 through 9 for making the moon vase on page 100.

2 | Note where the sphere starts to curve in toward the top. Use your needle tool to cut all the way around, removing the top of your sphere. (You can use this circle for a plate by refining the edge.)

3 | Add a coil over the inside seam, where the top and bottom halves join, just as you did on the outside seam.

4 | Blend the coil to eliminate the seam on the inside of the pitcher. You can use a plastic rib to help smooth. You may need to go back to the outside seam and smooth again. (As you use pressure to smooth the outside seam, the inside seam may bulge and vice versa. It's a delicate back and forth.)

5 | Cover the pitcher with plastic to keep it from drying while you work on the spout.

6 | Follow the steps for making a spout template on page 103. The rough rule for making a spout that pours well is to make sure the spout sticks out further than the belly of your pitcher and is level with the top. Unfortunately, the only way to really know if your pitcher pours well is after it's fired.

7 | Roll out a small piece of clay about a ¼" (6 mm) thick and, using your template, cut out the spout.

8 | Hold the spout gently where you want it on your pitcher and trace around the outside of it with your needle tool to mark its placement. Set the spout aside.

9 | Using your flexible knife, cut out the clay from the rim of the pitcher along the line you marked.

10 | Score and slip the ¼" (6 mm) below the cut on the pitcher and the edge of the spout.

11 | Attach the spout (with gentle pressure to keep from squishing it) onto the pitcher. (You will come back to the spout when it firms up and add coils, blending them in to eliminate the attachment seams.)

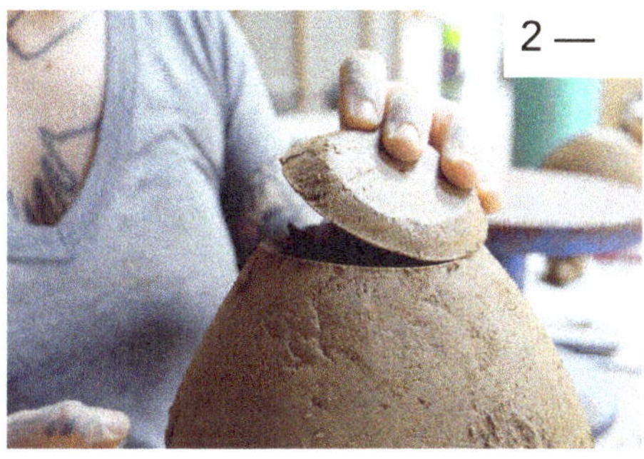

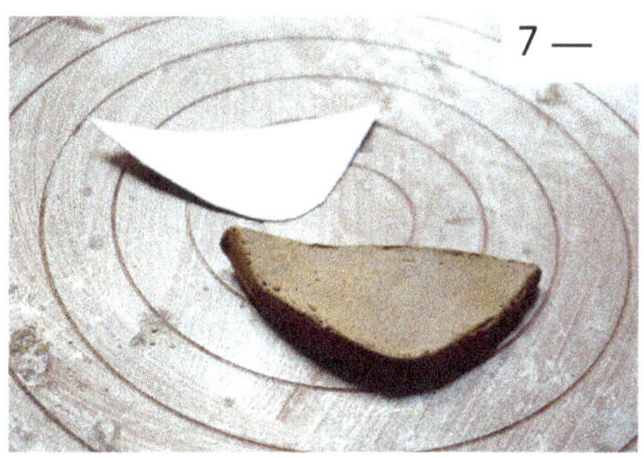

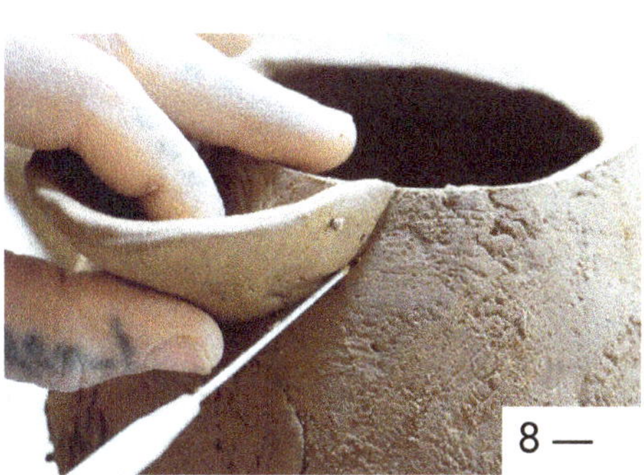

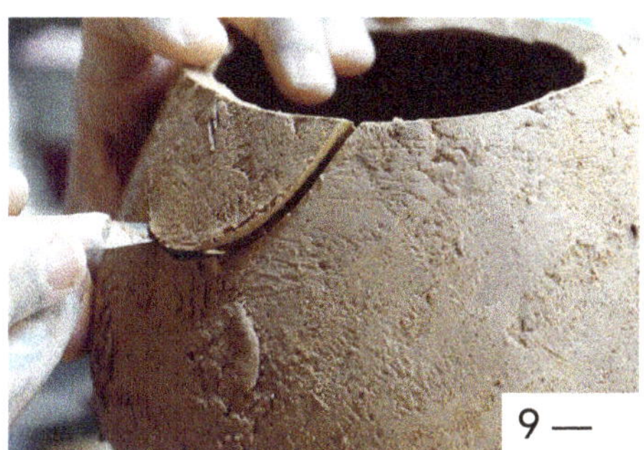

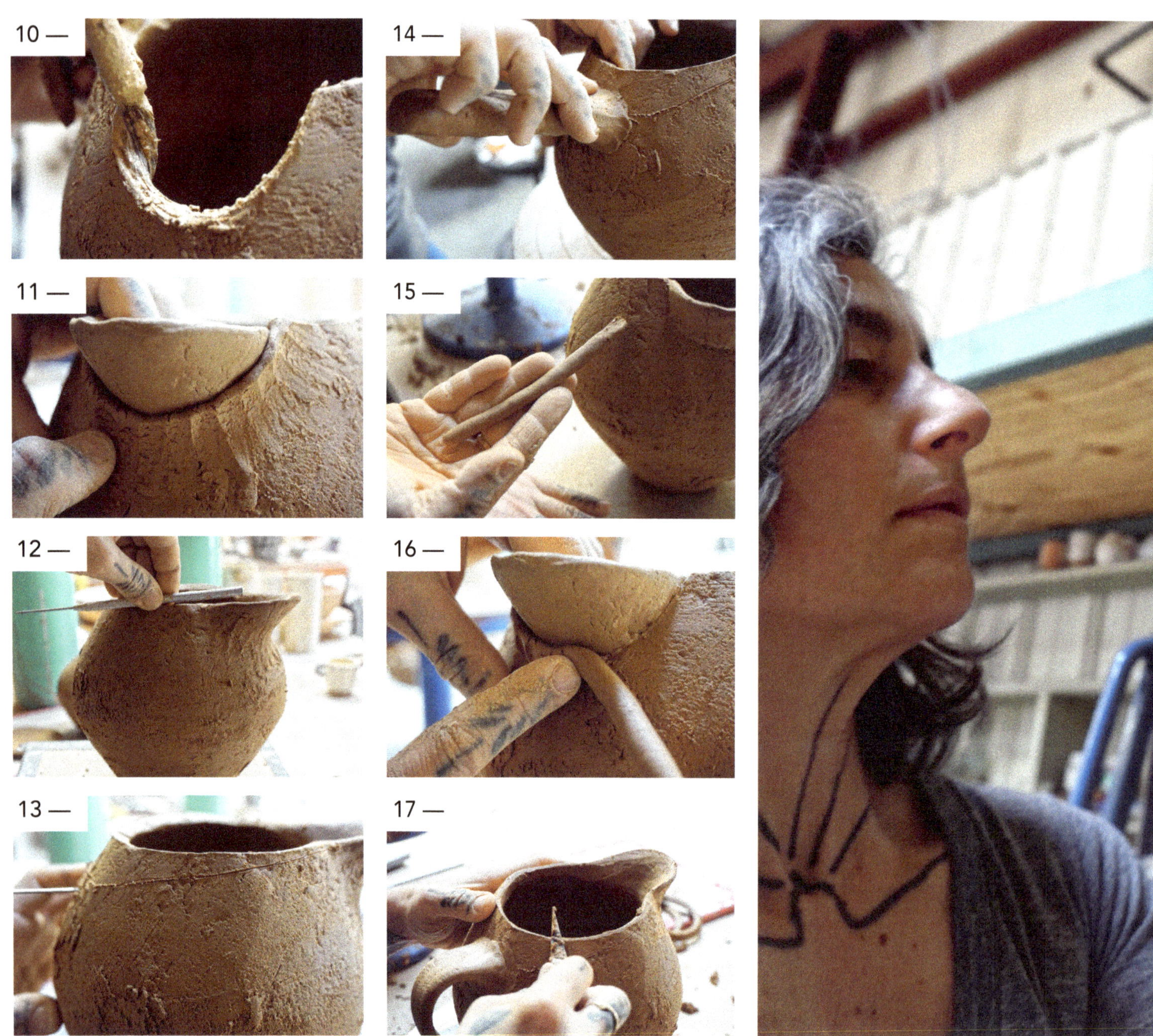

10 —

11 —

12 —

13 —

14 —

15 —

16 —

17 —

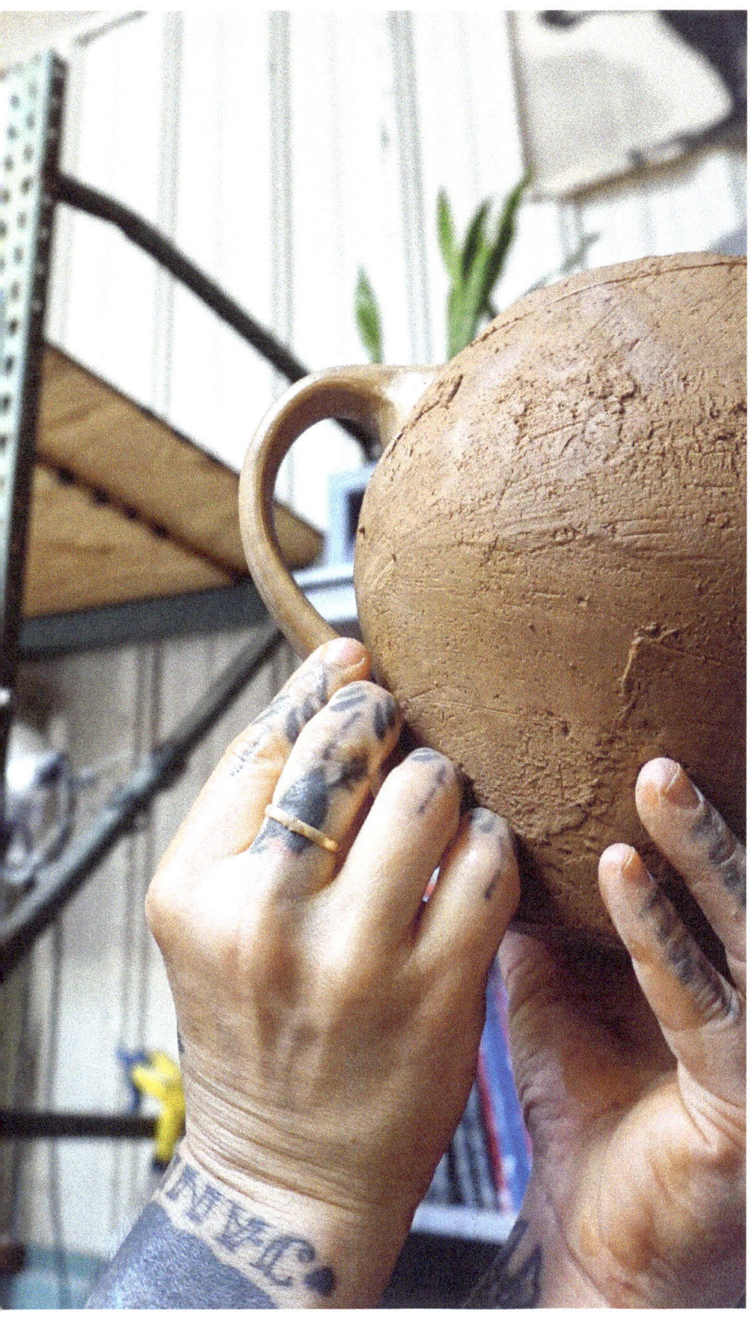

12 | While the spout is setting up, make the handle. Find a spot for the handle opposite the spout. I eyeball this by holding the pitcher with the spout on the far side and placing a stick above the middle of the spout to rest on the rim. I mark this point.

13 | To decide where to place the top of the handle, I turn the pitcher sideways and draw an imaginary line from the spout across the pitcher to the back. I like it when the top of the handle falls slightly lower than the spout in a gradual diagonal line.

14 | Decide where you want the handle to attach on the bottom. Consider the curve of your pitcher and where it visually makes sense for the handle to attach. Think of the pitcher filled with liquid and if it will be better to get all your fingers around the handle to hold and pour. There is no right or wrong here; it will just look right or wrong. It's a good idea to play with different placements and shapes using a practice handle. When you decide what kind of handle you want and where it goes, score and slip the attachment on your pitcher and add your handle.

15 | When your spout and handle are leather-hard, refine. Add a thin coil to the inside seam of the spout where it attaches to the pitcher. Blend it in, eliminating the attachment seam.

16 | Do the same on the outside of your spout.

17 | Using your flexible knife, carefully refine and taper the edge of your spout. Use the knife or a rib to refine, bevel, smooth, and finish your handle.

18 | I wrap the handle, rim, and spout in plastic to slow down their drying. You might have cracking issues if these dry too fast.

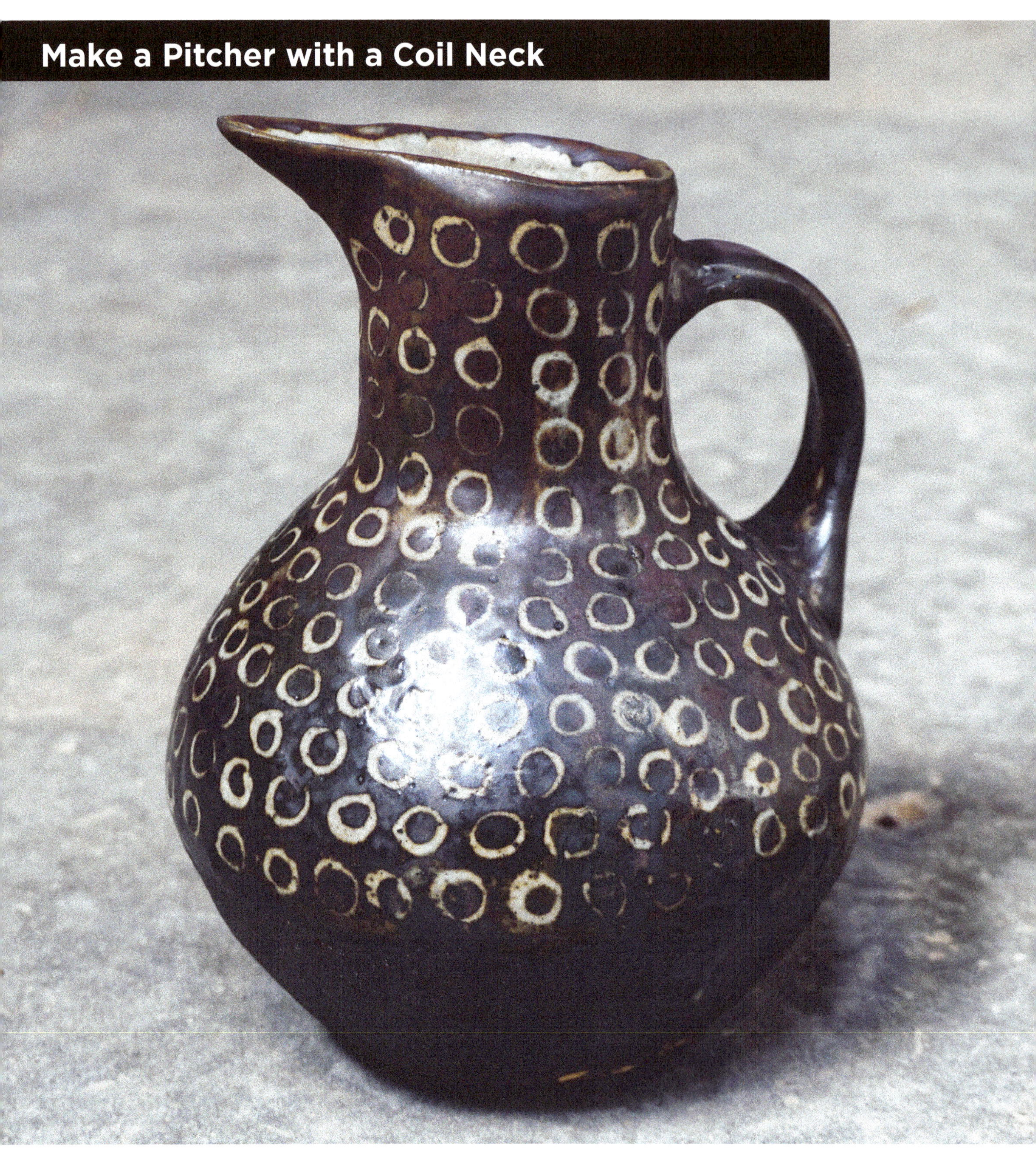

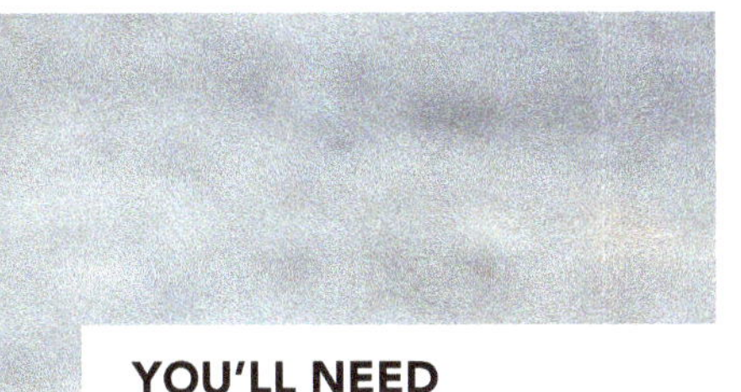

YOU'LL NEED

- ☑ Surform
- ☑ Flexible knife
- ☑ Plastic ribs
- ☑ Mason jar or other tall prop
- ☑ Slab roller, rolling pin, or slab sticks
- ☑ Ware board
- ☑ Serrated rib
- ☑ Slip

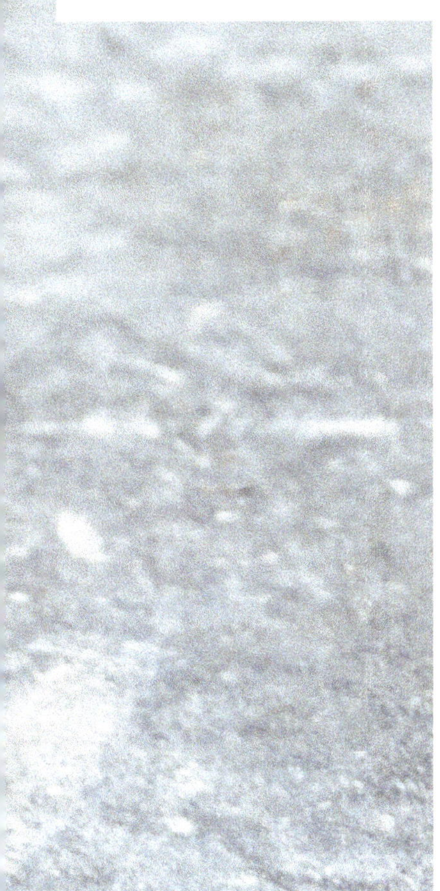

1 | Start the pitcher as in step 1 of the previous pitcher on page 107.

2 | In step 2, make a hole in the top of the pitcher with your needle tool and decide how wide you want your opening.

3 | Cut out the opening.

4 | Add coils to build your neck, following directions for the coil-neck vase on page 104.

5 | When the neck is the desired height, follow steps 6-18 of the previous pitcher on page 107 for adding a spout and handle.

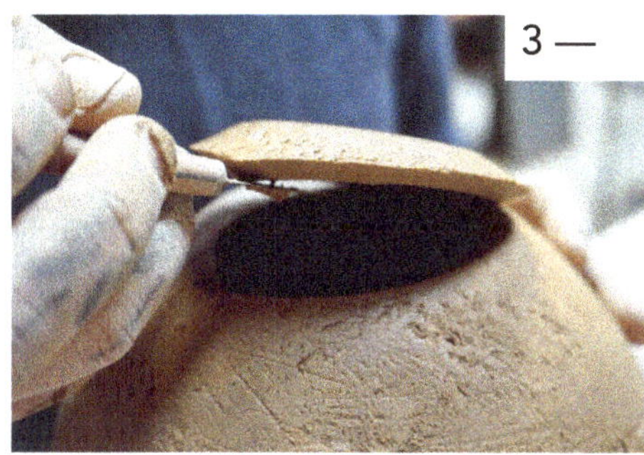

3 —

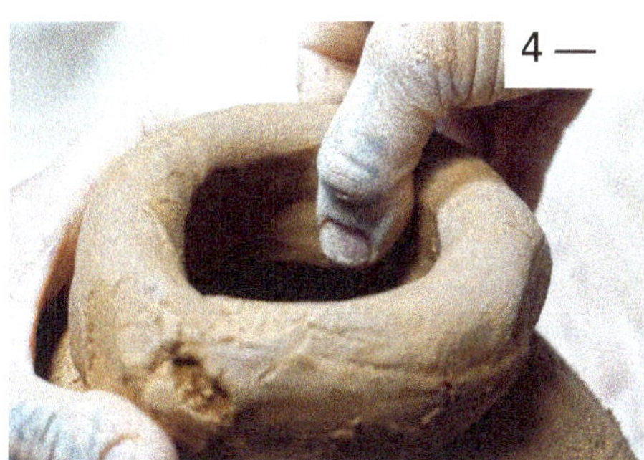

4 —

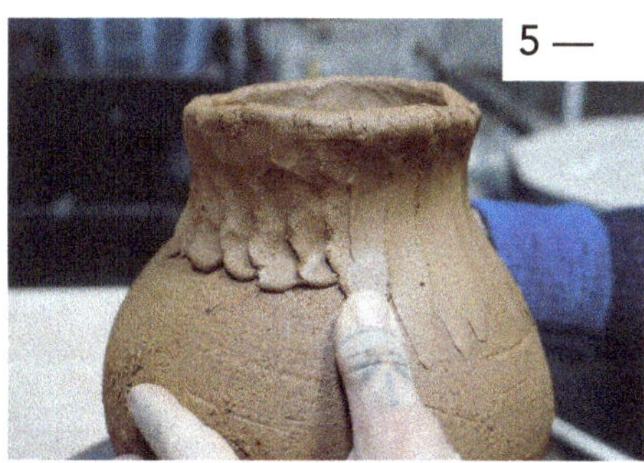

5 —

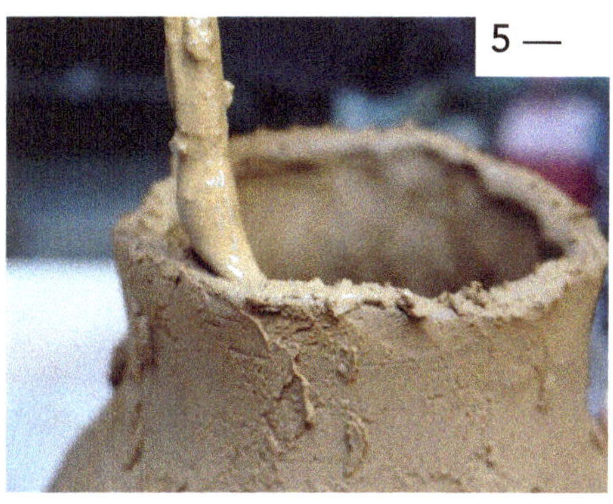

5 —

Guest Potter Interview: Candice Methe-Hess
Commanding Presence in Handbuilt Forms

Candice Methe-Hess received her BFA from Northern Arizona University in 2011 and her MFA in clay from the University of Minnesota in 2015. She works from Helena, Montana, where she teaches at the Archie Bray Foundation for Ceramic Arts and shows her work at the Red Lodge Clay Center. In 2016 she received a Warren MacKenzie Advancement Award through Northern Clay and traveled to Ghana, West Africa, for a month to learn indigenous clay methods and practices with the women in the northern part of the country.

MW: YOUR POTS LOOK LIKE ANCIENT VESSELS MADE BY AN EDUCATED MODERN HUMAN. DO YOU LOOK AT A LOT OF HISTORIC FORMS?

CMH: I do look at a lot of historic forms spanning many cultures. I look at historic pieces from Africa, Japan, and a lot of Native American work as well. I am not just looking at clay, though—I am looking at wood, textiles, and basketry as well.

MW: HOW HAS YOUR CERAMIC EDUCATION INFORMED YOUR WORK?

CMH: When I first began my graduate education, I felt that my work was really missing something—fundamentally and foundationally. I had acquired skills, but I hadn't found my voice yet. Being in a supportive environment that helped push my boundaries and understanding of the material was very beneficial. What I also appreciated from my time at the University of Minnesota, Minneapolis, is that it is a contemporary art–based program, which I also believed would be important for me to understand. All the graduate students had their studios together, so I had the opportunity to see and experience how artists of other mediums interact with their practices. With clay, we have a very long history that precedes us that we can explore, but it's also imperative to understand the times in which we live.

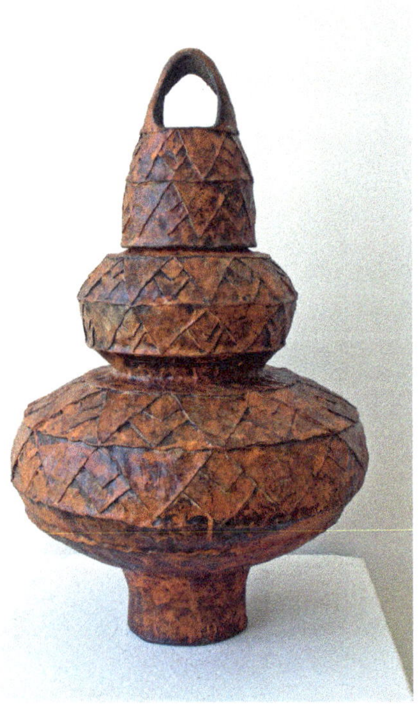

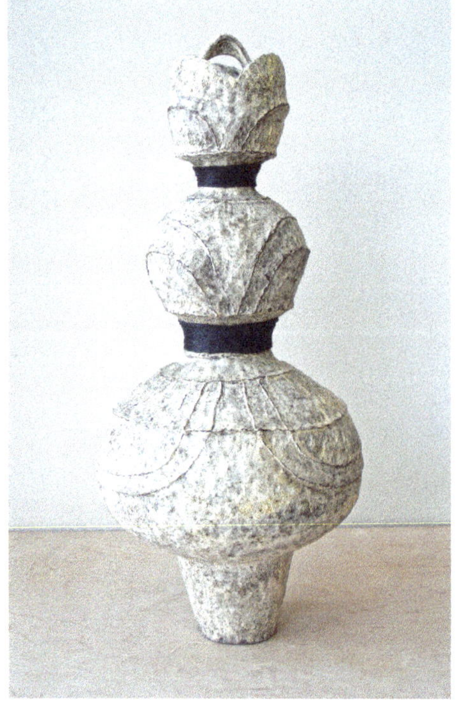

MW: YOU MAKE VERY LARGE VESSELS, YET, UNLIKE MOST LARGE-SCALE CERAMICS I'VE SEEN, YOURS HAVE A FEMININE QUALITY. THEY HAVE A STRENGTH AND PRESENCE THAT DOESN'T COMPROMISE THEIR DELICATE GRACE. I PICTURE YOUR PIECES COMMANDING A PRESENCE IN A SPACE NOT UNLIKE A LIVING BEING. DO YOU AGREE?

CMH: I do agree. We do see a lot of masculine forms in large vessels, and I think that is based in tradition and function: a lot of men make these large forms. When I started making large work, which was very much by accident, I quickly recognized its relationship with the human form—both through making the pieces and through proximity. It's a component of my work that I feel is important: I'm constantly exploring it and taking it into consideration. I think the vessel is the perfect metaphor for being human. When I create a piece, I feel that I am making an individual: the spirit of the moment and the material come together and are present in the work. I want my work to be voluminous and relatable.

> **"I look at historic pieces from Africa, Japan, and a lot of Native American work as well."**

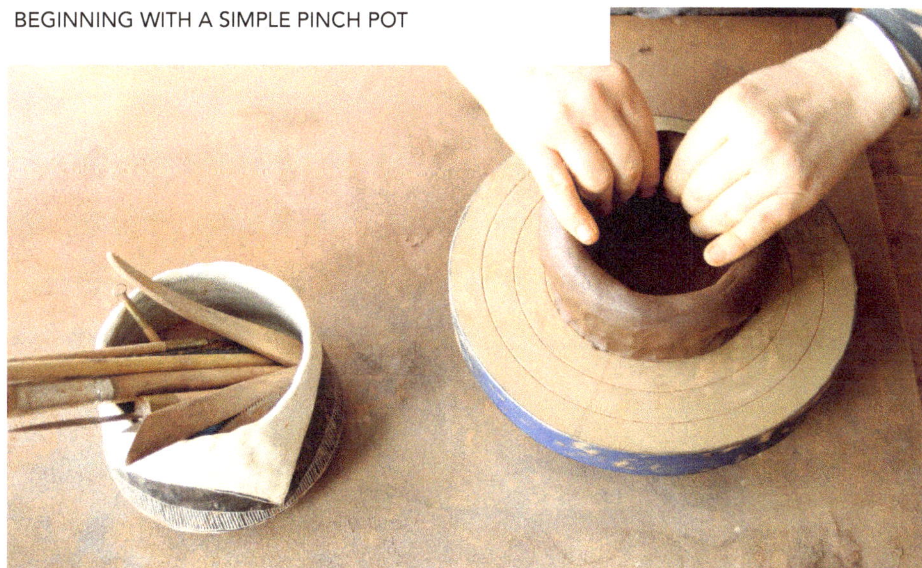

BEGINNING WITH A SIMPLE PINCH POT

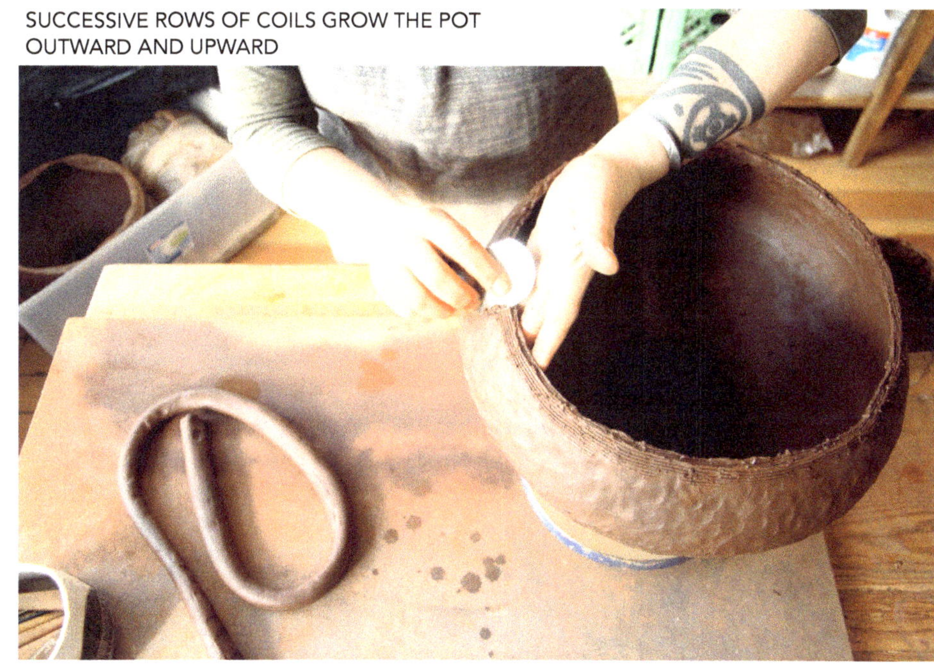

SUCCESSIVE ROWS OF COILS GROW THE POT OUTWARD AND UPWARD

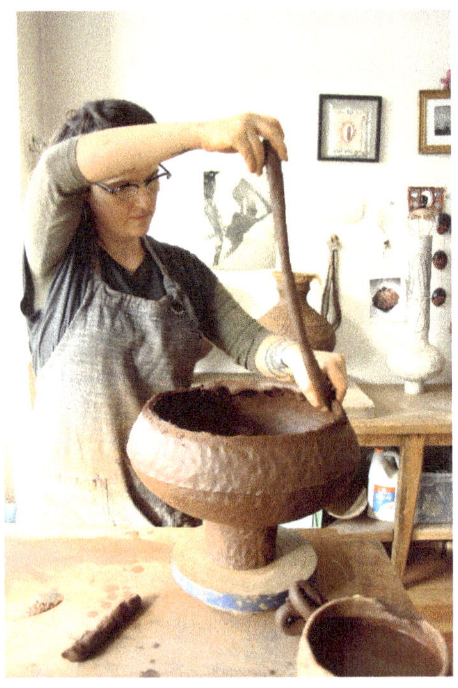

ADDING ANOTHER COIL

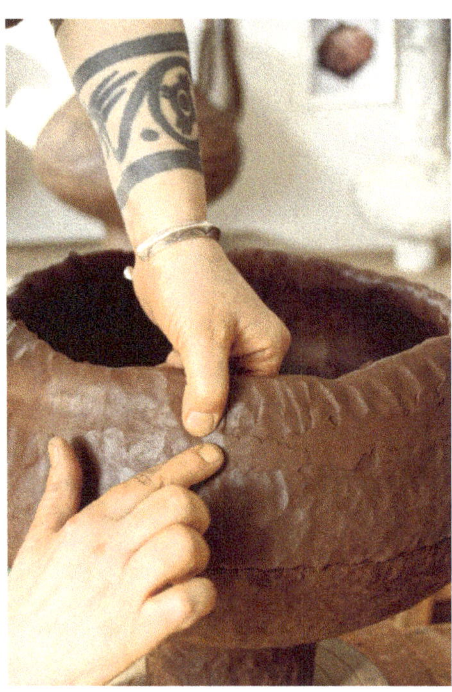

BLENDING A COIL

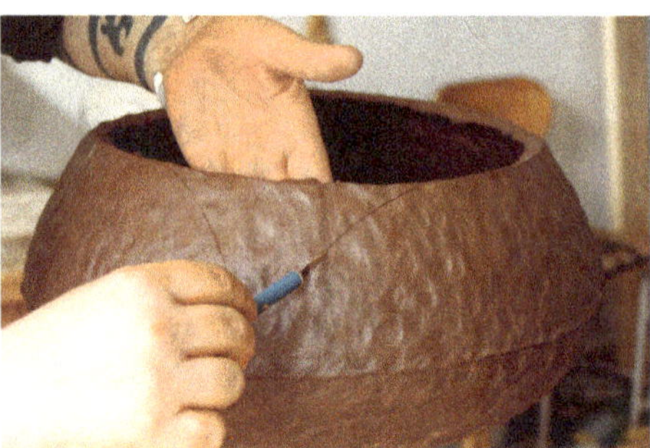

MARKING THE CUT-OUT SHAPE

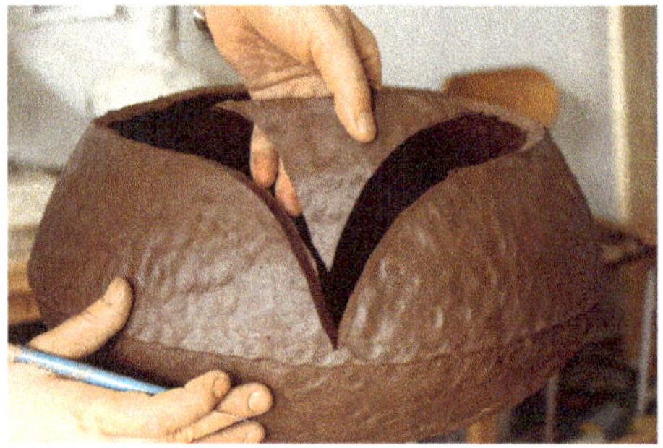

CUTTING OUT THE SHAPE

MW: WORKING ON SUCH A LARGE SCALE PRESENTS ITS OWN SET OF CHALLENGES. WHAT, IF ANY, DO YOU FACE AND HOW HAVE YOU DEALT WITH THEM?

CMH: As much as I love working large scale, it can become very technical very quickly! The challenges lie in firing the work, storage space, transportation, shipping, and all of those practical concerns. To work large scale, you have to be in an environment that supports you through those concerns, and that in itself can be challenging to come by.

MW: WHAT IS YOUR HANDBUILDING PROCESS?

CMH: I work in the round, from the bottom up, and build as I go through coil and pinch methods. The way I work is pretty straightforward and I use very few tools. For the lines, I will usually cut out the shapes and put them back together, leaving a little overlap as I build up. Sometimes I add a small coil to create the line.

MW: YOUR MUGS AND SMALLER-SCALE FORMS SEEM TO INFORM THE LARGER WORK, LIKE A MAQUETTE. IS THIS THE CASE?

CMH: No. Although it is all the same family, the smaller works I see as more functional, and their shapes are dictated by that. With the larger pieces, they are more "exhibition" and exploratory.

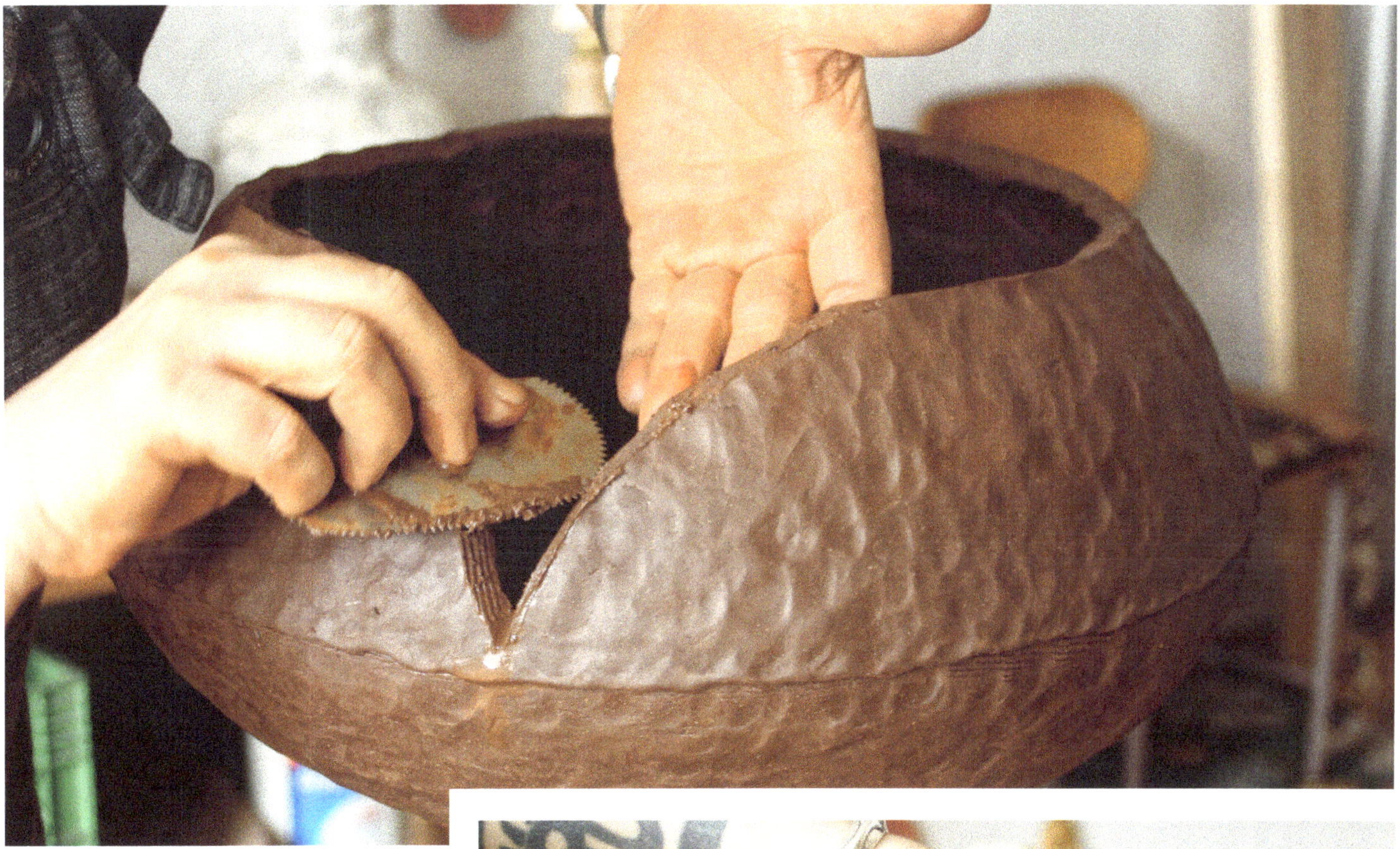

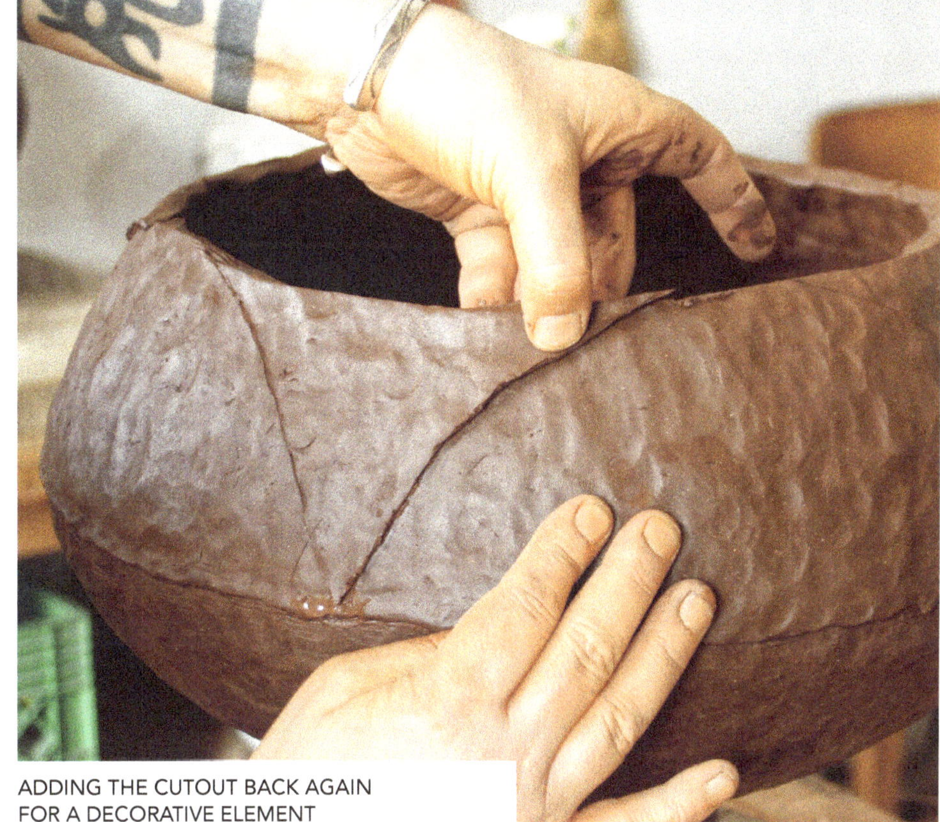

SCORING THE EDGE

MW: **WHAT ARE YOUR INFLUENCES?**

CMH: As I mentioned before, I look at a lot of African artwork, mostly carved wood pieces. I look at a lot of Zulu basketry as well. There is so much going on there in terms of scale, texture, form, and color. I gain inspiration through reading about the ways of life of ancient cultures, in terms of agriculture, architectural designs, cooking, rituals, and burials. Nature is always a bountiful place of inspiration, but I think my biggest influence comes from just making. The process of making fuels the ideas.

ADDING THE CUTOUT BACK AGAIN
FOR A DECORATIVE ELEMENT

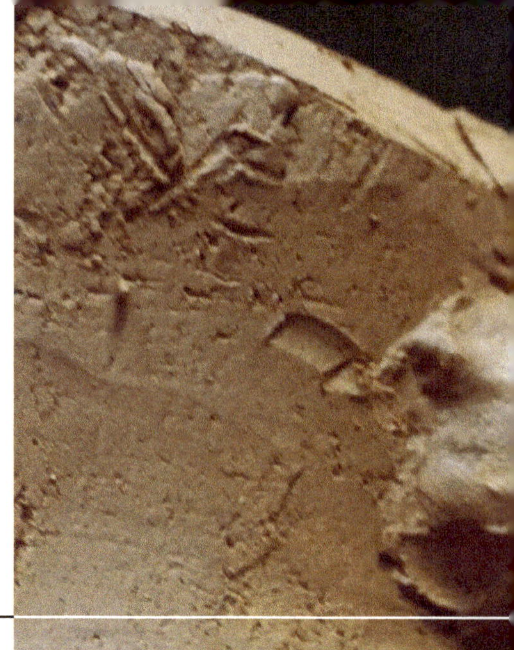
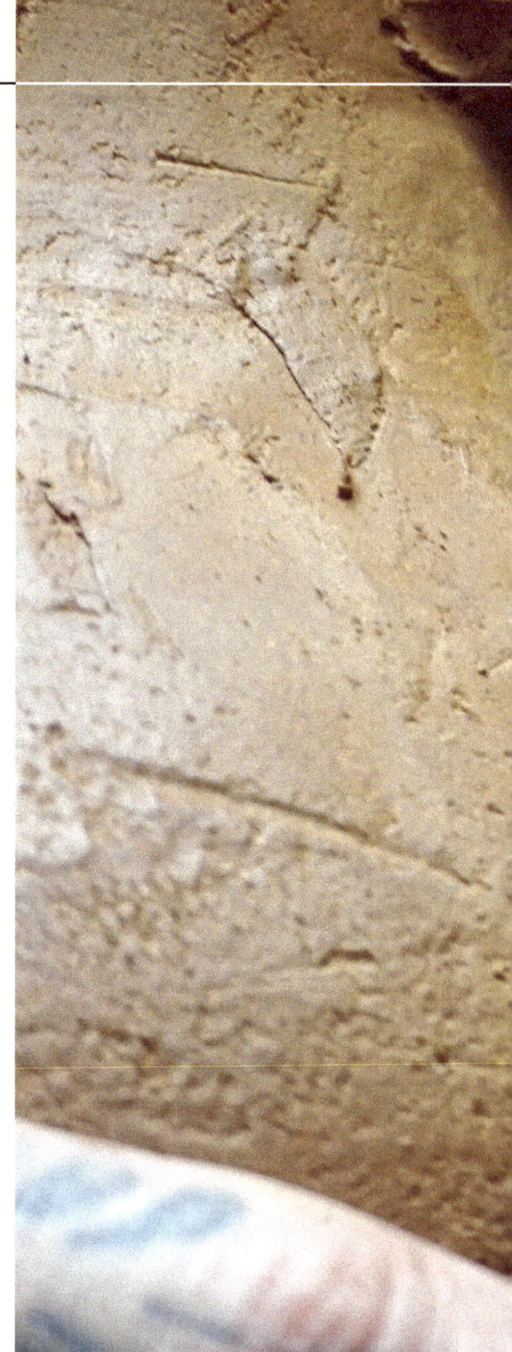

07

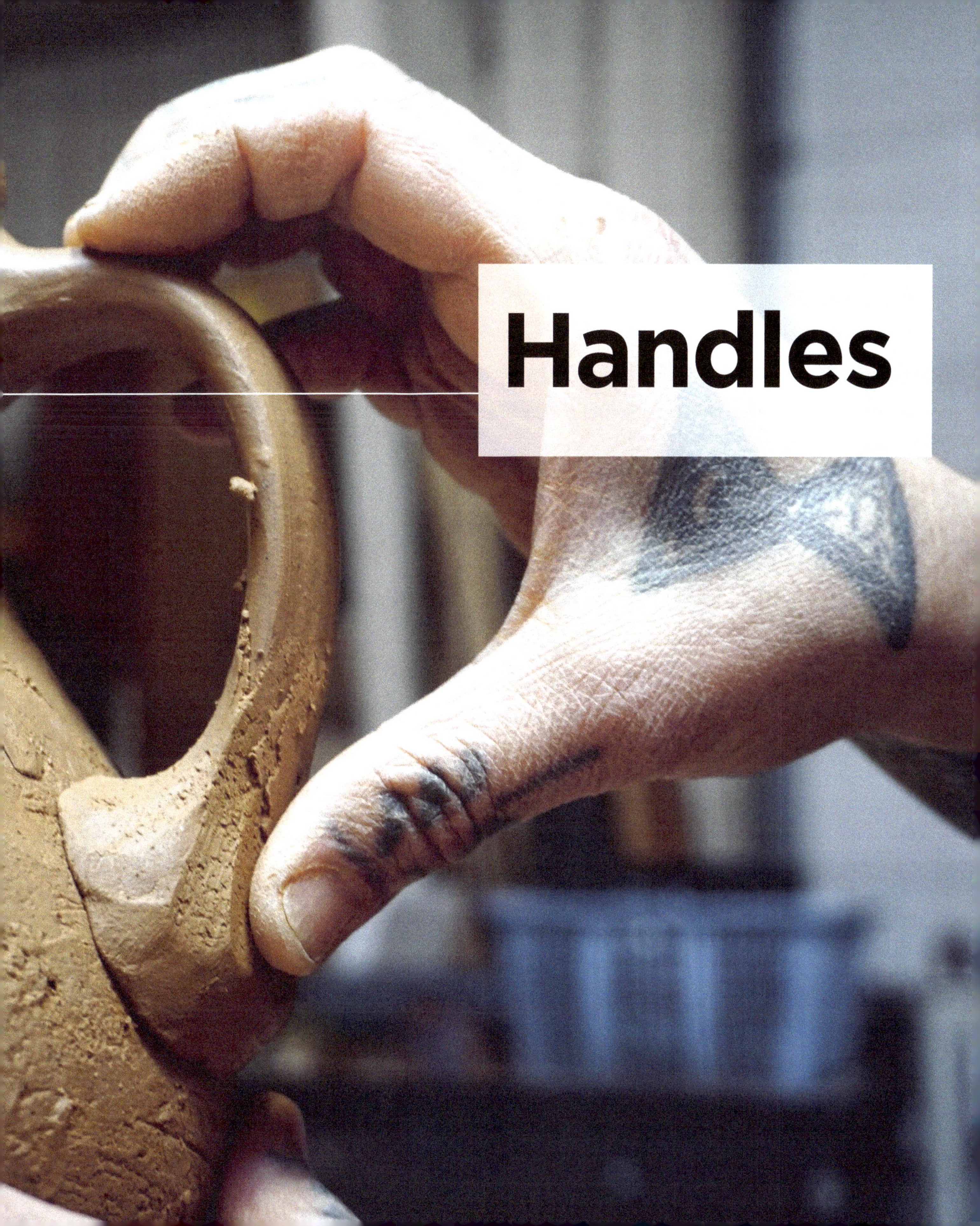
Handles

Making Handles

Handles can be decorative or functional, and they can really change the way a pot looks, feels, and functions. I enjoy making handles and think they're the most important component of certain types of pots.

I make many different styles of handles using a variety of methods. I'll tell you about the three I use most. For mugs and pitchers, I make handles by attaching a piece of clay and, using water, pulling the handle into shape from the pot. I also make handles from an attached coil. For carved trays and buckets, I often use a disc of clay and a hole punch.

Handles are as varied as pots. The best way to choose which style to use is to look at the pot and decide what would suit it best. You don't want to make a single style of handle and stick it on every pot you make.

YOU'LL NEED

- ☑ Serrated rib
- ☑ Plastic rib
- ☑ Slip
- ☑ Hole punch

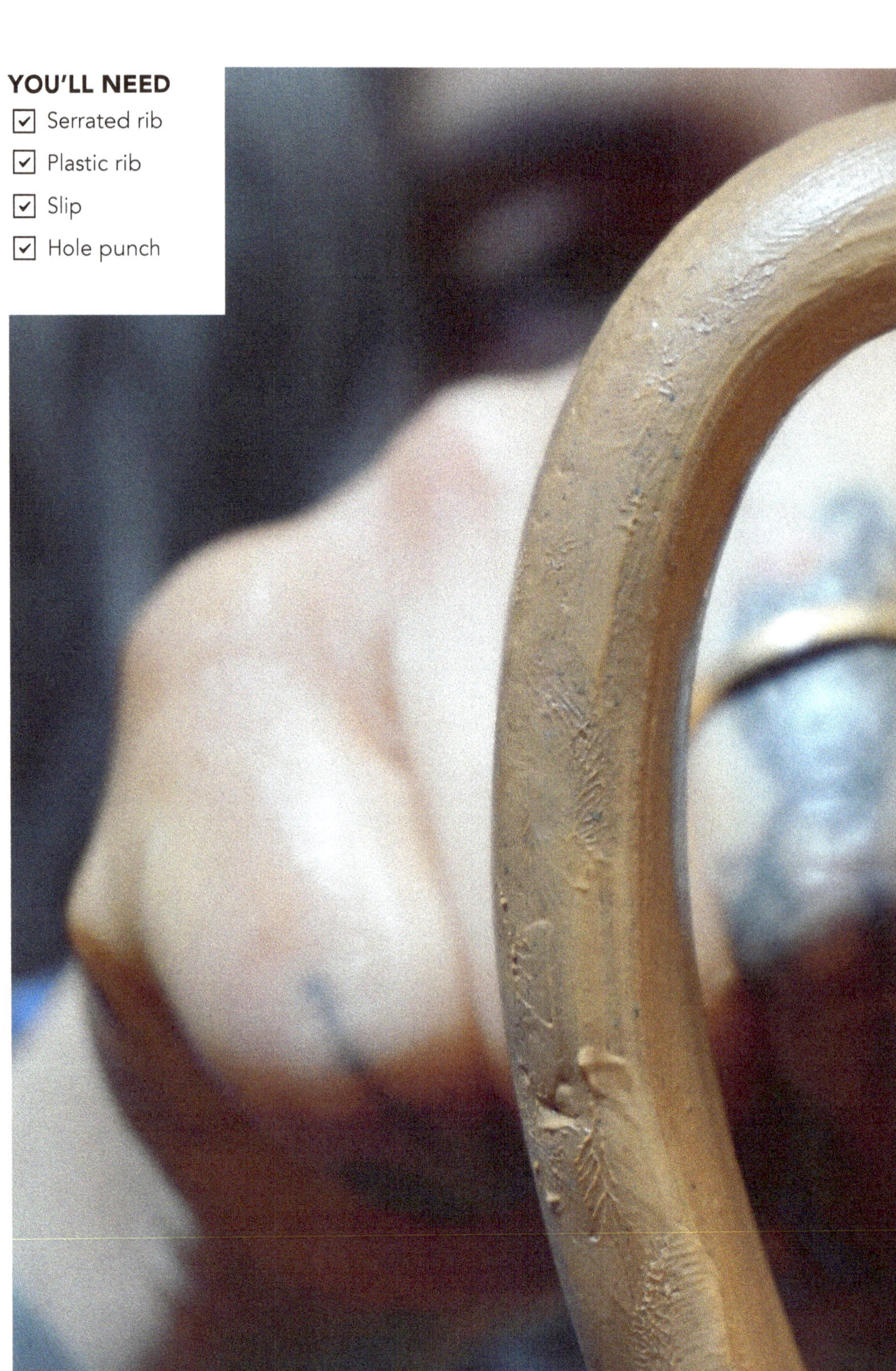

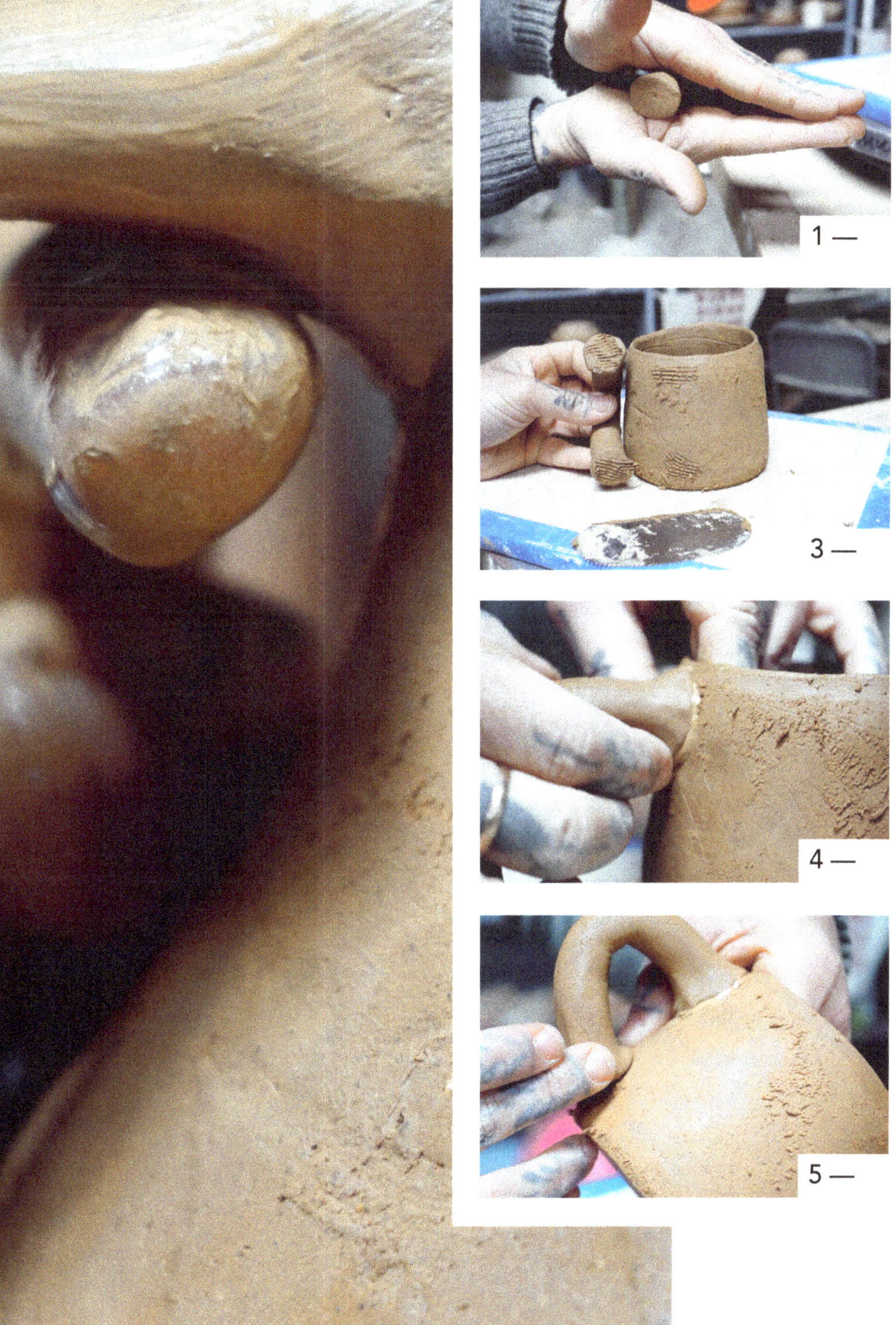

ATTACHED COIL HANDLES

1 | Roll out a coil thicker than you want your finished handle to be. Make it slightly thicker at the ends.

2 | Hold the coil in position to see if it's the right length and adjust if needed.

3 | Mark the place where you will attach the handle, and score and slip your pot.

4 | Score the ends of the coil. Push one end into the upper attachment spot. I like to do this by holding the coil just back from the ends with my fingertips, then pressing the end onto the surface to widen it. This provides a wider access point and gives you extra clay to push into the pot for a solid attachment. Use your fingers to press the coil all around the edge of the flattened end into the pot.

5 | Curve the coil down to meet the other end with the lower attachment spot. Push this end into place the same way. You can blend in this attachment or accentuate the seam. Let the coil dry to leather-hard, and refine with a flexible knife and a rib.

DISC HANDLES

1 | Roll a piece of clay into a ball. The size of the ball depends on how big you want the handle to be. If you are making multiple disc handles for a pot, prepare them all at the same time from equal-sized balls.

2 | Flatten the ball into a thick disc. Take the disc and press it down onto a surface to flatten one edge, making a solid U shape.

3 | Further press on the edge to make it wider than the rest of the disc, giving you a wide access point for attaching it.

4 | Score and slip the pot where the handle will go.

5 | Score the flat edge of the disc.

6 | Push the disc onto the pot, pressing the entire edge of the disc into the pot.

7 | Blend in or accentuate this attachment seam.

8 | Let the disc get to leather-hard. While supporting the disc and the pot, use the desired size of hole punch to make a hole in the middle of the disc.

9 | I go back in and cut the edges of the hole to bevel them so they don't look quite perfect. Use a knife and/or a rib to refine your handle.

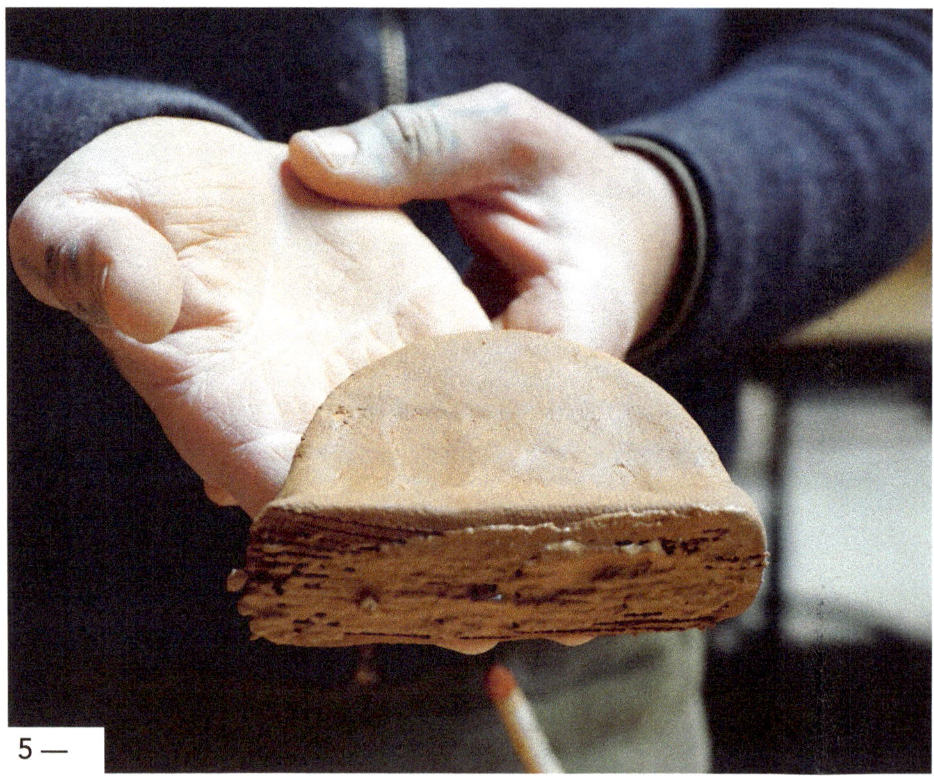

5 —

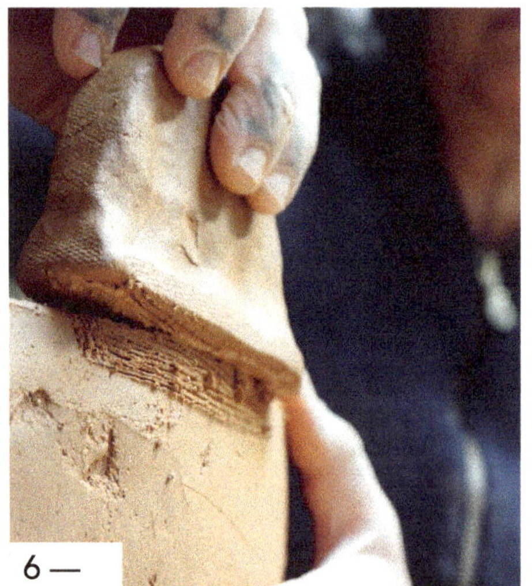

6 —

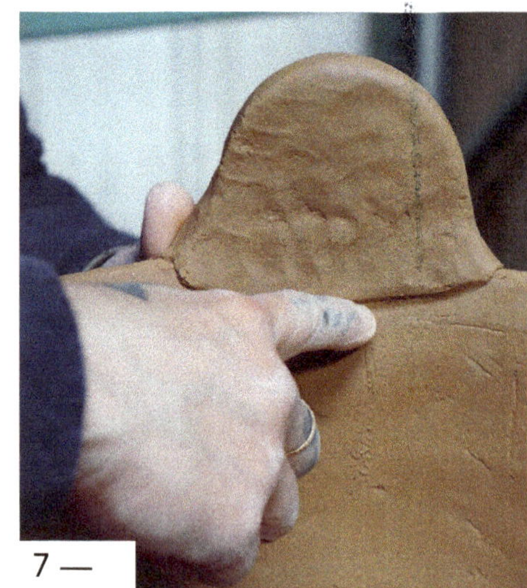

7 —

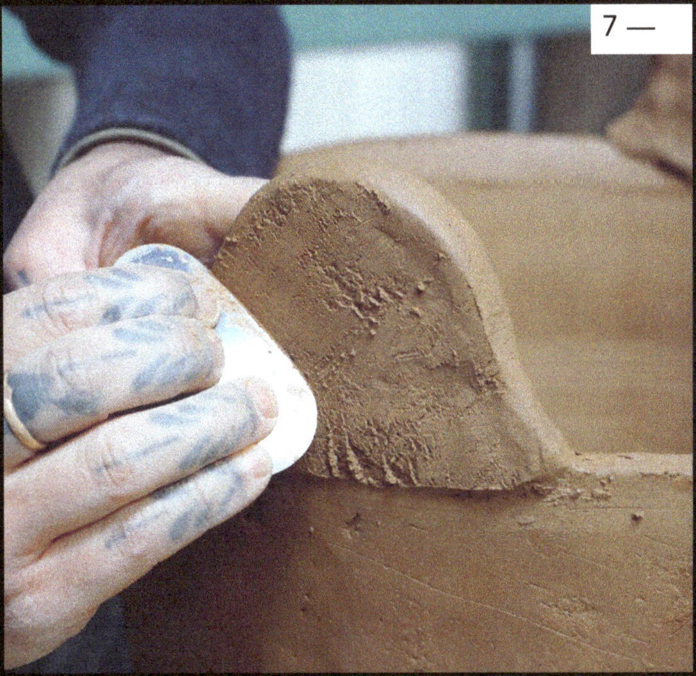

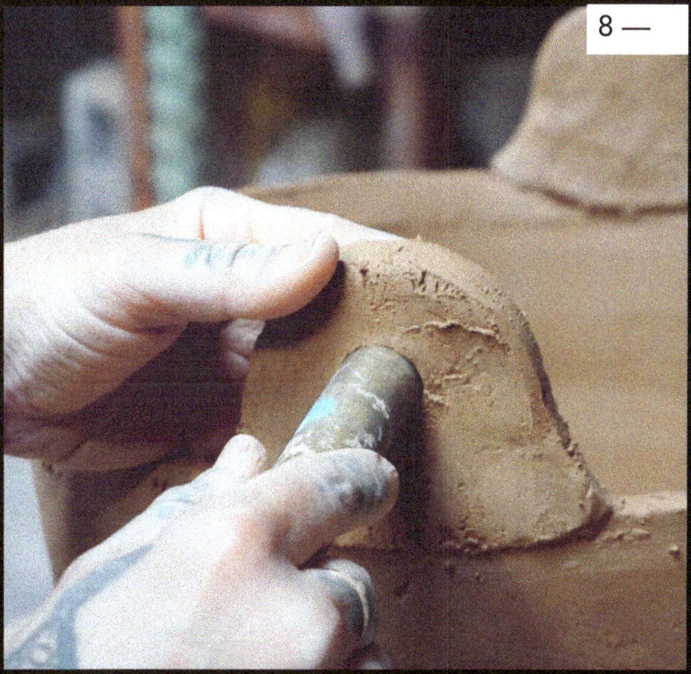

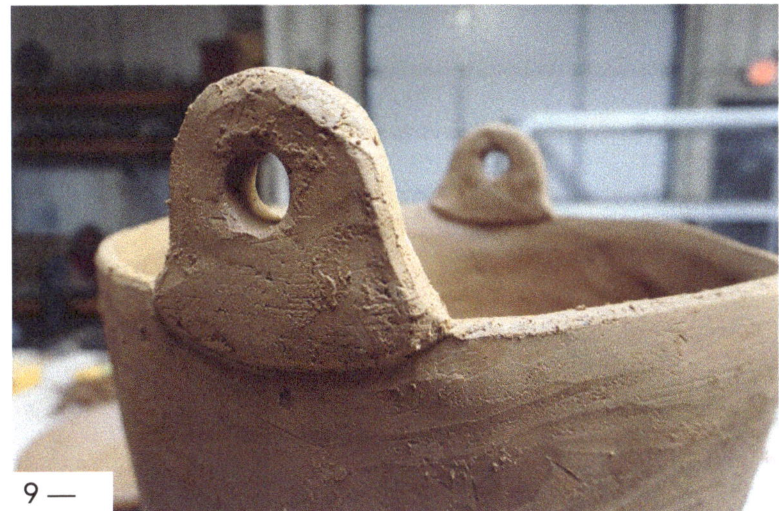

PULLED HANDLES

This type of handle can take a while to master, but it's my favorite method for handling mugs and pitchers. It takes experience to find the balance between the right amount of clay and the pressure. It's a learn-by-feel, more than by direction, process, but I will get you started with the basic instructions.

1 | Have a bucket of water ready. Shape a piece of clay into a thick, wide piece, kind of like a short, flat carrot. The size of this piece is dependent on the size of the mug or pitcher you're attaching it to. For a mug, start with at about 1" (2.5 cm) wide and 2" (5 cm) long.

2 | Press one end onto a surface to flatten and widen it. It's important to do this, so when you press it onto the pot you don't thin it out.

3 | Decide where it will attach at the top of your pot, and don't worry about where it will attach at the bottom yet.

4 | Score and slip your pot and the flattened spot on your piece of clay, and press it into the pot. Press into the outer edge of the clay, securing it to the pot without thinning out the rest of the handle.

> The first time I ever made a pulled handle, the teacher came by and said it looked like a piece of bacon. I was determined to get good at this method, so I threw fifty mugs on the wheel and proceeded to handle them all. I definitely cried out of sheer frustration.

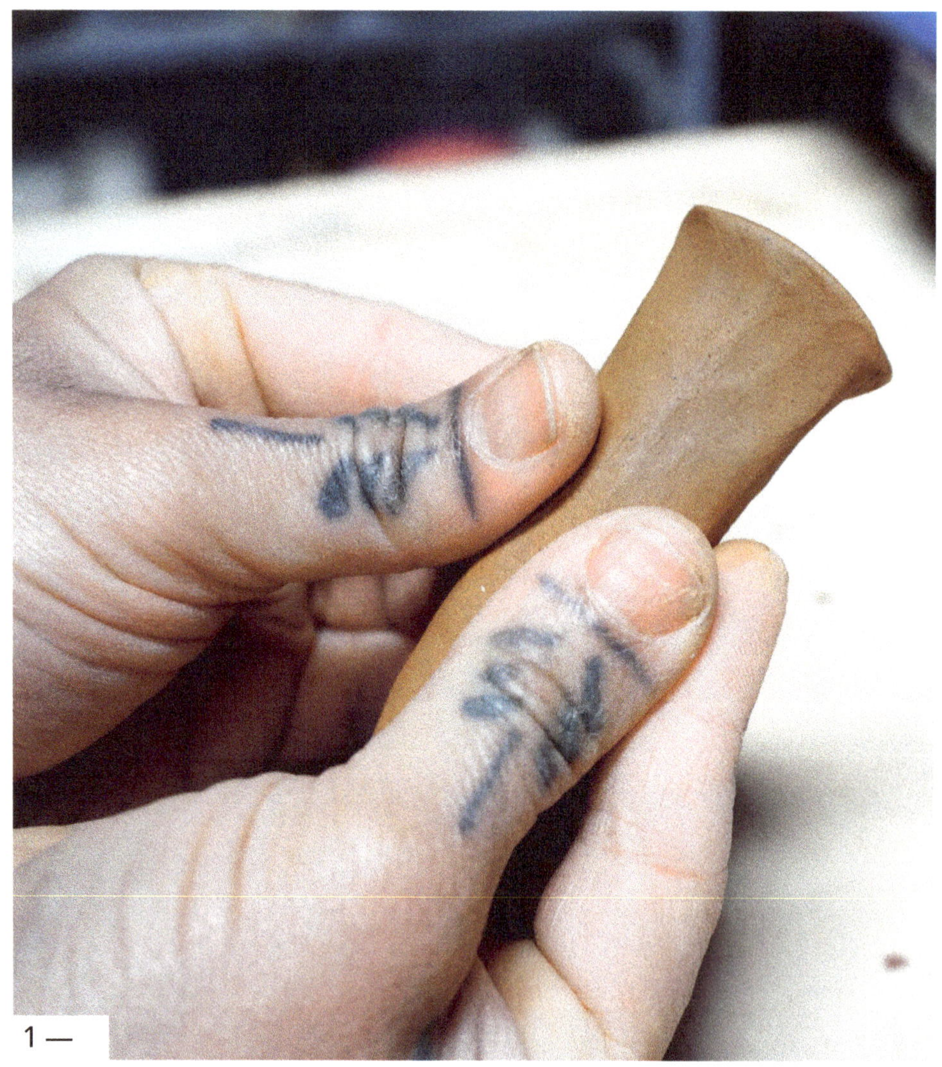

1 —

5 | When it is attached, hold the pot in front of you sideways with your nondominant hand so that the handle comes straight off your pot at a 90° angle. Submerge the handle quickly in the water.

6 | Pull it out of the water and use the angle where the thumb and forefinger of your dominant hand meet to grab the handle at the top near the attachment. Pull your fingers along the handle so that it slides through your hand. You need to use enough pressure to thin and lengthen the clay, but not so much that it gets too thin and breaks.

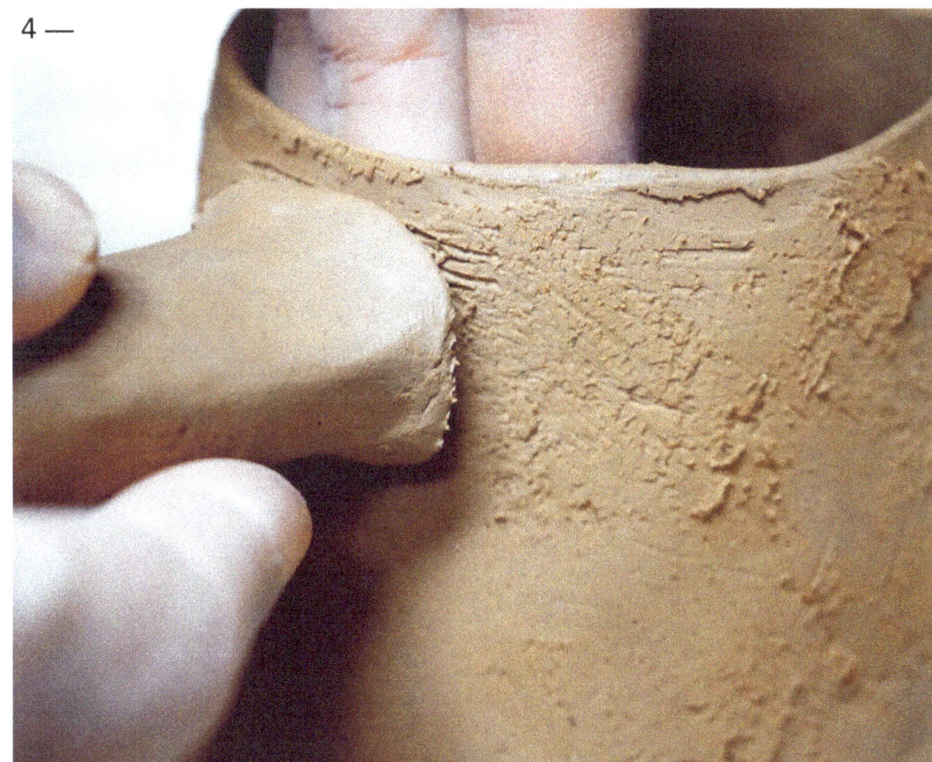

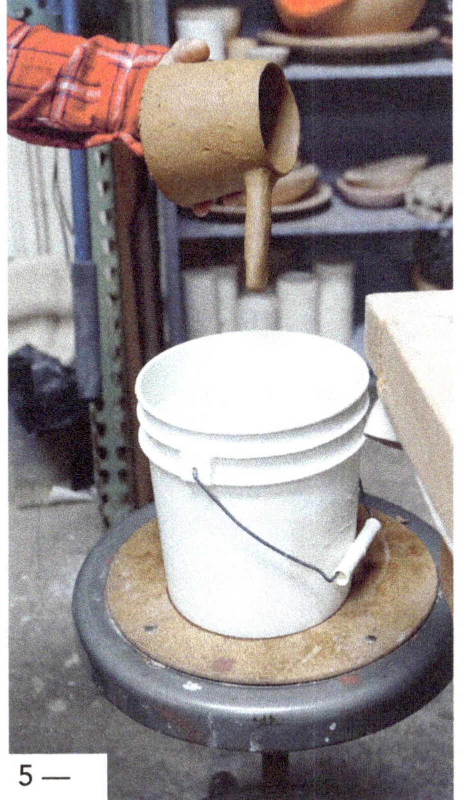

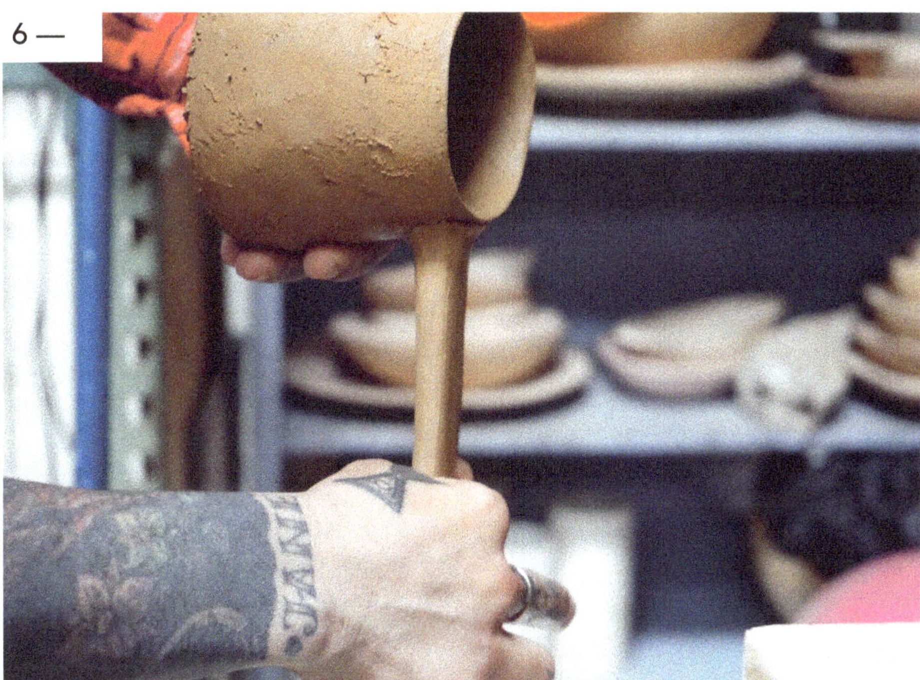

7 | Gradually and evenly thin and lengthen the handle with as many pulls as it takes to achieve the desired handle length and thickness, redipping in the water with every pull.

8 | To see where it will attach, I turn the pot right side up and let the handle fall naturally into place. If it's too short, I give it another pull. If it's too long, I cut off the excess. For some reason, I never score and slip this bottom attachment, and it's always fine.

9 | Once I push the bottom of the handle into place on the pot, I put it aside to get leather-hard. Normally, I backfill my handles to eliminate the gap on the inside of the bottom attachment. To do this, I roll a coil about the width of a pencil that wraps around the bottom of the handle where it meets the pot. Then I push the coil in and blend it into the handle and the pot so it disappears, filling in that gap and making a visually solid attachment.

Note: In my experience, it's best to slow dry pots with these types of handles.

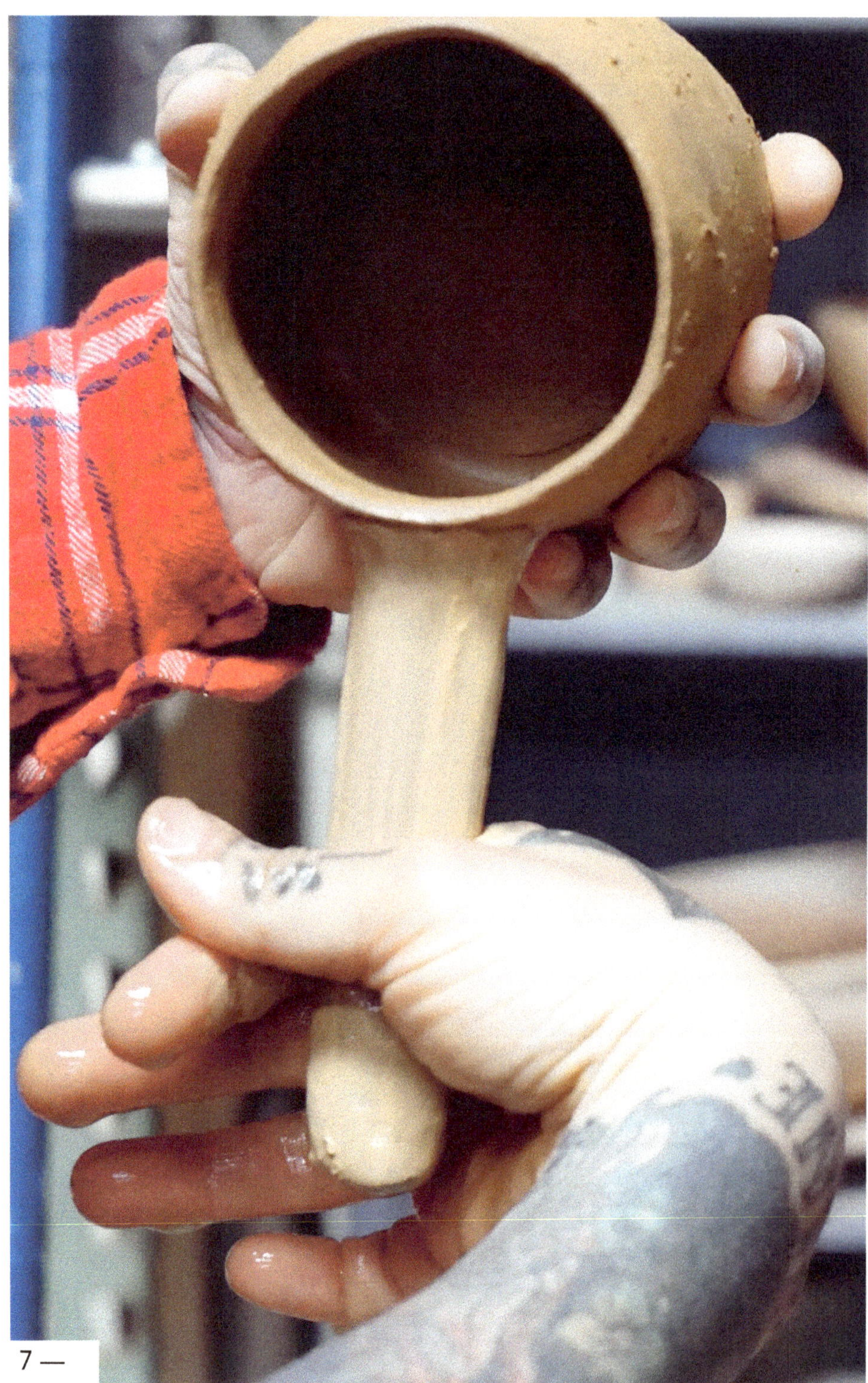
7 —

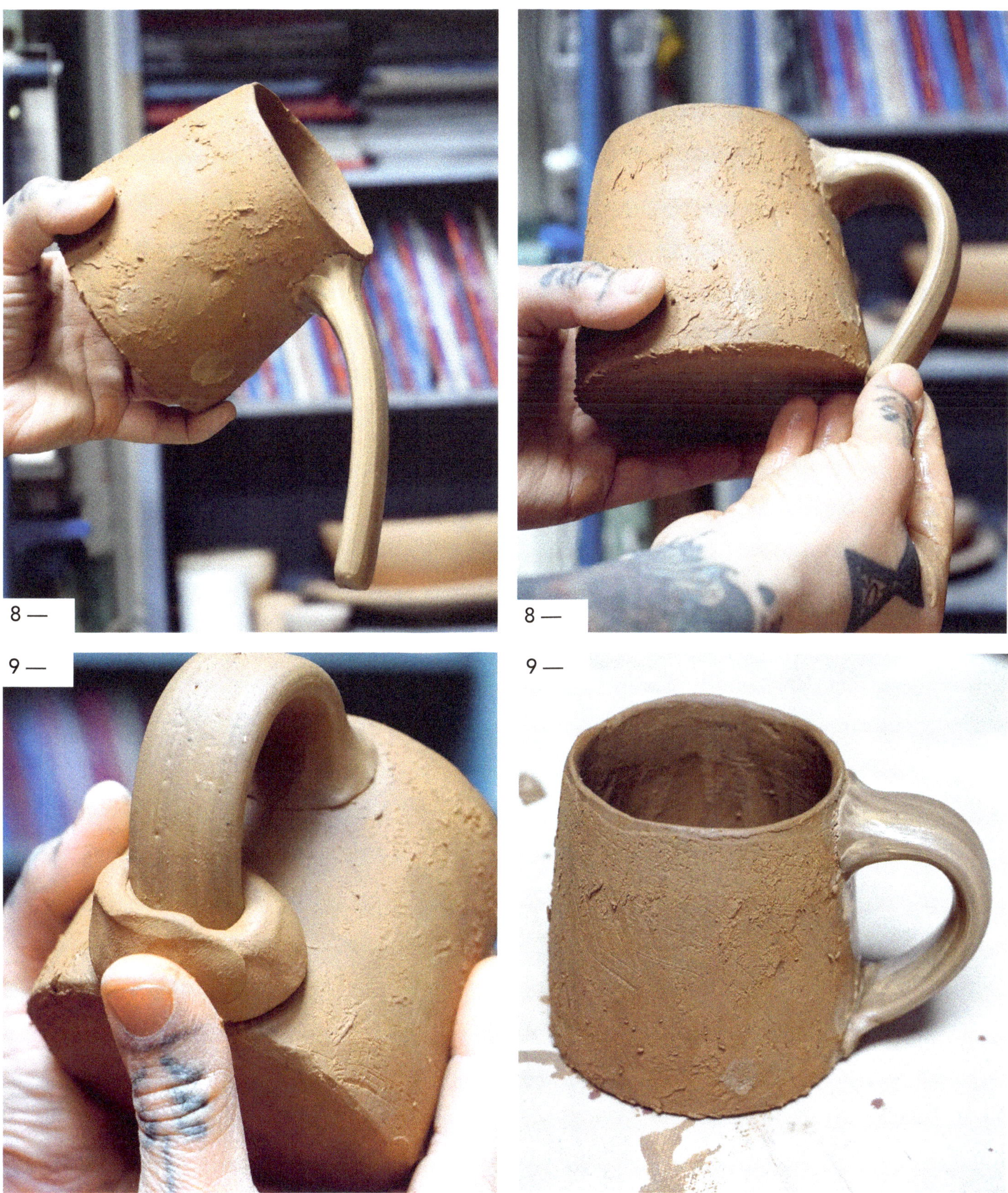

8 —
8 —
9 —
9 —

> Warren and I describe ourselves as artist potters. We make pots for use with an artistic intent because there is always an emotional resonance embedded in physical use. This artistic timber isn't necessarily comforting. Contravening convention can refresh one's perception. Artistic presence and physical use cannot be disentangled.

Our married and working relationship is delightfully tangled as well. We often tell people that in our professional life we work independently as artists, but we work together mechanically. We each make our own objects, but we will jointly mix clay and fire kilns, or take photographs and clean the studio together. When we are both in the groove of making, we will often ask each other's opinion. It's as if the other person's eye helps to confirm what we instinctively know. Sometimes, however, advice is vociferously ignored because its mere mention crystalizes a hidden intuition headed in an alternative direction.

We are always keeping our eyes open for useful materials. Warren has more of an engineering background, so he will look at soil and geological maps, search for technical data, and do calculations for clays and glazes. I (Catherine) am more intuitive and hands-on, so I will make little test pieces using found materials and try kooky things with a broad brush. This turns out to be a great balance for both of us. After he researched clay at Stancills, Warren got a twelve-ton dump-truck load. I make pickup-truck runs and fill up five-gallon buckets with diverse materials, concocting recipes as if they were this week's soup. You have a working formula that you then adapt to the new fresh materials. Then you taste and modify. Each method has its value and its shortcomings. We learn from each other all the time, and we jointly modify our process, aiming for freshness, excitement, and evocative results.

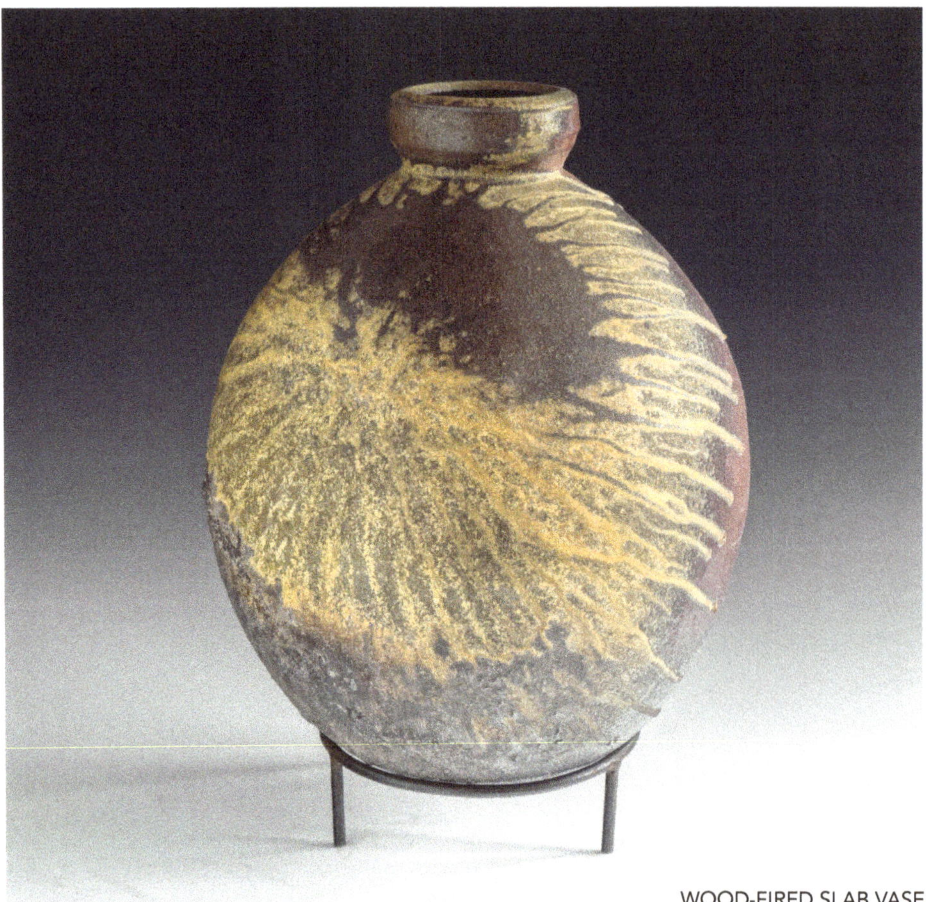

WOOD-FIRED SLAB VASE

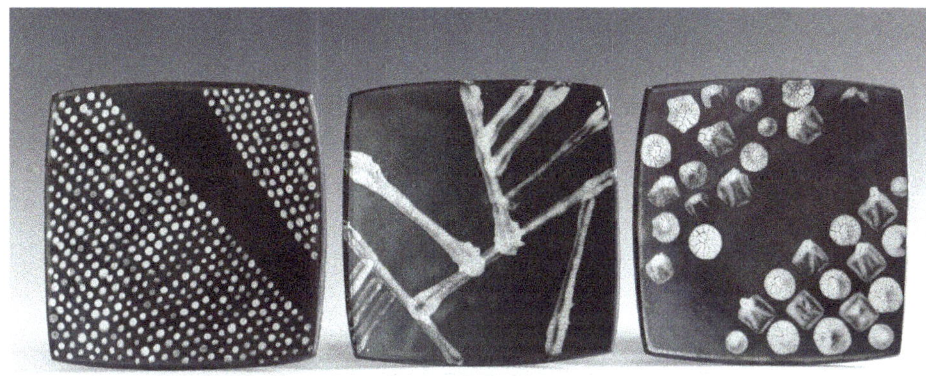

HEX PLATES

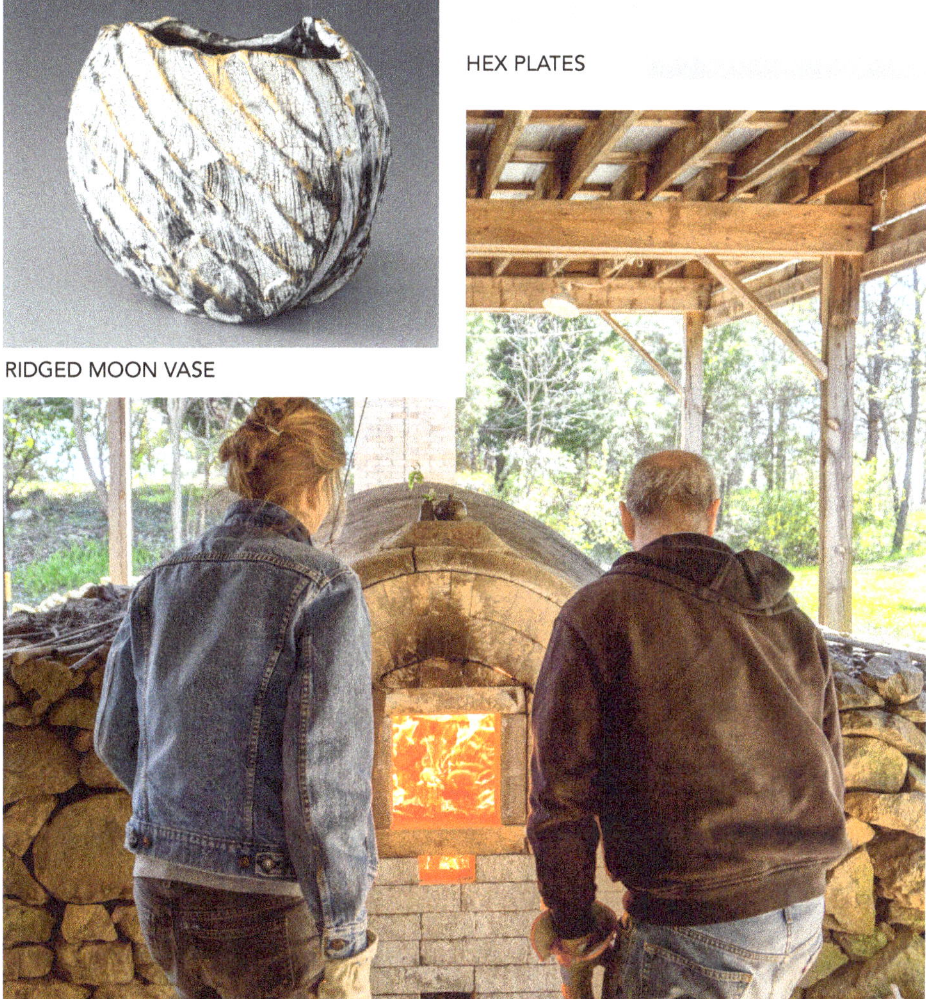

RIDGED MOON VASE

CATHERINE AND WARREN AT THEIR WOOD KILN

We have a wood-fired anagama kiln and a propane gas kiln for glazed work. The wood kiln is large and is fired once or twice a year. Each type of firing influences the other. The gas kiln has a faster turnaround, so ideas can be tested and then be more quickly refined.

The wood kiln is like navigating a huge ship that is slow to change course. It takes a long time to fill the anagama, fire it, and assess the results. We generally try to make clear changes slowly, yet each firing has its own flavor. We like the longer lead-up to firing the anagama. There is room to explore ideas and be innovative in the stacking. We do not use glaze, and so each object influences how the ash flows to the surrounding work. Warren often describes the flame moving through the kiln as being like a current moving through a stream; our pots are the boulders that disrupt the flow, causing the ash deposits and the different forms of flashing that interact with the character of the clay, thus creating the complex variety of natural ash, wood-fired glaze surfaces.

The longer we work, the more the line between what is thrown and what is handbuilt gets blurred. Handbuilt work is put on the wheel, while thrown parts get assembled off the wheel. The largest work is almost always coiled and paddled. It is stacked in the very front of the kiln, adjacent to the large firebox. These pots become partially covered with the massive bed of coals that fill the firebox as we reach cones 11 to 13. Plates are often fired in stacks of four to six (separated by clay wads that are removed after the firing). Plates are thrown, slab built, or even some combination of the two.

Because the wood kiln floor is cool, where less ash is deposited, we have found it useful to make our own patterns using ash, basalt rock dust, or porcelain clay dust. This has become one of my favorite stacking areas because there's a tight connection between the clay object and my ever-ongoing painting, drawing, and journaling.

The accompanying how-to images show one example of making a set of slab plates with a continuous porcelain clay dust drawing. These slab plates are directly influenced by our local landscape of rolling pastures with windblown grasses. I often feel that what I am looking at moves through my body and out my hands. Just as when I draw or paint, I am testing my hand against what I see.

In the dust print images, I prepared a set of circular, stiff slabs using our tabletop North Star slab roller and some circular, stainless steel pastry rings. With limited space, we like a slab roller that can be put away. I will do a drawing as a warm-up and plan, but I will often improvise off of a drawing once I'm actually working with clay. We have lots of simple bisque mold shapes that can be used as drape molds or as exterior molds to shape a curve and stiffen a slab. I use simple tools for a dust drawing: a kitchen sieve, a large roll of inexpensive paper, a wide drywall knife, a series of circular baking rings, a pencil, and plastic-tipped brushes. After the drawing is done, the slabs are placed on top, and the pressure applied by the rolling pin picks up the drawing.

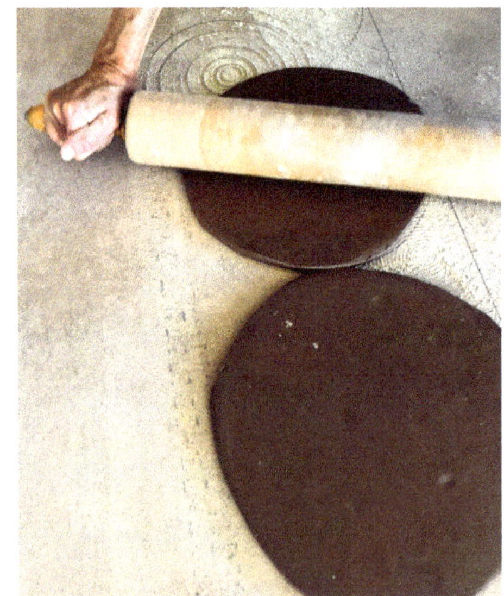

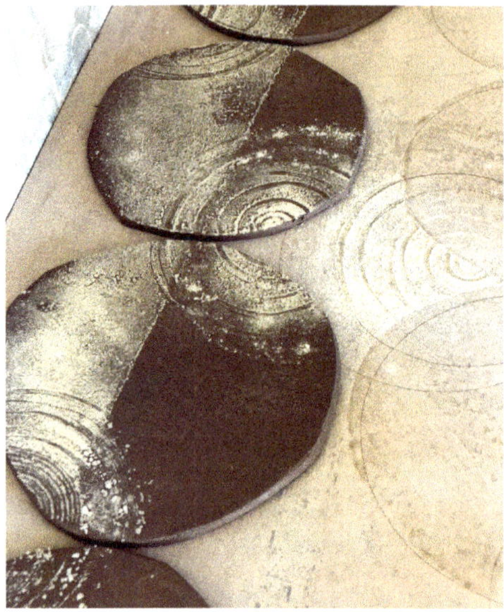

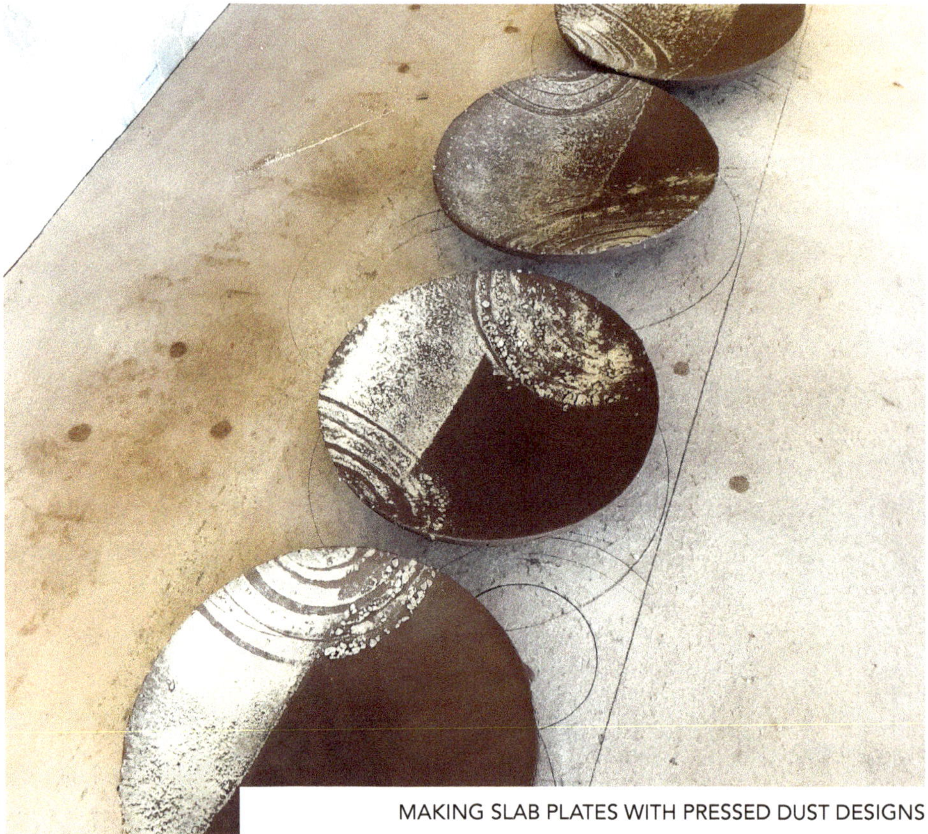

MAKING SLAB PLATES WITH PRESSED DUST DESIGNS

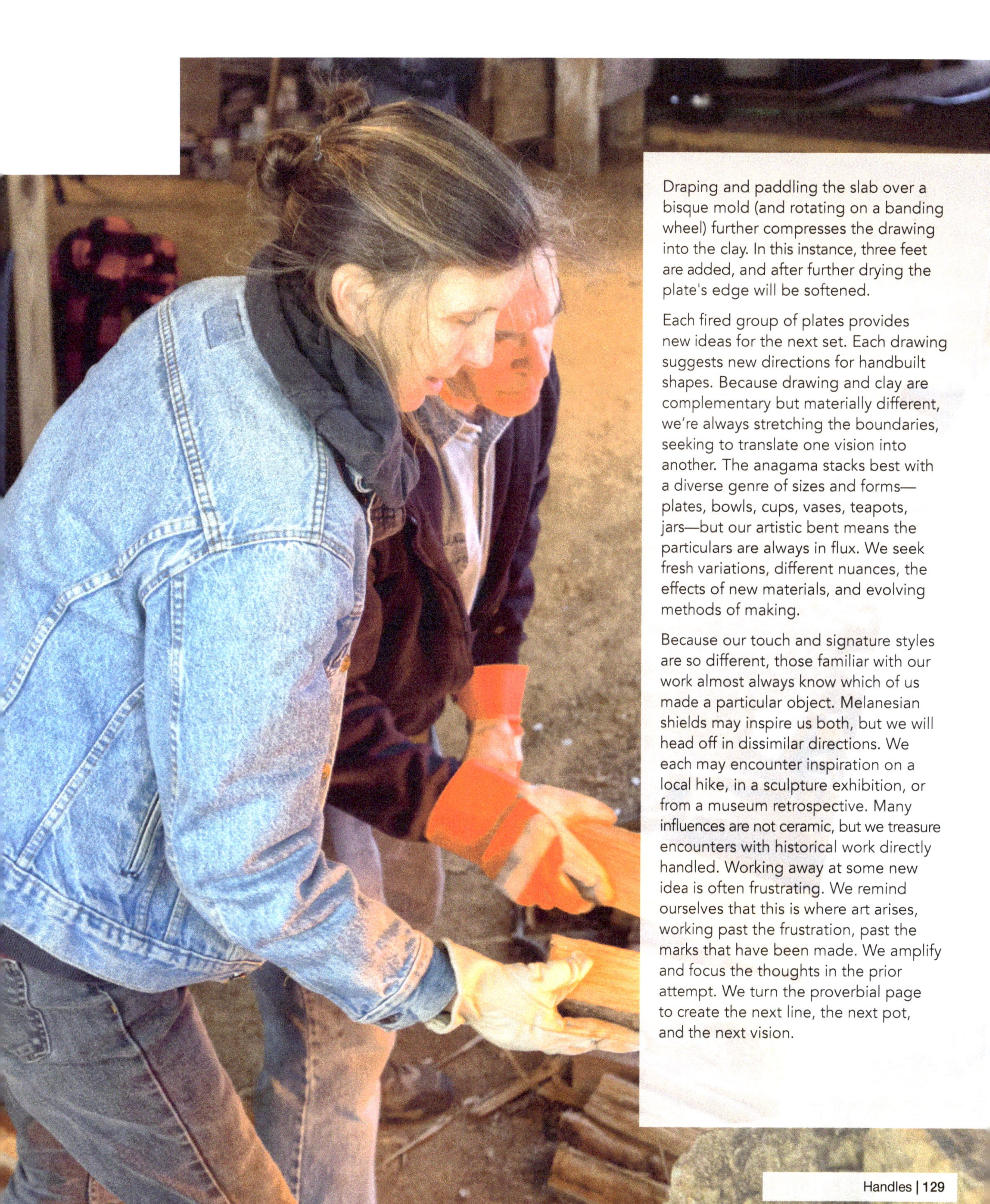

Draping and paddling the slab over a bisque mold (and rotating on a banding wheel) further compresses the drawing into the clay. In this instance, three feet are added, and after further drying the plate's edge will be softened.

Each fired group of plates provides new ideas for the next set. Each drawing suggests new directions for handbuilt shapes. Because drawing and clay are complementary but materially different, we're always stretching the boundaries, seeking to translate one vision into another. The anagama stacks best with a diverse genre of sizes and forms—plates, bowls, cups, vases, teapots, jars—but our artistic bent means the particulars are always in flux. We seek fresh variations, different nuances, the effects of new materials, and evolving methods of making.

Because our touch and signature styles are so different, those familiar with our work almost always know which of us made a particular object. Melanesian shields may inspire us both, but we will head off in dissimilar directions. We each may encounter inspiration on a local hike, in a sculpture exhibition, or from a museum retrospective. Many influences are not ceramic, but we treasure encounters with historical work directly handled. Working away at some new idea is often frustrating. We remind ourselves that this is where art arises, working past the frustration, past the marks that have been made. We amplify and focus the thoughts in the prior attempt. We turn the proverbial page to create the next line, the next pot, and the next vision.

08

Decorating Techniques

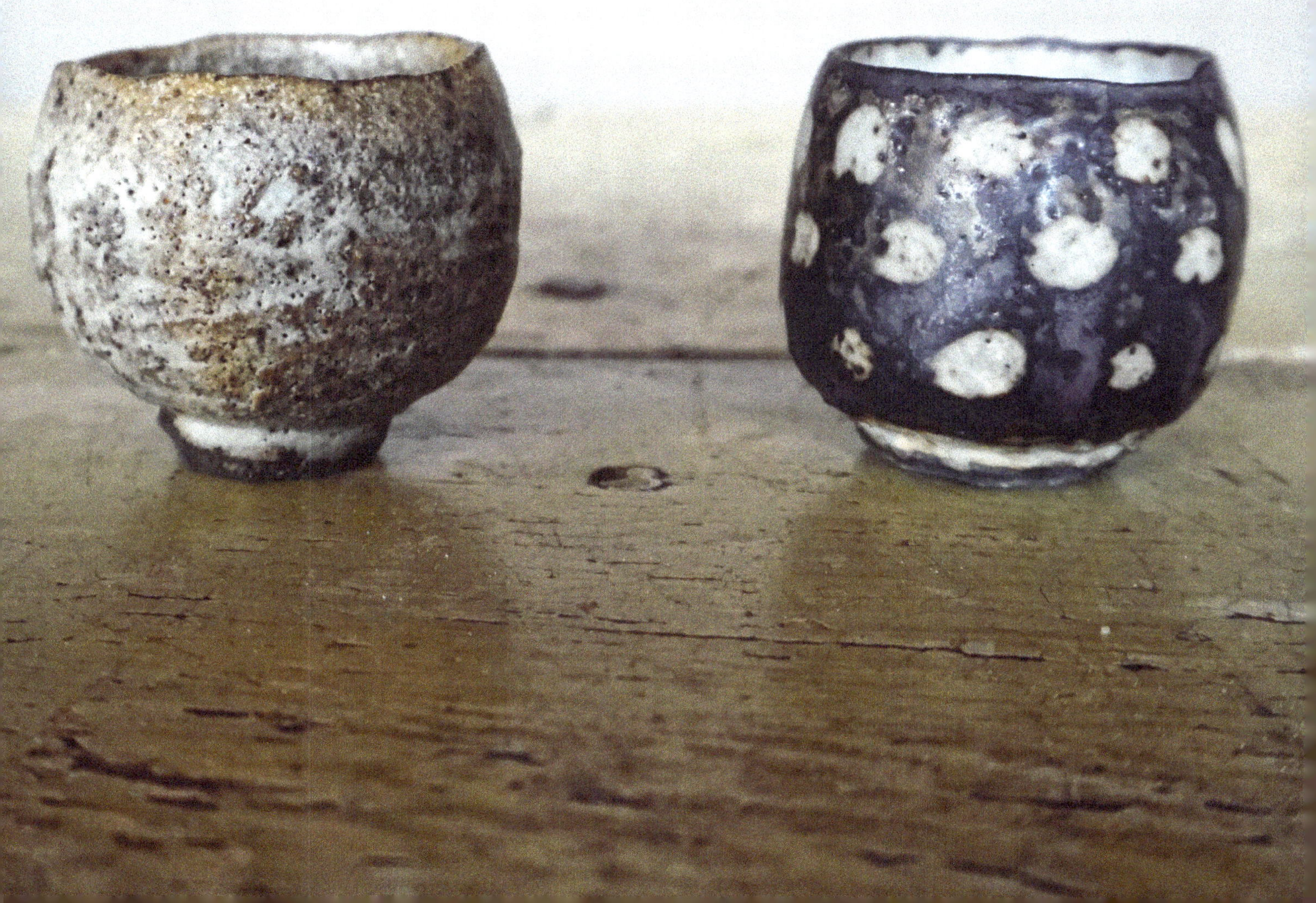

Types of Decorating Techniques

There are many ways to decorate your pots and they come from all over the world. Finger wipes through slip or glaze are a Korean technique best utilized in Onggi pots. Sgraffito is widely used and gives texture to decorating and is traditional in Italian pottery. Hakeme is a Japanese brush technique conveying movement, texture, and spontaneity.

There are carving techniques such as faceting and fluting that change the dynamic of a surface from flat or round to separate planes and edges evoking an architectural feel. Wax resist is a technique that lets you "draw" with a brush onto your pots before glazing for a raw clay design or between glazes for contrast in color.

I like to employ a lot of decorating techniques in my work, as some work better than others for certain pots and ideas.

HAKEME | A technique using a coarse brush to apply white slip.

FINGER WIPE | For this technique, you'll dip your pot in slip and immediately make marks through the slip by wiping your fingers through it.

The slip techniques above are best used with a clear or transparent glaze.

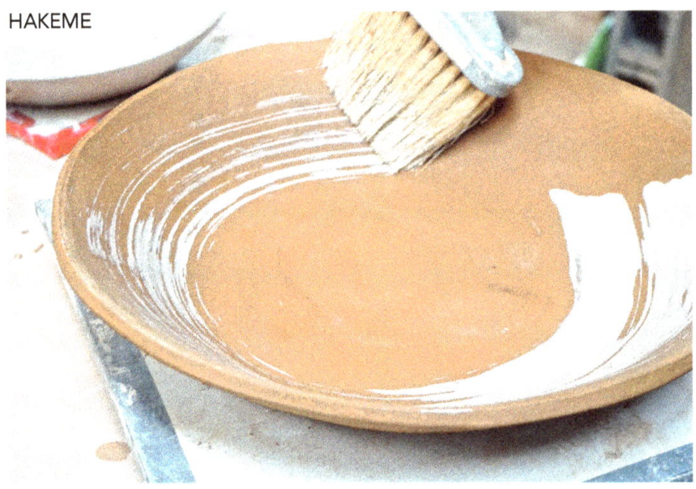

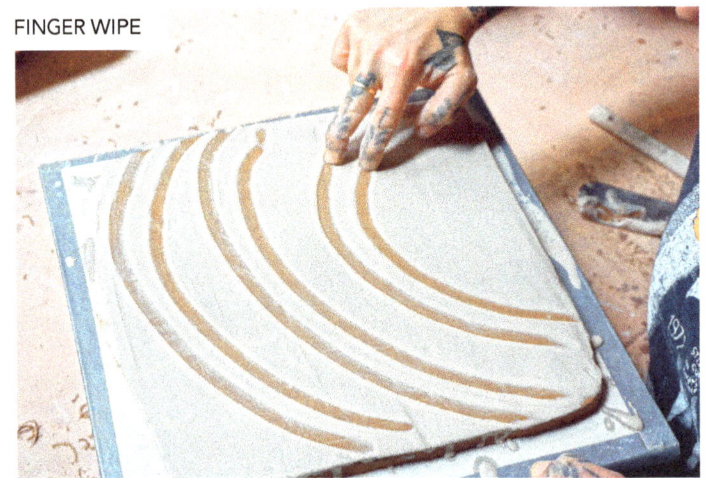

CARVING | I like to carve into the clay body to decorate. This is best done at leather-hard. I use a variety of carving tools, depending on the carving. There is a carving technique using an oval loop tool, called fluting, where I start from the bottom and drag the tool at an angle. The degree of the angle depends on how deep I want to go up to a stopping point. This removes strips of clay, like ridged stripes.

FACETING | This is another carving technique that removes wider strips of the clay wall to create flat panels all around the pot. There are special faceting tools, but a metal cheese slicer with a handle works well. Sometimes I carve the outside and don't glaze it at all. I also carve and then glaze on top. The glazes I use interact beautifully with the carvings, appearing darker or lighter in the raised and recessed areas.

SGRAFFITO | In Italian, sgraffito means "to scratch." This decorating technique is commonly used with slip in ceramics. Dip or brush slip onto your pot. I like to do this when the slip is still damp but not wet, when it's just tacky to the touch. You can use carving tools or a blunt-pointed tool, such as a dull pencil, to scratch through the slip to reveal the clay underneath. I don't like to use a very pointy, sharp tool because the scratched line is too fine and creates burrs.

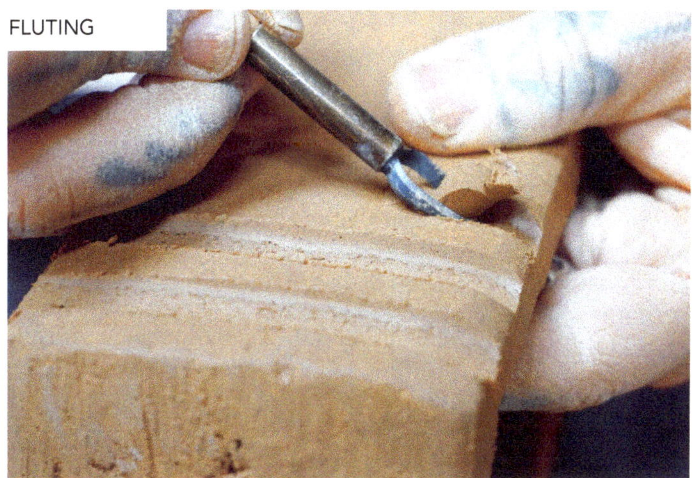

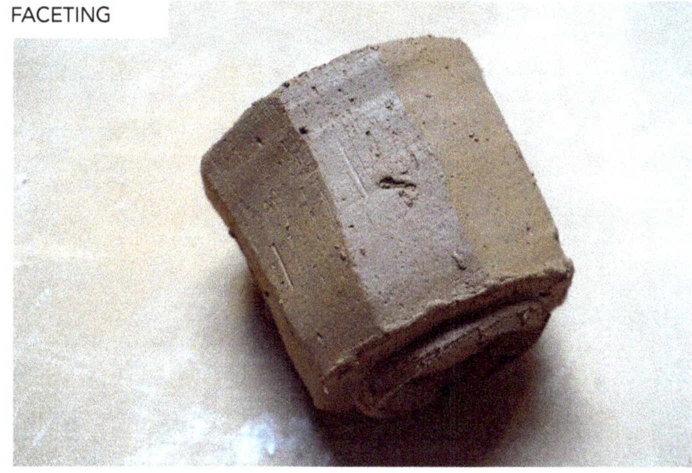

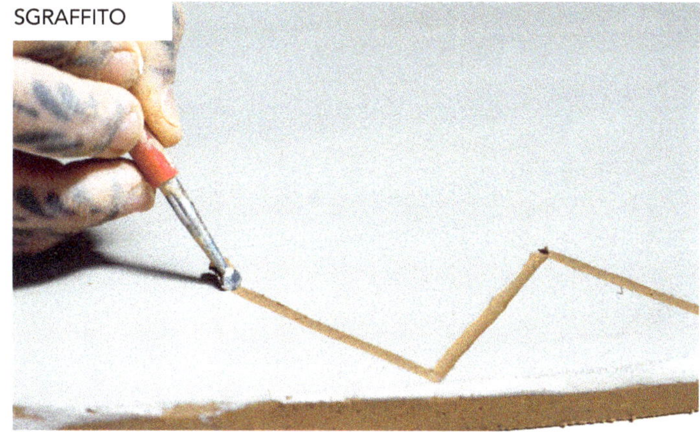

WAX RESIST | Wax resist is commonly used to decorate pottery between layers of glazes and washes. My "black-and-white" pots are made using this technique. I use wax on top of my glaze and under my iron wash. Wax resist can be applied between two glazes as well. Depending on your glaze, you may need to use Mobile or an oil-based wax instead of a water-based wax. Water-based wax on top of glazes can cause the glaze to peel.

You glaze, then paint your design in wax with a brush. Let it dry, then dip it into another glaze or use a brush to apply a wash. Wax resist can also be applied directly to a pot. Then the glaze is brushed on top of the resist. When it comes out of the kiln, the part that was decorated with wax will be raw clay.

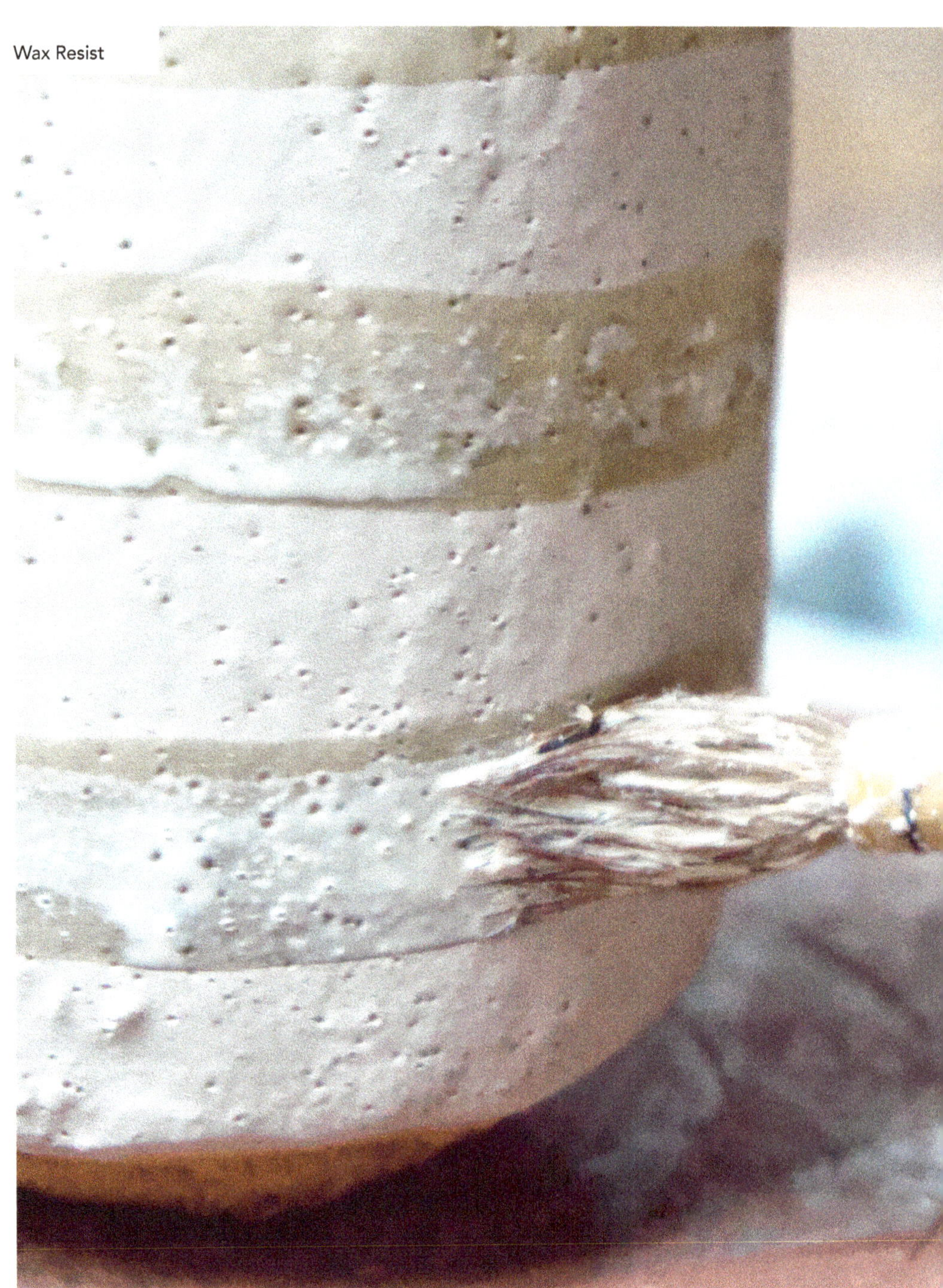

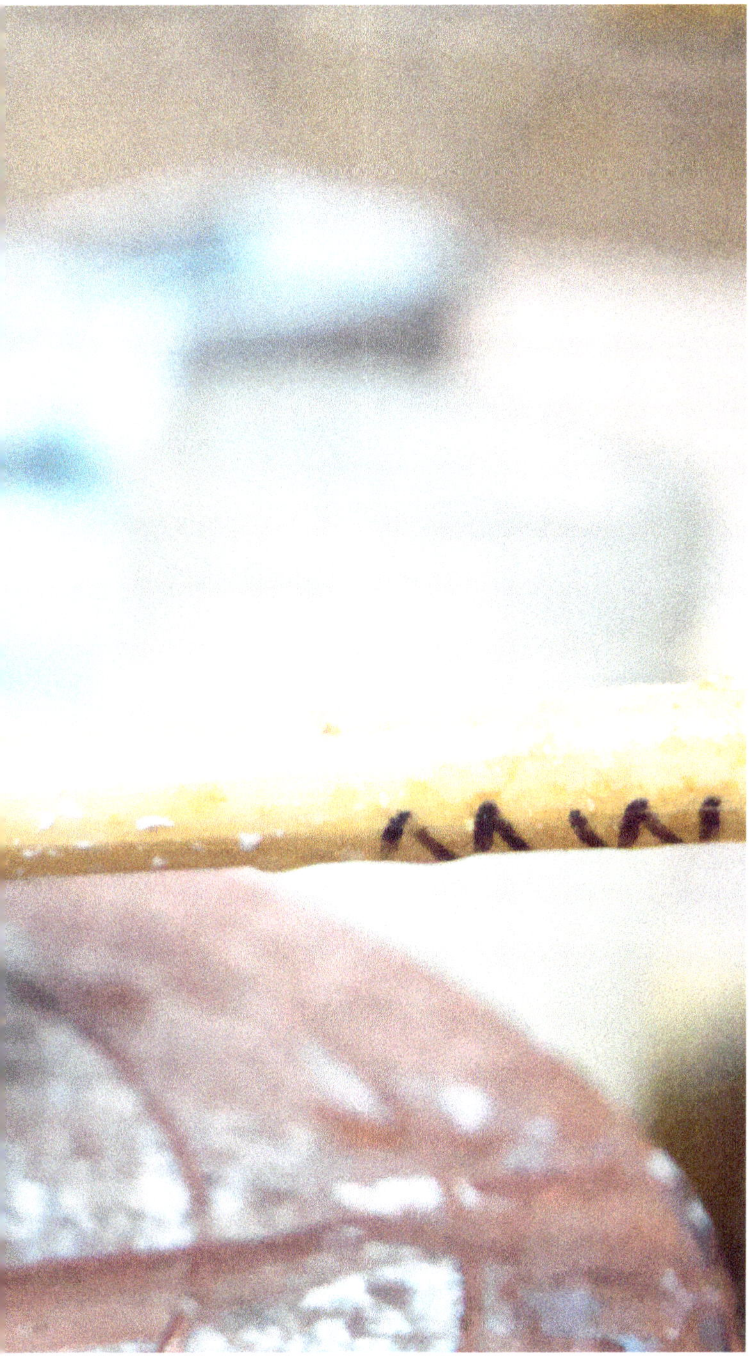

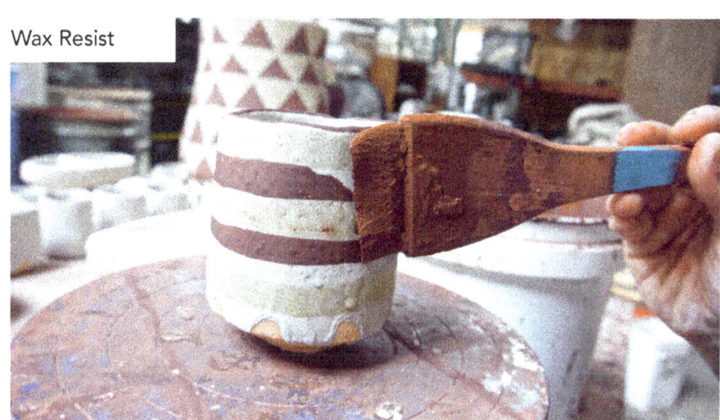
Wax Resist

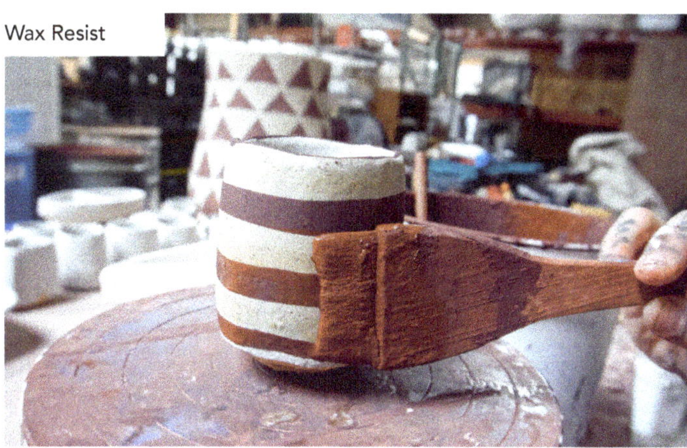
Wax Resist

Shawn Ireland established his pottery in Bakersville, North Carolina, in 1997. Working from a foundation of folk tradition, he makes pots with food, flowers, and candles in mind. For him, that involves using a variety of hand-processed local clays and glaze materials, single firing in a wood-burning kiln, and using a kick wheel. These ingredients promote surprises and keep his craft connected to the natural world.

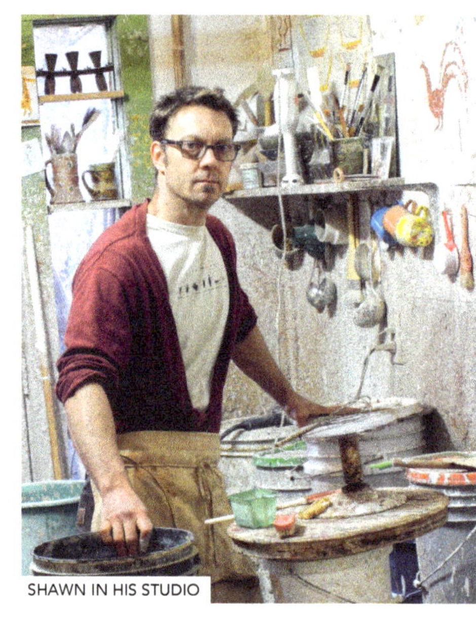
SHAWN IN HIS STUDIO

MW: YOU WERE ONE OF MY EARLIEST MENTORS AND CONTINUE TO BE ONE OF MY BIGGEST INFLUENCES. ROCK CREEK POTTERY WAS YOUR INSPIRATION FOR USING LOCAL CLAYS AND YOU WERE INSTRUMENTAL IN MY EXPLORATION INTO DIGGING AND TESTING WILD CLAY TO MAKE MY CLAY BODY. DESCRIBE HOW USING LOCAL MATERIALS INFORMS YOUR POTS.

SI: It has been exciting to see all of your experiences evolving into such a strong body of work. Will Ruggles and Douglass Rankin of Rock Creek Pottery were inspirational to me in so many ways. Reliable clay materials are crucial to functional pots, and they can be inspiring as well. Choosing local materials with consideration and with respect for their varied characteristics determines the beauty of the fired clay and glaze interface. Blending these materials, with their various particle sizes, by low-tech methods results in a lively, loamy textured clay, which is a pleasure to work with. In turn, textural unpredictability keeps me present while handling the clay. Wild materials promote a very real relationship with nature and a connection to the historic pots I admire.

> **"Choosing local materials with consideration and with respect for their varied characteristics determines the beauty of the fired clay and glaze interface."**

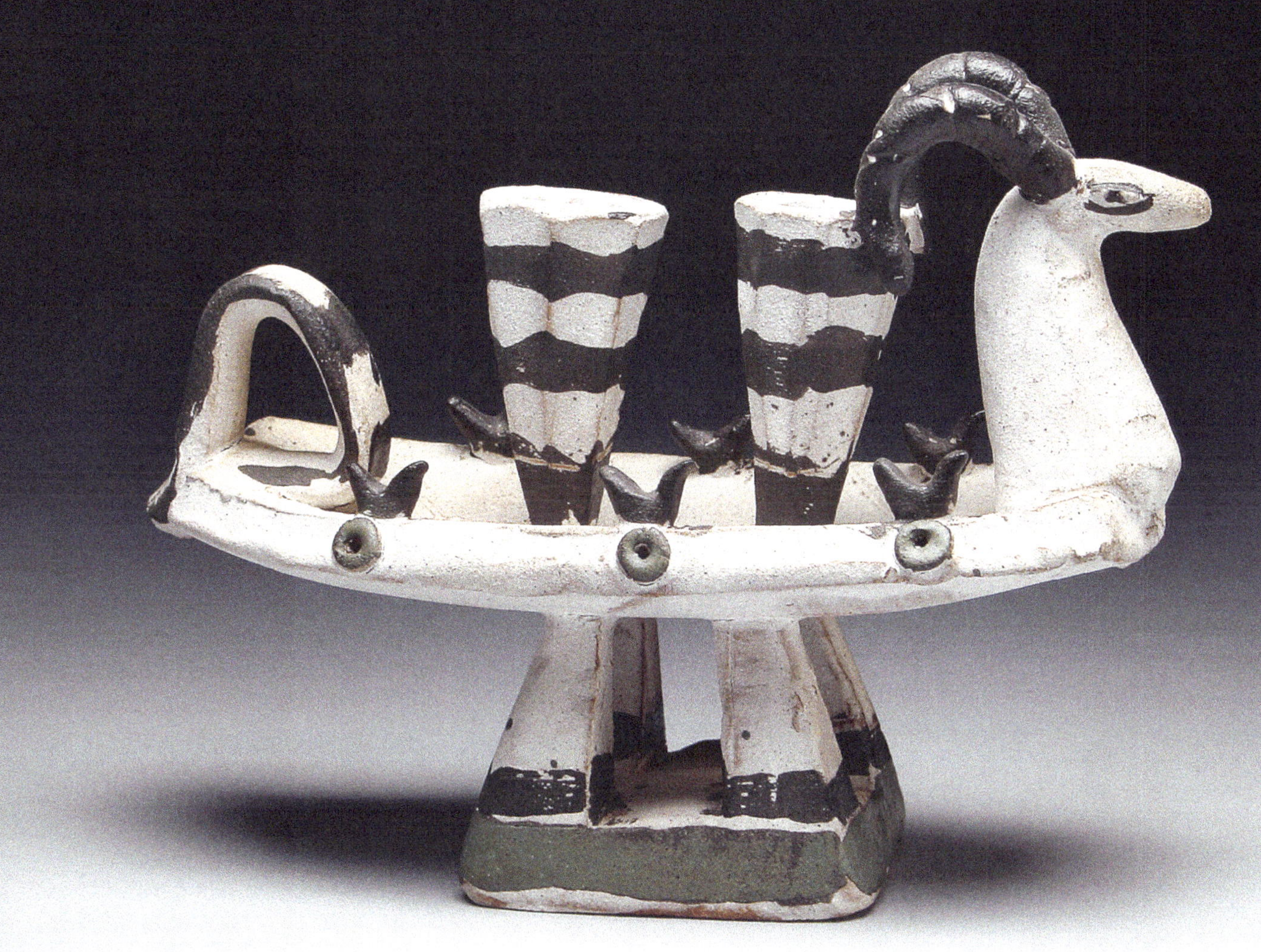

MW: YOU ARE ALSO A PAINTER. WHAT CAME FIRST, POTTERY OR PAINTING? DO THE TWO MEDIUMS COMPLEMENT EACH OTHER? HOW ARE YOUR PAINTINGS INFLUENCED BY YOUR POTTERY AND VICE VERSA?

SI: As a fine arts major at Kutztown University in the late 1980s, I took painting and a few clay classes. I got C's in clay and vowed to never throw again. Beginning in 1991 though, after a workshop at Penland School, Ruggles and Rankin and the intrigue of wood firing reinvigorated my interests in clay.

It wasn't until I was a Resident Artist at Penland from 1996 to 1999 that I returned to painting. I like bouncing back and forth between pottery's earth tones and bright paint colors. Good oils are made from only earth pigments and linseed oil. I'm as fascinated with their natural integrity as I am with clay materials. When I finally lost my fear of the "precious" notions of oil paint, I started using it as freely as clay. That's when painting became really captivating. My pots have become more colorful and eclectic since I began painting more often.

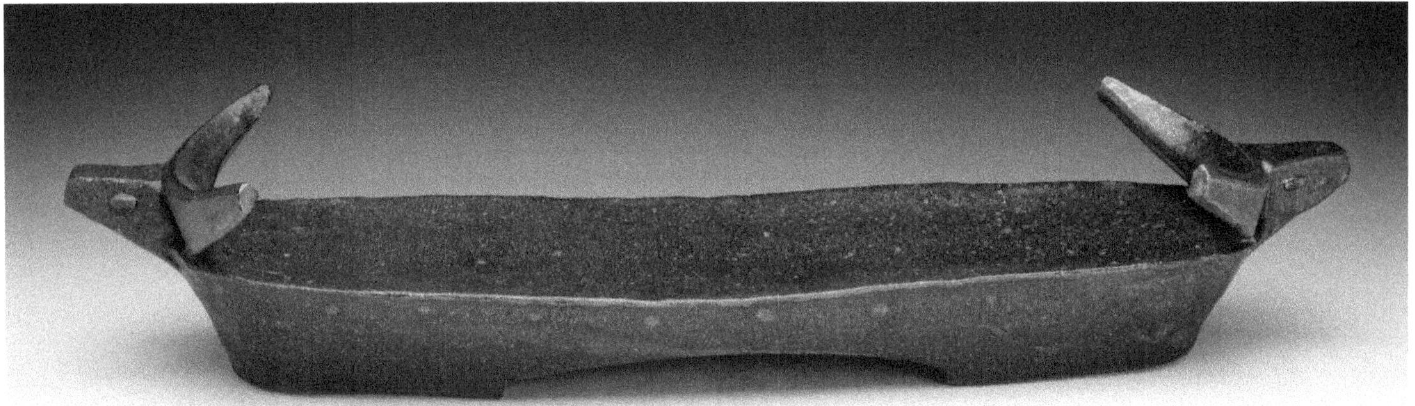

OX-HEAD TRAY

MW: ITALIAN FOLK POTTERY IS A BIG INFLUENCE IN YOUR WORK. HOW DID THIS COME TO BE? HOW HAS YOUR MODERN INTERPRETATION TAKEN THIS ART FORM AND MADE IT YOUR OWN?

SI: Since 2005, I have traveled often to Italy, where for two years I worked with the University of Georgia as their study abroad studio coordinator. Those years in Italy, with its abundant antique markets, were intoxicating. Italian folk pots encourage me to be less serious in the studio. Their casual clumsiness is so friendly and clay-like. Italian culture and years of repetition create this character and inspire me to be as free with clay. It's tricky to not have this desire for "looseness" look forced, though.

Caution provides yet another opportunity to be present when making. While these pots have influenced my stoneware for years, in 2017 I began making wood-fired earthenware after extensive testing. Earthenware clay moves differently than stoneware and it shrinks less, which, I believe, contributes to its retaining a soft surface quality. A multichambered kiln is useful if one likes to diversify. Though it can be challenging to juggle two clays and glaze palettes, they inform each other and refresh my eye.

MW: YOUR HOUSE, STUDIO, AND WOOD KILN ARE ALL SITUATED ON A BEAUTIFUL PIECE OF PROPERTY IN THE MOUNTAINS ADJACENT TO PENLAND SCHOOL OF CRAFTS. IT ALL SEEMS SO IDYLLIC. IS THIS HOW YOU PICTURED YOUR LIFE? DID POTTERY BUILD THIS LIFE?

SI: I was convinced from a young age that I would be an artist but had no plan other than undergrad followed by fame. Instead, I found myself in the restaurant business with my BFA. Via Penland, I discovered new paths I was compelled to follow. My teachers, Ruggles and Rankin, were hugely influential in my art and life choices, and they were proponents of trusting one's gut. My wife, Jo, and I love to create spaces and gardens reminiscent of Italy and South Africa, where she is from, because we want to live in a magical, natural place. Visiting customers seem to enjoy strolling around the gardens and kiln compound, which becomes memorable for them, and then pots go home with them. We are all nourished in this scenario.

MW: HOW DO YOU CONTINUE TO BE INSPIRED?

SI: I am inspired most by that feeling I get when a pot or painting somehow rings true to me. That feeling is so vital that I want to attempt it over and over. Also, world travel, books, museums, and fellow artists inspire me. And my antique treasures never let me down.

MW: YOUR ANIMAL POTS ARE FUNCTIONAL TABLETOP SCULPTURES, PAYING HOMAGE TO FOOD AND CELEBRATION IN A TIMELESS WORLD. I CAN SEE THEM IN A STONE COTTAGE IN THE COUNTRY IN SICILY AND IN A MODERN HIGH-RISE IN NEW YORK CITY. HOW DO YOU THINK YOU BRIDGE THIS PRIMITIVE AND MODERN GAP?

SI: If I bridge that, then I feel successful, but I don't really set out with that in mind. The animalware pots are a combination of all my art interests. There is no formula, but I aim for making them as crudely as possible, blending functional and sculptural elements. I keep working until a balance is struck where they emit an animated spirit while retaining evidence of their inherent materials and processes. I like to think my pots bring a bit of nature and its energy into the home.

SI: The coarse clay I use from Mitchell County, North Carolina, is not very plastic, but it works well when mixed with ball clay, Lizella clay from Georgia, and local feldspar. I mix materials in a cattle trough with a drill and shovel it into drying racks. A 1,500-pound batch is ready to use in about three weeks and yields one and a half kiln loads.

It takes me three months to fill my two-chambered 130-cubic-foot noborigama-style kiln with three to four hundred pots. I throw on a treadle kick wheel, but I also make many of my pots through slab building, hump molds, or handbuilding. Changing techniques allows me to change postures throughout the day, which is critical to a potter's physical health.

All my pots are raw glazed and single fired to cone 9–10, which takes eighteen to twenty hours when both chambers are stoneware, and less time when the second chamber is lower-temperature earthenware. Once the making cycle begins, I am generally a 9-to-5 potter, working five or six days a week. I like a routine and I love a list, taking great joy in checking off pots I make as the shelves fill up.

My firing schedule is determined by show and sale dates. With my own shop as my most consistent selling venue, it has always been a challenge to schedule firings coupled with wood and clay prep, show applications, and non-pottery life. Artists need time. I have never really fallen for the 24-hour clock, because something magic happens with time when one sets out with love, respect, and determination. Limitations can dissolve. I also think immersing yourself in art feeds you in some way that promotes positive energy.

People often remark that the wood-fired pottery process involves so much tedious labor. That's true, but beauty in the pots is the result. Being a potter and an artist is a creative lifestyle, rather than a job, and in every aspect, there is opportunity for connection to nature and for continued discovery.

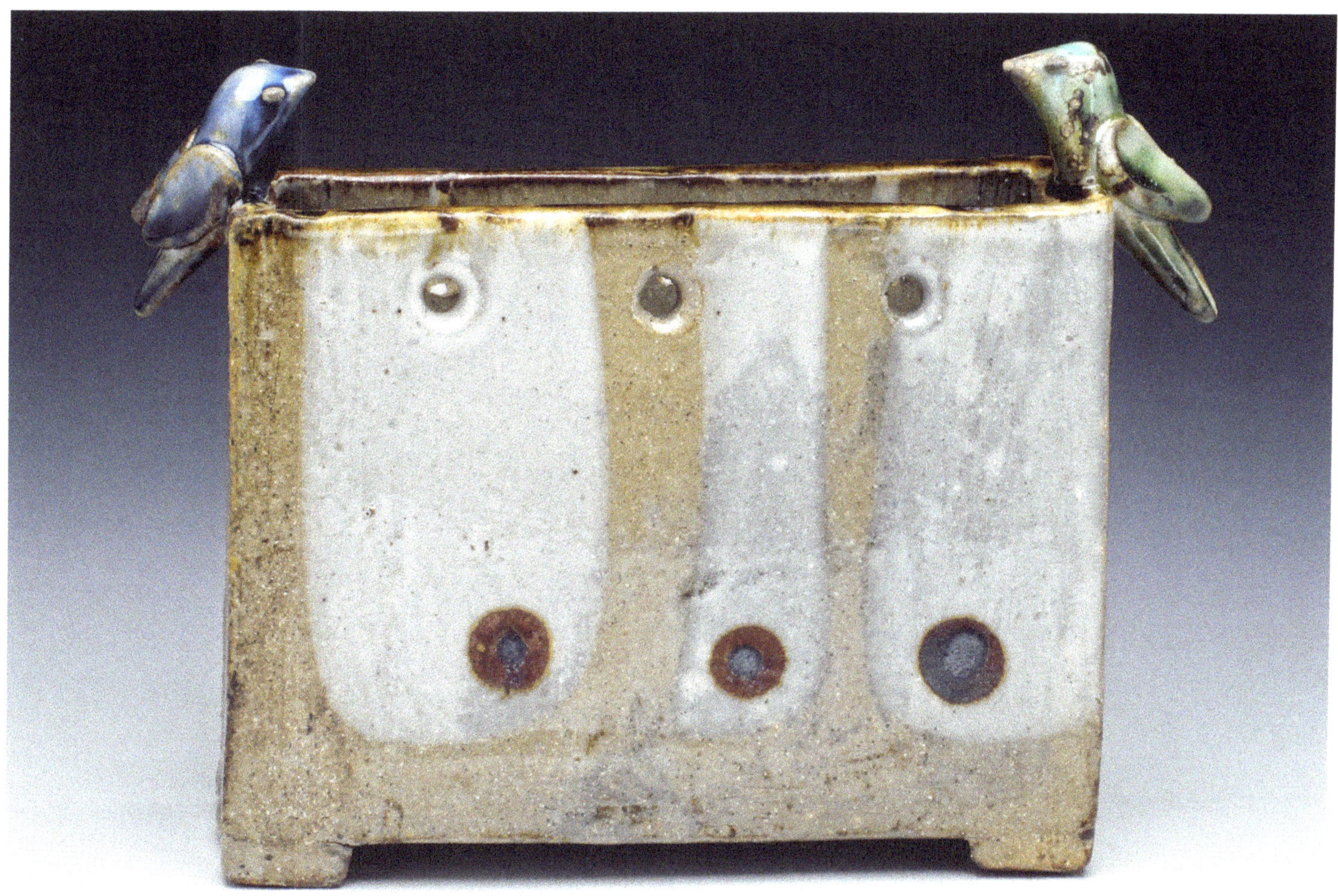

VASE WITH BIRDS

09

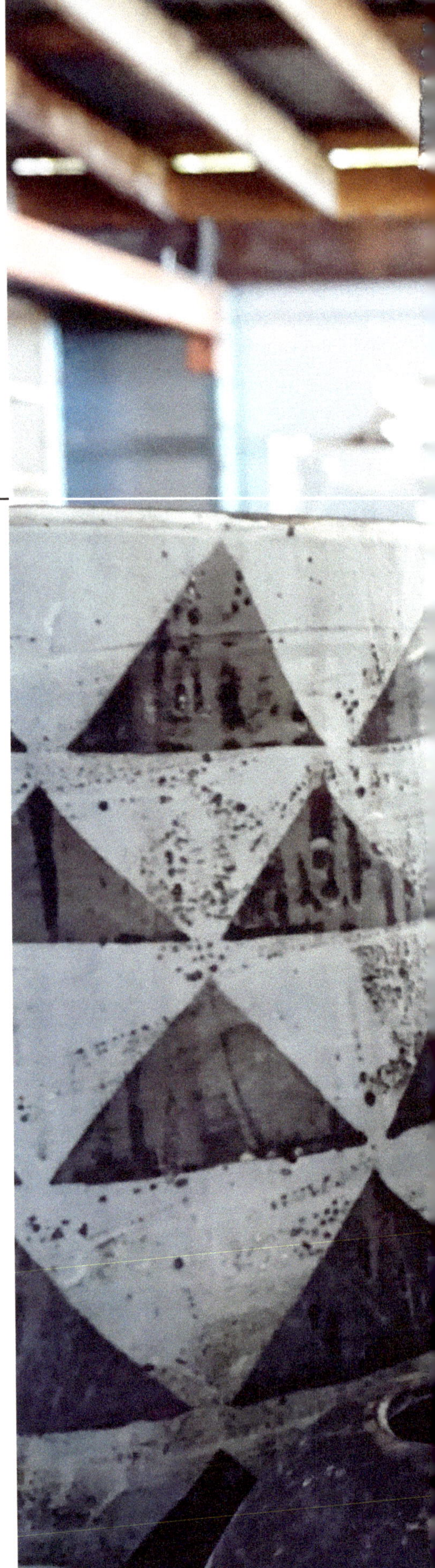

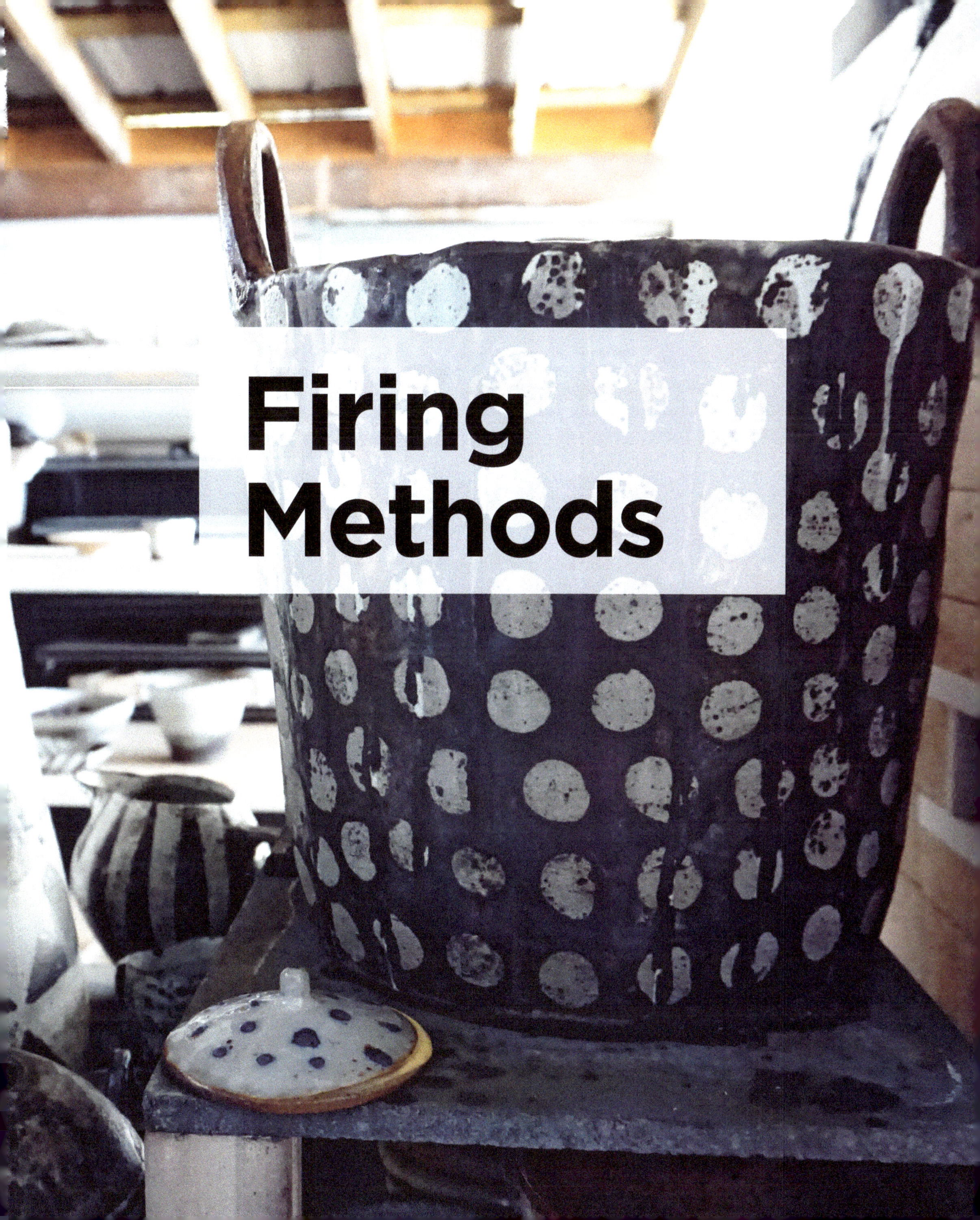

Firing
Methods

Firing and Cones

Crafts don't get much more elemental than pottery. Pots are made with materials dug out of the earth, formed by hand, and fused with fire. About the only difference between making pottery today and in ancient times is that potters now have gas and electric kilns available to them. To talk about firing pottery, we have to define a few essential terms: cones, bisque, slips, reduction, and the types of clay.

CONES | When you hear of cone 10 or cone 04 in ceramics, the term refers to a temperature-gauging system. Pyrometric cones are made from clays that melt at specific temperatures. They are used to measure the amount of heat absorbed by clay in the kiln. The numbers on cones designate temperatures, going from 022 to 01 at the lower range, and then from 1 to 23 and up at the higher range. You'll use cones in both your bisque firings and your glaze firings.

Even if you have a pyrometer—a sensing device that reads the temperature of surfaces—you will need to use cones in firings. They read temperature more accurately, and pyrometers can sometimes fail.

Cones are placed in a kiln in a shallow clay stand called a cone pack. You can make your own cone packs, and you should have them for several different areas in your kiln, such as the top and bottom peeps. Peeps are the spots in your kiln with a removable brick for checking cones. The bigger the kiln, the more peeps and the more areas of temperature fluctuation that need to be checked.

A cone indicates when the kiln reaches a certain temperature by melting. So, in preparing for a firing, you will use cones with a range of firing numbers.

Make a cone pack to hold them in the kiln. Shape 4 ounces (115 grams) of clay into a thick rectangle and pinch up the edges. Then pinch up two ridges that go from end to end though the middle. This will create a clay mound for holding the cones.

Use your needle tool to poke lots of holes all over the cone pack to encourage drying. Cone packs are not bisqued, so they must be bone-dry before they go in your kiln. I try to make them well in advance of a firing.

Stand the cones in the clay, going from the lowest to the highest temperature in two rows. I put the lowest in first—it will melt first, so put it in front so it doesn't melt onto the other cones. Behind that goes the second-lowest, then the third. Then I turn the cone pack and make another row facing the opposite direction, with the next highest cone until the highest cone is in the back. For instance, I use cone 012 at the lower range to determine when to put my kiln in reduction for body reduction, followed by several middle-range cones, such as 04 and 6, to make sure the kiln is firing evenly, and then 9, 10, and 11. I fire to cone 10, but my clay can handle cone 11.

It's a good idea to have a cone above your firing temperature, in the event your kiln is uneven. If cone 10 is down on the top but not even bending on the bottom I can continue to monitor cone 11.

The large Orton cones I use come in boxes of fifty. You can purchase them from most ceramic supply stores. You will want to buy cones that correspond to your firing schedule, regarding reduction and maximum firing temperature. If you want to start reduction at 012, then buy 012 cones. If you are using cone 10 clay, then buy cone 10 and cone 11.

A few in the middle will let you know if your kiln is even or what temperature you are in if you don't have a pyrometer or yours breaks during a firing.

Earthenware clays are low-fire, stoneware clays are mid- and high-fire, and porcelain clays are high-fire. If you buy clay from a commercial supplier, it will be rated by cones. Your clay, glaze, and firings all need to be the same cone rating. This applies to all firings: electric, gas, and wood. Electric kilns will be rated to a maximum cone temperature and the elements cannot exceed that temperature. Make sure, if you want to fire to cone 10 in an electric kiln, that it is rated for that.

MAKING A CONE PACK

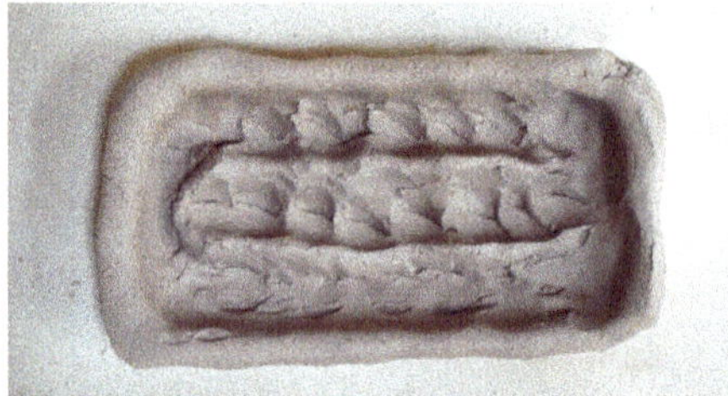

CONE PACK WITH CONES

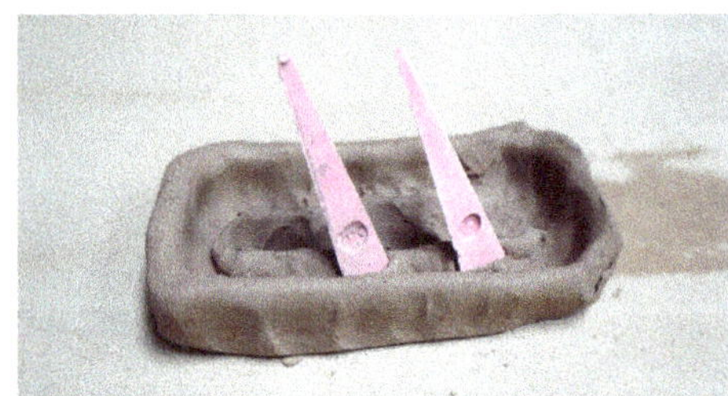

MELTED CONES AFTER FIRING

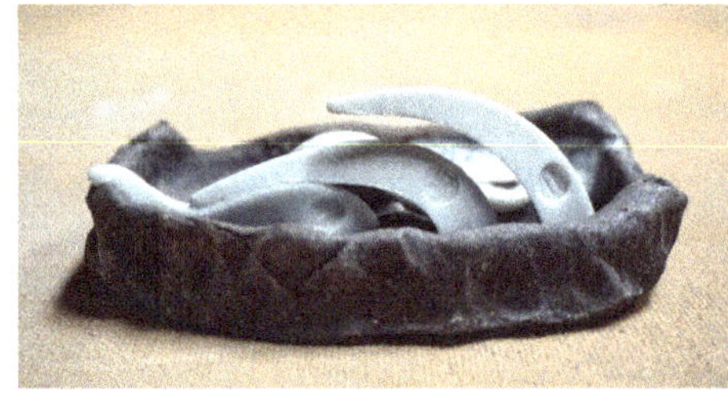

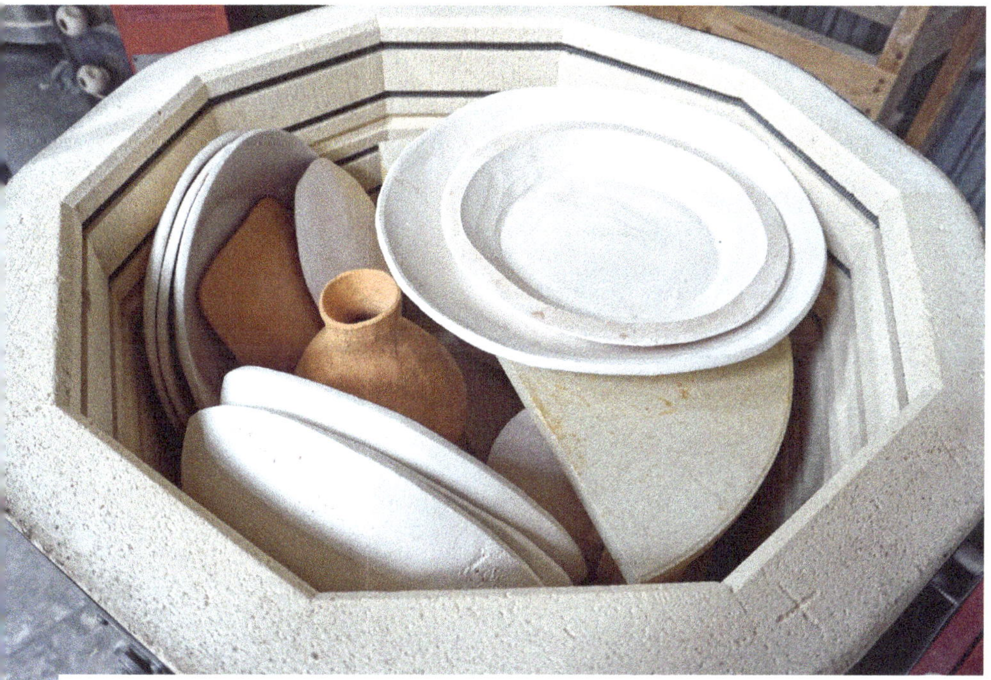

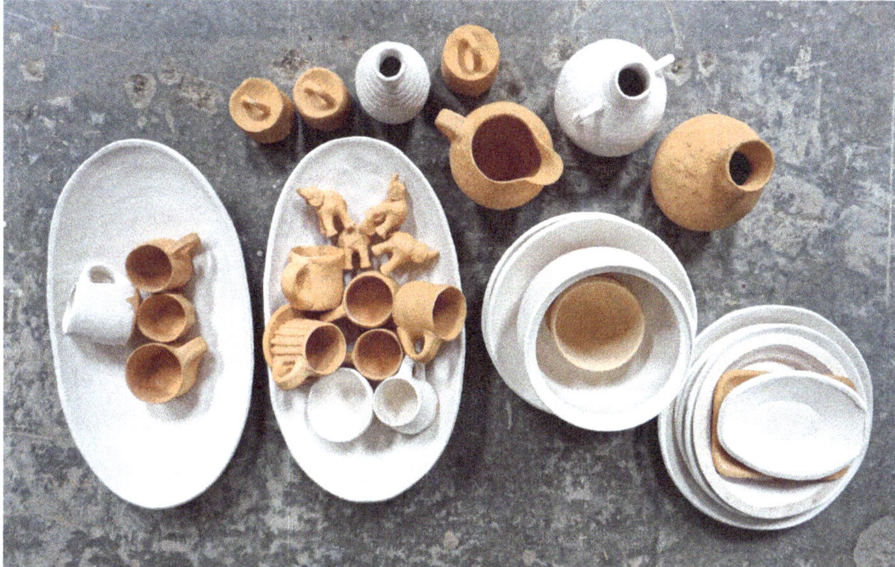

Most pottery goes through two transformative firings. The first, the bisque or biscuit firing, transforms the unfired clay—called greenware—into a hard, but still porous bisqueware. All the moisture and organic matter in the clay disappears during bisque firing—you may be surprised to find that your pots have shrunk. Once bisqueware has cooled, it's ready to be glazed. The porous surface of bisqueware can absorb glaze and is perfect for glaze adherence. Bisque firings are done at a lower cone temperature than glaze firings.

Greenware is ready to be bisqued when it is at least leather-hard, if not completely air-dry. How long that takes is completely dependent on the temperature and humidity levels in your workspace and the size and thickness of the pot. A small, thinner cup on a hot, dry day can dry in twenty-four hours. A larger, thicker pot in the winter or rainy weather can take weeks to fully dry. You'll want to monitor your greenware, turning it over, wrapping fast-drying parts, such as rims and handles, in plastic while it air-dries, to make sure that the pot dries evenly.

If you are firing pots that are not bone-dry, you will need to do a preheat hold—placing the pots in the kiln at a temperature below 200°F (93°C) to let them dry thoroughly. (Water boils at 212°F [100°C], and any water in the clay at this temperature can cause the pot to explode.) The preheat hold can last anywhere from a couple of hours to many hours, depending on how wet the clay is. I typically put leather-hard pots in a bisque with a 12– to 15–hour hold at 180°F (82°C). Pots run the risk of cracking if not dried slowly, especially larger, thicker pots or pots with a lot of attachments. The safest way, if you have the time, is to let the pots dry slowly.

I've explained a few things about slip in the section on glazes on pages 30–33. But slip goes hand in hand with bisque firing, so I'll return to it here. Slip is liquid clay, or slurry. It can be used to cover a pot, like a glaze, or you can paint it onto a pot with a brush for decoration. You can apply slip to greenware before bisque firing so that it fuses with the clay.

I apply my slip to leather-hard pots. Applying slip to bone-dry pots with attachments will likely make the attachments come apart. If you want to apply the slip to bone-dry pots, it's best to brush it on, rather than dipping the pots into the slip. The texture of the slip when fired can look like crazing when put on bone-dry pots and can be beautiful. I use a very iron-rich dark clay and a white slip to add another layer of color, and to provide depth and texture and whiten or brighten my glazes. There are slips formulated for bisqueware, but I do not use them.

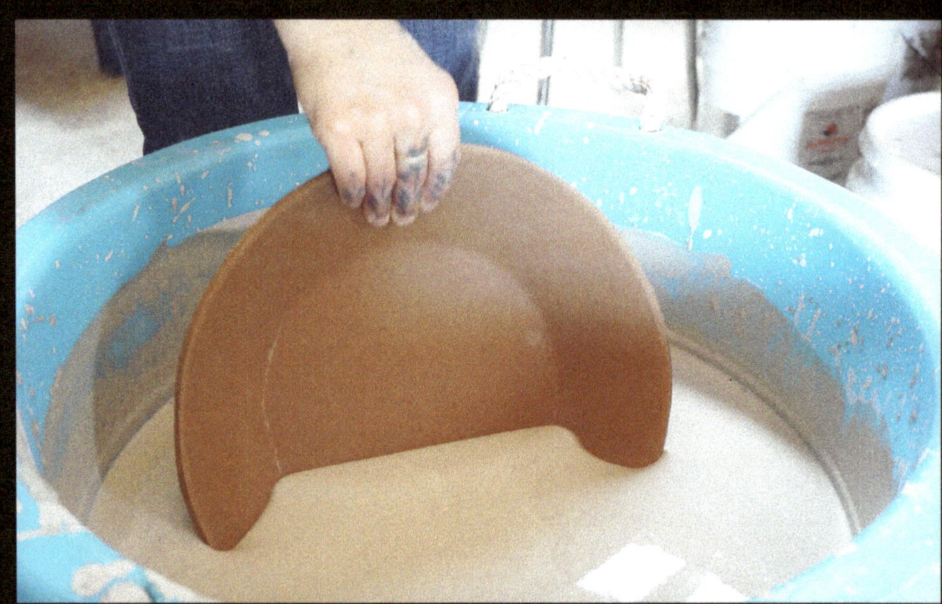

YOU CAN APPLY SLIP TO COVER A POT IN ITS ENTIRETY BY DIPPING IT.

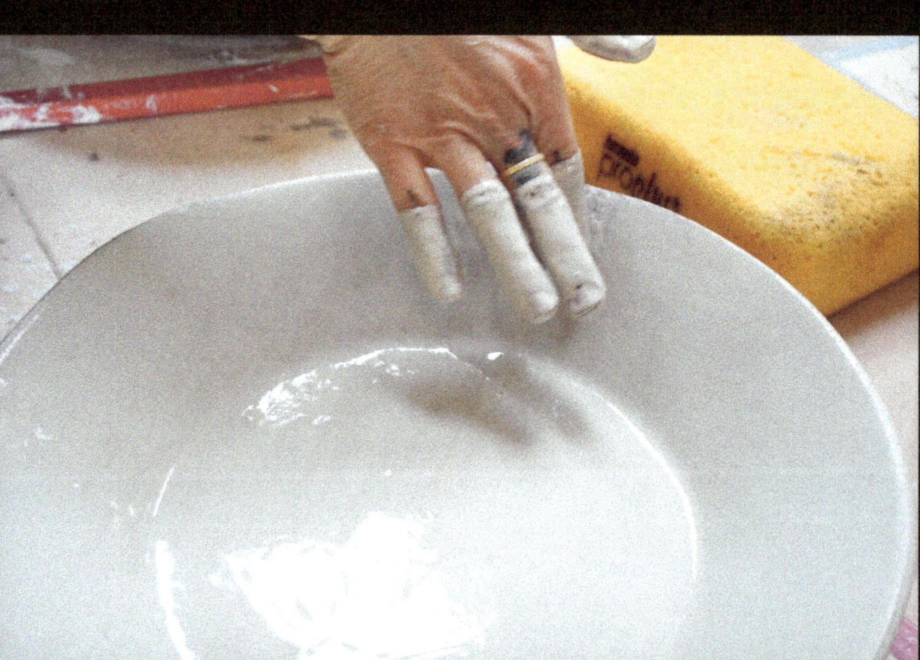

About Kilns

REDUCTION

In firing pottery, the term "reduction" refers to reducing or eliminating the amount of oxygen inside the kiln when the pots are fired and cooled. Glaze and clay react to oxygen, or the lack of it, and reduction firing creates wonderful variations in the finished pots.

A kiln—whether electric, gas, or wood-fired—is always rich in oxygen at the start of a firing. That is necessary, so that sulfur and organic compounds can be burned off. Electric kilns remain high in oxygen throughout the firing—you cannot reduce the amount of oxygen in an electric kiln. Gas and wood-fired kilns, on the other hand, can be adjusted. To a degree, you can control the outcome of the glazes. More about that in the gas kiln section ahead.

TYPES OF CLAY

There are generally three categories of clay bodies used in ceramics: earthenware, stoneware, and porcelain.

Earthenware is considered a low-fire clay, firing to cone 04 to 06. Earthenware clays are easily worked, and, after firing, remain somewhat soft—they chip easily and the surface can be scratched with a knife. Because it doesn't vitrify (become glasslike) in its low firing, earthenware remains porous—it must be glazed in order to hold water.

Stoneware clays include mid-fire and high-fire varieties: mid-range are generally cone 4 to 7, and high-fire cone 8 and above. There is a wide range of stoneware clays that range in color, from buff to light and medium grays and reds. High temperatures allow stoneware clays to vitrify or semi-vitrify during firing, so they are watertight when fired, and extremely durable. The clay I make is a stoneware clay.

Porcelain is the strongest, purest clay body used for high fire. Porcelain typically matures at cone 10 to cone 13. Porcelain is made of kaolin, which makes it less plastic. A clay body that is less plastic is known as "short" and can be challenging to work with. Porcelain is often described as "cream cheese." It tends to crack more easily and warp during firings. I do not use it.

If you want to mix different colored clay bodies, as in swirl ware, you will need to use clays that fire at the same temperature and you should test them together. The different clay bodies will need to have similar shrinkage rates.

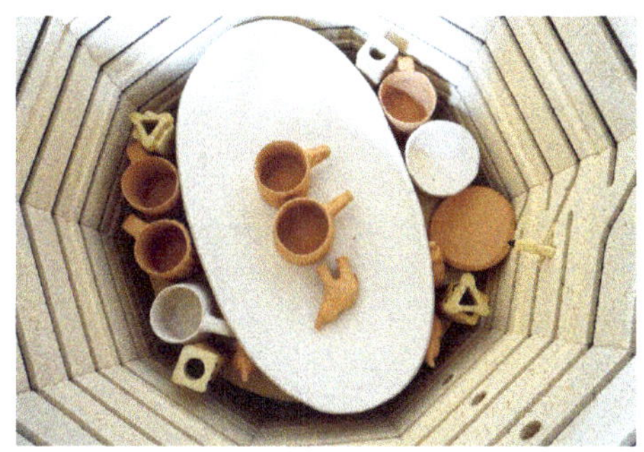

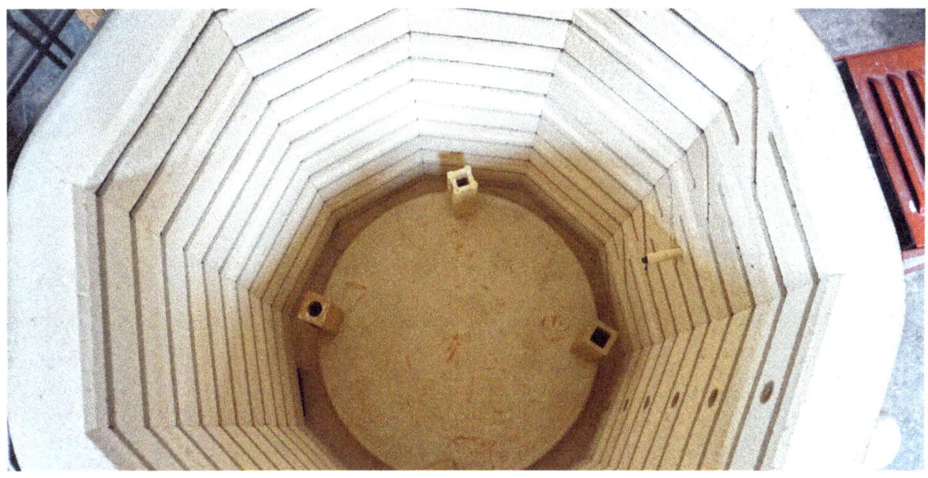

Kilns

CHOOSING A KILN

Not every potter gets to choose what type of kiln to work with. If you live in a large urban area, it's not likely that you can use a wood-fired kiln. In places like New York City, there are very strict laws and codes for using gas kilns as well. The costs associated with fulfilling city ordinances and codes is often prohibitive.

Luckily, potters tend to be a pretty generous and communal group, and in many communities there are lots of opportunities for helping and trading labor in exchange for kiln space. For the first eleven years of my pottery career, I bartered work-trade to get my pots into wood kilns, and I shared and rented communal gas kilns in town. Working communally is a great way to learn the varying methods of firing in many different types of kilns.

Wood and gas kilns are called atmospheric firings because the potter is able to control the amount of oxygen being let in during firing and cooling. So, a wide range of variations is possible, and beautiful, surprising results can be achieved.

Electric kilns fire in oxidation. You cannot do reduction firings, controlling the amount of oxygen, in an electric kiln without modification. You can, however, control the speed of cooling and soaking at high temperature to create interesting and varied results. Electric kilns are much more affordable than gas-fired kilns, and you can operate them in your home, garage, or basement. They can go up to cone 10, but not all do. The higher the temperature, the faster the elements wear out.

You can fire any kind of clay in an electric kiln.

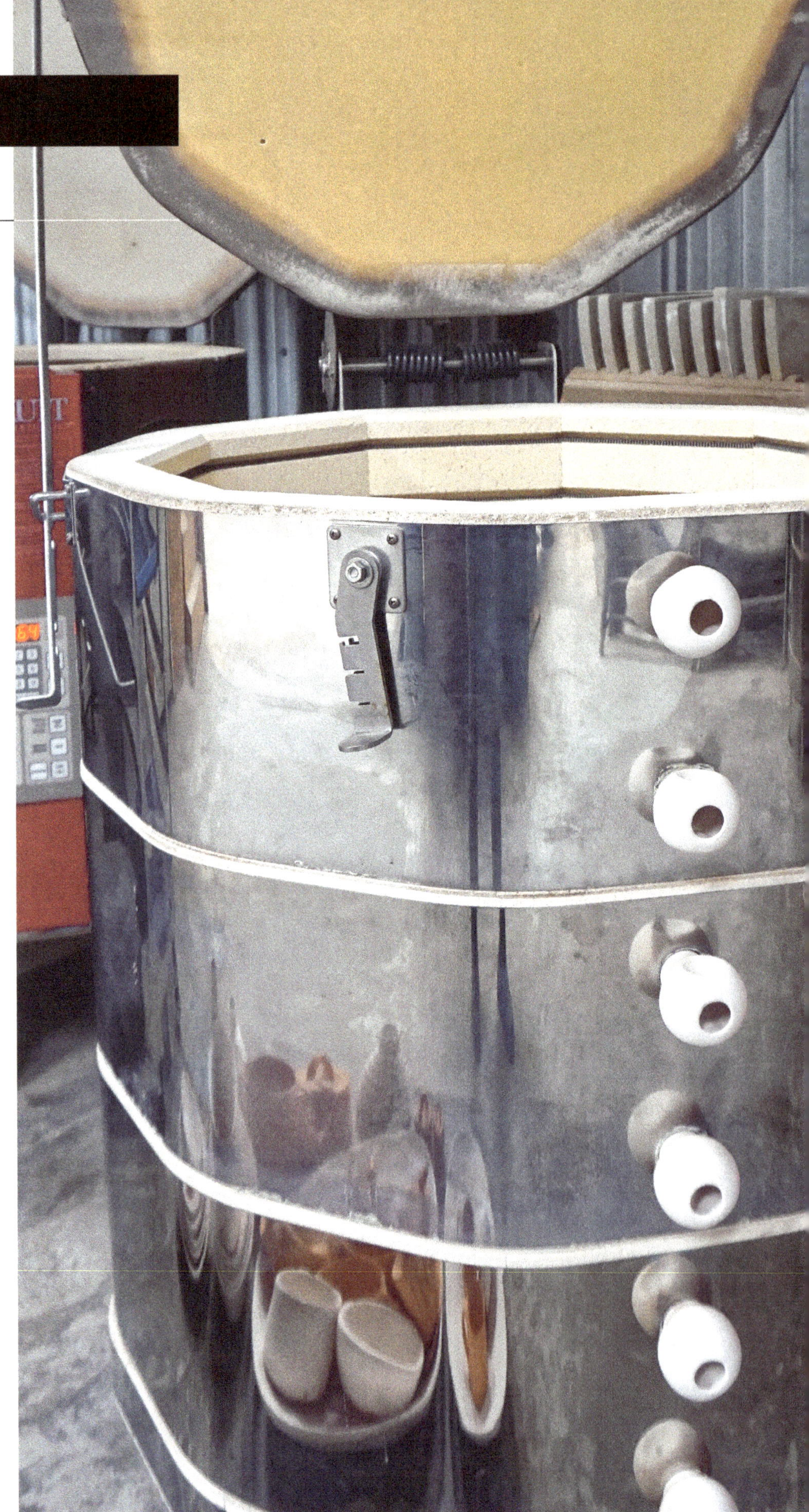

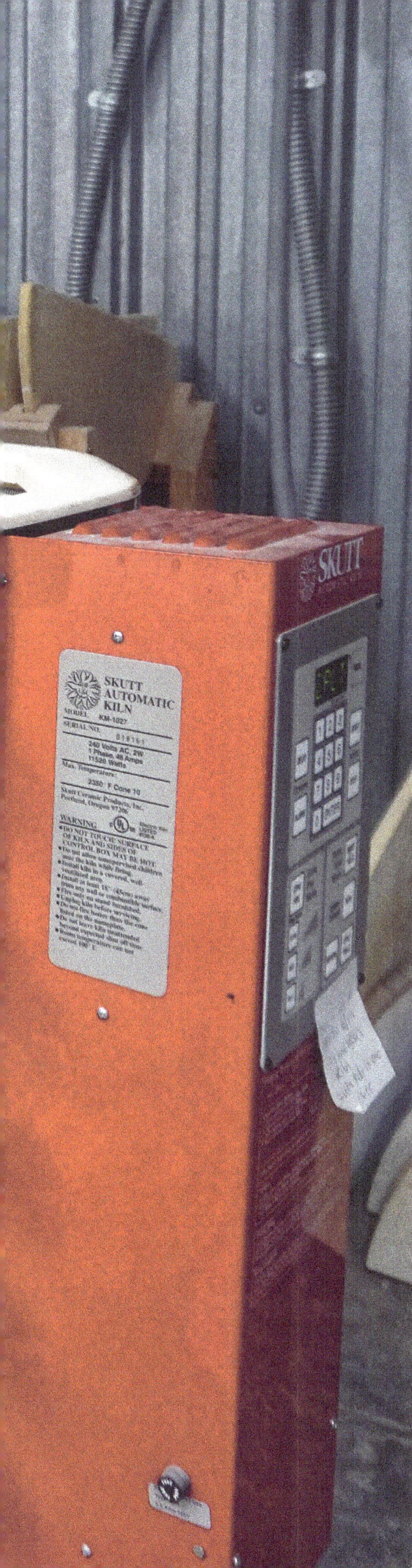

BISQUING IN AN ELECTRIC KILN

I use an electric kiln strictly for bisquing my pots. There are manual and computerized electric kilns. I use a computerized Skutt kiln for more freedom during firing and the ability to program a specific schedule.

A manual bisque kiln normally has separate controls in three segments: bottom, middle, and top. It also has a kiln sitter, which is a mechanism that holds a small cone; when the kiln reaches the temperature of the cone, it trips the kiln and shuts it down.

Electric kilns typically have multiple sections. These sections heat up independent of one another and let the kiln be turned on and heated up slowly. To fire a manual kiln for bisquing, you'll turn the segments on one at a time for specific amounts of time. To dry or hold work at a low temperature in a manual kiln, for instance, you turn on the control to low in the bottom segment for as many hours as needed. Then you turn the middle and top on low. This heats the kiln slowly from the bottom up. Then start back at the bottom by moving to medium and on up. How much time you leave between turn-ups varies. Your electric kiln should have instructions on how to fire it.

BISQUE SCHEDULE IN A MANUAL KILN

After the hold on low, I put the middle and top on low and wait three hours. Next, put the bottom on medium and wait an hour before turning the middle to medium, and then another hour before turning the top to medium. Wait three hours, then repeat with the bottom on high, waiting an hour between the middle and top turn-ups.

Stay near the kiln and wait for it to shut off to make sure the kiln sitter doesn't malfunction and overfire. I bisque to cone 06. To be safe with bisque firing, only fire bone-dry greenware. I sometimes vary from that rule and will bisque pots when they are leather-hard and still contain some moisture—but I had to blow up a few pots in order to figure out a formula for doing so. Water boils at 212°F (100°C), and if there is still moisture in the pot when it gets to this temperature it will blow up. To get around that, I put a hold on my kiln at 180°F (82°C) for up to fifteen hours, so that it finishes drying out in the kiln. The hold time depends on how moist and/or large the work is.

You cannot allow pieces of pottery to touch one another in a glaze firing, because the glazes will fuse them together. But in a bisque firing, with no glazes, it's all right if the pieces touch. I carefully stack pots on top of one another. It is important to fire bisque slowly through quartz inversion. Quartz inversion occurs at 1064°F (573°C). At this point, quartz crystals rearrange themselves into a slightly different order. Firing too fast through this phase can lead to cracking and other serious issues later in the glaze firing.

SLOW BISQUE PROGRAM FOR A COMPUTERIZED ELECTRIC KILN

SEGMENTS 4

SEGMENT 1 50°F PER HOUR TO 180°F HOLD (ENTER NUMBER OF HOURS)

SEGMENT 2 200°F PER HOUR TO 1000°F

SEGMENT 3 100°F PER HOUR TO 1300°F

SEGMENT 4 250°F PER HOUR TO 1828°F

GAS KILNS

After eleven years of using other people's kilns, I finally bought my own, a Bailey gas kiln. By that time, making pots had become my business and full-time job. It made more sense for me to buy a factory-made kiln than to build my own, which would require dealing with code, safety, and bureaucratic regulations that can be difficult and costly to navigate.

Having my own kiln changed everything about how I make pots. I now had the luxury of being able to fire how and when I wanted. I also had the opportunity to "get to know" my kiln and how it fires.

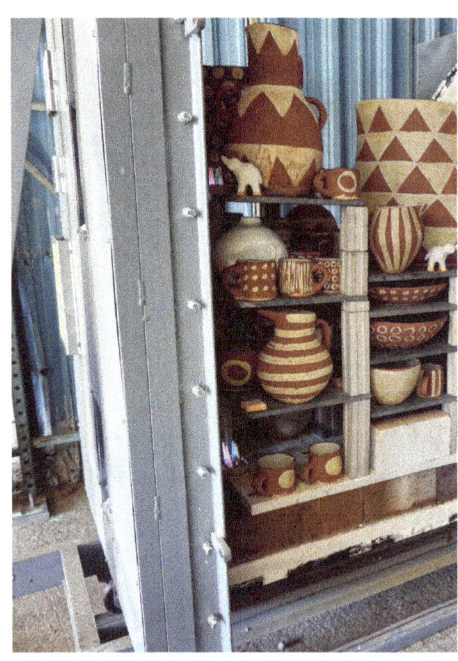

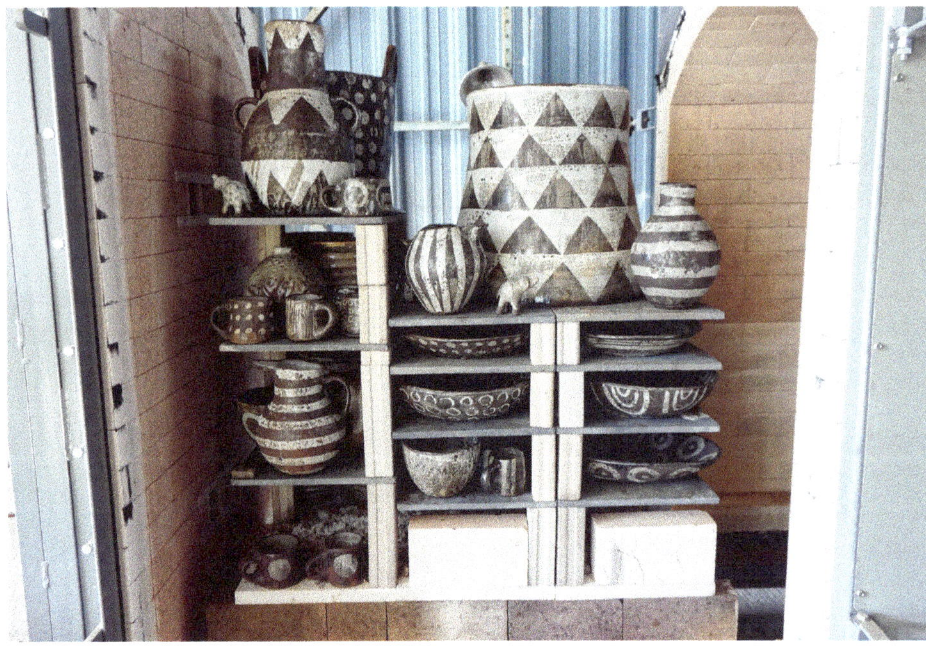

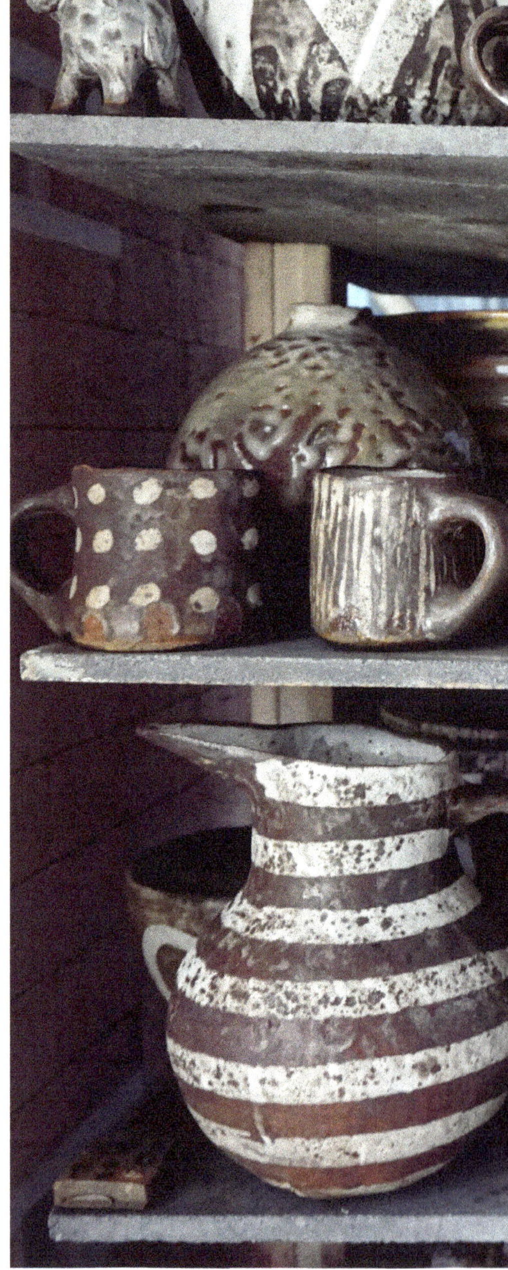

LOADING THE GAS KILN

Once my pots have been bisqued, cooled, and glazed, I'm ready to fire them. Loading a glaze kiln involves thought and patience. When I load my bisque kiln, I am trying to fit as many pots as possible, carefully stacking and balancing them to get them all in; loading the glaze kiln is completely different. The pieces cannot touch each other, or they will fuse permanently one to another during the firing.

It took me a few firings to get to know my kiln and how the temperature and reduction varied in different parts of the kiln during firing. Some areas got hotter, some more reduced. Knowing all of this helps me make decisions about where to place certain pots.

My kiln is a cart kiln. The stacking area is on a cart that attaches to the kiln door and rolls in and out of the kiln on a track. I have 18 cubic feet of stacking space. This holds about 100 to 150 pots in a typical mix of platters, cups, bowls, and pitchers.

I start by putting my cone pack on the bottom in front of the peep. My kiln takes three 12" × 18" (30.5 × 45.7 cm) shelves per level, but these can be staggered. On the first level I leave an empty channel from the front to the back, because I'll need space to add wood sticks during the cooling (more about that in the reduction-cooling section ahead).

I load the kiln by putting pots of similar heights on a shelf, being careful that none of the pots touch each other. I insert stilt supports that are at least a ½" (1.25 cm) taller than the tallest pot on that shelf and when the shelf is full, I add another shelf that sits on top of the stilts. When using stilts, it's important to use three to a shelf and that they occupy the same spot on each shelf from the bottom up. If the stilts are in different places on each shelf, they won't provide enough strength, which can cause a shelf to break in the firing. I continue to stack in this fashion until I reach the top.

REDUCTION FIRING AND COOLING

My gas kiln is easy to fire. It takes me about twelve hours to get to cone 10. I use the R1 reduction firing schedule in John Britt's book *The Complete Guide to High-Fire Glazes*. It is a schedule based on degrees per hour and reduction. It calls for a heavy reduction around cone 012, then a medium reduction until it reaches cone 10.

The way I reduce my kiln is to push the damper in a few inches to limit the amount of oxygen coming into the kiln. When the kiln is deprived of oxygen, it enters a reduced atmosphere. This reduction can be light to heavy and can have huge effects on clay bodies and glazing.

When and how much you reduce the oxygen matters. Body reduction, which affects the clay body, happens at 012. Different glazes react to how and when reduction is introduced. Iron, for instance, reacts very strongly to reduction. Iron-rich clay bodies will vary from light orange to black, with purples, reds, browns, and all variations of those colors within them, from light to dark. You can see a great example of this is in old factory bricks. If you look at a brick wall of an old building, you will see these colors varied throughout the bricks. They were made from an iron-rich clay and in the firing, were all exposed to a different amount of reduction.

KEEP A KILN LOG

The best way to figure out how much reduction, and when to do it, is to experiment and keep good kiln logs for each firing. Referencing these notes is key to understanding what is happening and how to adjust or repeat your firings.

Curiously, once I figured out how to fire for the look I wanted from my clay and glazes, I got bored! Instead of feeling excited with the anticipation of discovery when I'd open a kiln, the pots just looked the same each time! That was nice, of course, but nice pots are not all I am after. I want strange pots. Weird pots. How-did-this-happen pots. Whoa pots! I want pots that make me think about what I'm doing and inspire me to try new things. And I want pots that teach me lessons and encourage me to grow. Creativity is a living beast and needs to be fed or it will die. Feeling anxious that I would be stuck or bored or uninspired, I took down the pots from my keeper shelf.

My keeper shelf houses a collection of pots that I've kept over the years. These are pots that were exceptional or so strange that it was unlikely I'd ever achieve their finished look again. The collection has become a reference of my forms, glazes, and firings.

REDUCTION COOLING

I looked at some plates that I kept from a reduction-cooled wood firing that I participated in a few years back. In this process, the kiln is kept in reduction throughout the cooling. A true reduction cooling would allow no oxygen. This firing allowed some oxygen, so technically, it would be called a controlled cooling. I studied these plates, each of which had a different glaze. They were the start of something that wasn't quite realized yet.

When I decided to keep these plates, I had a sense that they were important to keep, even though I didn't understand why. But when I looked at them again now, I knew instantly that I wanted to reduction cool my gas kiln. I started to do some research on the process but couldn't find too much about it. There aren't a lot of potters doing reduction cooling, and the ones that do mainly use wood kilns.

I got a few questions answered and some loose guidelines, but that was all. I decided to just go for it. We fired the kiln up to temperature about 2350°F (1287°C) as normal, but then, instead of sealing up the burner ports and pushing in the damper and calling it done, as we had in all previous firings, we sealed up one burner port and kept the gas on low in the other. We pushed the damper all the way in, so as not to let in any oxygen, and we pulled out the peeps every so often to register how much flame was coming out of the hole.

The amount of flame exiting from the peep hole is a good indication of the degree of the kiln's reduction. We didn't know how much reduction to give it, so we just guessed. We kept it quite well reduced. We had already learned previously that for the clay to go black,

we needed to cool in reduction until 1550°F (843°C). We used an oxyprobe, which reads the level of oxygen in the kiln, and we kept that number at about 700.

It took twelve hours to reduction cool the kiln. It was a twenty-four-hour firing, all in all. After a very long day of waiting for the kiln to be cool enough (200°F [93°C]) to open, we—both excited and nervous—opened the kiln. WOW! It worked!! It was incredible.

RICH BLACK TO ROBIN'S-EGG BLUE

Due to the reduction in the cooling, my iron-rich clay body went black. Normally in a reduction firing without a controlled cooling, my clay would get a nice red color, similar to brick. My Ru celadon went from its previous shiny greenish color to an icy, matte robin's-egg blue. My iron decoration on the ash-glazed pots was a rich black, with varying shades within it.

The pots looked old, spooky, smoky, and rich. I hadn't expected such beautiful results the first time through. I also hadn't known what I wanted out of the pots until I had it, but I felt like I'd achieved the unknowable result that I was hoping for.

This first successful experiment was encouraging. It motivated us to keep going with it. We have since reduction cooled all of our kilns, and the work has changed and evolved because of this new way of firing. Over the next year and a half, we experimented and achieved so much variation. The clay body alone has come out red, purple, and black in different firings.

When I bought my own kiln, we needed to do some adjusting and experimenting to get those same sorts of results.

We were dependent on the oxyprobe, and the slightest adjustments put our oxygen numbers out of range. Too much reduction, and the clay had an anemic look and the glazes looked washed out. Not enough reduction, and everything went purple. It was really hard to achieve a good firing.

REDUCTION COOLING WITH WOOD IN THE GAS KILN

For over a year we struggled—there were many good firings, but there were also many that weren't great. Our dependency on the oxyprobe wasn't working for us either. We decided to cool the kiln with wood instead of gas. When it was time for the cooling, we turned off the gas, pushed in the damper, and covered the flame ports.

We had long, skinny scraps of wood from the waste of a cabinet shop. We stuck one piece into the bottom peep. We no longer needed the oxyprobe and relied instead on the flame coming out of the peep. When the stick burned down and a short 1 to 2 inch (2.5 to 5 cm) flame flickered out, we fed another stick. It was about a stick every ten minutes to keep it in reduction. At around 1900°F (1037°C), we introduced oxygen by letting the kiln clear out by opening the damper for a couple of minutes. This seemed to make the blacks richer.

The kiln dropped to 1550°F (843°C) in half the time, and it's much more fun to feed wood and look at flame instead of staring at a fluctuating number on an oxyprobe. We don't even use the oxyprobe for the cooling anymore.

When we unload the kiln, we just sweep up the ash from the wood and there is no damage to the kiln.

The potters I reached out to who are doing reduction cooling and making beautiful, interesting work are Lindsay Oesterritter, John Neely, Eric Knoche, Ernest Gentry, and Warren Frederick.

WOOD KILNS

I have participated in many wood firings with local wood-fire potters. The potters Will Ruggles and Douglass Rankin of Rock Creek Pottery left a powerful and lasting mark on the potters of western North Carolina. They have moved on to Santa Fe, New Mexico, and are not currently making pottery, but during their years here, they not only wood fired their pottery, but also designed kilns. Many wood-fire potters in western North Carolina have kilns designed by them.

There are many great and informative books on wood firing and kiln design/construction. My experience is limited and the subject is vast. The more you know, the more there is to know. Each wood kiln fires differently, and while there are certain rules about how to achieve heat, evenness, and other practicalities, there is no one formula that applies. You learn how your particular kiln fires by loading the pots in specific ways, keeping notes, listening to the fire, watching the color and density of the smoke, and doing lots of firings.

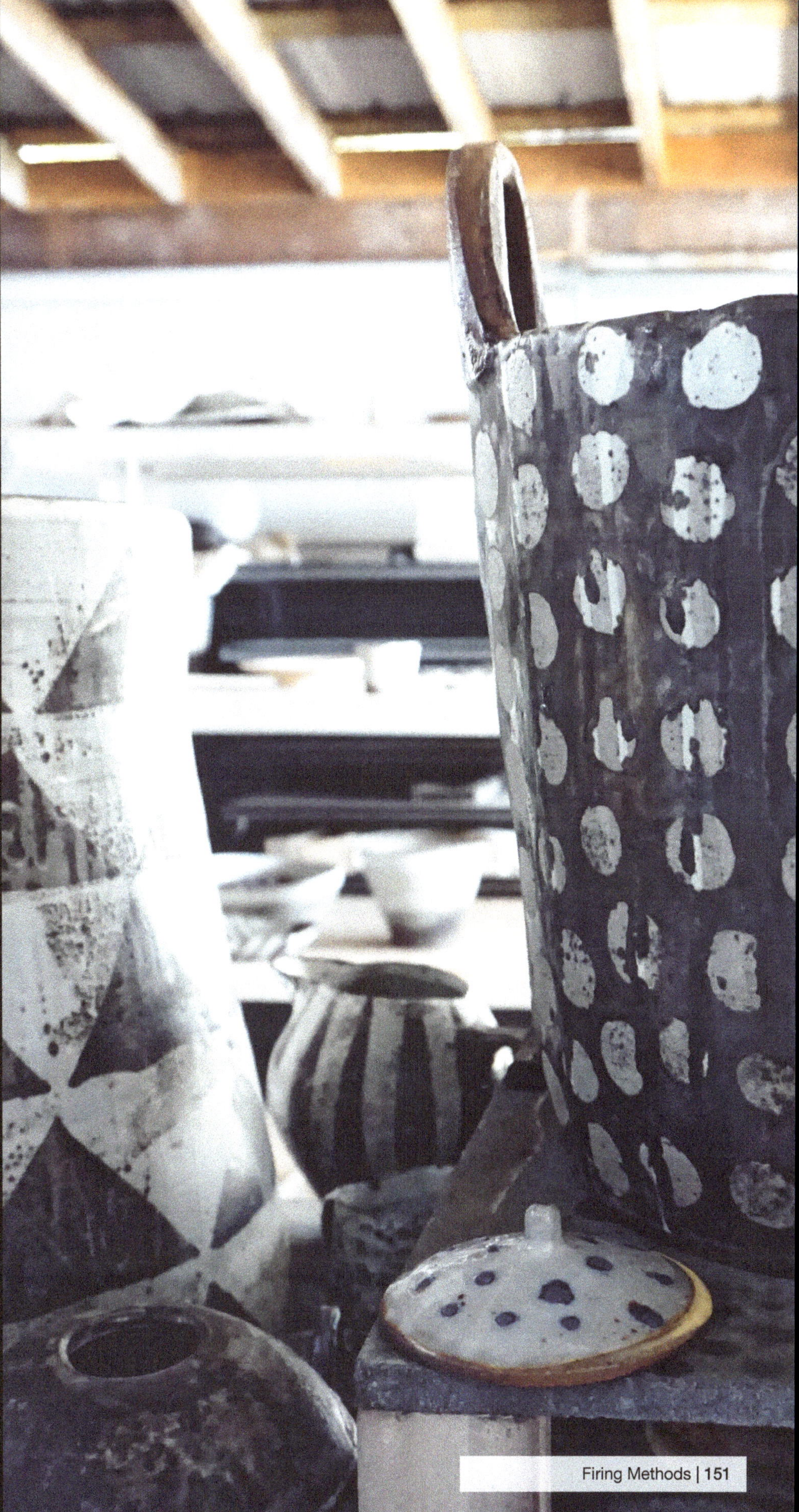

The Heart of the Studio: Elijah Cody Ferguson

I can't complete this book without writing about Elijah. He is my partner in the studio and my partner in life. The pottery studio is no longer a one-person operation and he does most of the hard work, making clay, glazes, and slips; firing kilns; and rebuilding pugmills and filter presses. When I quit my job in the service industry and decided to go for being a full-time potter, he came on board full time, too.

Elijah is from Boise, Idaho. We met in Arkansas through mutual friends when I went out to dig clay one spring. That summer he came to visit me in North Carolina and never left. He had been working in construction, and now he uses his endless skills at building, welding, woodworking, and fixing machinery to make our production more efficient. He is tireless.

Elijah is a self-taught potter who first discovered his love of making pottery in high school. He is always testing glazes, digging local clays, and adding rocks and ash and other ingredients to pots to see what will happen. He has a curiosity about life that has found an interesting home in pottery and he makes beautiful, fearless pots. It makes sense that using wild clays, rocks, ash, and minerals would drive his creativity, as it matches his deep love for the natural world. He loves the forest and is always telling me the names of different plants, rocks, trees, and mushrooms. I nicknamed him nature boy.

He has taught me so much about patience, quiet, and love. His good-natured, easygoing self is a necessary balance to my tendencies of hyper-focus, stress, and anxiety. He is constantly reminding me that "we got this" and it's going to be fine. I need that.

A family pottery business is hard, never-ending work, and we love every minute of it. It is a gift to wake up every day and be excited about what we do. The privilege of being potters for a living is not lost on us and we are grateful for it. We get to travel all over the country doing shows, and work surrounded by other creatives, our dogs, and a garden. This living lets us appreciate all that we have and do.

Pottery is a lesson in slowing down, listening, paying attention, humility, love, patience, and time.

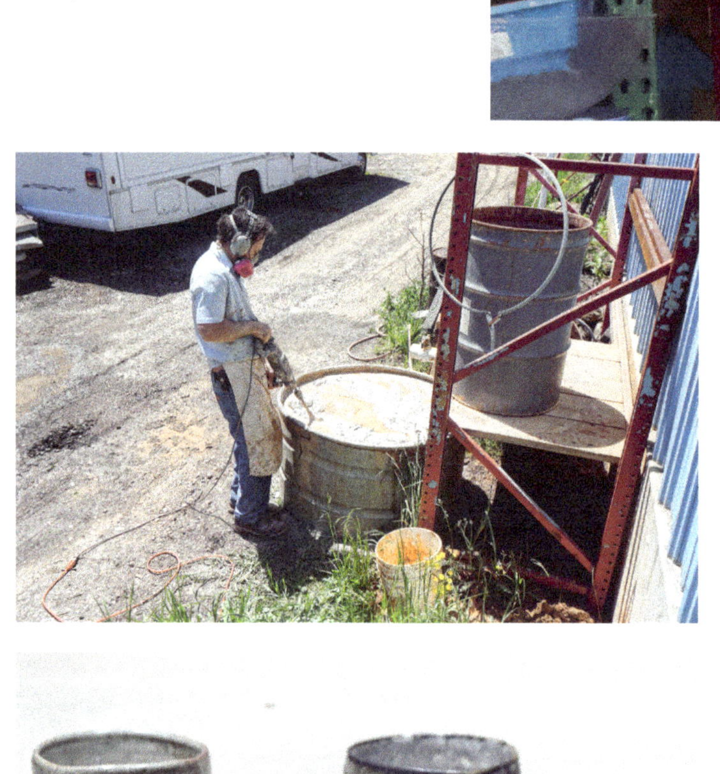

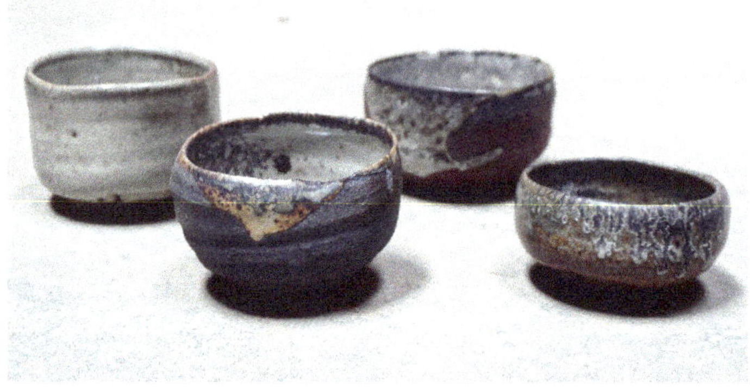

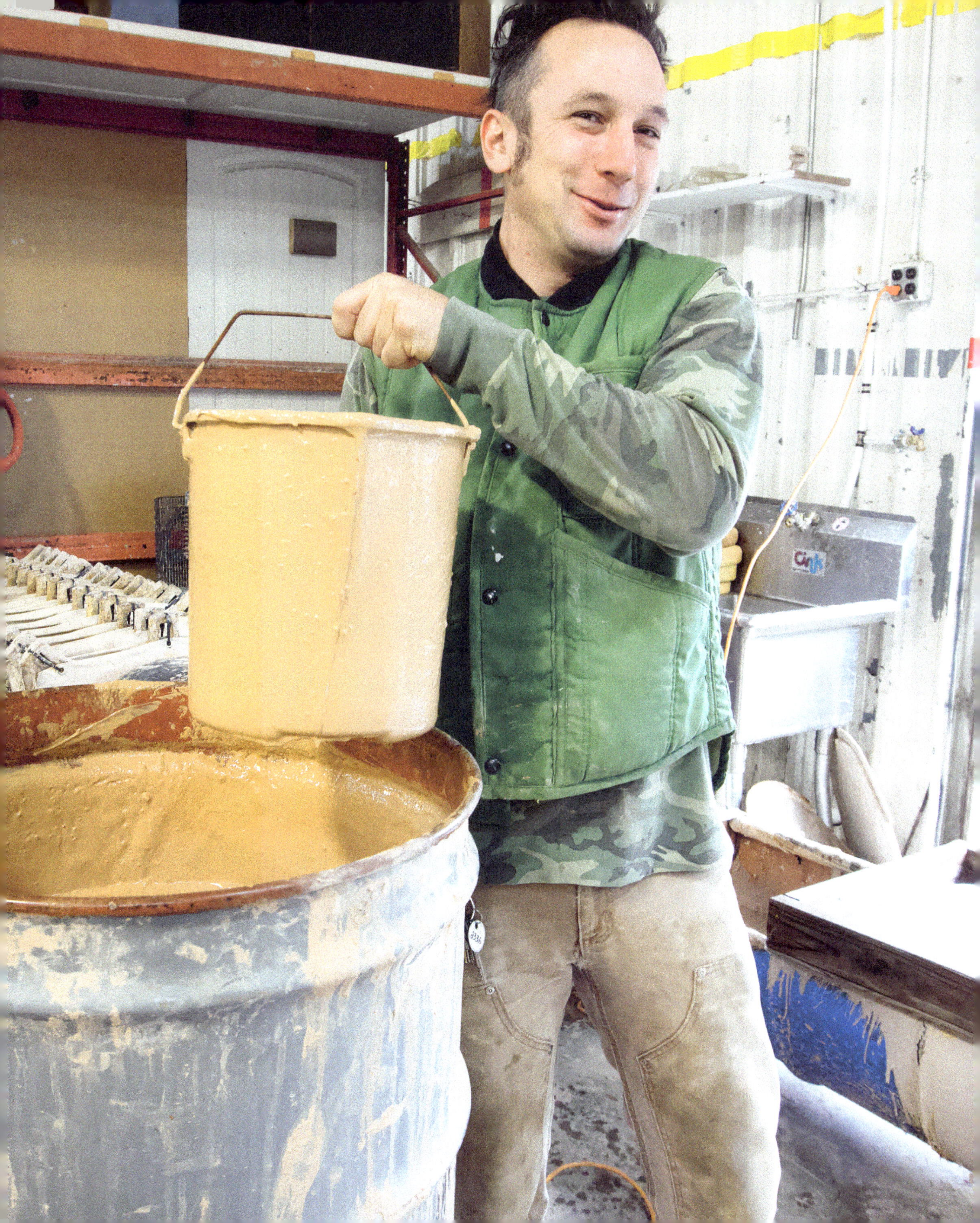

www.sheffield-pottery.com/Orton-Cone-Chart-s/314.htm

www.ceramicartsnetwork.org/daily/firing-techniques/electric-kiln-firing/quartz-inversion-and-other-important-stages-of-firing-pottery

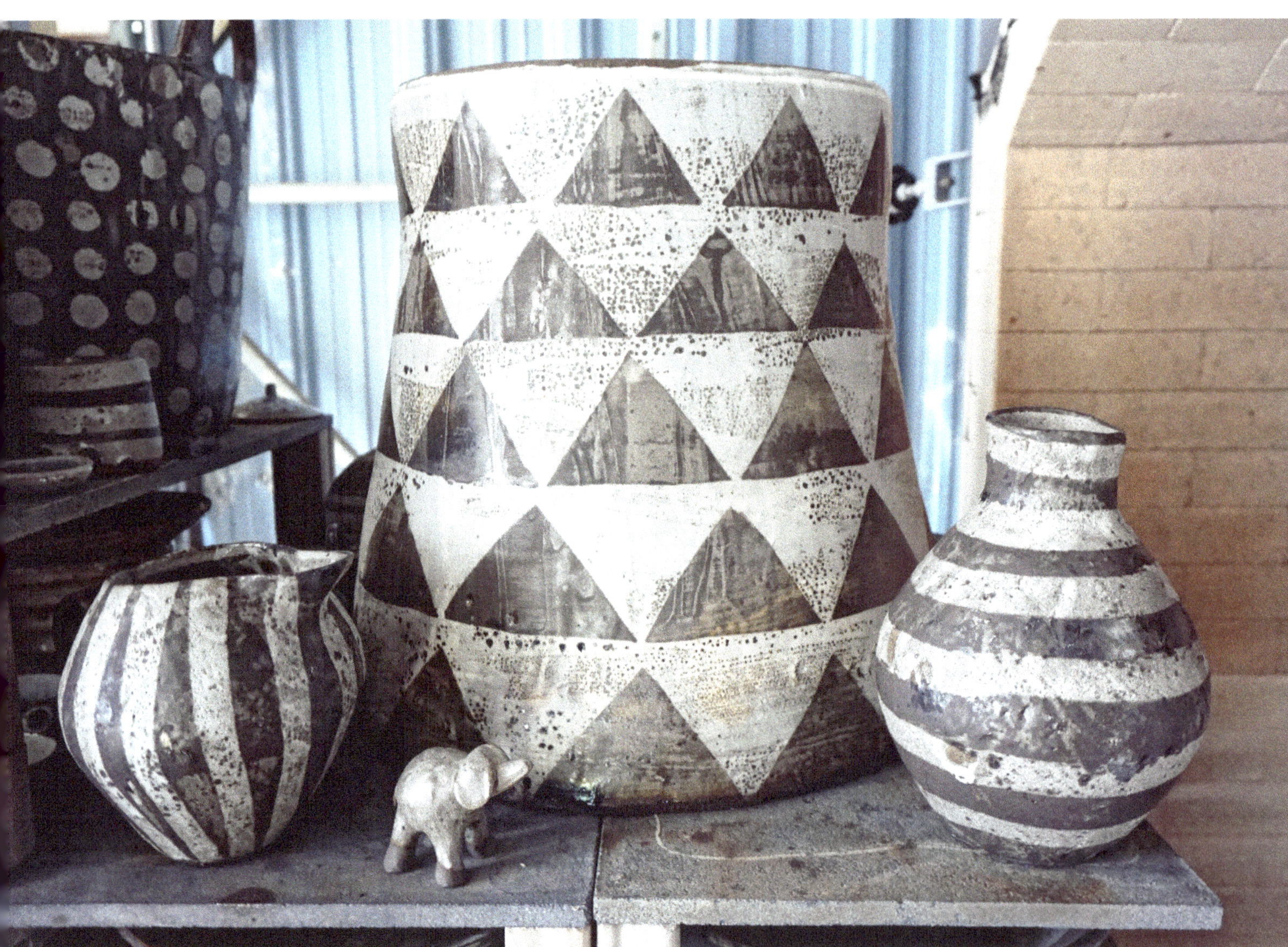

A POTTER'S WAY & WORK | by Shoji Hamada

THE JAPANESE POTTERY HANDBOOK | by Penny Simpson, Lucy Kitto, and Kanji Sodeoka

THE UNKNOWN CRAFTSMAN | by Soetsu Yanagi

KILNS | by Daniel Rhodes

GLAZES FROM NATURAL SOURCES | by Brian Sutherland

CLAY AND GLAZES FOR THE POTTER | by Daniel Rhodes

ASH GLAZES | by Phil Rogers

THE COMPLETE GUIDE TO HIGH-FIRE GLAZES | by John Britt

THE KILN BOOK | by Frederick L. Olsen

OUT OF THE EARTH, INTO THE FIRE | by Mimi Obstler

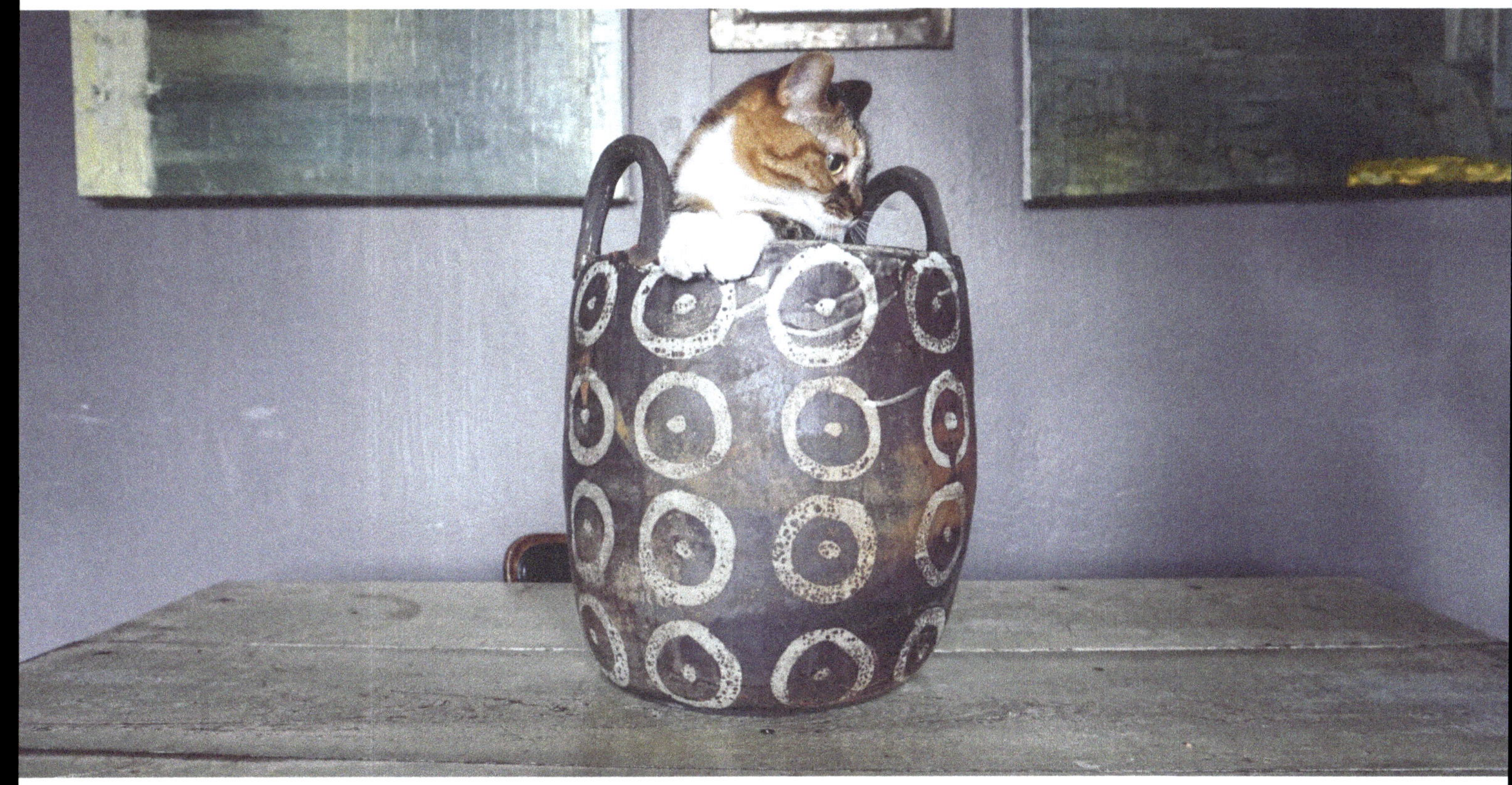

Acknowledgments

I would like to thank Becca Floyd for the encouragement she gave me right out of the gate. I still hear your voice regularly in my studio. Thanks to Shawn Ireland and Bandana Pottery for all of their generous help, sharing of knowledge and resources, and teaching me how to wood-fire kilns with calm, humor, and grace. Thank you, Lindsay Rogers, for being so smart and always patiently answering my never-ending questions. Thank you to all of the rest of the contributing potters in the book for being willing to share your techniques and practices without hesitation. Thank you, podcasts and punk rock music, for providing my head a place to go during all the thousands of studio hours. Thank you to Stephanie Pierce, my best friend, because we all need one of them in this life. Thank you to my daughter for motivating me to take my first pottery class when she was five months old because she cried so much. Most of all, I want to thank my partner, Elijah Cody Ferguson, without whom none of this would even be happening, because I would still be waiting tables and making pottery on the side. He does all the behind-the-scenes hard work that comes along with being a full-time potter. He makes the clay, slip, and glazes; builds the booth for shows; drives the bus out west, up north, and all over the country and back to help set up, break down, and sell pots at shows. He does the night shift on the kiln and keeps everything fixed and the studio running with his never-ending talents. He also cooks, cleans, and does laundry. He's sweet, funny, kind, and selfless, and I'll never know how I got so incredibly lucky to find him.

And, don't let me forget, thanks to my mom for always believing in me and being proud.

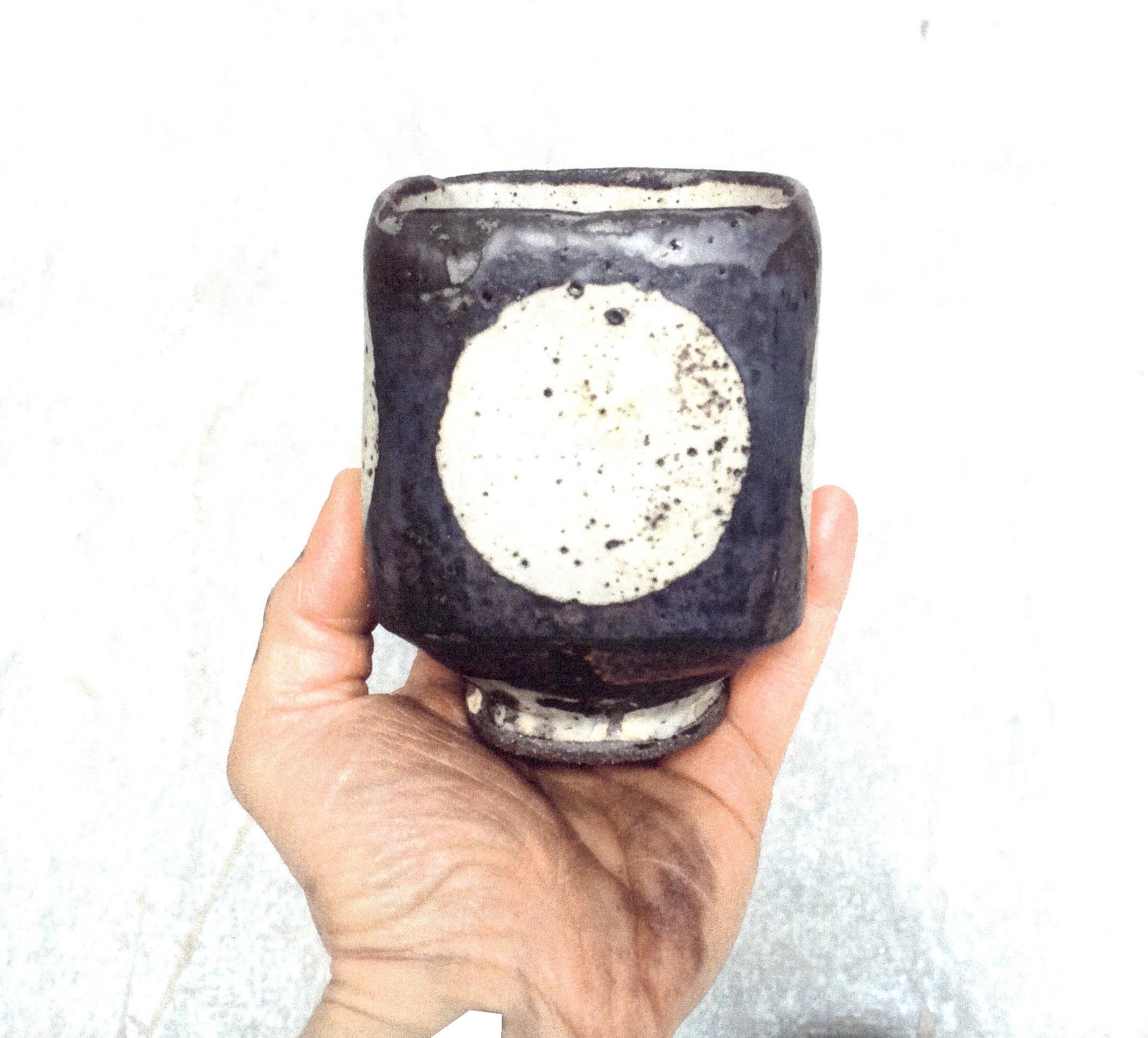

About the Author

Melissa Weiss is a full-time studio potter living and working in Asheville, North Carolina. She lives with her partner, daughter, two cats, and two dogs. While she has no formal education in ceramics, she received a BFA in photography from the School of Visual Arts in 2000. She travels around the country participating in craft shows, art fairs, and teaching workshops. She spends lots of time running, hunting for mushrooms, and in general exploring in the national forests that surround her town. She hopes she will be making pottery forever and ever.

You can follow her on Instagram **@melissaweisspottery**

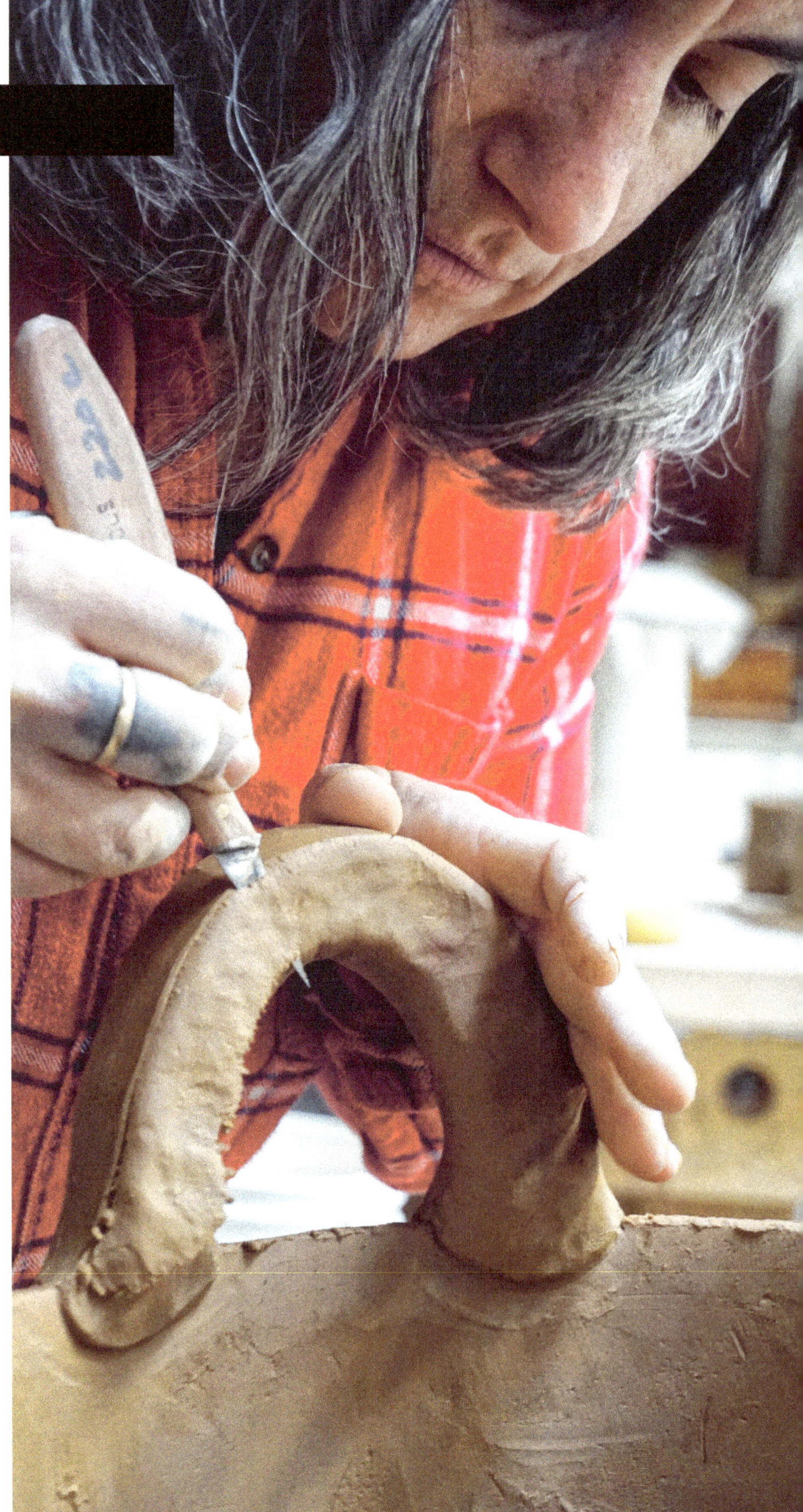

Index

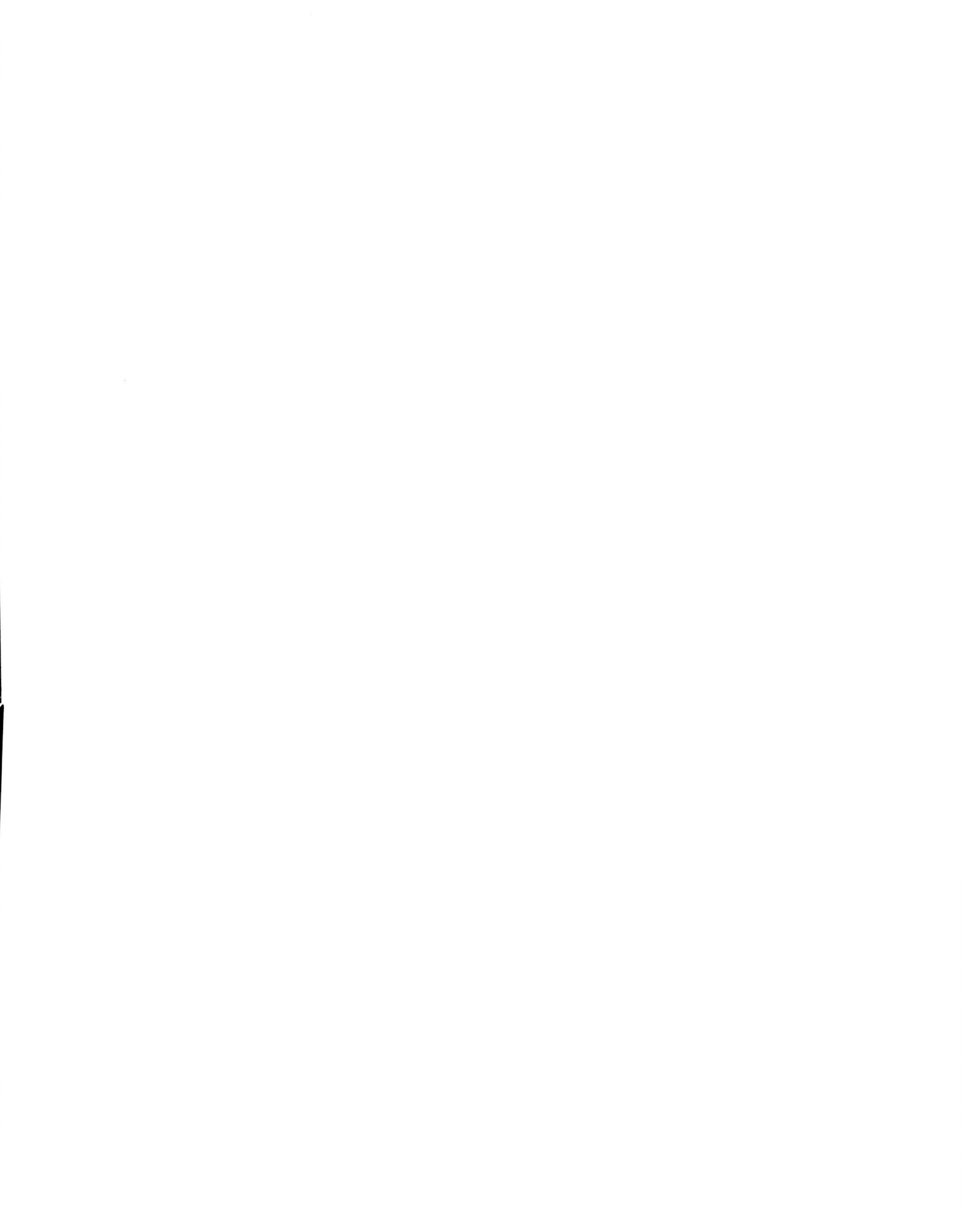

www.ingramcontent.com/pod-product-compliance
Ingram Content Group UK Ltd.
Pitfield, Milton Keynes, MK11 3LW, UK
UKHW050125260126
467270UK00009B/124